The Golden Age

Ballet in Soviet Russia 1917-1991

Dedicated to

Clement, for his wit, wisdom, guidance and friendship

Pasha, to whom I owe everything

and

Nina Theologovna

The Golden Age
Ballet in Soviet Russia 1917-1991

Gerald Dowler

DANCE BOOKS

Published in 2021 by:

Dance Books Ltd
Southwold House
Isington Road
Binsted
Hampshire
GU34 4PH

© 2021 Gerald Dowler

ISBN: 978-1-85273-155-7

Contents

	List of illustrations	vi
	Foreword	x
	Introduction	1
1.	Ancien Régime – before 1917	4
	Theatres and Schools	5
2.	Red Dawn – 1917	13
	The Status Quo	13
3.	From Tsar to Commissar – 1917-1924	17
	Ballet Schools	44
4.	Dancing through the Terror – 1924-1941	53
	Dancers of the first Golden Age	64
5.	War and Thaw – 1941-1956	110
6.	Cold War Dances – 1956-1962	138
	Dancers of the second Golden Age	157
7.	The Time of Troubles – 1962-1977	196
	Dancers of the third Golden Age	229
8.	A Window on the West – 1977-1991	234
	Postscript	264
	Conclusion	269
	Appendices	271
	Bibliography	276
	Index	294

List of Illustrations

BETWEEN pp. 52/53

1920 - *Swan Lake*, Act II, Bolshoi. Leonid Zhukov as Siegfried.

c.1920 - *Giselle*, Act II, Bolshoi. Courtesy of *Dancing Times*

Vasily Tikhomirov at the Bolshoi Ballet School with Lev Potekhin, Vera Svetinskaya, Viktor Smoltsov, Anastasia Abramova, etc. in 1910.

Imperial Theatre School, Rossi Street, St Petersburg in the early 1900s.

Alexander Gorsky, Fyodor Lopukhov, Mikhail Fokine, Georgy Balanchivadze

1924 – *The Red Whirlwind*, GATOB.

1925 - *Joseph the Beautiful*, Bolshoi.

Le Corsaire, Bolshoi - Ekaterina Geltser as Medora and Vasily Tikhomirov as Conrad.

c.1923 - Members of the Young Ballet (Georgy Balanchivadze seated).

1925-26 - *Pulcinella*, GATOB. Courtesy of *Dancing Times*

1927 - *The Ice Maiden*, GATOB. Olga Mungalova in the title role and Pyotr Gusev as Asak.

1927 - Tatiana Vecheslova and Leonid Yakobson

1928 – Bolshoi ballerinas Nina Podgoretskaya, Lyubov Bank, Valentina Kudryavtseva, Anastasia Abramova

1930 - *The Footballer*, Bolshoi. Asaf Messerer in the title role.

1928 - *The Red Poppy*, Act I Sailors' Dance, Bolshoi. Courtesy of *Dancing Times*

1930 - *The Footballer*, Bolshoi. Courtesy of *Dancing Times*

1930 - *The Golden Age*, GATOB.

1931 - *The Bolt*, GATOB. In rehearsal

1931 - *The Bolt*, GATOB. In the workshops

1932 – *Giselle*, Act I, Bolshoi. Courtesy of *Dancing Times*

1932 – *The Flames of Paris*, GATOB. Courtesy of *Dancing Times*

1935 - *Three Fat Men*, Bolshoi. Courtesy of *Dancing Times*

1934 - *The Fountain of Bakhchisarai*, GATOB. Courtesy of *Dancing Times*

1935 - *Three Fat Men*, Bolshoi. Olga Lepeshinskaya as Suok. Courtesy of *Dancing Times*

1936 - *Swan Lake*, Bolshoi. Marina Semyonova as Odette. Courtesy of *Dancing Times*

1936 - *The Sleeping Beauty*, Act I, Bolshoi. Marina Semyonova as Aurora. Courtesy of *Dancing Times*

1936 - *The Bright Stream*, Bolshoi.

1937 - *The Nutcracker*, Bolshoi. Marina Semyonova as Masha and Mikhail Gabovich as the Prince. Courtesy of *Dancing Times*

Sergey Prokofiev, Leonid Lavrovsky, Dmitry Shostakovich, Konstantin Sergeyev

1939 - *Laurencia*, Kirov. Natalia Dudinskaya in the title role. Courtesy of *Dancing Times*

BETWEEN pp. 114/115

1939 - *Swan Lake*, Kirov. Galina Ulanova as Odette and Konstantin Sergeyev as Siegfried. Courtesy of *Dancing Times*

1940 - *Romeo and Juliet*, Kirov. Andrey Lopukhov as Mercutio. Courtesy of *Dancing Times*

1940 - *Romeo and Juliet*. Courtesy of *Dancing Times*

1940 - *Taras Bulba*, Kirov. Mikhail Dudko in the title role.

1941 - *Straussiana*, MALEGOT.

1941 - Leningrad Choreographic School in Platoshino near Perm.

1944 - Maly Opera and Ballet Theatre.

1945 – Victory. 9th May celebrations outside the Bolshoi Theatre.

1945 - *Cinderella*, Bolshoi. Galina Ulanova in the title role. Courtesy of *Dancing Times*

1946 - *Cinderella*, Kirov. Natalia Dudinskaya in the title role and Konstantin Sergeyev as the Prince.

1947 - *The Sleeping Beauty*, Bolshoi. Galina Ulanova as Aurora, Mikhail Gabovich as the Prince, Cherkasov as the King and Evgenia Biber as the Queen. Courtesy of *Dancing Times*

1946 - *Heart of the Hills*, Kirov. Vakhtang Chabukiani as Djardje. Courtesy of *Dancing Times*

1947 - Elizaveta Gerdt (seated), Maya Plisetskaya, Vladimir Preobrazhensky in rehearsal at the Bolshoi.

1948 - *The Little Stork*, Bolshoi. Courtesy of *Dancing Times*

1948 - *La Bayadère*, Kirov. Vakhtang Chabukiani as Solor. Courtesy of *Dancing Times*

1949 - *Youth*, MALEGOT.

1948 - Agrippina Vaganova and her class, LHU. Courtesy of *Dancing Times*

1949 - *The Bronze Horseman*, Bolshoi. Raisa Struchkova and Alexei Ermolayev.

1950 - *Swan Lake*, Act II, Bolshoi. RIA Novosti archive, image #854874 Anatoliy Garanin CC-BY-SA 3.0

1953 - *Swan Lake*, MALEGOT. Violetta Bovt as Odile, Alexey Chichinadze as Siegfried and Alexander Klein as Rothbart.

1953 - *The Seven Beauties*, MALEGOT.

1951 - *La Bayadère*, Act I, Kirov. Natalia Dudinskaya as Nikiya. Courtesy of *Dancing Times*

1950s - *Don Quixote*, Bolshoi. Maya Plisetskaya as Kitri. Courtesy of *Dancing Times*

1950s - *Moszkowsky Waltz*, Bolshoi. Raisa Struchkova and Alexander Lapauri. Courtesy of *Dancing Times*

1954 - Raisa Struchkova as Aurora in *The Sleeping Beauty*, RIA Novosti archive, image #644728 Umnov CC-BY-SA 3.0

1956 - Nikolai Fadeyechev as Siegfried in *Swan Lake*, RIA Novosti archive, image #672496 Umnov CC-BY-SA 3.0

BETWEEN pp. 196/197

c.1950 - *Swan Lake*, Act III, Bolshoi. Alexey Ermolayev as Siegfried and Galina Ulanova as Odile. Courtesy of *Dancing Times*

1955 - *Amulet of Freedom*, Latvian Opera and Ballet Theatre.

1951 – Ekaterina Maximova, Vladimir Vasiliev and Alla Mankevich at the Bolshoi Ballet School.

1950 – *The Sleeping Beauty*. Irina Kolpakova as Aurora.

c.1956 – Rudolf Nureyev with Alexander Pushkin, Natalia Kamkova and Alla Sizova, LHU.

c. 1957 - *The Stone Flower*, Kirov. Alla Shelest as Katerina. Courtesy of *Dancing Times*

1956 – Poster for the Bolshoi *Romeo and Juliet* at Covent Garden.

1954 - Galina Ulanova and Yuri Zhdanov in Romeo and Juliet RIA Novosti archive, image #11591 Umnov CC-BY-SA 3.0

1956 - *Romeo and Juliet*, the ball scene, Bolshoi. Courtesy of *Dancing Times*

1957 - *Gayaneh*, Sabre Dance, Bolshoi. Courtesy of *Dancing Times*

1958 - *Swan Lake*, MALEGOT. Māris Liepa as Siegfried and Violetta Bovt as Odette.

1959 - *The Stone Flower*, Bolshoi. Maya Plisetskaya as the Mistress of the Copper Mountain and Nikolai Fadeyechev as Danila.

1959 - *Coast of Hope*, Kirov. Alla Osipenko and Askold Makarov. Courtesy of *Dancing Times*

1961 - *Leningrad Symphony*, Kirov. Courtesy of *Dancing Times*

Yuri Faier - 1958 caricature.

1960 - *The Little Humpbacked Horse*, Bolshoi. Alexander Radunsky as the Khan and Rimma Karelskaya as the Tsar Maiden.

1961 - *Chopiniana*, Bolshoi. Galina Ulanova. Courtesy of *Dancing Times*

1962 - Mikhail Baryshnikov aged 14 at LHU.

1961 - Rudolf Nureyev as Solor in *La Bayadère*, Act III in Paris.

Māris Liepa teaching at the Bolshoi Ballet School.

1962 - George Balanchine and Vakhtang Chabukiani.

1960 - Arrival of the Bolshoi Ballet at Schiphol airport. Amsterdam (Nina Timofeyeva extreme left).

1962 - *Spartacus*, Bolshoi. Shamil Yagudin (right) as a Gladiator. Courtesy of *Dancing Times*

1962 - *Spartacus*, Kirov. Courtesy of *Dancing Times*

1962 - *Spartacus*, Bolshoi. Mikhail Lavrovsky as a Slave. Courtesy of *Dancing Times*

The Fountain of Bakhchisarai, Bolshoi. Alexander Lapauri as Khan Girey in 1954. Courtesy of *Dancing Times*

Gayaneh, Bolshoi - Nikolai Fadeyechev as Armen. Late 1950s.

1962 - *The Bedbug*, Kirov. Dmitry Vovk and Elena Selivanova.

1964 – *Cinderella*, Kirov. Natalia Makarova as an Ugly Sister. Courtesy of *Dancing Times*

1963 - Ekaterina Maximova as Maria in *The Fountain of Bakhchisarai* - RIA Novosti archive, image #521299 V. Blioh CC-BY-SA 3.0

1966 - Vladimir Vasiliev as the Prince in Yuri Grigorovich's *The Nutcracker*. RIA Novosti archive, image #709789 Alexander Makarov CC-BY-SA 3.0

1966 - *Giselle*, Act I, Kirov. Yuri Soloviev as Albrecht. Courtesy of *Dancing Times*

1965 – *The Legend of Love*, Kirov. Alla Osipenko and Vladilen Semyonov. Courtesy of *Dancing Times*

1966 - *The Rite of Spring*, Bolshoi. Nina Sorokina and Yuri Vladimirov. Courtesy of *Dancing Times*

1967 - *Carmen Suite*, Bolshoi. Maya Plisetskaya as Carmen and Nikolai Fadeyechev as Don José.

1967 - Leonid Lavrovsky in a rehearsal of *Paganini* with Yaroslav Sekh in the title role. Courtesy of *Dancing Times*

1961 - *The Nutcracker*, Novosibirsk Ballet. Nikita Dolgushin as the Prince. Courtesy of *Dancing Times*

1968 - Kirov Mens' Class including Soloviev (second from right). Courtesy of *Dancing Times*

BETWEEN pp. 244/245

1968 - *Spartacus*, Act III, Bolshoi. Boris Akimov as Crassus. Courtesy of *Dancing Times*

1967 - Oleg Vinogradov in rehearsal for *Asel* with Nina Timofeyeva, Bolshoi. Courtesy of *Dancing Times*

Galina Ulanova coaching *Swan Lake* with Māris Liepa, Bolshoi.

1969 - Mikhail Baryshnikov in *Vestris* at the first Moscow International Ballet Competition. Courtesy of *Dancing Times*

1969 - Jury members of I International Ballet Dancers Contest, Moscow RIA Novosti archive, image #842769 Alexander Makarov CC-BY-SA 3.0

Hamlet, Act II, Kirov. Mikhail Baryshnikov. Courtesy of *Dancing Times*

Hamlet, Kirov. Elena Evteyeva as Ophelia. Courtesy of *Dancing Times*

1970 - *Hamlet*, Act I, Kirov. Mikhail Baryshnikov in the title role. Courtesy of *Dancing Times*

1972 - Yuri Grigorovich, Pyotr Gusev, Galina Ulanova and Fyodor Lopukhov. Courtesy of *Dancing Times*

The Stone Flower, Kirov. John Markovsky and Alla Osipenko in rehearsal. Courtesy of *Dancing Times*

1974 - *The Prodigal Son*, Kirov. Mikhail Baryshnikov in the title role.

1972 - *Anna Karenina*, Bolshoi. Maya Plisetskaya in the title role.

1974 - *Yaroslavna*, MALEGOT. Tatiana Fesenko in the title role.

1977 - Third Moscow International Ballet Competition "During contest days." RIA Novosti archive, image #843299 Alexander Makarov

1975 - Yuri Grigorovich during a rehearsal. Courtesy of *Dancing Times*

Natalia Kasatkina and Vladimir Vasilyov in rehearsal.

1975 - *Ivan the Terrible*, Bolshoi. Curtain call. Courtesy of *Dancing Times*

1976 - *Angara*, Bolshoi. Natalia Bessmertnova as Valya and Vladimir Vasiliev as Sergey.

Vladimir Vasiliev and Alexey Ermolayev in rehearsal, Bolshoi.

Yuri Grigorovich in rehearsal with Vladimir Vasiliev.

Stanislav Isayev in the studio.

1979 - Irina Kolpakova in the studio, Kirov. Courtesy of *Dancing Times*

Nathalie, ou la Laitière suisse, Moscow Classical Ballet. Ekaterina Maximova as Nathalie and Stanislav Isayev as Oswald.

1978 – *Notre-Dame de Paris*, Kirov.

1979 – *Icarus*. Ekaterina Maximova and Vladimir Vasiliev. Courtesy of *Dancing Times*

1980 - *The Seagull*, Bolshoi. Maya Plisetskaya as Nina Zarechnaya and Alexander Bogatyrev as Treplyov. Courtesy of *Dancing Times*

1982 - *The Golden Age*, Bolshoi. Irek Mukhamedov as Boris and Natalia Bessmertnova as Rita. Courtesy of *Dancing Times*

1984 - Stanislav Isayev. Moscow Classical Ballet. Courtesy of *Dancing Times*

1982 - *The Golden Age*, Bolshoi. Yuri Vetrov, Tatiana Gorlikova and Vasily Vorokhobko. Courtesy of *Dancing Times*

Ivan the Terrible, Bolshoi. Irek Mukhamedov in the title role. Courtesy of *Dancing Times*

1989 – *Petrushka*, Kirov. Andris Liepa in the title role.

Don Quixote, Kirov. Farukh Ruzimatov as Basilio and Elena Pankova as Kitri.

Foreword

I have coronavirus to thank for this book. Spurred on by national lockdown in England in March 2020, I brought forward a project which I had pencilled in for later in the year and probably after, namely an overview of ballet in Soviet Russia.

The germ of the idea came with the 2017 centenary of the Russian Revolution which I proposed to mark with some articles for my 'home' publication *Dancing Times*. I must thank Jonathan Gray, the editor of the magazine for the decision to commission me to write an analysis of how the social and political upheavals affected the world of ballet in Russia. It was the start of a long and illuminating period of research for me during which I learned so much about the less-than straightforward narrative which played itself out in the USSR. Putting into practice the adage 'never start something you don't intend to finish' and encouraged by positive reactions to my articles, I proposed more, and Jonathan went with me, commissioning several series of articles which took the readers of *Dancing Times* to the fall of the Soviet Union in 1991.

The idea of turning fourteen 1800-word essays into a book slowly germinated in my mind and finally took root with invaluable advice from Dance Books' David Leonard and the spread of the dread virus; on day one of lockdown, I opened a new computer file and started. The world of Soviet ballet has been my daily companion during the difficult months of the pandemic, and for that I am truly grateful.

Researching the material has been illuminating in so many ways. The last time such a book was attempted was in the middle of the 1960s, one, from either side of the Iron Curtain. Both studies are superb; Natalia Roslavleva's *Era of Russian Ballet*, which shows a very 'Soviet' perspective and Mary Grace Swift's *The Art of Dance in the USSR* which tells the story 'from the other side'. My own efforts will tend towards the latter by simple virtue of where I live and the languages I speak and read. Of course, there was over a quarter of a century of Soviet Russian ballet to look at after the publication of both surveys. There is no other overview. Russian sources tend to be very good on individuals and their achievements but do not look at the bigger picture; a manifestation of the state's discouragement of personal interpretation, which some would argue did not cease with the fall of communism.

Some individual investigations have been invaluable: *Balanchine and the Lost Muse* by Elizabeth Kendall which provided so much detail about the Petrograd Ballet School and dance life during the early 1920s; *Like a Bomb Going Off*, Janice Ross's appreciation of choreographer Leonid Yakobson; *Soviet*

Choreographers in the 1920s by Elizabeth Souritz; Gennady Smakov's *The Great Russian Dancers* for details and appreciations of important artists; Christina Ezrahi's selective but fascinating *Swans of the Kremlin*. Stéphanie Gonçalves' excellent work in French on the foreign tours by major ballet companies across the Iron Curtain from the mid-1950s must also be highlighted. The opportunity to trawl through decades of *Dancing Times'* reviews and appreciations was too good to turn down and yielded important reviews from Russia as well as the UK. The miracle of online translation engines allowed unfettered access to the Russian language ballet encyclopaedias, even if knowledge of what the title of a ballet was in Cyrillic script was essential to find its entry in an alphabetically-arranged reference work. Some facts have been impossible to pin down, not least the chronology of the directors of the Mariinsky/Kirov and Bolshoi companies and their schools. Enquiries to Russia and several archives drew a blank – no one seems to know who was director of the Bolshoi from 1930 to 1935...

My admiration is boundless for the dancers and teachers of the Soviet Union who first saved and then took their artform to new heights. Their achievements were astounding, often secured in difficult and dangerous circumstances. Diaghilev's Ballets Russes is rightly credited with bringing the art of ballet back to the West, and it is true that the impresario's death in 1929 released a diaspora of artistry which shaped the dance world. However, the Russian revolution was as important in spreading both the word and the talent – George Balanchine would never have left Russia had the home situation not been so precarious. But Soviet Russian ballet itself occupies as great a role, the Ying to the West's Yang. The modern view of ballet is shaped by the glamorous visits and tours by Russian companies which began in the mid-1950s during the cultural 'thaw' and by the trinity of Soviet defectors – Rudolf Nureyev, Natalia Makarova and Mikhail Baryshnikov. Western dancers and audiences had never seen the like. Thirty years after the fall of the communist state, Russia still produces dancers of superlative schooling and artistry, successors to the golden ages of Asylmuratova, Dudinskaya, Kolpakova, Maximova, Plisetskaya and Ulanova, Chabukiani, Ermolayev, Mukhamedov, Sergeyev, Soloviev and Vasiliev.

This book's title of *The Golden Age* seemed to me a perfect description of ballet in Russia during the Soviet period. Additionally, two works of that same name bookend it in time: *The Golden Age* of 1930, premièred in Leningrad some thirteen years after the Russian revolution, and that of 1982 which opened in Moscow nine years before the fall of the Communist regime.

I have adopted the Oxford style of transliteration from Russian unless there is a generally accepted alternative in common usage. In the footnotes, where a dancer is described as having graduated into a company, it is from that ensemble's own school; when this was not the case, the details have been provided. Asterisks have been used to indicate a subsequent biographical entry in the main body of the text. In the biographical sections of notable dancers, the entries have been ordered by company, gender and date of birth.

I have to express my sincere thanks to Jonathan Gray, Editor of *Dancing Times*, for his unfailing support, generosity with his time, good humour and friendship. I am extremely grateful that he gave me access to the *Dancing Times* picture archive from which the majority of the images are drawn. I must also thank Mikhail Messerer whose encyclopaedic knowledge led to invaluable suggestions and corrections – Misha, you have my profound respect and admiration – and to Margaret Willis, whose eagle eyes spotted countless mistakes and slip-ups and who undertook a read-through with characteristic enthusiasm and good-humour. Liz Morrell has been the most patient and knowledgeable of editors, full of helpful suggestions and guidance; to her, my sincere and heartfelt thanks.

Clement Crisp has been a constant support, lending encouragement and advice, and not a little inspiration. His extraordinary experience and memory of nigh on seven decades of Russian ballet opened up paths of investigation and interest. As a role model for a dance writer, he cannot be bettered. This book is, in no small part, a thank you to Clement.

Finally, my undying thanks go to my lifelong partner Paul, who has provided tea by the gallon, a peaceful home environment and discreet absence when I have been engrossed in the minutiae of casts and chronologies. His patience, his unfailing support and love are without equal. This book is, in many ways, a tribute to what we have become together.

Introduction

For ballet-goers today, the history of twentieth-century Russian ballet appears seamless – the February and October revolutions of 1917 signalled the hand-over of classical dance from the tsars of Empire to the commissars of the Republic under whom the art form would continue to grow and prosper, albeit with a new Soviet ideological and propaganda purpose. Nothing could be further from the truth.

In fact, Russian classical dance and its two national centres, the Mariinsky Theatre in Petrograd (ex-St Petersburg) and the Bolshoi in Moscow, almost didn't make it, ballet's baby nearly thrown out with the revolutionary bath water. And before ballet was to become a jewel in the Soviet artistic crown, used as a powerful propaganda tool both internally and around the world, it had to face numerous challenges, not least of which was to establish a reason for existing other than for the entertainment of the Tsar and his court. It needed to justify itself to survive. The huge financial cost associated with ballet performances had to be defended during the period of economic collapse and desperate shortages in the years which followed the revolution, and even when those particularly dark days had passed, the question of how classical dancing fitted into the Soviet cultural policy of education and indoctrination had to be addressed. The 1920s saw a period of both choreographic experimentation and preservation of the pre-revolutionary repertoire, phenomena which did not always sit comfortably alongside one another. Once the question of the validity of classical ballet in the new Russia was settled, the need to make the art form contribute to the Soviet ideal became ever more pressing as the decade went on. In terms of who would dance on stage, the stabilisation of dance training was another feature of this period, and the graduation of young Soviet artists of quality into the performing ensembles was seen as a guarantee of ballet's continuing existence.

After Lenin's[1] death in 1924, Stalin's[2] ever-tightening grip on power

---

1   Born Vladimir Ulyanov in 1870 in Simbirsk, in Ulyanovsk, Lenin embraced Marxism in 1887 after his brother Alexander's execution for plotting to assassinate Tsar Alexander III. He became a leading figure in the post-1903 Bolshevik splinter group and actively sought to promote world-wide revolution during the First World War. In 1917 he took control of the new government, by 1923 becoming Chairman of the Council of People's Commissars of the Soviet Union. He died in Gorky, Moscow in early 1924.

2   Born in Gori, Georgia in 1878 as Ioseb Dzughashvili, Stalin became a Marxist in his youth and rose through the Bolshevik party, securing ultimate power after Lenin's death against other contenders including Trotsky. His tenure ended with his death, having ruled

meant that the Russian ballet world had to contend with ideological shifts throughout the 1930s and weather political storms which brought down many prominent individuals. However, the regime's decision to make ballet a motor for disseminating Soviet influence and power led to the establishment of many new centres of teaching and performance around the republics of the USSR. The decade witnessed a first golden age in terms of the number and quality of dancers emerging from the schools while the companies had to contend with the establishment of 'socialist realism' as the dominant imperative in stage works.

The invasion of Russia by Germany in 1941 sent ballet largely into internal exile in remote locations far from the theatres of war, but the determination to maintain both the companies and their schools remained strong even in the direst of times. Victory meant that the socio-political imperative was re-imposed in the second half of the decade, with greater focus on the artists' ideological purity. Stalin's death in 1953 brought Khrushchev's[3] 'thaw' and the beginnings of experimentation with non-narrative dance. It was also the decade of the first artistic contacts with the West since the 1930s with visits by foreign companies to the Soviet Union and the Bolshoi Ballet's first season abroad in London in 1956, events which led to a broadening of the Soviet ballet consciousness and first-hand experience of other classical dance traditions.

The 1960s saw the second golden age of Soviet ballet with a roster of artists of the highest ability and artistry produced by the ballet schools. They were marked by the first high-profile defection by Rudolf Nureyev in 1961 and by continuing experimentation with choreographic styles and approaches, often by newly formed small-scale ensembles. During the 1970s further defections and a general ossification in approach and repertoire characterised the Bolshoi and Kirov ballets, the Soviet Union's two major companies. There was, however, greater creativity in smaller ensembles and the decade witnessed growing dissatisfaction being openly expressed by frustrated dancers. The Soviet ballet world was opened up as part of Mikhail Gorbachev's[4] relaxation of Soviet society in the mid-1980s; for the first time,

---

the Soviet Union with unpredictable harshness, overseeing purges and terrors but leading the country to victory against Germany. He died in his Kuntsevo dacha in 1953.

3   Born in 1894 in Kalinovka, near Ukraine, Nikita Khrushchev joined the Bolsheviks in 1918 and rose through the party structure, ultimately taking control of the USSR after a power struggle subsequent to Stalin's death in 1953. His eleven years in power saw a relative relaxation of state control and repression as well as a more international perspective in foreign affairs. He travelled extensively abroad and engaged actively in the Cold War with the USA and its allies. He was removed from power in 1964 and allowed to retire. He died near Moscow in 1971.

4   Born in 1931 in the village of Privolnoye near Stavropol, Mikhail Gorbachev rose through the Communist Party's structure, joining the ruling Politburo in 1979 and

dancers were able to travel to perform abroad with far greater freedom and the Russian companies began to embrace the work of foreign choreographers and to begin to make claim to a Western dance heritage which had until then been closed to them.

With the fall of communism and the end of the USSR in 1991, Russian ballet once again found itself struggling to find a purpose and a clear artistic voice in a newly-formed society; that struggle is arguably not over yet. Nevertheless, the legacy of seventy-four years of communism is too important and too valuable to be cast aside – in ballet terms, it was a period of astonishing achievement. The challenge remains for today's Russian ballet to find its place in modern culture and society whilst acknowledging the extraordinary legacy of the golden age of the Soviet era.

---

elected General Secretary in 1985 after the death of Konstantin Chernenko. Committed to significant economic and social reforms, he instituted a policy of perestroika (restructuring) to address the former and glasnost (openness) for the latter. He ultimately allowed the democratic movements of 1989 in Eastern Bloc countries but was unable to prevent the dissolution of the Soviet Union in 1991 and he resigned his office. He was the eighth and last leader of the Soviet Union.

1
Ancien Régime

Before 1917

The Imperial Era

Prior to the revolutions of 1917, ballet as an art form had existed in Russia since the reign of Peter the Great, although it was his heir, the Empress Anna who in 1738 established the first dance school which ultimately became the famed Imperial Theatre School in St Petersburg. In 1734 the French *maître de ballet* Jean-Baptiste Landé[5] arrived in St Petersburg and was engaged to train noble-born boys from the military *Corps des Cadets* to appear in danced interludes in operas given at court. Such was the success of his training that in 1737 he petitioned the empress to establish a dance school which he opened the following year, admitting "from among the children of the court servants: twelve slim girls in their teens, and the same number of youths. Their care was taken up by the court."[6] In another example of Russian cultural emulation of the West, in 1766 the Empress Catherine II (the Great) created the Imperial Directorate which established three state theatres in the capital St Petersburg: a Russian ensemble, a French drama company and a Franco-Italian opera and ballet troupe (the last of which took the name, in subsequent years, of Mariinsky, Kirov and Mariinsky once again). Additionally, ballet was to be seen until the revolution at two other theatres: the Bolshoi in Moscow and the Weikl in Warsaw (then under Russian rule). Command performances for the Imperial family also took place in the Hermitage Theatre of the Winter Palace in St Petersburg and at the nearby Imperial residences of Pavlovsk and Tsarskoe Selo. Ballet was, therefore, an entirely imperial construct from the very outset, something which lasted until the abdication of Tsar Nicholas II and the end of Romanov rule in 1917.[7]

---

5   Of unknown birth date, French-born Landé danced in Paris, Dresden and in Stockholm where he held the post of royal dancing master between 1721 and 1727. He first went to St Petersburg in 1734 to arrange a performance for young aristocrats and remained in Russia until his death there in 1748.

6   van Stahlinin, 'Nachrichten von der Tanzkunst und Ballet in Russland' (News of the Art of Dance and Ballet in Russia) as quoted by Starikova in 'From the Biography of the First Russian Ballet Company.'

7   Born in St Petersburg in 1868, Nicholas acceded to the throne in 1894. He abdicated in March 1917, bringing three centuries of Romanov rule to an end. He was murdered by the Bolsheviks in Ekaterinburg in July 1918. He was the last Russian tsar.

Theatres and Schools

St Petersburg

In St Petersburg, the Imperial Bolshoi Kamenny (Stone) Theatre for opera and ballet was built in 1783; it was situated on Carousel Square, renamed Theatre Square in honour of the building. Rebuilt in 1802, it burned down in 1811 and was again reconstructed, finally reopening in 1836 when the theatre was given over exclusively to opera and ballet.

Alberto Cavos[8] (russified to Albert Kavos) designed and built the wooden Equestrian Circus Theatre between 1848 and 1849 which burned down ten years later; it was in 1860 that Cavos' reconstructed theatre was renamed 'Mariinsky' after its patroness, the Empress Maria Alexandrovna and where in 1870 the Imperial Ballet began to perform. It was designated the company's principal venue in 1886 and the building was extensively renovated. A lavish inauguration performance took place in February during which *Les Pilules magiques* (The Magic Pills), a *ballet féerie*,[9] set to the music of Léon (or Ludwig) Minkus[10] by *Marius Petipa, was premièred, featuring the Russian ballerina Evgenia Sokolova.[11] The last dance performances at the Bolshoi Kamenny Theatre took place in 1886 after which the building was deemed unsafe; it was rebuilt in 1896 by the Russian Musical Society and now houses the St Petersburg Conservatoire.

The Imperial Theatre School of St Petersburg where young dancers received their training was initially located in the Winter Palace itself and then in a building on Nevsky Prospect. It moved to a new location in 1836 within the beautifully proportioned neo-classical architectural ensemble of what came to be known as Theatre Street (now Rossi Street, named after its

---

8   Born in St Petersburg in 1800 to Venetian-born parents, Cavos studied in Padua, Italy before returning to Russia to practise architecture. He became the country's principal theatre architect, designing and building the Mariinsky, Bolshoi and Mikhailovsky theatres as well as numerous buildings in St Petersburg. He died in Peterhof in 1863.

9   A genre of fantasy ballet which emphasised spectacle and stage effects.

10 Born in Vienna in 1826, Minkus spent nearly his whole life in Russia, beginning as conductor of Prince Yusupov's private serf orchestra in 1853. After a period as a violinist at the Bolshoi, he was official ballet composer for the Mariinsky between 1869 and 1886. He collaborated extensively with Petipa and wrote the scores for *Don Quixote* and *La Bayadère* among many others. His compositions were intensely danceable and contained memorable melodies. He retired in 1886 and returned to Vienna in 1891 where he worked at the Court Opera. He died in the city in 1917.

11 Born in St Petersburg in 1850, Sokolova graduated from the Imperial Theatre School into the city's Bolshoi Theatre and rose to become a principal dancer noted for her lyricism and expressivity. She created several roles and retired from dancing in 1886 after which she taught at the Mariinsky/GATOB until her death in Leningrad in 1925. Her students included Anna Pavlova, Vera Trefilova, Tamara Karsavina and Lyubov Egorova.

architect Carlo Rossi[12]). It remains there today as The Vaganova Academy of Russian Ballet.

Moscow

While dance in St Petersburg was always intended for the pleasure of the monarch and his or her court, in the old capital Moscow, rarely in favour with the ruling elite, matters were different. In 1780, the privately-run Petrovsky Theatre acquired the imperial licence to present entertainments granted only four years before to Prince Pyotr Urusov. Under the Englishman Michael Maddox it began producing plays and operas but was destroyed by fire in 1805. The Arbat Theatre, also called the New Imperial, was used for opera and ballet between 1808 and 1812. After its destruction during the French assault on Moscow in 1812, the old Petrovsky was rebuilt during the 1820s as the New Bolshoi (big) Theatre with a seating capacity of over 2000. It in turn burnt down in 1853 and was rebuilt on an even-grander scale in 1856 by Cavos. It is this building which, after several restoration projects, stands to this day.

The Bolshoi Ballet School traced its origins to the Moscow Foundling Home which, under the direct patronage of Catherine II, was instructed in 1773 to provide dancing classes for its children. The engagement of the Italian dancer and ballet master Filippo Beccari[13] is taken as the date of the school's founding; within three years 24 of his 62 students were engaged as soloists and the rest as corps de ballet dancers. He was succeeded in 1778 by Léopold Paradis[14] whose pupils are known to have appeared at the Petrovsky Theatre from 1784 onwards, the same year the school came under the theatre's direct supervision. In 1806, the renamed Moscow Imperial Theatre College came under the control of the newly-formed Office of the Imperial Theatres and in 1863 moved to a new location on Neglinnaya Street.

Independent theatrical ensembles also developed from the mid-eighteenth century onwards, often taking serfs from the properties of the great aristocratic families and training them in the performing arts; these were

---

12 Born in Naples in 1775, Carlo di Giovanni Rossi came to Russia as a child with his ballerina mother Guertroude Rossi-Le Picq. He studied architecture with the Admiralty Board and in Italy before beginning to practise in St Petersburg in 1806. He rapidly came to be in demand for his grand building style, the Mikhailovsky Palace, General Staff Building and Alexandrinsky Theatre being some of his most notable creations. He died in St Petersburg in 1849.

13 Beccari's date and place of birth are unknown, as is the year of his arrival in Russia. He is known to have danced at the St Petersburg Court Theatre before his appointment in Moscow. The date of his death is also unknown.

14 Born in Vienna on a date unknown, Paradis moved to Russia in 1759 to dance in the St Petersburg ballet company under *premier danseur* Franz Hilferding in whose productions he appeared. He took over from Beccari at the Moscow Orphanage in 1778. He died in 1782 in an unknown location.

fertile recruiting grounds for the imperial theatres which bought up several ensembles in times of economic hardship – in 1806 the newly-established Imperial Theatres of Moscow acquired thirty-six serf dancers and musicians from the noble Stolypin estate.

French ballet masters

From the mid-1700s onwards, Russia became a destination for foreign ballet masters and dancers alike, drawn by lucrative performing contracts. Italy may have been the cradle of ballet in the sixteenth century, but the art form itself came of age in France; thus, a long list of French men and women made their way east alongside artists from other European centres of dance to make money and gain a reputation. In 1786, dancer and choreographer Charles Le Picq[15] moved to St Petersburg, taking up the post of ballet master which he held until 1798. He staged ballets by Dauberval and Noverre as well as several of his own creation. Charles-Louis Didelot[16] became the Director of the Imperial Ballet in 1801 and remained in post for some twenty-eight years with a brief hiatus occasioned by Napoleon's invasion of and subsequent defeat by Russia. The ensuing patriotism ensured that ballet in Russia took a decidedly domestic turn, the focus becoming that of making it a home-grown art form. However, even for hardened Russophiles, the lure of the star of Romantic ballet,[17] Marie Taglioni,[18] was too great and from 1837 she spent a full five years in the capital performing *La Sylphide* – the *sine qua non* of the dance style – countless times, which opened the gates again for French ballet. *Giselle* was first staged in St Petersburg in 1842, featuring Russian ballerina

---

15 Born in Naples in 1744 (some sources indicate Strasbourg in 1749), Le Picq studied with Noverre in Stuttgart before embarking on a European career in 1764. He danced as a premier danseur at the Paris Opéra between 1776 and 1781 before moving first to Naples and then to London. He died in St Petersburg in 1806.

16 Born in Stockholm in 1767, Didelot studied dance in the Swedish capital and then in Paris under Dauberval, Noverre and both Gaetano and Auguste Vestris. He danced in Paris, Stockholm and London during the 1780s and 90s and in 1801 went to St Petersburg where he remained for ten years, introducing French technique and insisting on expressivity in performance. He left for Western Europe between 1811 and 1816 before returning again to Russia. He finally retired in 1834, having created over 50 ballets including *The Prisoner of the Caucasus* (1823) and overseen the first performances of Dauberval's *La Fille mal gardée*. He died in Kiev in 1837.

17 A style of dancing popular in the 1830s and 1840s which offered exotic fantasies, often with an emphasis on the supernatural.

18 Born in Stockholm in 1804, Taglioni studied dance with her father Filippo in Vienna and with Coulon in Paris. She debuted in Vienna in 1822 and was a star dancer in Paris from 1827 to 1837. She created numerous roles and came to epitomise the ethereality of Romantic dancing. After her return from Russia, she retired briefly but then returned to Paris where she became Inspectrice de la Danse between 1859 and 1870. She died in Marseille in 1884.

Elena Andreyanova[19] who scored a personal triumph in the title role.

Jules Perrot[20] arrived in St Petersburg in 1848 as imperial ballet master; he immediately restaged the work, having been involved with its creation in Paris in 1841, and in 1850 his production featured the creator of the title role, Carlotta Grisi,[21] as part of her season in Russia. In 1849 he also staged *Esmeralda*, his danced version of Victor Hugo's 1831 novel *Notre-Dame de Paris* (*The Hunchback of Notre Dame*) with Fanny Elssler[22] triumphing in the title role. Perrot created ballets which focussed on drama and narrative, and he found willing and talented interpreters during his eleven years in Russia.

Perrot was replaced in 1859 by another Frenchman, Arthur Saint-Léon[23] who held the post for ten years, distinguishing himself as a prolific choreographer and producer who moved away from Perrot's drama-focussed style to a more dance-oriented approach with brilliant, musical movement. In 1864 he premièred *The Little Humpbacked Horse* to music by Cesare Pugni.[24]

---

19   Born in St Petersburg in 1819, Andreyanova danced from 1837 to 1855. Noted not only for her ethereal dancing but also her expressivity, she performed a wide repertoire; she was Marius Petipa's partner for his Russian debut in 1847 in the ballet *Paquita*. She was one of the first Russian dancers to appear abroad, notably in Paris and London. She retired from the stage in 1855 and died in Paris in 1857.

20   Born in Lyon, France in 1810, Perrot studied dance in his home city and then under Vestris. He performed extensively in both Paris and London and became Taglioni's favourite stage partner. In 1834, he met Carlotta Grisi who became his lover and new dancing partner and created many works for her, including the solos in *Giselle* in 1841. He was ballet master at His Majesty's Theatre, London between 1843 and 1848 and then in St Petersburg from 1848 until 1859. As a choreographer he integrated dance into the drama of the ballets he created. He died in Paramé, near Saint-Malo, France in 1892.

21   Born in Visinada, Croatia in 1819, Grisi studied at the ballet school of La Scala, Milan and joined the corps de ballet aged ten. In 1834 she met Jules Perrot who created numerous roles for her, most notably that of Giselle. She was a guest ballerina in London throughout the 1840s and in St Petersburg between 1850 and 1853. She retired from dancing in 1854 and died in St Jean, Switzerland in 1899.

22   Born in Vienna in 1810, Elssler studied first at the Theater an der Wien and also under Vestris. Having danced in several European capitals, she settled in Paris in 1834 where she danced at the Opéra until 1840, feted as a sensuous and expressive dancer. She toured for another 11 years, including to America and Cuba before retiring from the stage in 1851. She died in Vienna in 1884.

23   Born in Paris in 1821, Saint-Léon studied under his father in Tuscany and in Stuttgart, debuted as a dancer in Munich in 1835 and subsequently danced throughout Europe, considered as something of a virtuoso both in dancing and on the violin. He worked as a choreographer in Paris and Lisbon before taking up the position of ballet master in St Petersburg where he remained for ten years. He died in Paris in 1870.

24   Born in Genoa in 1802, Pugni wrote over 300 ballets, the first of which was for La Scala, Milan in 1823. In 1843 he became composer for Her Majesty's Theatre, London where he collaborated with choreographers Perrot and Saint-Léon. In 1851 he became Ballet Composer in St Petersburg and continued to create music for successive ballet masters, including Petipa, until his death in the city in 1870.

He returned to Paris in 1869 where he created *Coppélia* at the Opéra in 1870, the year of his death.

He was succeeded by another Frenchman Marius Petipa[25] who had first arrived in St Petersburg in 1847 as a dancer and ballet master, like so many others, to make his fortune. The younger brother of the distinguished Paris Opéra dancer Lucien Petipa, the first Albrecht in *Giselle*, Marius became the defining choreographic voice of Russian ballet, rising to the post of *premier maître de ballet* (Chief Ballet Master) which he held for thirty-four years. Petipa created over sixty works, of which several form the cornerstones of today's performing repertoire in Russia and around the world: *Swan Lake, The Sleeping Beauty, La Bayadère, Don Quixote*.

Petipa and beyond

Petipa occupied the post of the Imperial Theatres' Chief Ballet Master from 1869 to 1903 and transformed ballet into the tsar's prized jewel. Over the course of his long creative career, his choreographic style changed with the tastes of the times, away from the *ballet féerie* towards a more symphonic approach, weaving dance numbers into the narrative of dance and mime. Under him, the Imperial Theatre School began to produce Russian dancers of the greatest artistry and technical accomplishment who would replace the foreign stars who had initially dominated. His ballets came to occupy a central place in the performing repertoire and were soon considered the benchmarks of classical style. Moreover, they were the motors for the advance in dance technique, as teachers and students sought to offer Petipa what he required for his works.

The impetus of Petipa's artistry meant that, despite his retirement early in the century, Russian ballet continued to be graced with dancers of the highest order during the first decade and a half of the twentieth century. The dancers of the first Paris seasons of Sergey Diaghilev's[26] Ballets Russes[27] were

---

25 Born into a family of dancers in Marseille in 1818, Petipa trained with his father Jean Antoine and with Vestris in Paris, he danced in Europe and North America throughout the 1830s and 40s before travelling to St Petersburg in 1847, often appearing with the ballerina Fanny Elssler. In 1850 he became Perrot's assistant and in 1855 created his first major work *The Star of Granada*. In 1862 he was appointed ballet master and choreographed his first success *La Fille du Pharaon*. He was made Chief Ballet Master in 1869, a post he held until his retirement in 1903. He died in Gurzuf, Crimea in 1910.

26 Born in Novgorod in 1872, Diaghilev studied Law in St Petersburg before entering the city's artistic circles; in 1899 he co-founded the art magazine *Mir iskusstva* and became assistant to the director of the Imperial Theatres. He became an impresario, staging an exhibition of Russian art in Paris in 1905, followed by theatrical seasons which ultimately focussed on dance. He established the Ballets Russes company in 1909 which lasted until his death in Venice in 1929; it was one of the most notable artistic enterprises of the twentieth century.

27 The company formed in 1909 by Diaghilev to bring Russian dance to the West which

all products of the Imperial Theatre School and artists of the Imperial theatres themselves.

Ballet as a form may have started in Italy and been developed in France, but by the eve of the 1917 revolution, it was emphatically Russian. Nowhere else in the world was there such talent, training and artistry as in the Russian Empire and in St Petersburg's Mariinsky Theatre in particular.

Poland

Poland left Russian rule at the end of the First World War in 1918 to become a sovereign state. As a country it had been partitioned at the end of the eighteenth century by the Hapsburg, Prussian and Russian monarchies and had been subject to further Russian expansion. Ballet first came to Poland principally from the West and a local 'Romantic' dance tradition grew up but the process of balletic russification accelerated towards the end of the nineteenth century with increasing emphasis on Mariinsky repertoire; Lev Ivanov,[28] St Petersburg's second *maître de ballet*, staged several works in Warsaw. From 1893 Mariinsky ballerinas appeared as guest artists – Matilda Kschessinskaya,[29] Tamara Karsavina[30] and Anna Pavlova[31] all appeared

---

became a cradle for new design, music and choreography for the twenty years of its existence. Its first seasons took place in Paris. It influenced greatly the nature and style of ballet in the West for much of the twentieth century.

28   Born in Moscow in 1834, Ivanov joined the Mariinsky Theatre as a dancer in 1850, rising to the rank of principal in 1869. He became company *régisseur* in 1882 and assumed the position of second ballet master three years later, all while continuing to appear as a celebrated character dancer. He choreographed many productions including *The Nutcracker* in 1892 and the 'white' lakeside acts II and IV of the 1895 *Swan Lake*. Such was his ability and creativity that many believe that he would be better known had it not been for the dominance of Marius Petipa. He died in St Petersburg in 1901.

29   Born in Ligovo, near St Petersburg in 1872, the daughter of the character dancer Felix Kschessinsky (Feliks Krzesiński in Polish), Kschessinskaya (or Kschessinska) graduated into the Mariinsky in 1890, rising to the rank of prima ballerina in 1893. She was nominated *prima ballerina assoluta* in 1895. The first Russian dancer to master the feat of performing thirty-two consecutive *fouettés*, she was a brilliant technician with a strong stage personality. She left Russia in 1920, opening a school in Paris in 1929. She was titled the Princess Romanovskaya-Krasinskaya after her marriage to the Grand Duke Andrey Romanov. She died in Paris in 1971.

30   Born in St Petersburg in 1885, Karsavina graduated into the Mariinsky company in 1902 as a soloist, attaining the rank of ballerina in 1909. She became the star of Diaghilev's Ballets Russes, creating many major roles for the ensemble. She left Russia in 1918 on her marriage to a British diplomat and settled in the UK, dancing again for Diaghilev and the early days of Ballet Rambert. She became vice-president of the Royal Academy of Dancing between 1946 and 1955 and was a distinguished coach of many of her former roles. She died in Beaconsfield in 1978.

31   Born in St Petersburg in 1881, Pavlova became a ballerina of legendary status. She graduated into the Mariinsky in 1899 and was made a ballerina in 1905. She began to tour abroad in 1908, appearing with Diaghilev from 1909 to 1911. She left the Mariinsky

at the Weikl. Warsaw saw its first production of *Swan Lake* in 1900, the choreography largely that of Rafael Grassi, the Italian company director; when Mariinsky ballet-master Enrico Cecchetti[32] became director in 1902 he set about establishing even closer artistic ties with St Petersburg.

The several appearances by Isadora Duncan[33] in Poland between 1904 and 1907 in concert performances with the Warsaw Philharmonic Orchestra led to a general questioning of the validity of the expensive art of ballet and a vogue in smaller-scale dance enterprises. However, in 1908 Mikhail Fokine,[34] dancer and budding choreographer at the Mariinsky, staged two of his ballets in Warsaw, *Eunice*, a 'Roman' ballet set in the time of the Emperor Nero and *Chopiniana* (known in the West as *Les Sylphides*), which had both premièred in St Petersburg the year before. Both works had Polish connections – the former was based on Henryk Sienkiewicz's novel *Quo Vadis*, the latter set to orchestrated piano music by the Polish 'national' composer Fryderyk Chopin. *Eunice* was widely appreciated while *Chopiniana* was generally seen as a sacrilegious treatment of the composer's music.

The Polish ballet company continued to be beset by problems, with the regular haemorrhaging of the best dancing talent to St Petersburg made worse by Diaghilev and Pavlova's active recruitment for his Ballets Russes and her eponymously-named company throughout the 1910s. The ballet ensemble contributed to the Teatr Weikl's celebration of three hundred years of Romanov rule in March 1913 with a performance of Fokine's *Schéhérazade*

---

in 1913, having bought a home in London two years before. She toured extensively around the world with her own company until 1929 bringing ballet to tens of thousands. She gave her last performance in 1930 and died of pneumonia in The Hague in 1931.

32   Born in Rome in 1850, Cecchetti was a noted dancer, mime artist and one of the greatest ballet teachers. He studied in Florence with Lepri and debuted at La Scala, Milan in 1870. He toured extensively thereafter and debuted at the Mariinsky in 1887 as a dancer – his presence and superb technique led to an immediate offer of a principal dancer contract. He taught at the Imperial Theatre School from 1892 to 1902 and opened his own school in 1906. He appeared and taught for Diaghilev between 1909 and 1918 before settling to teach in London. As a performer he created many notable roles including Carabosse and The Blue Bird in *The Sleeping Beauty* (1890). He died in Milan in 1928.

33   Born in San Francisco in 1877, Duncan pioneered 'free dance', basing her creations on flowing, natural movement. She studied Ancient Greek art which influenced her style greatly, and her performances, though carefully prepared, were characterised by seeming spontaneity. She opened a school near Berlin in 1905, the first of many managed either by her or her followers. After her first visit in 1904, she toured frequently to Russia, was an ardent supporter of the new Soviet state after 1917 and opened a school in Moscow in 1921. She died in Nice in 1927.

34   Born in St Petersburg in 1880, Fokine graduated into the Mariinsky Theatre in 1898 where he rose to be a First Soloist by 1904. He began to teach in 1902 and to choreograph in 1905. A ballet reformer, and ultimately one of the most important choreographers of the first half of the twentieth century, he found greatest fame in his work outside Russia with Diaghilev's Ballets Russes. He left Russia for good in 1918 and pursued a freelance career around the world thereafter. He died in New York in 1942.

and continued on a modest scale until the war with a limited number of performances. Poland ceased to be part of Russia in 1918 and therefore leaves the scope of this book.

2

Red Dawn

1917

The status quo

Repertoire

In 1917, Russian ballet was wide and varied despite being dominated by the works of Marius Petipa, twenty of which were still in the active repertoire. These ranged from the early exoticism of *La Fille du Pharaon*, through the classical purity of *La Bayadère* to the rich orchestral scores of Tchaikovsky (*Swan Lake*, *The Sleeping Beauty*) and Glazunov (*Raymonda*). Petipa's long tenure, his aesthetic and the demands of his choreography had shaped the Imperial ballet and its style in a way made possible only by that combination, a phenomenon rarely replicated in subsequent times – Frederick Ashton[35] at The Sadler's Wells/Royal Ballet, *George Balanchine at New York City Ballet and John Cranko[36] at Stuttgart Ballet are perhaps the only other examples.

From earlier times remained a repertoire of works: *La Fille mal gardée* (created in 1789 by Dauberval), known in Russia as *Vain Precautions*; *Giselle* (Perrot and Coralli); *Le Corsaire* (choreographed by Frenchman Joseph Mazilier, the original James in *La Sylphide*, who worked as a ballet master in St Petersburg for the 1851-2 season); *Esmeralda* (Perrot); *The Little Humpbacked Horse* and *Coppélia* (Saint-Léon). However, they, as with almost every ballet, had been adjusted, altered and reworked over the decades by successive ballet masters. From 1885, Petipa's second-in-command had been Lev Ivanov, but what remained of his choreography on the eve of revolution was limited: *Swan Lake* Acts II and IV (the lakeside scenes) – the most famous and long-lasting of his creations – *The Nutcracker*, *The Magic Flute* and an interpolated section in *The Little Humpbacked Horse*.

---

35 Founder Choreographer of The Royal Ballet and one of the most significant dance-makers of the twentieth century, Ashton was born in Ecuador in 1904. He was captivated by a performance by Anna Pavlova and trained by Massine, Nijinska and Rambert. He began to choreograph for Rambert in 1926 and moved to Ninette de Valois' Vic-Wells Ballet in 1935. He is credited with creating the English style through his many ballets for the company. He died in Suffolk in 1988.

36 Born in Rustenburg, South Africa in 1927, Cranko trained locally and then at the Sadler's Wells School. He showed choreographic talent early and created several works in the UK, including *Pineapple Poll* and *The Lady and the Fool*, with foreign companies and for revue and cabaret. He took over the directorship of the Stuttgart Ballet in 1961 where he created both a rich repertoire of his works and a world-renowned company of superlative dance-actors. He died by accident on a flight back to the UK from the USA in 1973.

Mikhail Fokine was a rare example of a choreographer allowed some room to innovate at the St Petersburg Mariinsky company in the years leading up to 1917, even if his most radical experiments were conducted in Western Europe for Diaghilev's Ballets Russes. Disillusioned with the limited performing opportunities with the ballet company, he took up a teaching position at the Imperial Theatre School at the age of twenty-two. In 1904 he wrote to the director of the theatre outlining what he saw as the need for reform: "In place of the traditional dualism, the ballet must have a complete unity of expression, a unity which is made up of a harmonious blending of the three elements—music, painting and the plastique art... dancing should be interpretive. It should not degenerate into mere gymnastics... it should explain the spirit..."[37] He started to choreograph the following year and persevered despite resistance from the Mariinsky's more conservative elements. In 1917 the active Fokine repertoire comprised *Chopiniana*, his plotless *ballet blanc* of mood and atmosphere, *Le Pavillon d'Armide* and *The Dying Swan* solo (1907), the *commedia dell'arte*-inspired *Le Carnaval* (1910), the exotic *Une Nuit d'Égypte* (1908), the 'Polovtsian Dances' from Borodin's opera *Prince Igor* (1909) and *Islamey* (1912), the mythological narrative in *Eros* (1915) and the Spanish movement of *Jota Aragonesa* (1916). Fokine's *Petrushka* was only mounted after the revolution in 1920. The Petrograd[38] production was by Leonid Leontiev[39] and featured *Elena Lukom as the Ballerina and Leontiev himself in the title role. *The Firebird* would only be performed with movement by other choreographers, starting with *Fyodor Lopukhov's version for GATOB (the ex-Mariinsky) in 1921.

Creating movement initially very much outside the imperial ballet was the figure of Boris Romanov,[40] a character and mime soloist at the Mariinsky who had been very much influenced before the revolution by the avant-gardism

---

37 From 'Fokine's Revolutionary Platform', http://www.michelfokine.com/id63.html

38 St Petersburg was renamed Petrograd in 1914 at the beginning of the war with Germany.

39 Born in St Petersburg in 1885, Leontiev trained with Nikolai Legat and graduated into the Mariinsky in 1903, soon revealing himself to be a superlative mime artist and performing there until 1941. He appeared with Diaghilev's Ballets Russes in Paris between 1908 and 1910. He taught at the Imperial Theatre School from 1911 to 1916 and at its successor from 1918 to 1941, serving as its director between 1918 and 1920 and of the company in 1920 and again between 1922 and 1925. He revived and produced many ballets. He died in Molotov (now Perm) in 1942.

40 Born in St Petersburg in 1891, Romanov graduated in 1909 and joined the Mariinsky Theatre, becoming an admired character dancer. He was director of the Mariinsky company from 1918 to 1920 when he left Russia with his wife, ballerina *Elena Smirnova, and led the Russian Romantic Theatre in Berlin from 1921 to 1926 before becoming Pavlova's ballet master and later worked in the same role at the Teatro Colón, Buenos Aires between 1928 and 34. He was ballet master of New York's Metropolitan Opera House from 1938 to 42, and again between 1945 and 50. He died in New York in 1957.

of the 'Stray Dog' artists' cabaret[41] and the Expressionist movement.[42] From 1914 onwards he became a house choreographer at the Mariinsky. His choreographic style owed much to Fokine, but he also displayed a growing satirical and grotesque side with such ballets as *What happened to The Ballerina, the Chinese and the Jumpers* (1914) and *The Dream of Pierrot* (1917) which displayed a macabre sensibility. A Mariinsky work which survived the revolution was his *Andalusiana*, first created in 1914, which channelled violence, eroticism and blood-lust in a tale of Hispanic high emotion.

In Moscow, *premier maître de ballet* *Alexander Gorsky held sway, as he had done since the turn of the century and would continue to do until 1924. He had moulded the repertoire of the Bolshoi very much as he had seen fit, despite the theatre being an integral part of the Imperial Theatres and under the notional hegemony of the Mariinsky management. He was in essence a revisionist, influenced greatly by the radical ideas of the Moscow Art Theatre,[43] Konstantin Stanislavsky[44] and other innovators working in the old capital. For Gorsky, realism, believability and narrative coherence were paramount, and he set about refashioning the old ballets along those lines; he revised *Vain Precautions* seven times, *Swan Lake* and *Giselle* five, among many others; it was his re-ordered and re-focussed production of *Don Quixote* in 1900 which formed the basis of the ballet as we know it today. The Bolshoi Theatre re-opened after the 1917 February revolution with Gorsky's new version of Petipa's *La Bayadère* with new music to replace much of Ludwig Minkus' score and wholesale rechoreographing of the dances.

---

41   Established in St Petersburg in 1911 by Boris Pronin, the 'Stray Dog' became a notable meeting place for artists and poets who felt alien to aristocratic society and tastes. It was closed down in 1915 by the authorities.

42   Originating in Dresden in 1905 with the founding of 'Die Brücke' (the Bridge) by four artists, Expressionism rapidly spread across the world as a movement which prized showing the world subjectively. Emotional experience carried greater importance than physical reality. Exponents of expressionist dance later in the twentieth century included Mary Wigman, Rudolf von Laban, and Pina Bausch.

43   Founded in 1898 by theatre practitioner Konstantin Stanislavsky and playwright and director Vladimir Nemirovich-Danchenko, the Moscow Art Theatre (MHAT) was conceived as a venue for naturalistic theatre (in contrast to melodrama) and became hugely influential in the development of the art form worldwide.

44   Born in Moscow in 1863, Stanislavsky trained and performed as a stage actor until the age of thirty-three when he co-founded the Moscow Art Theatre with Vladimir Nemirovich-Danchenko which rapidly gained acclaim for extending the possibilities of theatre with a focus on naturalistic and emotionally credible acting. He also established his 'method' which has influenced world theatre. He died in Moscow in 1938.

Companies

Described in 1930 by Commissar for Enlightenment Anatoly Lunacharsky[45] as a 'golden rattle' for the amusement of the tsars, classical ballet had long enjoyed exalted cultural status in the Russian empire. Its two centres at St Petersburg's Mariinsky and the Bolshoi in Moscow were designated Imperial Theatres, the artists in the service of the Tsar himself. Indeed, choreographer George Balanchine,[46] who in 1913 entered the Imperial Theatre School at the age of nine, remembered being driven in carriages bearing the double-headed imperial eagle to appear at the Mariinsky Theatre. Audiences at both theatres comprised the upper strata of Russian society – the nobility and military – with less well-off, but nevertheless educated, elements seated in the higher-up seats, many of which were passed on from one generation to the next. The Mariinsky Theatre was particularly favoured by members of the Imperial family who were not only often seen in the grand State Box but also, in the case of a particular Grand Duke, in the fashionable second tier or *bel étage* from where there was direct access back stage. Alexandra Danilova,[47] one of the most notable ballerinas of the mid-twentieth century, remembered an alcove which the performers passed on the way to the stage which was where distinguished guests would smoke and talk with their favoured artists during the intervals: "generally, there were at least two or three grand dukes, we would drop in deep curtsey as we ran past"[48] she recalled.

---

45 Born in 1875 in Poltava, Ukraine, Lunacharsky became a Marxist at the age of fifteen and was an early supporter of Lenin. He moved to Paris in 1913, returning to Russia after the revolution and in 1918 was appointed People's Commissar for the Commissariat for Enlightenment (*Narkompros*) in the first Soviet government. He remained in that position until 1929 after which he represented the USSR at the League of Nations. He died in France in 1933 on his way to Spain to take up the post of Russian ambassador.

46 Born in St Petersburg in 1904, Georgy Balanchivadze (he would later take the name Balanchine) was one of the twentieth century's greatest choreographers. He graduated from the Petrograd Ballet School in 1921 into the Mariinsky company. He left Russia in 1924 and by 1925 was chief choreographer of Diaghilev's Ballets Busses where he met Igor Stravinsky, who became a life-long collaborator. In 1933 he went to the United States where he founded the School of American Ballet and the company which later became New York City Ballet. He made more than 200 ballets. He died in New York in 1983.

47 Born in Peterhof in 1903, Danilova graduated into GATOB (ex-Mariinsky) in 1921, rising to the rank of soloist the year after. She left Russia with Georges Balanchine in 1924 and danced with Diaghilev's Ballets Russes until 1929. From 1933 to 1938 she was ballerina with de Basil's Ballets Russes and thereafter prima ballerina with the Ballet Russe de Monte Carlo until 1955. Technically strong, she was a charming and witty dancer who danced a wide variety of roles. She created major roles in several Massine and Balanchine works. She taught at the School of American Ballet from 1964 to 1989 and died in New York in 1997.

48 Danilova, *Choura: The Memoirs of Alexandra Danilova*, p.29

3

From Tsar to Commissar

1917-1924

Revolution

Russia's revolution let loose a myriad of experimenters in the world of dance, as the control exercised over the art form evaporated. From the very outset, however, it was also a world threatened by the political and social ideologies which had brought down Tsar Nicholas and destroyed the fabric of Russian society; some questioned whether ballet should exist at all in the new Soviet era. The first years after 1917 presented many challenges, from the material – non-payment of dancers, shortages of both food and fuel – to the philosophical, artistic and aesthetic. Before the control which the Soviet state would increasingly impose on classical dance, there was to be an existential struggle for the art form itself. Russian ballet had somehow to free itself from its close association with the deposed monarchy and, also, through training, perpetuate itself with new practitioners. No national policy existed – it was, at best, a piecemeal and uncoordinated approach – and those who emerged as ballet's greatest advocates did so in the face of often virulent opposition. That they succeeded in preserving classical dance in Russia at all is surprising enough; that post-revolutionary Russia became, once again, the recognised epicentre of the art form is nothing short of miraculous.

Early days

In 1917 and during the first few years thereafter, ballet can be split into three interwoven strands: the vicissitudes of the two former imperial companies and their theatres, the dance-makers, choreographers and directors who shaped the repertoire and, finally, the dancers themselves. Far from effecting a smooth transition, the revolution and its messy aftermath came close to dealing a fatal blow to classical dancing in Russia, partly as a result of the circumstances around them, partly from ideological hostility.

Faced with the abdication of the Tsar after the February Revolution, the establishment of the Provisional Government and the Bolsheviks' October putsch in St Petersburg, the dancers of the imperial theatres were deprived of their raison d'être; few if any could have failed to appreciate their precarious position as former members of the imperial household in a new society in which the social order and hierarchy of which they were once a part had been swept aside.

The so-called moderate February revolution had little effect on day-to-day dance life. As violent protests broke out in Petrograd, the Mariinsky company initially continued to perform – on 26th February, Saint-Léon's *La Source* was the last ballet to be shown before the theatre closed the next day. Soon after the Tsar's abdication on 2nd March, Mikhail Lvov, a member of the Duma (parliament), was appointed to look after the former imperial theatres in St Petersburg. The Mariinsky (performing opera and ballet), the Alexandrinsky (Russian drama) and the Mikhailovsky (French and German classical theatre) all re-opened on the 12th, suitably de-imperialised and renamed as 'state theatres', imperial double-headed eagle emblems covered in red cloth, ushers' uniforms now grey and programmes featuring a lyre instead of the Tsar's coat of arms. The dancers of the now ex-Mariinsky Theatre and the students at the ex-Imperial Theatre School continued to be in demand, not only for scheduled ballet performances, but also for celebratory galas and events elsewhere – fifteen older boys from the school were involved in the city's May Day celebrations, held on 18th April given the disjunct between Western and Eastern calendars (the Gregorian calendar was adopted on 14th February 1918, Russia 'losing' two weeks in the process). On 19th March Alexander Gorsky's new version of *La Bayadère* was the first ballet to be shown at the re-opened Bolshoi Theatre. One victim of the February revolution was Matilda Kschessinskaya, the Mariinsky's *prima ballerina assoluta*,[49] who had long been intimately associated with several male members of the Imperial family and who in 1921 would marry in exile one of the tsar's cousins, the Grand Duke Andrey Romanov. Her luxurious town house in St Petersburg was ransacked by revolutionaries who saw her as a symbol of the old order.

However, as early as in April, not only material concerns about the future of ballet in general were being raised: "Ballet is ruined...This exotic plant can only exist in a special atmosphere, which now no longer exists" wrote a commentator in the magazine *Epikur*.[50]

The October revolution had a very different effect on the Bolshoi Theatre and School, ex-Mariinsky Theatre and the newly-renamed Petrograd Ballet School which all closed shortly after the outbreak of Bolshevik violence. During 1917, between the two coups d'état, the old aristocratic administration, seeing the writing on the wall for society as they knew it, melted away and clear responsibility for the theatres was only fully assumed in late November 1917 by the newly-formed People's Commissariat for

---

49 Very rarely awarded and without any agreed process to do so, the rank of *prima ballerina assoluta*, denoting exceptional talent, was given twice by the Mariinsky in imperial times (to contemporaries Pierina Legnani and Matilda Kschessinskaya) and twice by the Bolshoi in the Soviet era (to Galina Ulanova and then Maya Plisetskaya). There have been no others.

50 Swift, *The Art of Ballet in the USSR*, p.27

Enlightenment or *Narkompros* which, by a stroke of luck for the future of ballet in Russia, was headed by Anatoly Lunacharsky. The Bolshoi Theatre re-opened on 21st November, the Mariinsky somewhat later owing to continuing civil unrest; by early 1918, however, ballet performances were again being staged regularly in Petrograd.

Anatoly Lunacharsky

Politically, Lunacharsky was a committed Marxist who had lived in in political exile in Europe since 1906 but who had also fallen in love with the 'bourgeois' art forms he experienced there, not least of which was the 1912 Ballets Russes Paris season. His return to Russia in the spring of 1917 was followed in the autumn by the receipt of the culture portfolio from Lenin; he was resisted on many fronts, not least by the arts and educational institutions he nominally controlled. The stakes were high, given the prevalence of a revolutionary desire to sweep aside everything associated with the empire in order to start afresh, something which most decidedly included ballet. A cultured man, it was Lunacharsky who time and time again argued the case for dance at the highest levels, with Lenin and other members of the ruling *Sovnarkom* (Council of People's Commissars), insisting that to throw out all of the past would be wrong; better to appropriate it for the new communist Russia. In a speech given in March 1921 he spoke about the importance of what had been achieved in ballet under the tsars:

> "To lose this thread, to allow it to break before being used as the foundation of a new artistic culture – belonging to the people – this would be a great calamity, and, if it depends on the will of certain persons – a great crime... Can ballet be abolished in Russia? No, this will never happen."[51]

Certainly, his speeches in favour of ballet's survival carried immense power. *Fyodor Lopukhov wrote:

> "It is difficult to say what argued better for Soviet power, the content of Lunacharksy's speeches or he himself – a passionate orator, able to conquer the auditorium not so much by his ideas...as by the emotional conviction which always impressed the artists."[52]

If anyone can be seen as the saviour of classical dance in Russia, it is Anatoly Lunacharsky.

Survival

Crucial to the early days of survival was the entertainment that ballet performances gave to the workers; the repertoires of the newly-revolutionary

---

51 Lunacharsky, 'The Art Education of Soviet Schoolchildren' p.170
52 As quoted by Devereux, *Dancing Times*, January 1988,

theatres did not change from those under Tsar Nicholas II, with the established works featuring most prominently – the Bolshoi re-opened with *La Bayadère* and began its 1917-18 season with that most regal of ballets *The Sleeping Beauty*.

"For ballet this was an especially dangerous moment" wrote choreographer and director Fyodor Lopukhov many years later in *Sixty Years in Ballet*, as he remembered appearing in the first performances at the ex-Mariinsky after the theatres had re-opened. "There was an age-old conviction that ballet was for the chosen few, for the summit of society, for courtiers and aristocrats... it was said to be an inescapable attribute of Tsarism, incapable of relating to the stormy real issues of the day...What would happen? Would they laugh at our ballerinas, 'half-nakedly waving legs'? ...Would they get angry at the stage power of princes, princesses, fairies and evil geniuses? What were such persons to them?"[53] he recalled the dancers wondering.

In addition to the rude physical overhaul undergone by the theatres themselves to remove all imperial connotations, the audience became increasingly proletarian; gone were the nobles and diplomats of the past and in came factory workers, ordinary soldiers and sailors. That, in itself, was remarkable as most Russians at the time would have had no concept of what ballet was, many never having entered a theatre. Lopukhov recalled:

"When the auditorium designed for the cream of metropolitan society filled with workers and peasants in grey overcoats, in leather jackets, with kerchief on their heads, in working and military clothing, some even with rifles – our hearts thumped. The first minutes intensified anxiety. Previously the audience had not come in like this. The hall had filled noisily, its patrons met each other, laughed, called across, foreign languages were heard. The new public appeared silent, concentrated, frowning...only afterwards did we understand that here we beheld an unprecedented attitude to the theatre: to its old habitués the theatre appeared a long-familiar vanity fair, but to the new – an unknown, secret and awesome temple."[54]

The need to escape the pressures and challenges of everyday life cannot be ignored as a raison d'être for classical ballet: "When the revolution was over, the arts attracted people. There was a feeling of survival, and an impulse to seek beauty"[55] observed former Bolshoi ballerina Sulamith Messerer[56] in 1989.

---

53   As quoted by Devereux, *Dancing Times*, January 1988
54   ibid.
55   As quoted by Finch in *Dancing Times*, November 1989
56   Born in 1908, Messerer graduated in 1926 from the Bolshoi Ballet School into the company where she enjoyed a dancing career of some twenty-five years and was particularly noted for her vivacious on-stage personality. Her first leading role was Lisa in *Vain Precautions* with her brother Asaf as Colas in 1930. In 1933, they became the first

Post-revolution evenings at the ballet certainly proved popular, and both free performances for trades unions and visits by dancers to factories spread the word about dance. Not everyone was entirely happy about the change: in Petrograd, the critic Konstantin Ostrozsky observed that his fellow audience members were now more "accustomed to balalaika songs from a coach house and a record player in a tearoom."[57] However, he grudgingly attested to their enthusiasm, as did the city's pre-eminent dance commentator Alexander Pleshcheyev[58] in March 1918:

> "This season I considered as a question of 'to be or not to be?' for the ballet. The question of whether the ballet would survive on the state stage or would be wiped out as an amusement and caprice of its elect admirers, was in the air of the theatre. the new audience, the masses who flocked to the ballet and chose it as an accessible art...the popular audience is sensitive, responsive and perceptive."[59]

The number of performances increased, from under 50 a year at the tsarist Mariinsky to around 70 by the 1919-20 season. In the early days at least, ballet provided a popular escape from the harshness of daily life characterised by limited access to food or heating, a fact recognised by Lenin who argued that "it is too early yet to put the bourgeois artistic heritage in an archive."[60] There was still a place, it seemed, for the fantasy and spectacle of the old imperial ballet, which an examination of the ex-Mariinsky's repertoire of the 1918-19 season shows was in plentiful supply. Eighteen ballets were staged, all revivals of existing works, which included *Swan Lake*, *The Sleeping Beauty* and *Giselle* as well as other Petipa works *Esmeralda*, *Bluebeard*, *Le Halte de Cavalerie*, *Le Talisman* and Fokine's *Eros*. The next season also saw the return of Petipa's *Les Millions d'Arlequin*, Ivanov's *The Nutcracker* and Fokine's *Le Carnaval*. The picture was similar in Moscow: the 1917-18 season featured the familiar pre-revolution ballets *La Bayadère*, *The Magic Mirror*, *Don Quixote*, *The Little Humpbacked Horse*, *Coppélia*, *Le Corsaire*, *Swan Lake*, *Raymonda*, *The Sleeping Beauty*, *Vain Precautions* and Gorsky's 1913 work *Love is Quick!*

Soviet dancers to tour Western Europe. She was also an Olympic swimmer and held the Soviet 100 metre front crawl record between 1927 and 1930. She began teaching in 1938 and continued to be much sought-after as such both before and after her defection from the USSR in 1980 until her death in London in 2004.

57 As quoted by Souritz, *Soviet Choreographers of the 1920s*, p.43

58 Born in St Petersburg in 1858, Pleshcheyev started as a dramatic actor and then turned to writing plays for the stages of the capital. From 1876, he published stories, travel sketches and memoirs and wrote for several newspapers. In 1896 he published *Our Ballet*, a history of ballet in Russia. He emigrated to France in 1919 where he continued to write until his death in Paris in 1938.

59 As quoted by Souritz, *Soviet Choreographers of the 1920s*, p.44

60 Morrison, 'The Bolshoi and the Revolution', p.6

However, productions suffered from reduced company forces and the absence of experienced principal dancers which resulted in the simplification or excision of some dances – in February 1920, Petrograd witnessed a revival of *The Sleeping Beauty* without the character of the Bluebird in Act III.

Life was consistently challenging for the theatres and their staff – conditions became extremely difficult, with little to no heating and limited access to electricity outside performance hours. Food was initially in desperately short supply, with the resulting effect on the health and strength of the dancers, and there were many instances of them accepting food as payment for their performances rather than all-but-useless bank notes. In November 1919 a deal was struck by the management of the ex-Mariinsky and Alexandrinsky theatres with the Red Army under which the theatre personnel would receive military grade rations (on-stage performers 'front' grade, backstage staff 'rear' grade) in return for entertainment for the troops by then fighting a ferocious civil war against the anti-Bolshevik White Army. It marked a turning point in the theatres' ailing fortunes, given the severe shortages in society at large.

The ideological threat

In terms of the future of the theatres and their companies, however, the ideological threat became even more severe than material shortages. In an interview given in 1917, Bolshoi director Alexander Gorsky emphasised that ballet could successfully be 'popular' theatre but, soon after the revolution, there were numerous and loud voices who argued vociferously in favour of shutting down the theatres altogether. "The most serious threat to the theatre came from the hard-line Bolsheviks who, for financial, political, and aesthetic reasons, saw no reason to finance the arts"[61] observed Elena Malinovskaya,[62] a loyal administrator whom Lunacharsky appointed director of the Bolshoi Theatre in late 1919. Theatre as a whole was considered in some quarters as ideologically suspect, operas and ballet in particular further stained by being elitist, tsarist entertainments. During the 1918-19 financial crisis, Vladimir Galkin, the commissar for Moscow's schools, pushed strongly for the redirection of resources away from the Bolshoi, arguing that fuel should be used to heat labourers and not "diamond-clad baronesses".[63] Articles among which 'Should the Bolshoi Exist?' and 'Is the Bolshoi Theatre necessary?' continued to be published, arguing that its purpose and viability

---

61 ibid p.9

62 Born in Moscow in 1875, Malinovskaya first organised the artistic and educational department of the Moscow City Council in February 1917 and became Commissar for Moscow theatres after the October revolution. She set up Stanislavsky's Opera Studio in 1918. She was Director of the Bolshoi Theatre from 1919 to 1924 and again from 1930 to 1935. She died in Moscow in 1942.

63 Morrison, 'The Bolshoi and the Revolution', p.6.

had ceased to exist even before the revolution and in 1919 the newspaper *Pravda* accused the Bolshoi company of isolating itself from its audiences, providing sweet fairy tales instead of the reality of the proletarian struggle. But the Bolshoi continued to exist, as did the ex-Mariinsky, and their status was further consolidated by the conferment of the title 'Academic' in 1919 after the nationalisation of all theatrical property and the establishment of *Tsentroteatr* or the Central Theatre Committee whose president was none other than Lunacharsky himself. In 1920, the ex-Mariinsky was renamed the State Academic Theatre for Opera and Ballet (Gosudarstvenny Akademichesky Teatre Opery I Baleta), shortened to the acronym GATOB and often referred to simply as 'Ak'. Key to their continuing survival was the fact that dancers performed frequently during cultural evenings organised by trades unions and workers' organisations – Tamara Karsavina, a star of the Ballets Russes and principal dancer of the ex-Mariinsky, appeared frequently in such performances before her emigration to the United Kingdom in 1918:

> "Under the new regime artists were treated with great consideration. Maybe from motives of policy, *panem et circensis*. If bread was scarce, shows were liberally given to the people; we were constantly commanded to perform in suburban theatres for a public of soldiers and workmen."[64]

In the early years after the revolution, financial constraints often threatened the theatres and their ensembles with closure and disbandment. By 1921 Lenin ordered Lunacharsky to 'lay all the theatres in the grave' in favour of educating the illiterate masses, and in late 1922 swingeing cuts in subsidies almost shut the doors of both ballet institutions for good. The early 1920s were the time of greatest threat; the country's economic collapse left the expensive art form of ballet open to the accusation of being simply unviable. In late 1921 Lunacharsky mounted a vigorous defence, accepting the cost but emphasising how far the theatres had gone in reducing their deficit (reducing it nine-fold), the potential bill of pensioning off employees and their success in attracting a new, proletarian audience; in March 1922 the Politburo decided against closure. These were such unpredictable and changing times that this seemingly definitive decision proved to be far from the end of Lunacharsky's struggle: by the autumn of the same year the nation's financial situation had worsened to such an extent that a new Politburo mandate was given to cut state subsidy to the Bolshoi and GATOB, even if it entailed their closure which did in fact almost happen. In November, notices of redundancy were posted in both the Moscow and Petrograd theatres and the threat of complete closure was only averted by directors Malinovskaya in Moscow and Ivan Ekskuzovich[65] in Petrograd undertaking

---
64 Swift, *The Art of the Dance in the USSR*, p.35
65 Born in 1882, in Elizavetgrad, now Kropyvnytskyy, Ukraine, Ekskuzovich graduated

to make the necessary internal cuts in order to comply with the financial imperatives. By means of a reduction in production and maintenance costs and an increase in seat prices, they ensured that this was the last instance of such an existential threat to both theatres. Ekskuzovich proved as important to the survival of the ex-Mariinsky theatre companies and the ballet school; a friend of Lunacharsky, he had been entrusted with Petrograd's theatres in 1918 and proved himself a dogged defender of the arts during the difficult years which followed.

With Lunacharsky's repeated defence staving off the immediate, material threats to the old imperial theatres, a more insistent menace emerged – the belief that ballet was ideologically useless to the revolution. The argument did not arise only at that moment; it tapped into the calls in some quarters for a wholesale cultural overhaul which had begun at the end of the nineteenth century with the desire to look forward and not back in the arts – 'Boots, Not Raphael' was one slogan. Post-revolutionary fervour saw calls by literary futurists to dump all pre-revolution artists 'from the steamer of modernity'. Ballet was in a particularly weak position because, while other theatrical forms had moved towards realistic depictions of social ills, and visual art had also started to explore abstraction, it had continued to live in a hierarchical, bejewelled fantasy world. "The ballet is not sick...it is senile," observed a writer in a Petrograd newspaper in November 1922, "classical ballet as a form has become obsolete".[66]

New work was rare in the first years after the revolution, indeed from 1921 onwards, GATOB even embarked upon revivals of the best of the old repertoire. However much this may have pleased some in the audiences, there was no escaping the reality that society had changed completely and that ballet needed to play its part in the creation of new Soviet culture. Lunacharsky himself, while fending off the most extreme attacks, was not himself in favour of a wholesale preservation of the past. His fervent belief was that Russia's pre-revolutionary bourgeois culture needed to be refocussed to serve the needs of the new socialist state, and central to those needs was the creation of new masterpieces grown from the best of the past in order to take their place as central planks of a new repertoire which would support and reflect the ideals of the revolution. In a speech in 1921 he stated:

> "We need the old art not only because it is valuable in itself, pleasant and perfect. We need it because new candles are lit from this torch and because

---

from the St Petersburg Institute of Civil Engineering in 1909. In 1918 he was put in charge of Petrograd's theatres and from 1923 to 1928 oversaw all theatres in the RSFSR. He died during the Siege of Leningrad in 1942.

66   As quoted by Souritz, *Soviet Choreographers of the 1920s*, p.48

new generations, growing around such artists, thus inherit the traditions of the school."[67]

This specific challenge to ballet in Russia was to alter its very raison d'être. The process could not have been more daunting even though dancers were being sent out with increasing frequency to perform for soldiers and workers in everything from cinemas to factories. Ballet could not remain as pure entertainment; it needed to educate the society it served. In short, it had to look to the present and the future, to the realities of a new way of life and to move away from the escapist fantasies and myths of the past. For that to happen, it needed artistic directors and choreographers to create and shape the repertoire.

Post-revolution dance-makers

It would be a mistake to assume that the revolution signalled an absolute break in the artistic life of Russia. Many choreographer-directors did leave, none more devastatingly so at the time than Mikhail Fokine, the firebrand of a modern, forward-looking movement in classical dance. It is worth noting that, in addition to being famous in the West as choreographer to Diaghilev's Ballets Russes for which he had created such works as *The Firebird*, *Petrushka* and *Schéhérazade*, Fokine also enjoyed considerable prestige in his native Russia. After the revolution, many hoped that he would take the helm of the ex-Mariinsky company as ballet master-in-chief and chief choreographer, leading the company in a new artistic world. He decided not to do so, the reasons for which were murky at the time, but it was said that he had demanded excessively high remuneration, unquestioned stagings of his future works and the promotion to ballerina rank of his wife, Vera Fokina, a soloist in the company. There was considerable resistance to the content and tone of his demands and a subsequent delay in any agreement; Fokine left for Stockholm in March 1918 to mount his ballet *Petrushka* and it was initially intended that he would return in the autumn but, on account of the worsening political situation, he decided that was not possible and ultimately made his way to the United States. He never returned to Russia.

Change in the world of the arts was already in full motion before the political and social upheavals of the revolution. Artists had travelled to and from Europe; Russia was not ignorant of the innovations taking place in Paris, Berlin and Vienna, and it must be remembered that Sergey Diaghilev himself at the forefront of the avant-garde and the *Mir iskusstva* (World of Art) movement.[68] The years leading up to 1917 had seen an explosion of

---

67 Roslavleva, *Era of the Russian Ballet*, p.191
68 Founded in 1898 by a group of students who included Alexandre Benois and Léon Bakst, *Mir iskusstva* also launched a magazine of the same name with Sergey Diaghilev as its editor in chief. The movement organised six major exhibitions of Russian art between

rebellious, modern, forward-looking artists in a range of movements, from Cubists and Futurists to Constructivists and Suprematists. Konstantin Stanislavsky had founded the Moscow Arts Theatre as far back as 1898 and had set about revolutionising theatre practice; in 1913 the poet Vladimir Mayakovsky[69] was one of the many signatories of the Futurist manifesto 'A Slap in the Face of the Public', and in 1915, Kazimir Malevich[70] had exhibited his first *Black Square* at the 'Last Futurist Exhibition 0,10'. This was the so-called 'Silver Age' in Russian arts. In the world of classical dance, a debate had arisen about its future and growing discontent was voiced about the increasingly moribund state of choreographic invention at the imperial theatres. Within those two institutions there were modernisers who wished to refresh and revitalise the art form, and outside, independent dance-makers whose groups and ensembles sought to experiment and to bring modern life and society into what was considered an increasingly outdated genre.

It would be wrong to underestimate the ongoing influence of Isadora Duncan, who had first appeared to great acclaim in St Petersburg during the winter of 1904-5. The freedom she brought to her movements and her focus on spontaneity and liberation were widely admired. Her first Russian recital comprised abstract dances solely to Fryderyk Chopin and within two years at the Mariinsky, Fokine created his own plotless ballet *Chopiniana* to the same composer. Duncan's alternative vision of movement, free and classless, as well as her radical political views, made her the darling of the early days of the revolution – in 1921 Lunacharsky invited her to found a school in Moscow which she enthusiastically did; it continued until 1949. Duncan's approach spawned several 'free' dance schools and collectives such as the Studio of Vera Maya in Moscow which began in 1917.

The revolution created what would be a short-lived artistic vacuum for dance in Russia. With the challenge of keeping society and the economy going after the enforced departure of an entire ruling class and a wholesale

---

1899 and 1906. It was re-founded in 1910 and its last exhibition was held in Paris in 1927. Rejecting the aesthetic of the industrial era, it focussed primarily on folk art and theatrical design.

69 Born in 1893 in Baghdati in the Kutais Governorate, Mayakovsky became a poet, playwright, artist and actor. Before the revolution, he was a noted member of the Futurist movement. He was a committed socialist from a young age, spending eleven months in custody in 1909 for smuggling female activists out of prison. From 1917 he was an ardent supporter of the Soviet/Communist ideal, an enthusiasm which waned with increasing censorship and state control of the arts. He committed suicide in Moscow in 1930.

70 Born in Kiev, Ukraine in 1879, Malevich studied at the Moscow School of Painting, Sculpture, and Architecture from 1904 to 1910 and assimilated Impressionism, Symbolism and Cubism before conceiving of Suprematism, a belief in art divorced from natural forms. An enthusiastic supporter of the revolution, he worked in several capacities before losing influence in the mid-1920s as Socialist Realism became the dominant movement. He died in Leningrad in 1935.

change in the social structure, it was several years before the Soviet governmental machine was strong enough and had sufficient time to turn its attention fully to ballet. In essence, a dance free-for-all developed outside the two old imperial theatres. Duncan was not alone, as practitioners of various dance forms and theories, from Dalcroze eurhythmics to folk dancing, vied for attention and exposure in a variety of venues and locations.

An array of dance-makers emerged such as Nikolai Foregger[71] who evoked the contemporary spirit of industrialisation and modernity and experimented with what he termed the 'machine dance' in which human bodies represented parts of a mechanical whole. He sought to make "dances of the pavement, of rushing motor-cars, the accuracy of machine work, the speed of the present-day crowd, the grandeur of skyscrapers".[72] Foregger believed movement could express struggle and victory and need not be allied to music; in 1924, he created *Dance of Machines* in which his dancers played parts in a giant mechanism. Lev Lukin,[73] a trained pianist, established the Free Ballet Studio (later called the Moscow Free Ballet) in 1920. Considered to the left of the avant-garde, he combined acrobatics, classical and plastique dance to liberate the expressivity of the human body and to establish a synergy between music and movement. Starting with *Sarcasms* and *Fleetingness* to music by Prokofiev, Lukin produced several experimental works over the four years of the ensemble's existence.

In Fokine's absence, three major choreographic figures emerged in the early years of post-revolutionary Russia (a fourth was to leave the country before he could influence the form) who must, in different ways, share the credit for saving classical dancing in the early post-revolutionary years. It was they who sought to reconcile the fundamental ideological conflict at the heart of the art form, that between the ornamental aspect of dancing (i.e., the sight of bodies in motion) which included feats of virtuosity, and the narrative and dramatic side. Petipa had shown the two largely without trying to reconcile them, mime and character dancing contrasting with the 'pure' movement of his *ballets blancs*, as exemplified by the *jardin animé* scene of the last act of *Le Corsaire*.

---

[71] Born in Kiev in 1892, Foregger became fascinated by the constructivist movement and invented and taught his own system of physical movement inspired by the motions of machines. He founded his own ensemble Mastfor in 1920. He was chief régisseur in Kharkov from 1929 to 1934 and then in Kuibyshev between 1938 and 1939. He died in 1939 in either Moscow or Kuibyshev.

[72] Swift, *The Art of the Dance in the USSR*, p.45

[73] Born in Moscow in 1892, Lukin graduated in piano from the Gnesins Musical School in 1910 before studying at the Moscow Conservatoire and joining a ballet class. After the closure of the Moscow Free Ballet in 1924, he worked at the Baku Workers' Theatre and headed Moscow's Duncan School between 1936 and 1944. During the war, he worked as the head of the Pacific Fleet Ensemble and in peace time he staged dances for operettas and worked in a circus. He died in Moscow in 1961.

Alexander Gorsky

Of huge importance in trying to reconcile the two elements of classical dancing was Alexander Gorsky. Born in St Petersburg in 1871, he graduated from the Imperial Theatre School in 1889 and joined the Mariinsky company, rising to the rank of soloist by 1895. He began to teach and stage ballets the year after, moving to Moscow in 1900 to become the company's *premier danseur* and *régisseur*, and then its *premier maître de ballet*, or director, in 1902. Gorsky worked closely with the theatre director Konstantin Stanislavsky, and was hugely influenced by him, prizing realism in performance above all. On his arrival in Moscow, he re-staged much of Petipa's work in a more naturalistic way – it is from his 1900 revision of *Don Quixote* that all of today's productions are derived. He emphasised mime, attempted to bring psychological truth to interpretations through more contemporary, everyday gesture and inflection, and prized a clear, dramatic impetus. In 1917 he was, in essence, demoted with the election of *Vasily Tikhomirov as head of the ballet company in his stead; Gorsky continued as choreographer. His work became more experimental, leading to increasing conflicts with the conservative elements at the Bolshoi, led by Tikhomirov. During the summer months of 1918, feeling that he could only create freely away from the theatre, he presented a season at Moscow's Aquarium Garden Theatre during which he created several new works with a number of Bolshoi dancers.

A very early success of sorts in terms of the creation of a new Soviet ballet and perhaps a reason to believe that such new works could be created successfully dated to June 1918 when, as part of the celebrations of the first anniversary of the October Revolution, Gorsky staged *Stenka Razin*. The seventeenth century Don Cossack leader who rebelled against tsarist rule was a major folk hero and his story was eagerly taken up in Soviet times, appearing frequently in verse and play forms. In dance terms, Mikhail Fokine had created a work of the same name in 1916 to Alexander Glazunov's[74] symphonic poem for a benefit performance at the Mariinsky Theatre, and two years later Gorsky decided to use the same music in Moscow for what was a hastily assembled production in which it is alleged that the company's leading ballerinas *Ekaterina Geltser and Alexandra Balashova[75] refused to

---

74 Born in St Petersburg in 1865, Glazunov was a musical child prodigy and studied privately with Rimsky-Korsakov. In adulthood, he found early fame as a composer and conductor; in addition to symphonies and other forms, his ballet scores *Raymonda* (1898) and *The Seasons* (1900) were especially popular. He was director of the St Petersburg (later Petrograd, later Leningrad) Conservatoire from 1905 and, nominally, until 1930 and oversaw Shostakovich's education there. He left Russia in 1928 on a musical tour and settled in France in 1929. He died in Neuilly-sur-Seine in 1936.

75 Born in Moscow in 1887, Balashova graduated from the Bolshoi Ballet School into the company in 1905 and came to excel in the major ballerina roles, notably Aurora in *The Sleeping Beauty* and Odette/Odile in *Swan Lake*. She left Russia in 1922 and settled in Paris,

appear. At the first performance Razin was performed by Alexey Bulgakov[76] and the Persian princess by Maria Reisen.[77] The first of Russia's post-revolutionary ballets, it was a modest success, receiving three performances and a further eleven in revival in 1922.

Gorsky essayed a radical new interpretation of *The Nutcracker* in May 1919, a project he had started to work on as early as 1912, which focussed the entire narrative through the eyes of the child Clara; to emphasise this approach, he cast Valentina Kudryavtseva,[78] then only fifteen years old, in the role. In 1920 at the Bolshoi, he worked with Vladimir Nemirovich-Danchenko,[79] a distinguished theatre director and co-founder of the Moscow Art Theatre, on a revision of *Swan Lake* which focussed on a logical progression of the narrative; in this they were enacting a decision in 1919 to bring the two theatres into an artistic union, the former taking responsibility for directorial work at the latter. This was the first *Swan Lake* to show Odette and Siegfried triumph over Rothbart and Odile (the famous dual role was split and danced by Elena Ilyushchenko[80] as Odette and Maria Reisen as Odile

---

first dancing at the Paris Opéra before opening her own school. She died in Paris in 1979.

76 Born in St Petersburg in 1872, Bulgakov graduated into the Mariinsky Ballet where he danced until 1909 as a noted character artist. Between 1909 and 1914, he appeared with the Ballets Russes in numerous roles. He joined the Bolshoi Ballet in 1911 and performed there until 1949. He taught mime at the Bolshoi School between 1926 and 1929. He died in Moscow in 1949

77 Born in Moscow in 1892, Reisen graduated into the Bolshoi in 1909 and performed at the theatre until 1950. She participated in Diaghilev's Ballets Russes Paris seasons between 1910 to 1912. Her first major role at the Bolshoi was in 1918 as Giselle. She possessed a fine technique and was an expressive stage artist. She coached and taught at the Bolshoi company from 1938 to 1948 and at the Bolshoi School from 1950 to 1952. She died in Moscow in 1969.

78 Born in Moscow in 1904, Kudryavtseva graduated into the Bolshoi Ballet in 1920, establishing herself as a lyrical and graceful dancer. An enthusiastic experimenter with Goleizovsky in the early 1920s, she fell victim to Stalin's refocussing of the Bolshoi from 1930 onwards. In 1939, she staged *Giselle* for the open-air stage of Gorky's Park's 'Island of Dance'. She taught at the Bolshoi Ballet between 1941 and 1943 after which she left the company altogether. She died in Moscow in 1951.

79 Born in Ozurgeti, Georgia in 1858, Nemirovich-Danchenko studied at Moscow University, abandoning his studies in 1879 to work in the theatre, firstly as a critic, then as a writer, teacher and director focussing on longer, organised rehearsals and a less rigid acting style; he worked closely with Konstantin Stanislavsky and his 'Method' system of acting. He encouraged both Anton Chekhov and Maxim Gorky to write for the theatre. In 1919, he established the Moscow Art Theatre with Stanislavsky, and a Musical Studio which later became the Nemirovich-Danchenko Musical Theatre. He died in Moscow in 1943.

80 Born in Tiflis, Georgia in 1904, Ilyushchenko graduated into the Bolshoi in 1919 where she appeared until 1959. She worked extensively with Kasyan Goleizovsky in the early 1920s and was a member of his studio. She danced a wide variety of roles at the Bolshoi and created The Lady in Oransky's *The Footballer* in 1930. She died in Moscow in 1987.

alongside Leonid Zhukov[81] as Siegfried). In 1922, Gorsky mounted a new version of *Giselle* at Moscow's New Theatre which brought many radical ideas to the stage not least of which was an appeal to naturalism on stage – he exhorted Reisen as Giselle to die "with your legs apart, not placing one on the other".[82] There was an emphasis on dramatic realism and the social inequality inherent in the tale of a philandering aristocrat and a naïve village girl; the supernatural element of Act II was jettisoned, the wraith-like *Wilis* becoming human mourners for Giselle's death. Transferring to the Bolshoi main stage in 1924, Gorsky's production lasted until 1934 when a return to the traditional production and choreographic text was made. In seeking to relax classical dance and give it new life through added meaning, Gorsky pointed the way forward – ballet classics survived in the new Soviet Russia as a result of some apposite re-focussing to make them ideologically acceptable.

Gorsky scored an unqualified success for the Bolshoi in November 1922 with *Ever Fresh Flowers*, a children's ballet performed by children to music by Tchaikovsky and interpolations by Boris Asafiev.[83] Lunacharsky was so impressed by the portrayal of a bright and hopeful future under communism, with songs and marches in praise of the eternal freshness of the revolutionary ideal, that he urged Lenin to attend the second night of "the experimental and enormously successful revolutionary children's production".[84]

Gorsky's time at the Bolshoi was far from easy, his attempts to modernise encountering stiff internal opposition, and his mental health declined to the extent that in his final months he could be seen shuffling around the backstage corridors of the Bolshoi Theatre before finally being committed to an asylum. He died in 1924, but his ideas lived on with theatre directors

---

81 Born in Moscow in 1890, Zhukov graduated into the Bolshoi in 1909 where he performed until 1926 and then again from 1931 to 1934 and 1942 to 1946. A brilliant partner and dancer with an airy jump, he performed leading roles across the repertoire, often with his wife Maria Reisen. In the 1923, he created two unsuccessful ballets, *Capriccio Espagnol* and *Schéhérazade* for the company, and was company manager between 1922 and 1924. In later years he appeared in character parts. He also worked as ballet master in Ukraine, Kazakhstan, Tatarstan and Kyrgyzstan. He died in Moscow in 1951.

82 As quoted by Souritz, *Soviet Choreographers in the 1920s*, p.140

83 Born in St Petersburg in 1884, Asafiev became a rehearsal pianist at the Mariinsky in 1910 and, after the revolution, a favoured composer of the Soviet regime, writing scores for some twenty-seven ballets which included Zakharov's *The Fountain of Bakhchisarai* and Lavrovsky's *The Prisoner of the Caucasus*. He was a writer, musical critic and one of founders of Soviet musicology; Prokofiev dedicated his First Symphony to Asafiev. He died in Moscow in 1949.

84 Lunacharsky as quoted by Souritz in, *Soviet Choreographers of the 1920s*, p.152

Stanislavsky and Sergey Radlov[85] and, through them, influenced the next generation of choreographers.

After Gorsky's death, there was no single choreographer at the Bolshoi able to take his place. Essential, however, in shaping the repertoire and preserving much of the heritage was *premier danseur* Vasily Tikhomirov and ballerina Ekaterina Geltser who represented the traditionalist element in the company, often in direct opposition to Gorsky's innovations.

Kasyan Goleizovsky

A dance-maker of considerable influence and a man of immense personal charisma was Kasyan Goleizovsky. Born in Moscow in 1892, he first trained locally and then at St Petersburg's Imperial Theatre School, graduating into the Mariinsky in 1909 before moving the following year to the Bolshoi Ballet where he danced until 1918. Increasingly frustrated by what he considered the conservatism of style and performance, he stepped away from the company at the age of twenty-six, in favour of establishing his own ensemble; with his own dancers, he sought to extend the classical idiom, blending it with external elements such as gymnastics, and worked towards greater fluidity of movement. His treatment of the human body would come across to modern audiences as surprisingly familiar: he used both turned-out and parallel feet, placed dancers on the floor, employed complicated lifts and partnering and favoured minimal costuming. Working during the early years after the revolution in the artistic cabarets of Moscow such as The Bat[86] and the Mamontovsky Theatre of Miniatures,[87] he developed a dark, sexual side to his choreography which he explored further at The Quest, his own studio established in 1916. He was encouraged and supported by the experimental director and impresario Vsevolod Meyerhold[88] and used the

---

85   Born in St Petersburg, Russia in 1892, Radlov gravitated to the theatre after graduating in History and Geography from the city's university, working with Vsevolod Meyerhold in his workshop between 1913 to 1917. After the revolution, he became a distinguished theatre director in which capacity he became director of GATOB (ex-Mariinsky) in 1932. Having emigrated to Paris during the war, he returned to the USSR in 1945, was accused of treason and sent to a gulag for eight years. He was released in 1953 but banned from Moscow and Leningrad. He died in Riga in 1958.

86   Founded in Moscow in 1908 as a basement theatre club by the actor-director Nikita Baliev, The Bat developed a repertoire of songs, poems, parodies and dramatisations of literary classics. The enterprise closed in 1922. Baliev emigrated from Russia and continued to present programmes in Europe and the USA until his death in 1936.

87   Founded in Moscow in 1911 by playwright Sergey Mamontov and a group of theatre-lovers, the Mamontovsky Theatre of Miniatures presented one-act plays and entertainments until its closure in 1915.

88   Born in 1874 in Penza Oblast, Meyerhold studied theatre under Vladimir Nemirovich-Danchenko and became an actor at the Moscow Art Theatre before becoming a fervent symbolist. He welcomed the revolution and worked closely with Lunacharsky from

music of modernist composers such as Nikolai Medtner.[89] Goleizovsky was very much a product of the pre-revolutionary innovation and protest which had characterised the intelligentsia, and his creations in the early 1920s clearly demonstrated both aspects, showing that he took the upheavals in society as an opportunity to leave nineteenth-century academicism behind and create a genuinely new style of ballet. However, he functioned very much on an individual level, focussing on personal emotions and desires rather than the needs or wishes of the masses, which would set him increasingly at odds with the prevailing cultural climate. Between 1921 and 1925, he brought together dancers in an ensemble which became known as the Moscow Chamber Studio in order to realise his theories in dance. In 1922 his *Salomé* showed almost-naked performers in near-pornographic poses and movements, and *Faun*, set to the Debussy score used by Nijinsky for Diaghilev in 1912, was a deliberately non-narrative, non-realistic production in striking abstract designs which sought simply to arouse emotion in its audience. Goleizovsky's star shone briefly at the Bolshoi; initially praised for the contemporaneity of his work, he was effectively censured off the stage by 1927 and was reduced to working on concert programmes and in music halls. He experienced something of a rehabilitation in the early 1960s and once more worked at the Bolshoi before his death in 1970. His work was nevertheless hugely influential on both dancers and choreographers alike.

Fyodor Lopukhov

If there is one individual who can be said to have contributed the most to the preservation in Russia of classical dance through choreography, it must be Fyodor Lopukhov; he is best known to British dancers and audiences as the creator of the Lilac Fairy's Prologue solo in *The Sleeping Beauty* and as brother to dancer Lydia Lopokova.[90] He was born in St Petersburg in 1886

the outset. In 1920, he founded his own theatre which employed methods of scenic constructivism and circus-style effects. He replaced Stanislavsky at the Stanislavsky and Nemirovich-Danchenko Music Theatre in 1938 before being arrested, tortured and executed in the Great Purge of 1940.

89 Born in Moscow in 1880, Medtner graduated from the Moscow Conservatoire in 1900 and, despite his virtuoso piano technique, he quickly focussed on composition. He wrote in many forms for the piano, including sonatas, chamber ensembles and three orchestral concerti. He emigrated to the United Kingdom in 1936 and died in London in 1951.

90 Born in St Petersburg in 1891, Lopokova graduated into the Mariinsky in 1909. She joined Diaghilev the following year and remained with the Ballets Russes until 1929. She created roles in several of Massine's ballets. A vivacious, musical dancer, she settled in London having married the economist John Maynard Keynes and was a founder member of the Camargo Society, dancing in its performances and those of the Vic-Wells Ballet. She appeared as an actress on the London stage and founded the Cambridge Arts Theatre in 1935. She was sister to Fyodor and Andrey Lopukhov. She died in Seaford, England in 1981.

and trained at the Imperial Theatre School, joining the Mariinsky company in 1905 where he became a celebrated character dancer. After brief spells at the Bolshoi (where he trained further with Gorsky) and abroad, he turned increasingly to staging and choreography; by the early 1920s, he had emerged as a respected *répétiteur* and, following the departure of Leonid Leontiev in 1922, Lopukhov replaced him as director of the GATOB (ex-Mariinsky) ballet company. The nature of classical dance in Petrograd was different from that in Moscow – no concerted modernisation à la Gorsky had taken place, and, by general consensus, the old pre-revolution ballet productions which continued to entertain the new proletarian audience were, by the early 1920s, struggling under textual alterations, excisions and reductions in numbers as well as everyday wear and tear. In addition, the now former capital bristled with those intent on preserving the past at all costs. It was into this tricky situation that Lopukhov, who allied practical talents with serious thought about what dance was and could achieve, plunged. Central to his aims was his belief that it was the relationship between music and dance that was paramount and that movement should not merely accompany the score but rather exist within it. To that end, his original choreography showed not only steps from the classical canon but also outside influences, the better to achieve a new fusion of movement. In 1921, he presented his own version of *The Firebird*, using Stravinsky's[91] 1910 score but taking the visual element away from Fokine's fantastical exoticism and presenting something altogether more allegorical. His prime aim was to fuse movement and music, which was commented upon favourably in reviews of the October première. Elena Lukom created the role of the Firebird and *Boris Shavrov that of Ivan Tsarevich.

Lopukhov's choreographic thoughts and experiments were exemplified by *Dance Symphony* or *The Magnificence of the Universe* in March 1923 set to Beethoven's Fourth Symphony. As a production, it was a failure, lasting for one performance, but it was a work which showed the way for the 'pure' dance which came to dominate twentieth century ballet, through the symphonic works of Léonide Massine[92] and the abstraction of Balanchine (who himself

---

91 Born in Oranienbaum near St Petersburg in 1882, Stravinsky was one of the twentieth century's most important and influential composers. Having studied composition with Rimsky-Korsakov he came to international prominence with three scores for the Ballets Russes: *The Firebird* (1910), *Petrushka* (1911) and *Le Sacre du Printemps* (1913). He ultimately moved to United States where he forged a close artistic bond with George Balanchine, composing many works for his New York City Ballet company. He died in New York in 1971.

92 Born in Moscow in 1895, Massine graduated into the Bolshoi in 1912 but then joined Diaghilev's Ballets Russes two years later. He started to choreograph the following year and went on to become one of the twentieth century's most successful and influential dance-makers as well as a much sought-after dancer. Many of his greatest roles were

danced in the production). Lopukhov sought to explore themes of universal significance through the music of Beethoven in a totally non-narrative fashion. The symphony's four movements were named 'Introduction' (which included episodes called 'The Birth of Light' and 'The Birth of the Sun'), 'Life in Death and Death in Life', 'Thermal Energy' and 'The Joy of Existence' which concluded with 'Eternal Motion' for the entire cast. That cast comprised young company dancers including future giants of the ballet world Georgy Balanchivadze, Alexandra Danilova, *Pyotr Gusev and Leonid Lavrovsky.[93] *The Magnificence of the Universe*, unsuccessful as it may have been, was a form of artistic credo from Lopukhov who sought to show that dance movement possesses inherent meaning and is not beholden to narrative or emotion. In 1925, he published *Paths of The Ballet-Master* which today reads as a manifesto for what became abstract ballet choreography as we know it. He wrote of "dance symphonies, with dance dominant, dance free of the close limitations of the story and accessories with which the old ballets were encumbered. The art of dancing is great for the very reason that it is capable, through the medium of choreography, of creating situation and surroundings that are in reality unseen, but felt. The art of dancing is capable of making the spectator experience such phenomena as wind or lightning far more strongly than scenic illusions of the same things."[94]

Lopukhov and the Classics

It was in his reappraisal of the pre-revolutionary canon that Lopukhov made his greatest and most lasting mark. From the outset, he sought to restore Petipa, but was unafraid to 'improve' where he saw fit. In doing so, he unquestionably did much to save a repertoire which would have either literally fallen apart or, in later years, been deemed 'un-patriotic'. His declaration to "remove from Petipa's ballet everything borrowed and alien"[95] was followed by decisive action, as he re-staged staples of the repertoire, from ballets by Petipa and Ivanov to those by Fokine. In 1922, Lopukhov's revival of *The Sleeping Beauty*, the acme of imperial Russia's dance classicism, was a major event; aided by Leontiev and character dancer

---

created for himself in ballets he made principally for the Ballets Russes and the Ballet Russe de Monte Carlo. He died in Weske bei Borken, Germany in 1979.

93 Born Ivanov in St Petersburg in 1905, Lavrovsky graduated into GATOB in 1922 and danced several major roles. In 1930 he produced his first choreographic work on the students of the Leningrad Ballet School, and in 1934 *Fadetta*, his first full-length ballet. He directed the Maly company from 1935-38, the Kirov from 1938-44, creating the first Soviet *Romeo and Juliet* in 1940. He directed the Bolshoi Ballet from 1944-55 and again from 1957 (or 1959)-64, choreographing throughout. He was one of the most important figures in Soviet ballet history. He died in Paris in 1967.

94 Roslavleva, *Era of the Russian Ballet*, pp.203-4

95 Souritz, *Soviet Choreographers of the 1920s*, p.257

Alexander Bocharov,[96] he worked hard to bring back the best of the original and even restored the usually cut hunting scene in Act II. At the première Aurora was danced by *Elizaveta Gerdt and Prince Désiré by *Mikhail Dudko. Reactions were mixed, with many of the Petrograd 'old guard' responding negatively to his streamlining and seemingly arbitrary approach to what many considered sacred text. However, Alexandre Benois[97] penned the article 'Piety or Blasphemy' in November 1922 in support of Lopukhov's artistic policy and against the vociferous criticism from some quarters. The director-choreographer continued undaunted, restoring and refreshing where he saw fit: he tackled *Raymonda* later in 1922 – "in those days we ached with desire to bring stage versions back to the literary original"[98] – with Gerdt and Dudko as Raymonda and Jean de Brienne, and used the same pairing as the Sugar Plum Fairy and the Prince in *The Nutcracker* in April 1923. Lopukhov also staged a version of Gorsky's *Don Quixote* in the autumn of 1923, this time showcasing Olga Spessivtseva[99] as Kitri-Dulcinea, partnered by Dudko as Basilio. Whereas in the West, many of these ballets have come through the notebooks of the émigré *régisseur* Nikolai Sergeyev,[100] in Leningrad it was Lopukhov who, at a crucial time when a performing tradition could have been lost, was in a position and of a mind to preserve what he could. He also faced opposition

---

96 Born in St Petersburg in 1886, Bocharov graduated into the Mariinsky in 1904 where he danced in the corps de ballet for ten years before becoming a noted character artist. He danced with the Anna Pavlova company in 1908 and 1909. In the early 1920s, he taught at Volynsky's 'Baltflot' school and continued to appear with GATOB/the Kirov until 1947, teaching at the school until his death in Leningrad in 1956.

97 Born in St Petersburg in 1870, Benois first studied law before turning to art; in 1899 he co-founded the art magazine *Mir iskusstva*. He was the first artistic director of the Ballets Russes and worked with Diaghilev from 1909 to 1911 when he returned to design for the Mariinsky Theatre. After the revolution, he served as curator of the Old Masters gallery in Petrograd/Leningrad's Hermitage Museum from 1918 to 1926. He left Russia in 1927 and settled in France. He died in Paris in 1960.

98 As quoted by Devereux, *Dance and Dancers*, February 1988

99 Born in Rostov in 1895, Spessivtseva was one of the greatest classical dancers. She graduated into the Mariinsky company in 1913 and was made ballerina in 1918. She frequently guested abroad and, after her definitive departure from Russia in 1924, she became an *étoile* at the Paris Opéra until 1932. She appeared around the world throughout the 1930s, dancing her last performance in Buenos Aires in 1939. She settled in the USA that same year and in 1943 suffered a nervous breakdown, remaining in a mental hospital for twenty years until moving to a Russian settlement, Tolstoy Farm, New Jersey where she died in 1991.

100 Born in St Petersburg in 1876, Sergeyev graduated into the Mariinsky in 1894 and rose to the rank of soloist in 1904. He became *régisseur général* between 1914-18. He left Russia at the revolution taking with him his notations of twenty-one productions from which he provided stagings from the 1920s onwards for several Western ballet companies including the Vic-Wells/Sadler's Wells Ballet Company in the UK. He bequeathed his notations to Mona Inglesby who later sold them to the Harvard Library in the USA. He died in Nice in 1951.

from more revolutionary individuals who pushed for radical reworkings of the old repertoire and even its rejection, but Lopukhov's approach won out, achieving his goal of saving great works for future audiences and dancers. Not everything was a success; in 1929, his experimental second production of *The Nutcracker*[101] never found favour and was dropped the following season, thereby opening the door for new versions in later years. The battle over the past was, however, far from over and the 1930s would see further attacks on ballet as an insufficiently revolutionary art form.

Georgy Balanchivadze

Georgy Balanchivadze (later George Balanchine) was a choreographer who ultimately found his future outside Russia but who soaked up the artistic influences around him before his emigration in 1924. Born in St Petersburg in 1904, he studied at the Petrograd Ballet School until his graduation into the GATOB company in 1921. Unlike the older choreographers Gorsky and Fokine, the young Balanchivadze was not taken by Isadora Duncan, later describing her in a magazine interview as "...absolutely unbelievable – a drunken, fat woman who for hours was rolling around like a pig".[102] He was however impressed by Fokine and by *Chopiniana* in particular, the plotless ballet of atmosphere attracting the future master of abstract dance. Balanchivadze created his first dance work in 1920 while in his teens, a pas de deux named *Night*, set to Anton Rubinstein's[103] Violin and Piano Sonata in B flat, featuring fellow students Olga Mungalova[104] and Pyotr Gusev who later became husband and wife. During his graduation year, he was captivated when he saw a performance during the Petrograd October arts festival by Goleizovsky's Moscow Chamber Studio ensemble which featured the sexually explicit *Salomé* and the suites *Medtneriana* and *Scriabiniana*. He later stated that what he witnessed had given impetus to and inspiration for his own creations; in 1921 he formed his own ensemble, the Petrograd Young Academic Ballet or Young Ballet[105] for short which put together infrequent

101   Olga Mungalova created the role of Masha, Boris Shavrov (some sources say Pyotr Gusev) was the Nutcracker and Leonid Leontiev appeared as Drosselmeyer.

102   Taper, *Balanchine*, p.59

103   Born in Vikhvatinets, Podolia Governorate in 1829, Rubinstein became one of most important figures in Russian music, being a virtuoso pianist of the highest rank, a conductor and teacher; he taught composition to Tchaikovsky. He founded the St Petersburg Conservatoire. He died in the city in 1894.

104   Born in Perm in 1905, Mungalova graduated from the Petrograd Theatre School in 1923, having been a pupil of Olga Preobrazhenskaya and Agrippina Vaganova. A member of Balanchine's Young Ballet, she became a favoured dancer of Lopukhov; in 1927 she created the title role in his *Ice Maiden* and danced with GATOB/Kirov until her death in 1942 during the Siege of Leningrad.

105   The Young Ballet (Molodoi Balet) was an ensemble of enthusiastic artists whose composition changed from month to month. Its most significant members were

concerts of new work. Balanchivadze's experimentation provoked negative reaction: the prominent balletomane and critic Akim Volynsky[106] saw both he and Goleizovsky as betraying the classical tradition and the GATOB management began to be unsympathetic towards the young dance-maker whose works owed much to the older choreographer in his choice of music and use of non-balletic steps, acrobatic lifts and even bare feet. Its increasing hostility, ultimately leading to a company ban on dancers performing his work, undoubtedly contributed to Balanchivadze's decision to leave the country in 1924. The Young Ballet was invited to tour to Germany which, despite the death in suspicious circumstances of dancer Lydia Ivanova[107] prior to departure, they embarked upon, deciding once in Berlin not to return. The great choreographer-to-be George Balanchine was thus lost to Soviet Russia.

Dancers after the revolution

When the cruiser Aurora's shots rang out and the revolution began to roll, the majority of Petrograd's dancers were gripped by fear, fear they would be without work, without means of existence. The more so as civil war, foreign intervention and blockade extended the destruction and living conditions became worse and worse. The company shrank drastically – some sickened, some died, some left in vain quest for a 'quiet haven'. Panic and terror tore at the artists of the former Imperial Theatres. Those who had once been in positions of power advised only one thing: "Flee abroad as fast as you can. Here ruin awaits all."[108]

1917 – Vera Trefilova; 1918 – Lyubov Egorova, Tamara Karsavina; 1919 – Pyotr (Pierre) Vladimirov; 1920 – Felia Dubrovska, Matilda Kschessinskaya;

choreographers Georgy Balanchivadze, Vasily Vainonen, Pyotr Gusev and Leonid Lavrovsky, dancers Alexandra Danilova, Lydia Ivanova, Alexey Ermolayev, Andrei Lopukhov, Mikhail Mikhailov, Nina Mlodzinskaya, Nina Stukolkina, theatre designers Tatiana Bruni and Vladimir Dmitriev and ballet historians Yuri Slonimsky and Marietta Frangopulo.

106 Born in Zhitomir, Ukraine in 1865, Volynsky became a notable art historian and ballet critic. His writings carried great influence. He was an outspoken critic of Mikhail Fokine's choreographic innovations. He stayed in Russia after the 1917 revolution, becoming Chairman of the Leningrad section of the Writers' Union between 1920 and 1924 and publishing *Problems of Russian Ballet* in 1923 and *The Book of Exultation: A Primer in the Classical Dance* in 1926, the year of his death in Leningrad.

107 Born in St Petersburg in 1903, Ivanova graduated into GATOB in 1921 and quickly made her mark as an individual and gifted dancer whose vivid stage presence and explosive jump distinguished her from the others. She rapidly added solo roles to her dancing repertoire and became a firm favourite of both the critics and the audience. She participated in Lopukhov's *Dance Symphony* and Balanchine's first forays into choreography. She died in Leningrad in 1924 in mysterious circumstances on the eve of her departure abroad.

108 Lopukhov quoted by Devereux, *Dancing Times*, January 1988.

1921 – Sofia Fedorova, Olga Preobrazhenskaya, Ludmilla Schollar, Anatoly Vilzak; 1922 – Nikolai Legat, Bronislava Nijinska; 1923 – Serge Lifar, Mikhail Mordkin, Olga Spessivtseva; 1924 – Georgy Balanchivadze, Alexandra Danilova. The roll call of émigrés after October 1917 is one comprising ballet legends, which, in terms of the first fragile years after the Bolshevik revolution, signified a drain of talent and experience which in itself threatened to deal a death blow to classical dancing in Russia. Not only were the finest dancers fleeing the country, but also ballet masters, teachers and coaches – the very people who perpetuate the art form; it is estimated that forty percent of Russia's ballet personnel left after the revolution. Those who emigrated recognised that their world had, in essence, come to an end, many were terrified what the future held politically, socially and artistically both for them and for Russia.

Moscow and the Bolshoi

In Moscow, Vasily Tikhomirov, the Bolshoi Ballet's senior *premier danseur*, remained, becoming a favoured artist of the new regime. Born in Moscow in 1876, Tikhomirov studied at the Bolshoi School and then in St Petersburg, initially joining the Mariinsky company then returning to Moscow in 1893 – in 1899, he was the Bolshoi's first Bluebird in *The Sleeping Beauty*. He rose to be the ensemble's leading male dancer, Jean de Brienne in *Raymonda* and Conrad in *Le Corsaire* being among his best roles. A member of the Bolshoi's Artistic Council, Tikhomirov became company director in 1926 the year after assuming control of the Bolshoi Ballet School where he had taught since 1896. His devotion to the school and his clear conviction of what was needed to produce dancers of quality did much to preserve traditions and to establish what even today is recognised as the Bolshoi dance style in terms of the dancers' technical and dramatic qualities. The Bolshoi Ballet School had re-opened in 1920 and by 1925 numbered some fifty-three students who had come from the numerous private and semi-private studios in the capital. In 1922, Tikhomirov put together a list of technical requirements which the students had to satisfy in order to pass from one grade to another, as well as a further list for trained dancers applying for positions at the Bolshoi Ballet itself.

Born in 1876, Ekaterina Geltser was a product of the imperial ballet system, training firstly at the Imperial Theatre College in her native Moscow before being sent to St Petersburg in 1896 to work with Christian Johansson[109]

---

[109] Born in Stockholm in 1817, Johansson studied at the Royal Swedish Ballet School and under Bournonville in Copenhagen; he partnered Taglioni as a *premier danseur* in Stockholm in 1837. In 1841 he joined the Mariinsky in St Petersburg where he danced until 1869. Thereafter, he became chief teacher at the Imperial Theatre School where he taught Kschessinskaya, Gerdt, Legat, Vaganova, Pavlova and Karsavina. He died in St Petersburg in 1903.

and Petipa. She returned two years later and rose slowly through the ranks, partly on account of a poor relationship with Gorsky, the company director. Her dancing carried great power thanks to her talent for characterisation; she was "a vehement ballerina"[110] in the words of Lopukhov, a 'dancing Brünnhilde' in the opinion of the critics. At the revolution, she declared herself for the Bolsheviks and engaged enthusiastically with everything that was asked of her in terms of performances for the troops and the workers. Theatre director Konstantin Stanislavsky observed to her:

> "It seems we can be assured that Russian ballet has escaped deadly danger. Its salvation is deeply indebted to you, to your keen devotion to the art, the enormousness of your achievement, your tirelessness, your sparkling technique, and that fire within you that has enabled you to create enduring, living characters and maintain ballet's high standards."[111]

Both Tikhomirov and Geltser, who were dance partners and sometime spouses, were in essence traditionalists, and set generally against the modernisation of the repertoire that Alexander Gorsky, later *Asaf Messerer and subsequently a young generation of artists attempted. However, they devoted themselves wholeheartedly to the new Russia, and served both as role-models for the new Soviet dancer and as vital links with the traditions of the past. Lunacharsky spoke fulsomely at a jubilee to mark Geltser's twenty-five years with the company, praising her as a repository of the knowledge and artistry which she had brought to the service of the state. Messerer gave Geltser and Tikhomirov full credit for their central role in saving classical dance in Moscow:

> "Both of them constituted the solid 'academic wing' in the Moscow ballet. And if the 'Akballet' managed to avoid disintegration in spite of all the attacks, then this is (their) great merit."[112]

Petrograd and the Mariinsky

The Mariinsky company saw the most significant contraction, from around 220 members before the revolution to 134 by the 1919-20 season. Additionally, while much focus was placed on the theatres and what they performed to their new proletarian audiences, very little was said or done about the schools which would furnish the dancers of the future. As with administration and choreography, individuals emerged who we can now identify as saviours of an art form threatened with extinction. However, at the time, the situation looked bleak:

---

110 As quoted by Smakov, *The Great Russian Dancers*, p.81
111 Morrison, *Bolshoi Confidential*, p.242
112 Messerer, *Dance. Think. Time*

"The flight abroad of nearly all the former Mariinsky's ballet stars naturally intensified the doubts of the remaining. How to work, if Fokine, Romanov and Legat[113] were overseas. Without ballet masters, ballerinas and *premiers danseurs* the theatre could not operate."[114]

Not every dancer left – the devotion felt by many to Mother Russia was not to be underestimated – and the outbreak of the First World War had, after all, prompted many dancers to return to their homeland out of patriotism, dancers like Tamara Karsavina and choreographers such as Mikhail Fokine. Their subsequent decision to leave, as for countless others, was not an easy one, and for some, no matter how hard life in Russia proved to be, one that they could never take.

Mariinsky/GATOB dancers

Viktor Semyonov was born in St Petersburg in 1892 and joined the Mariinsky in 1912 where he danced until 1929. A dancer of unforced, elegant bravura, he quickly rose to be a noted *danseur noble*, appearing in all the major roles of the repertoire. In 1930 he joined the Bolshoi company with his then wife *Marina Semyonova and became a principal dancer and teacher. He retired from dancing in 1931 and devoted himself to teaching, which, throughout the 1930s he did at the Bolshoi, the Moscow Art College and the Stanislavsky and Nemirovich-Danchenko Theatre. From 1939 to 1944 he taught dance to the Red Banner Ensemble. He died in Moscow in 1944.

A 1919 émigré who danced for just over one year after the revolution was the virtuoso male dancer Pyotr (or Pierre) Vladimirov. Born in St Petersburg in 1893, he graduated into the Mariinsky in 1911 where, owing to his prodigious technique and huge jump, he inherited many of Nijinsky's roles. He was made a principal dancer in 1915 and created roles in Fokine's *Francesca da Rimini* and *Eros* that year. He left Russia in 1920 and joined the Ballets Russes, dancing Prince Désiré on the first night of *The Sleeping Princess* in London in 1921 and he subsequently toured with several companies throughout the 1920s. He eventually settled in New York where he taught at the School of American Ballet from 1934 to 1967 as one of the USA's most influential ballet pedagogues. He died in New York in 1970.

---

113 Born in St Petersburg in 1869, Nikolai Legat graduated in 1888 and joined the Mariinsky Theatre, appearing in the first production of *The Nutcracker* and partnering Kschessinskaya, Pavlova and Trefilova. He was considered to possess a brilliant technique and was an outstanding *danseur noble*. Alongside his brother Sergei, he succeeded Petipa as ballet master in 1903 but concentrated on teaching – among his pupils were Preobrazhenskaya, Egorova, Vaganova, Nijinsky and Bolm. He left Russia in 1923, was briefly ballet master to Diaghilev's Ballets Russes before settling in London in 1926. He opened a successful school, numbering Danilova, de Valois, Markova, Dolin, Eglevsky and Fonteyn among his pupils. He died in London in 1937.

114 Lopukhov quoted by Devereux, *Dancing Times*, January 1988.

Born in St Petersburg in 1900, Boris Shavrov graduated into the ex-Mariinsky in 1918 and, partly owing to the drain in dancing talent, assumed leading roles early into his career and became one of the most important male dancers in Leningrad throughout the 1920s. Favoured by Fyodor Lopukhov on account of his strong classical technique and unforced, masculine presence, he created the roles of Ivan Tsarevich in the choreographer's *The Firebird* in 1921 and the Prince in *The Nutcracker* in 1928. He was the regular stage partner of ballerina Elena Lukom. He retired from dancing in 1938 and continued in character roles until 1964. He taught from 1918 onwards and was artistic director of the Leningrad Choreographic School in 1930 and 1931. He died in Leningrad in 1975.

Born in St Petersburg in 1902, Mikhail Dudko graduated into the ex-Mariinsky company in 1920 where he established himself as a dancer of quality, partnering ballerina Elizaveta Gerdt. He was much favoured by Lopukhov in his re-stagings of the classics on account of his noble presence. He enjoyed a fruitful career until 1941. His reputation as a handsome, lyrical performer was destroyed after the Second World War: found guilty of collaboration with the Germans when he had, in fact, been forced by them to work in a theatrical troupe in occupied territory, he spent eight years in a gulag after which he worked at the ballet companies in Ufa, Novosibirsk and Tbilisi from 1953 to 1962. He was not permitted to return to his native Leningrad; that only happened at the end of his life – he died there in 1982, still in disgrace.

Born in St Petersburg in 1904, Pyotr Gusev first studied with *Olga Preobrazhenskaya before joining the Petrograd Ballet School from where he graduated in 1922. He danced with GATOB from 1924 until 1934 and with Lopukhov at the Maly from 1931 onwards; he was also a member of Balanchivadze's Young Ballet in the early 1920s. Following Lopukhov, he joined the Bolshoi in 1935, becoming a highly admired principal dancer, renowned for his exemplary partnering. He retired from dancing in 1945 to become a respected ballet master, although he had taught from the early 1920s. He was director of the Kirov Ballet between 1945 and 1950, the Bolshoi from 1955 to 1957, the MALEGOT ballet company from 1960 to 1962 and then the Novosibirsk Ballet. He staged many revivals of classical ballets. He died in Leningrad in 1987.

In 1917, the ex-Mariinsky company could field only one officially-ranked ballerina, Elena Smirnova. Born in St Petersburg in 1888, she graduated in 1906 into the company, having been praised while still a student for her performance as Hymen in *Acis and Galatea* the year before. By 1912 she was performing Kitri in *Don Quixote* and Swanilda in *Coppélia* and her debut as Aurora in *The Sleeping Beauty* in 1914 was widely acclaimed for its classical purity. Her extraordinary technique allowed her to begin a classical variation with sixteen *entrechats six*. In 1919 she created the role of Rosa in Alexander Chekrygin's[115] unsuccessful *Romance of the Rose*. GATOB lost its prima ballerina in 1920 when, with her husband Boris Romanov, Smirnova emigrated firstly to Romania, then to Berlin where they founded the Russian Romantic Theatre and finally settled in Buenos Aires in 1928, where she taught at the newly-created dance department of the National Conservatoire. She died there in 1934.

Elena Lukom was another admirable company dancer. Born in St Petersburg in 1891, she graduated in 1909 and participated in the early Diaghilev Paris seasons, attaining the rank of ballerina at the ex-Mariinsky in 1918. A highly versatile artist who danced a range of disparate leading roles from the lyrical Giselle to the dramatic Esmeralda, she eventually became a highly respected teacher who passed on her purity of training and style to many, including Kirov ballerina *Irina Kolpakova who fondly remembered her teacher's reminiscences as a pre-revolution dancer. She was perhaps the last of the 'pure' imperial ballerinas, although, choosing to remain in Russia, she actively embraced the new Soviet ideas and values. She danced until 1941 and taught at the company between 1953 and 1965. She died in Leningrad in 1968.

Born in St Petersburg in 1891, the daughter of the Imperial Theatres' famed *premier danseur noble* Pavel, Elizaveta Gerdt graduated into the Mariinsky in 1908 alongside her classmate Vaslav Nijinsky and was his regular dance partner before he left Russia in 1911. She danced her first ballerina role in 1917, very much stepping into the void left by her departed senior colleagues, and rapidly acquired some fifteen lead roles as a result. She danced until 1928 when she retired from the stage and started teaching, firstly in Leningrad and then, from 1935 onwards, in Moscow where she trained some of the most notable of the company's ballerinas. She and a handful of her contemporaries kept ballet knowledge and tradition alive, albeit sometimes by the thinnest of threads, and did so until the Second World War and beyond; Gerdt taught until her death in Moscow in 1975.

These dancers, however accomplished, were not enough to prevent the developing view that the Petrograd troupe was in decline. Audience numbers were falling away as numerous stage spaces, often located in cabaret theatres, proliferated and drew away both spectators and performers. It was the return of Olga Spessivtseva in 1922 which arrested the process and helped bring the people of Petrograd back to the theatre they now knew as GATOB. She had

---

115   Born in St Petersburg in 1884, Chekrygin graduated into the Mariinsky in 1902 where he performed until 1923 as a valued character dancer. He was a house choreographer for operas and operettas at the Maly Theatre between 1923 and 1929 and took up a position as artist and choreographer at the Bolshoi in 1930. From 1930 to 1941 he taught at the Bolshoi School. He died in Tashkent in 1942.

left Russia frequently to dance with Diaghilev's Ballets Russes, but always returned; after the harsh performing conditions endured during the 1919-20 season, she was named principal dancer alongside Gerdt and Lukom but succumbed to tuberculosis and had to travel to the Caucasus to convalesce. In 1921, she had starred as Aurora on the opening night of Diaghilev's financially catastrophic yet artistically triumphant 1921 London production of *The Sleeping Princess*, the now-standard three double pirouettes into a fish dive during the *entrée* of the Act III Grand Pas inserted on account of her technical abilities. Ex-Mariinsky ballerinas Lyubov Egorova,[116] Lydia Lopokova and Vera Trefilova[117] also appeared in the role. The following year, Spessivtseva provided a much-needed boost to an arguably second division roster of principal dancers in Petrograd: aged twenty-seven, and at the height of her powers, she returned to the stage of GATOB, dancing in the classics of the repertoire *Giselle*, *Esmeralda*, *Don Quixote* and *Chopiniana*. She appeared with either her old partner Semyonov "un danseur magnifique, mais un piètre mime" (a magnificent dancer but a poor mime) or Shavrov, "un excellent artiste, un très bon mime, mais un danseur plutôt faible"[118] (an excellent artist, a very good mime but a rather weak dancer) and she succeeded in re-energising both the ballets and the audience. Spessivtseva's star quality, her technical accomplishments and her glamorous personality also had their effect on young dancers for whom she was a real inspiration – the rising Alexandra Danilova and Lydia Ivanova at last had a role-model. Spessivtseva was not, however, to serve Soviet ballet for long and left Russia for good in 1924 at first with an invitation from Diaghilev to appear with the Ballets Russes and then appearing in the title role in *Giselle* at the Paris Opéra in its new 'historic' production.

---

116 Born in St Petersburg in 1880, Egorova graduated into the Mariinsky in 1898. Her dancing was characterised by lyrical simplicity and she was a noted Odette and Giselle. Having moved to Paris at the revolution, she appeared with Diaghilev's Ballets Russes. She opened her own school in 1923 and counted Lifar, Anton Dolin, George Skibine and Janine Charrat among her pupils. In 1937 she founded the Ballets de la Jeunesse company and she also taught at the Royal Danish Ballet where she mounted *Aurora's Wedding*. On her marriage she became the Princess Nikita Troubetskoy. She died in Paris in 1972.

117 Born in St Petersburg (or possibly Vladikavkaz) in 1875, Trefilova graduated into the Mariinsky in 1894, becoming a soloist in 1901 and principal in 1904. A dancer of great expressivity, she was considered the finest Aurora in *The Sleeping Beauty* since the role's creator Carlotta Brianza. A victim of Kschessinskaya's hostility, she resigned from the company in 1910 and became an actress, appearing at the Mikhailovsky Theatre in 1915. In 1917 she left Russia and established a school in Paris. In 1924 at the age of almost fifty, she appeared to great acclaim with the Ballets Russes as Odette-Odile in *Swan Lake*. She retired in 1926 and died in Paris in 1943.

118 Schaikevitch, *Olga Spissivtzeva : magicienne envoûtée*, p.57

Company Teachers

There were still distinguished teachers left working with the company. A great ballerina passing on her knowledge was Ekaterina Vazem,[119] a fabled *terre-à-terre* virtuosa with a formidable technique, who, in her mid-seventies, continued to give a daily class at the ex-Mariinsky known for its difficulty and strength-building qualities; it started with sixteen *grands fondus développés* at the barre and another sixteen in the centre. Spessivtseva herself worked closely with the imperial-era ballerina Evgenia Sokolova who, having had a highly distinguished dancing career, had become an equally respected and sought-after teacher.

Ballet Schools

Petrograd

Dance training in Petrograd was initially threatened by the revolution – the city's Imperial Theatre School in Rossi Street was dissolved by the Bolsheviks. However, the pressures on a new and precarious revolutionary government preoccupied with war with Germany, economic collapse, civil war and social disintegration gave Anatoly Lunacharsky some breathing space, as the focus and efforts of his fellow commissars were directed elsewhere. He took the decision to re-establish the state theatres and the ballet school under the stewardship of his personal friend Ivan Ekskuzovich who had the soldiers billeted at the school sent elsewhere and ensured that it re-opened. One day Lunacharsky paid a visit to Rossi Street and addressed the students: "Don't worry. Now is a very hard time, but we will keep your school, whatever it takes. Study! Master the art of ballet, so you can use it to serve our people!"[120] The school was left in a mess after the soldiers' departure, but teaching began again, even if the building itself was barely heated. Ekskuzovich repurposed the old Mikhailovsky Theatre as a showcase for the ballet students where the people of Petrograd could see performances by the young dancers who until so recently had been the personal property of the Tsar. Both he and Lunacharsky continued to present classical dance to the populace in the hope of anchoring the art form in their consciousness; the summer of 1918 saw a number of small-scale performances by both students and company dancers – all over the city, dance was often shown on makeshift stages. Lunacharsky's desire to make classical dance a feature of new Soviet Russian culture meant that the years after the revolution also saw a proliferation of private and

---

119   Born in Moscow in 1848, Vazem graduated into the St Petersburg Bolshoi Theatre in 1867 where she danced until 1884, one of the first Russians to rival the virtuosity of the Italian dancers. She was Petipa's favourite Russian ballerina and was the first Nikiya in his *La Bayadère*. She taught at the Imperial Theatre School from 1886 to 1896, counting Pavlova and Vaganova among her students. She died in Leningrad in 1937.

120   Kendall, *Balanchine and the Lost Muse*, p.120

state-sponsored dance schools (some organised by the Commissariat for Enlightenment itself), such training no longer to be the preserve of the upper classes.

The curriculum at the ex-Imperial Theatre School changed with the revolution: boys and girls had some classes together for the first time, character dancing was introduced with a class taken by Alexander Shiryaev[121] who also established a theatre studio at the school which trained the students for appearances at theatres around the city and at workers' factory clubs.

Time and again Lunacharsky and Ekskuzovich reacted with speed to political shifts which threatened the school and, indeed, the main ballet company. When the 1918-19 school year started late because of the social upheavals of counter-revolutionary activity and the subsequent 'Red Terror', the school's coffers were empty, with little or no prospect of being filled by the state; the decision to house the Narkompros School of Drama in the Rossi Street building's unused third floor meant that food and fuel became available for the ballet school housed in the two floors below. The new Soviet state strongly favoured theatre as a channel through which to promote and disseminate its political ideals, so it was a fortunate alliance indeed for the students and their teachers. This was a turning point for the school whose existence had been at best precarious since the previous year's revolution. In November 1918, it was officially renamed the 'Petrograd State Theatre (Ballet) School of the Department of Property of the Council of People's Commissars of the Russian Republic' and in March 1919, ex-Mariinsky dancer Andrey Oblakov[122] became the new director and oversaw increasing stability in the lives of the students, even if there were ongoing challenges with staffing. A notable success was achieved in persuading Olga Preobrazhenskaya,[123] ex-prima ballerina of the Mariinsky, to return to the

---

121 Born in St Petersburg in 1867, Shiryaev graduated into the Mariinsky in 1885 and became a character dancer of distinction. In 1896 he became choreographic assistant to Petipa and, on Ivanov's death in 1901, his deputy. He was dismissed from the company in 1905 and only returned after the 1917 revolution, having travelled extensively abroad. He taught character acting at the school from 1918 onwards and in 1939 co-wrote *The Fundamentals of Character Dance* with Lopukhov and Bocharov. He died in Leningrad in 1941.

122 Born in St Petersburg in 1874, Oblakov graduated into the Mariinsky in 1892 where he danced until 1907. He taught ballet thereafter in several institutions as well as ballroom dancing to officer cadets up until the revolution. The date and place of his death are unknown.

123 Born in St Petersburg in 1871, Preobrazhenskaya (or Preobrazhenska) graduated in 1889 and rose to the rank of prima ballerina in 1900. A splendid technician and a versatile performer, she appeared some 700 times at the Mariinsky. She taught from 1914 onwards and left Russia in 1921, settling in Paris in 1923 and becoming one of the most sought-after teachers there, numbering Irina Baronova, Tamara Toumanova and Igor Youskevitch among her pupils. She died in Saint-Mandé near Paris in 1962.

faculty. She had taught at the school since her retirement from the stage in 1914 before returning to dancing in the spring of 1918 and to oversee her own private dance school. Another teacher taken on under Oblakov was *Agrippina Vaganova; both she and Preobrazhenskaya transferred from Akim Volynsky's School of Russian Ballet. By 1921, the Petrograd Choreographic School's future was secure and it was even granted use of Princess Zinaida Yusupova's former dacha in Detskoe (formerly Tsarskoe) Selo so that its pupils could enjoy a summer holiday away from the city.

Akim Volynsky and the 'BaltFlot' School

Another figure who initially helped preserve classical dance in Petrograd was the critic, intellectual and champion of Russian Symbolism, Akim Volynsky, who in 1920 established his School of Russian Ballet, also known as the 'BaltFlot' School, on account of it being housed in the buildings of the Baltic Fleet in central Petrograd. Volynsky, a hugely controversial and consciously provocative figure, was fanatical about classical dance, having been the first seriously to analyse its technique as a critic and commentator in the newspaper *Stock Market News*. Leonid Leontiev, himself a former Imperial Theatre School student and Mariinsky dancer, first headed the ballet department of the Petrograd Choreographic School between 1918 and 1920 and then rose to become director of the ex-Mariinsky ballet company in early 1920. He proved himself to be its dogged defender in the face of increasingly bitter criticisms from Volynsky concerning the standards of training and dancing at both the school and the company. In truth Leontiev was having to deal with a much-diminished ensemble which had lost the majority of its senior dancers and experienced shortages of everything from food to heating wood. In order to promote his theories, Volynsky founded his own School of Russian Ballet and assembled such luminaries as the exceptional teacher Nikolai Legat and senior dancers Olga Preobrazhenskaya, Agrippina Vaganova and Maria Romanova.[124] Volynsky was convinced that it was time to move on from what he saw as the antique and formulaic Mariinsky curriculum, which produced dancers who were "soggy lumps of sugar",[125] and to add the theory of movement and a general understanding of the language of ballet to the curriculum. At the core of the new school's teaching was to be the purity of movement so prized by the traditionalist Volynsky; for Legat, the project offered the best possibility of keeping the flame of classical dancing alive, and he became his strongest ally.

---

124   Born in 1886 in St Petersburg, Romanova graduated into the Mariinsky company in 1903 where she eventually danced soloist roles with distinction. She taught at the Petrograd Choreographic School from 1917 onwards and at GATOB from 1930; she was her daughter Galina Ulanova's first teacher. She died in Leningrad in 1954.

125   As quoted by Meinertz, *Vera Volkova*, p.26

All did not go according plan for Volynsky and Legat, and by late 1923, Volynsky found himself enduring heavy criticism including from the young Georgy Balanchivadze who had watched a demonstration class and a performance of *The Nutcracker* by the 'BaltFlot' School and then wrote at length in *Teatr* magazine. Volynsky's criticisms of the type of innovation the young choreographer was demonstrating, his obsession with the degradation of technique and the quest to maintain its purity was the background for Balanchivadze to comment that "Backs – they have none; their feet don't point; their movements are coarse; their flexibility – is nil; their mime is impossibly faint."[126] Volynsky and Legat eventually lost their battle, the latter leaving Russia in 1922 after Lopukhov's appointment as director of the GATOB company, the former dying in 1926, having fallen foul of the increasingly political direction ballet was taking. He was accused of creating an art which did not conform to Soviet revolutionary principles and in 1925 his School of Russian Ballet was ordered to amalgamate with the ex-Imperial Theatre School, the very institution he had sought it to improve upon. It is perhaps worth noting that one of Volynsky's important graduates before the merger was Vera Volkova[127] who went on to be one of the most respected dance teachers of the middle of last century.

Agrippina Vaganova

Born in St Petersburg in 1879, and having trained with Pavel Gerdt, Ekaterina Vazem and Nikolai Legat at the Imperial Theatre School, Vaganova graduated into the Mariinsky in 1897 where she became a valued soloist; known as the 'queen of variations', she was celebrated for her technical strength, in particular her unsurpassed elevation and *batterie*. After her retirement from full-time dancing in 1918, the demand for teachers provided her with much-needed employment. From the outset, she started work on her own method which sought to fuse the two distinct elements of dance training at the time, the virtuosic Italian and the more lyrical French schools, in order to create dancers with a strong core and complete coordination of all parts of the body. Her method created dancers with an ability to soar into the air, something which Soviet choreographers would showcase in successive decades. This is the method which, in the years that followed her transfer from Volynsky's 'BaltFlot' school to the ex-Imperial Theatre School, now re-opened and re-named Petrograd State Choreographic Technical School (or Technicum), she

---

126 Kendall, *Balanchine and the Lost Muse*, p.208

127 Born in St Petersburg in 1904, Volkova danced with GATOB before leaving Russia to settle in Shanghai in 1929. She married Hugh Williams and moved to London where she taught at her own school and both the Sadler's Wells Ballet and its school. She became one of the most respected dancer teachers in the West. She moved to Copenhagen as Artistic Advisor to the Royal Danish Ballet in 1951 and continued to teach; her pupils there included Erik Bruhn and Peter Martins. She died in Copenhagen in 1975.

developed further and set about using in her teaching. It allowed her and her associates to produce new generations of superlative dancers. She adapted to the new Soviet society in Russia and was conscious to satisfy its ideological demands as well as the technical and artistic development of her students:

> "We set ourselves the task of training cadres not only of performers who know the technique of ballet dance – we cannot limit the goal of ballet education only to mastering the technology of art. We train and must train the creative workers of our Soviet theatres, armed not only with the knowledge of the basics of their skill and its virtuosity, but also with a common culture. We are obliged to release people not only politically literate, but also politically minded."[128]

Such were her achievements that the school has, since 1957, borne her name despite her never having been its director. She died in Leningrad in 1951.

Vladimir Ponomarev

In light of the emigration of increasing numbers of male dancers in the years after the revolution, the Petrograd School was also lucky to retain the services of Vladimir Ponomarev. Born in St Petersburg in 1892, he had graduated into the Mariinsky in 1910 and been made a principal dancer in 1912. He was an accomplished technician, a fine partner and possessed a noble stage presence. He remained in Russia after the revolution and continued to dance at GATOB. In the 1930s, he became a renowned character dancer and then went on to be a noted coach with the company, its assistant director between 1935 and 1938, director of the MALEGOT ensemble for 1938 and 1939 and director of the Kirov Ballet when evacuated to Molotov (now Perm) between 1941 and 1944. He began to teach at the school in 1913 and did so until his death, bringing vital continuity to the training given and responsible for a generation of superb dancers. He was also instrumental, alongside Vaganova, for reviving pre-revolutionary repertoire, from *Vain Precautions* (known in the West as *La Fille mal gardée*) in 1923, *Le Talisman* in 1926 to *La Bayadère* and *Don Quixote* in 1941. He died in Budapest in 1951.

Moscow

At the onset of the October revolution Moscow's Bolshoi Ballet School or Academy (strictly speaking, the dance section of the Moscow Imperial Theatre College) shut its doors and the fraught question of whether to re-open them at all was considered by the new authorities who were reluctant to pay state money for the tuition of students in an 'imperial' art form, let alone for their board and lodging. It was decided that the school needed to

---

128 Vaganova as quoted by Degen and Stupnikov: https://www.belcanto.ru/vaganova_academy.html

continue in order to prevent the departure of dancers from the new Soviet state, although, as in Petrograd, there was considerable resistance to change on the part of the teaching staff. The School closed again during the winter of 1918-19, a victim of the material shortages which beset the entire capital, however, after Vasily Tikhomirov's petition to Lunacharsky about the need to preserve ballet teaching, a committee was established by the Commissariat for Enlightenment to look at a potential overhaul of the curriculum which subsequently proposed greater focus on character and folk dancing as well as introducing athletic movement. The school re-opened only in 1920.

GITIS

In June 1923, the State Practical Institute of Choreography joined Moscow's State Institute of Theatrical Art (Gosudarstvenny Institut Teatralnovo Iskusstva), referred to by its acronym of GITIS, which itself had been formed the previous year by the amalgamation of the State Institute of Musical Drama and Vsevolod Meyerhold's State Theatrical Workshops. The purpose of GITIS was to train students in the three main branches of the theatrical arts: drama, opera and choreography. In 1924, it survived the closure of many existing theatrical institutions in Moscow and Leningrad on the orders of Sovnarkom, the nation's ruling committee, and in 1935 it added the teaching of production management, directing and acting to its functions. In 1934, it was renamed the Lunacharsky State Institute for Theatre Arts GITIS, a name it held until 1991 when it became the Russian Academy of Theatre Arts – GITIS. It became an important centre of dance education in Moscow and the Soviet state in general, affording training both to aspirant dancers unable to gain admittance to the Bolshoi Ballet School and to would-be choreographers.

Kiev – L'École de Mouvement

A rare example of early dance training taking place outside the two ballet centres of Petrograd/Leningrad and Moscow was the École de Mouvement (School of Movement) in the Ukrainian capital Kiev. Bronislava Nijinska, the younger sister of Vaslav Nijinsky, was also a dancer of considerable distinction; born in Minsk, Belarus in 1891, she entered the Imperial Theatre School in 1900 and graduated eight years later into the Mariinsky. Having danced alongside her brother in the early Paris seasons of Diaghilev's Ballets Russes (she created roles in Fokine's *Le Carnaval* and *Petrushka* in which he starred), she too left the Imperial theatres in 1911 following his resignation over the scandal of what had been considered his indecent costume in *Giselle*. Returning to Russia in 1914 after Nijinsky's split from Diaghilev, she appeared as a principal dancer at the Petrograd Private Opera Theatre and started to choreograph movement, while in 1917 she began to teach at a variety of theatrical institutions. After the revolution, Bolshoi director Elena Malinovskaya failed to persuade Nijinska to work as a teacher at the School, however the dancer-choreographer, who had settled in Kiev in 1916 when her husband Alexander Kochetovsky became ballet master and she a principal dancer at the City Theatre, chose rather to open her own École de Mouvement in 1919. It was a dance school which sought to combine her own Imperial Theatre technique with training for the innovative movement she had encountered with the Ballets Russes and which she was using and developing in her own work. She selected twenty students between the ages of sixteen and twenty with no previous training, the parlous economic times meaning that they paid for their tuition in fuel and food and there were no evening classes because of the lack of electricity.

Nijinska established a very 'modern' school, training her students not only in dance but other aspects of theatre, including production, costume design, make-up and visual art. It was, however, a short-lived enterprise, more notable for its formative influence not on the students but the choreographer herself who crystallised her ideas about what dance was and could be with observations set down in her choreographic notebook and her experiments carried out in the studios. Central to her view was that dance academicism did not address the essence of movement which is the transformation of static placement and gesture into a flow of continuous action. Thus, she sought to eliminate preparation and emphasise phrasing; Nijinska was reacting against the classical school which sought to freeze technique in time, something she shared with Balanchivadze and his Young Ballet, and both Lopukhov and Goleizovsky and their choreographic innovations. She was no iconoclast, however, rejecting the idea of jettisoning the past simply for the sake of it, while accepting the excitement generated by the creation of the genuinely new. Of people like Dalcroze and Duncan she observed:

> "Their ideas were brilliant and legitimate, but why create a new musical scale? All they had to do was add these ideas to the existing school and theory of dance."[129]

She emphasised expressivity of the torso and arms and strength particularly in the legs – jumps were emphasised (both she and her brother had been notable for their extraordinary facility in this) and both speed and fleetness of foot. Her choreography at this time was, in essence, abstract – one solo, *Fear*, which she herself danced, was set to silence.

A pupil who was to go on to have an immense influence on ballet in the West was the fifteen-year-old Serge Lifar[130] who persevered in his desire to

---

129 Nijinska; *A Dancer's Legacy*, p.20

130 Born in Kiev in 1905, Lifar joined the Ballets Russes in 1923, creating numerous parts including the title roles of *Apollon Musagète* in 1928 and *Le Fils Prodigue* in 1929.

be taught by Nijinska after an initial rejection. He was rewarded with a few months of intensive study in 1921 before, on hearing the news that her brother had been committed to a mental asylum in Vienna, she decided to leave for Austria. She placed her École de Mouvement in the hands of a senior student, and, taking a freight train with her mother to the Polish border, escaped Russian-controlled territory some six weeks later. They arrived in the Austrian capital after a further month and half of travel, marking the end of Nijinska's contribution to dance in Russia. Soon after, Lifar himself left the country in similar clandestine circumstances ultimately to dance in Paris for Diaghilev and his then ballet mistress, Nijinska.

Nijinska left Diaghilev in 1925 and worked as a freelance choreographer in France, England and Argentina before founding her own company in 1932. In 1937, she was artistic director of the short-lived Polish Ballet and in 1941, she opened a school in Los Angeles. She worked with the Grand Ballet du Marquis de Cuevas after 1945. She died in Pacific Palisades, California in 1972.

Conclusion

What the schools of Petrograd/Leningrad and Moscow achieved over the decades subsequent to the revolution in terms of producing dancers of world standard is well known. The first Soviet ballerina, wholly trained under the new regime, was Marina Semyonova, born in 1908 in St Petersburg, but whose entire dance education took place after the revolution, most notably with Vaganova from 1919 onwards and whose first star pupil she became. Semyonova was of vital importance to the Soviet regime which clearly saw the propaganda worth of a dancer of such refinement and nobility; she went on to become a teacher of enormous distinction. And there were to be so many more, from the defectors Rudolf Nureyev, Natalia Makarova, Mikhail Baryshnikov and Irek Mukhamedov to those who stayed, from Vakhtang Chabukiani, Konstantin Sergeyev and Vladimir Vasiliev to Galina Ulanova, Natalia Dudinskaya and Maya Plisetskaya.

That Russia, having undergone the most monumental of social upheavals, preserved ballet, the 'golden rattle' of the tsars, and transformed it into a truly Soviet art form is nothing short of astonishing. The story of that transformation and of those who fought to save classical dance from the threat of destruction is no less extraordinary. Realising that ballet relies upon knowledge and transmission of the past which its practitioners preserved even during even the most extreme of Stalinist times, they continued to evoke

---

After Diaghilev's death he joined the Paris Opéra Ballet and rose to become its director and chief choreographer. He left the Opéra in 1944 but returned as director again from 1947 to 1958. He wrote prolifically on dance, choreographed numerous ballets and was one of twentieth-century ballet's most important personages. He died in Lausanne in 1986.

and pass on the spirit of their imperial past. In essence, those 'children of the revolution' who trained in ballet lived double lives in which the realities of their daily Soviet existence were set alongside older memories and knowledge from their dance teachers. Several great Soviet-trained dancers have spoken and written about this phenomenon, which saw ex-dancers from tsarist times pass on what they knew, knowledge which invariably included reminiscences about individuals and a society swept away by the revolution. The paradox lay in the fact that it was as if, in a social structure which emphasised the construction of new ways of living, those in power tacitly acknowledged the need for the transmission of ideologically suspect information for the sole purpose of forming new generations of Soviet artists. Thus, the great Soviet ballerinas were encouraged to carry themselves as princesses, the *premiers danseurs* as princes, in perhaps the only circumstances in the USSR when such behaviour and attitudes were not actively suppressed.

1920 - *Swan Lake*, Act II, Bolshoi. Leonid Zhukov as Siegfried.

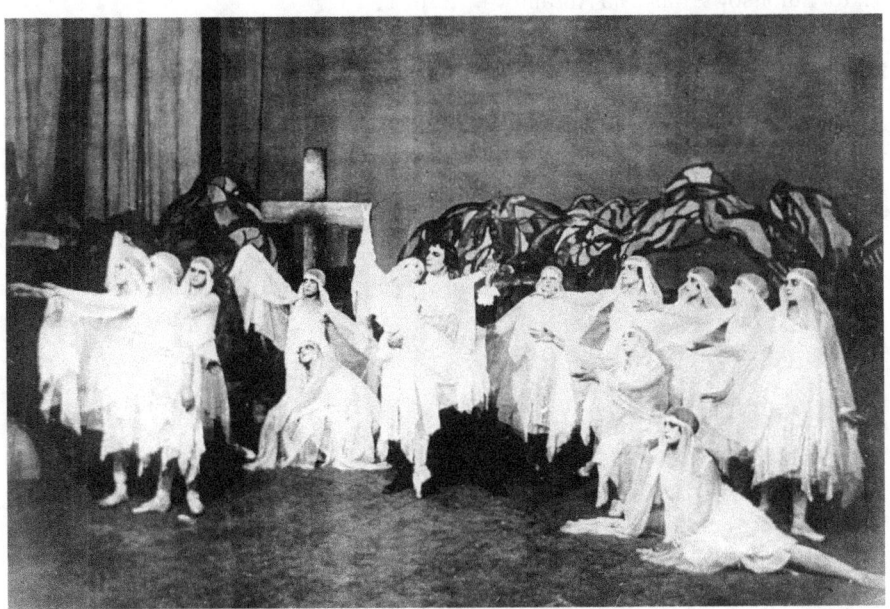

c.1920 *Giselle*, Act II, Bolshoi. Courtesy of *Dancing Times*

Vasily Tikhomirov at the Bolshoi Ballet School with Lev Potekhin, Vera Svetinskaya, Viktor Smoltsov, Anastasia Abramova, etc. in 1910.

Imperial Theatre School, Rossi Street, St Petersburg in the early 1900s.

Alexander Gorsky

Fyodor Lopukhov

Mikhail Fokine

Georgy Balanchivadze

1924 - *The Red Whirlwind*, GATOB.

Le Corsaire, Bolshoi - Ekaterina Geltser as Medora and Vasily Tikhomirov as Conrad.

c. 1923 Members of the Young Ballet (Georgy Balanchivadze seated).

1925 - *Joseph the Beautiful*, Bolshoi.

1925-26 - *Pulcinella*, GATOB. Courtesy of *Dancing Times*

1927 - *The Ice Maiden*, GATOB. Olga Mungalova in the title role and Pyotr Gusev as Asak.

1927 - Tatiana Vecheslova and Leonid Yakobson.

1928 - Bolshoi ballerinas Nina Podgoretskaya, Lyubov Bank, Valentina Kudryavtseva, Anastasia Abramova.

1930 - *The Footballer*, Bolshoi. Asaf Messerer in the title role.

1928 - *The Red Poppy* - Act I Sailors' Dance. Courtesy of *Dancing Times*

1930 - *The Footballer*, Bolshoi. Courtesy of *Dancing Times*

1930 - *The Golden Age*, GATOB.

1931 - *The Bolt*, GATOB. In rehearsal

1931 - *The Bolt*, GATOB. In the workshops

1932 - *Giselle*, Act I, Bolshoi. Courtesy of *Dancing Times*

1932 - *The Flames of Paris*, GATOB. Courtesy of *Dancing Times*

1935 - *Three Fat Men*, Bolshoi. Courtesy of *Dancing Times*

1934 - *The Fountain of Bakhchisarai*, GATOB. Courtesy of *Dancing Times*

1935 - *Three Fat Men*, Bolshoi. Olga Lepeshinskaya as Suok. Courtesy of *Dancing Times*

1936 - *Swan Lake*, Bolshoi. Marina Semyonova as Odette. Courtesy of *Dancing Times*

1936 - *The Sleeping Beauty*, Act I, Bolshoi. Marina Semyonova as Aurora. Courtesy of *Dancing Times*

1936 - *The Bright Stream*, Bolshoi.

1937 - *The Nutcracker*, Bolshoi. Marina Semyonova as Masha and Mikhail Gabovich as the Prince. Courtesy of *Dancing Times*

Sergey Prokofiev

Konstantin Sergeyev

Leonid Lavrovsky

Dmitry Shostakovich

1939 - *Laurencia*, Kirov. Natalia Dudinskaya in the title role. Courtesy of *Dancing Times*

4

Dancing through the Terror

1924-1941

Classical dance in Russia survived the 1917 revolution and its messy aftermath as the structure of the society which had supported it was dismantled and a new, Soviet future built. The years immediately after the revolution itself represented a period of cultural freedom, certainly relative to what was to follow. The state, increasingly sure in itself, its borders secured and the civil war won, began to turn its attention to every aspect of life, including the arts. If the survival of classical dancing after 1917 was something of an artistic miracle, the emergence of dancers of outstanding artistic talent and technical mastery in a golden age of ballet during the years of Stalin's terrifying autocracy was another phenomenon of equal importance. The extraordinary achievements of this period were built upon the shifting sands of political, cultural and artistic thought under an increasingly brutal and repressive regime.

From the onset of the Russian revolution, the figure of Anatoly Lunacharsky emerged as vital in the preservation of classical dancing. It was fortunate that he, a highly cultured man and a staunch defender of the value of 'high art', was appointed the first Commissar for Enlightenment responsible for, amongst much else, the Moscow and Petrograd theatres and their schools. Lunacharsky fought against fierce opposition for continued state funding of an art form perceived by many in the Communist party to be indissolubly linked to Imperial Russia. However, in the early years after the revolution that opposition was not in any way concerted, and Lunacharsky found that he was able to promote his position, sometimes at the highest level, even with Lenin himself. However, after Lenin's death and the victory of Stalin in a power struggle with Leon Trotsky,[131] increasing attention began to be paid to all aspects of Soviet life and the need for every function of society to promulgate state-sanctioned ideology. Ballet had to find a way to become a truly Soviet art form if it was to survive.

---

131   Born Lev Bronstein in Bereslavka, Ukraine in 1879, Trotsky was exiled twice to Siberia for revolutionary activities and met Lenin while in London in 1902. A leading Bolshevik, he headed the Petrograd Soviet at the 1917 revolution and, as head of the Red Army between 1918 and 1925, contributed to ultimate victory over the Whites in the civil war. After Lenin's death, he was removed from his offices by Stalin and went into exile in 1929. He was assassinated in Mexico City in 1940.

1924 – The Death of Lenin and the Twelfth Party Congress

Vladimir Lenin, the father of the 1917 revolution who had guided the first years of life in post-imperial Russia, died of a brain haemorrhage on 21st January 1924. His death provoked a political struggle for control of the USSR, a struggle ultimately won by Joseph Stalin.

The first changes in the state's attitude towards the arts came in 1924, following the Twelfth Party Congress resolution of late April of 1923 that theatre was to be used for the dissemination of communist propaganda. It marked the beginning of the politicisation of ballet and the increasing need for it to be seen to be at the service of the state and its societal goals. The chaos of the post-revolution period, the civil war and the questioning of what everything was for were over, and the communist regime, now far more confident in its own chances of survival, turned its attentions to acquiescence in all areas of society. In practical terms, increasing pressure was placed on the ballet companies to present new works which promoted communist values, although, in practice, little of such work that made its way to the stage met with any enthusiasm.

'Mammoth'

The state's desire to promote revolutionary values through the arts led to curious attempts to repurpose existing works. A production of *The Sleeping Beauty*, intended to replace Lopukhov's 1922 setting, was scheduled for the 1924/1925 season at GATOB; however, its libretto was to be completely rewritten. Nikolai Vinogradov,[132] director of 'Mammoth' or the Mammoth Workshop of Monumental Theatre, was tasked with creating a new storyline. His action was set in the fifteenth century and represented the first uprising of the proletariat. To the music of the Act I waltz, the people were to tear down the attributes of the authority of their ruling duke (the former Fairy Carabosse) and dance with new symbols of their labour. The astrologer-thinker (the Lilac Fairy) reveals their future with a wand. However, the Duke manages to kidnap Aurora, the Dawn of the Revolution who is put to sleep in "the city of the Commune in the gold of its riches, in the silver flame of electric fires and the red smoke of its factories". The leader of the people's uprising (the former Prince Désiré) finally sets "Aurora's coffin ablaze, releasing her as the beautiful dawn of World Revolution, rising in the scarlet glow of red banners". The production did not take place.

---

132   Born in St Petersburg in 1893, Vinogradov graduated from the Faculty of History and Philology of St. Petersburg University in 1914. He joined the Bolsheviks at the revolution and studied theatre with Meyerhold in 1918 and 1919. By 1923, he was a member of the artistic council of academic theatres in Leningrad and a stage director of GATOB, the year he founded Mammoth. He died in Leningrad in 1967.

1924 – the Death of Lydia Ivanova

On 16th June, GATOB soloist Lydia Ivanova was killed in a never-explained boating accident on the River Neva. A contemporary of Balanchivadze, Gusev and Danilova she was, like them, a member of the Young Ballet and had appeared in Lopukhov's 1923 *Dance Symphony* but it was her unquestionable star quality and modernity as a dancer which marked her out for future greatness. Just twenty years old and only in her third season with the company, she already represented an early hope of Soviet ballet. Her graduation performance from the school saw her in the title role of Pavel Gerdt's one-act *Graziella*, created for the ballerina Olga Preobrazhenskaya, by then Ivanova's teacher, and revived by her for her pupil. Ivanova was admitted into the company with the rank of second soloist, and she appeared across the repertoire, garnering much enthusiasm for her explosive jump and uncommon expressivity; by the end of her second season, she was something of a household name in Petrograd. Akim Volynsky saw in her the new-style dancer needed for the new Soviet ballet:

> "Our epoch demands that the iron and the copper – the true grit of the popular masses – ascend to the stars, not the ethereal reveries of individuals. Man himself has grown more severe, but even weightier: he yearns for the heights. And this is where Lida (sic) Ivanova's mission lay. She did not spread herself in the air like Pavlova, but performed *en tournant* in the arms of her partner as no other dancer before her."[133]

1924/1927 – *Whirlwinds*

In October 1924 Fyodor Lopukhov, director of the GATOB company of the newly-renamed city of Leningrad, produced *The Red Whirlwind*, a dance allegory representing the hurricane of Bolshevism blowing away the old values and the establishment of a new world based on communism. Naïve and unsure of its movement vocabulary, it met with harsh criticism and was for the choreographer his "greatest failure",[134] receiving just one performance. In Moscow, Kasyan Goleizovsky, who had exerted such an influence on the young Georgy Balanchivadze, attempted to produce his own work on the same theme in 1927. Entitled *The Whirlwind* (or *Smerch*), it was destined for the stage of the Bolshoi Theatre (whose name of 'big' had never needed to be changed). Like Lopukhov, Goleizovsky wanted a to create a work which was neither time nor place-specific, the monarch figure of his second scene not "the tsar of country X but 'an emblem of tsarism'."[135] However, owing to severe problems in rehearsals, an over-complicated approach and

---

133   Volynsky, *Ballet's Magic Kingdom*, p.125
134   Ezrahi, *Soviet Choreographers of the 1920s*, p.285
135   ibid, p.207

the unsuccessful depiction of the proletariat, the choreographer himself requested the management withdraw the ballet. The cancellation of Goleizovsky's *The Whirlwind* after one poorly-received performance sealed his fall from favour at the Bolshoi; other planned creations were decommissioned. He would only return to work with the company in the 1960s.

Soviet ballet and Constructivism

Constructivism started as a Russian movement which traced its origins back to 1915 and the artists Vladimir Tatlin[136] and Alexander Rodchenko[137] before expanding globally to become a highly influential artistic philosophy. Originating as a term from Kazimir Malevich's critique of Rodchenko's 'Construction Art', Constructivism was in essence a post-war, post-revolution development of Russian Futurism. At a time when the strictures of imperial society were swept aside, the arts in general began a period of experimentation which would only come to an end with the imposition of socialist realism under Stalin. The world of Russian ballet was not, as has been outlined in examining the choreographic ideas brought to the stage by the likes of Lopukhov and Goleizovsky, excluded from this phenomenon, and there was significant overlap as theories and practices in art and architecture came into the theatres through set and costume design.

Central to the Constructivists' manifesto of was the 'de-aestheticizing' of stage design, the excision of the decorative in favour of the essential, so dance was primarily influenced through set design which then became a springboard for sparer and often more mechanical movement. The first known constructivist stage design for dance was for Goleizovsky's Moscow-based Chamber Ballet – a 1922 work entitled *Transience* (or *Visions fugitives*) with music by Sergey Prokofiev,[138] although its author is unclear. Goleizovsky's *Salomé* and *Faun*, also from 1922, are better known. *Salomé* featured a scaffold against a background of triangular forms and moveable triangles were used to resemble pyramids and mountains; the designer was Nikolai Musatov.[139]

---

136   Born in Kharkov, Ukraine in 1885, Tatlin was one of the two most notable figures in the Soviet avant-garde art movement of the 1920s, influencing many important artists of the twentieth century. From the 1930s he worked for different theatres in Moscow. He died in Moscow in 1953.

137   Born in St Petersburg in 1891, Rodchenko was one of the most versatile of constructivist and productivist artists to emerge after the revolution. Much of the work of twentieth century graphic designers is a direct result of Rodchenko's work. He died in Moscow in 1956.

138   Born in Sontsovka, Ukraine in 1891. Prokofiev was one of the major composers of the twentieth century, working in a wide variety of forms from symphonies and concerti to operas and ballets. He left Russia at the revolution and enjoyed a flourishing international career before returning permanently in 1936. He died in Moscow in 1953.

139   Born in Moscow in 1895, Musatov studied theatre painting and worked extensively in theatre design thereafter, collaborating with Goleizovsky from 1922 to 1929 and working

However, the choreography was in no way 'constructivist', leading to a perceived disjunct between the stage picture and the movement. *Faun* was more coherent, with simple platforms, steps and criss-crossed white lines designed by Boris Erdman,[140] complemented by utilitarian costumes which for several dancers were made simply out of cord. Goleizovsky perhaps came closest to being a 'constructivist choreographer' with *Joseph the Beautiful* which was presented at the Bolshoi in 1925 with designs by Erdman. It possessed a remarkable set in Act II which used superimposed platforms to create the impression of a pyramid on which the dancers repeated phrases of movement again and again, contrasting Joseph's spirituality with the tyranny of the court of Pharaoh. In Petrograd/Leningrad, Lopukhov was far from the mainstream of the constructivist movement, but he also used multi-levelled and moveable set elements designed by Vladimir Dmitriev[141] which bore, nevertheless, its influence; in his 1929 designs for Lopukhov's Leningrad production of *The Nutcracker*, Dmitriev's moveable flat surfaces allowed him to create corridors down which dancers could run. There was, however, generally little coherence between design and the nature of the movement dancers were called upon to execute; Foregger's 'machine dances' were themselves never married to set design. The closest ballet came to becoming 'constructivist' was the 1927 Ballets Russes *Le Pas d'acier* created for Paris, with a set by Georgy Yakulov[142] featuring a high central rostrum with steps either side, the depiction of machine parts and outsize tools carried by the dancers. It was never seen in Russia. With the close of the 1920s, constructivism was, along with other experimental art movements in Russia, suppressed by an increasingly dictatorial regime, desperate to exert total influence over all areas of Soviet life.

---

at the Bolshoi Theatre from 1926 onwards. He also designed books and exhibitions. He died in Moscow in 1993.

140   Born in Mitau (now Jelgava), Latvia in 1899, Erdman was firstly an actor with the Moscow Chamber Theatre from 1917-18 before working in the circus section of *Narkompros*. He worked in experimental theatre during the 1920s before designing for circuses during the Second World War and then at the Stanislavsky Theatre from 1950 to his death in Moscow in 1960.

141   Born in Moscow in 1900, Dmitriev studied as an artist and came under the influence of Vsevolod Meyerhold. A prolific stage designer, he worked extensively with Sergey Radlov, shifting his scenic style to that of realism. He designed some 150 plays, operas and ballets before his death in Moscow in 1948.

142   Born in Tiflis in 1884, Yakulov studied at the Moscow School of Painting, Sculpture and Architecture from 1901 to 1903. He served in the Russo-Japanese War and was influenced by oriental styles. He also travelled to Italy and Paris and was involved with the 'Blue Rose' movement in Dresden in 1913. He worked extensively in theatre design. In 1925 he participated in the Paris Exposition Internationale des Arts Décoratifs and came to the attention of Diaghilev. He died in Yerevan, Armenia in 1928.

1925 – *Joseph the Beautiful*

In March 1925 Goleizovsky produced a new work for the Bolshoi, *Joseph the Beautiful*, based on the Old Testament's Genesis story of Jacob's son Joseph which he used to depict the theme of the moral purity of a hero who comes into conflict with the lack of spirituality of the world around him. Engaging the constructivist designer Boris Erdman and using a score commissioned from Sergey Vasilenko,[143] the choreographer created a series of tableaux in two acts with the dancers often arranged in sequences of poses on the multi-layered set, their bodies painted to fuse with the overall scenic concept. Movement ranged from the fluid to the acrobatic, and was often performed by dancers lying down – the cast was led by Vasily Efimov as Joseph, Alexey Bulgakov as Potiphar and Lyubov Bank[144] as his wife, Taiah. *Joseph the Beautiful* was presented at the Bolshoi's Experimental (later Filial) Theatre[145] alongside another new one-act Goleizovsky work, *Teolinda*, set to music by Franz Schubert which satirised classical dance; it featured Lyubov Bank in the role of Lisette. *Joseph* was subsequently staged in Odessa in 1926 and Kharkov in 1928 but, at the Bolshoi itself, despite 17 performances in its first season, it did not return. Reactions from the traditionalists were hostile, indeed, as the ballet was being prepared in early 1925, an attempt to ban the work on the grounds of violating the theatre's academic foundations was made, provoking a protest by several young dancers led by the future principal *Mikhail Gabovich and choreographer and director-to-be Igor Moiseyev.[146] Their subsequent dismissal from the company was countermanded by Lunacharsky himself. *Joseph the Beautiful* may have demonstrated

---

143 Born in Moscow in 1872, Vasilenko studied at the Moscow Conservatoire where he later became a professor, counting Aram Khachaturian among his students. A prolific composer in many forms, he composed several ballets, including *Mirandolina* for Vainonen in 1949. He died in Moscow in 1956.

144 Born in Moscow in 1903, Bank graduated into the Bolshoi Ballet in 1919 where she danced as a principal until 1947. Noted for her sculptural quality on stage and vivid acting skills, she danced the major roles of the repertoire including Kitri in *Don Quixote* and Nikiya in *La Bayadère*. She died in Moscow in 1984.

145 The Bolshoi Filial Theatre was opened in 1924 in the former Mamontov-Zimin Theatre to satisfying growing audience demand. It offered the same repertoire and dancers as the main Bolshoi Theatre. Ballet performances stopped in 1959; it is now the Moscow Operetta State Academic Theatre.

146 Born in Kiev in 1906, Moiseyev graduated from the Bolshoi Ballet School to the company in 1924 and remained a dancer there until 1939. He danced the title role in Goleizovsky's *Joseph the Beautiful* in 1925. He started choreography in the early 1930s (including acrobatic displays in Red Square), creating *Three Fat Men* for the Bolshoi in 1935 and the first Moscow version of *Spartacus* in 1958. He began to move into folk dancing in 1936, becoming director of the Moscow Theatre for Folk Art. He is credited with creating professional 'character' dance; his company toured the world with intelligent and successful programmes of his choreography. He died in Moscow in 2007.

Goleizovsky's avant-garde creativity but was ultimately considered a noble failure, even if Lunacharsky described it as "unquestionably interesting".[147]

Tikhomirov and Geltser at the Bolshoi

Despite the upheavals in Russian society, the old imperial ballets continued to enjoy great popularity, providing a degree of escapism for their audiences, an aspect of theatre which Lenin himself acknowledged in saying that "a theatre is necessary not so much for propaganda, as to rest hard workers after their daily work".[148] However, the failure of new works meant that the critics, those who believed ballet to be nothing more than an imperial 'golden rattle', could provide evidence that it was a dead art form. Tikhomirov had been the *premier danseur noble* of the Bolshoi Theatre and chose, alongside his wife and stage partner Ekaterina Geltser, to remain in Russia at the revolution. He was elected head of the ballet company after the February 1917 revolution, his star waxing as Gorsky's waned owing to increasing ill-health, a post Tikhomirov held until 1930. It was Tikhomirov who in January 1923 restored Petipa's famous 'Kingdom of the Shades' scene in *La Bayadère*, excised by Gorsky in his own production; he danced the role of Solor, Geltser was Nikiya and Bank, Gamzatti. In May of the following year he oversaw the revival of *The Sleeping Beauty* with Geltser as Aurora and himself as Prince Désiré and in February 1925, in order to mark the Bolshoi Theatre's centenary, he staged the second act of August Bournonville's *La Sylphide* with Geltser as The Sylph and himself as James. He was at heart a dance traditionalist, but made it clear from the outset that he also subscribed to the new political order, and in doing so, placed himself as someone who could perhaps fulfil Lunacharsky's ideal of preserving the best of the past in order to create the masterpieces of the future.

1926 – *Esmeralda*

To celebrate his thirty years at the Bolshoi, Tikhomirov staged *Esmeralda*, a ballet which had first been created by Jules Perrot in London in 1844 who had brought it to Russia in 1848. It was reworked by Petipa in 1886 and again by Gorsky as *Gudule's Daughter* in 1902; the narrative was that of Victor Hugo's *Notre-Dame de Paris*. On the advice of *Yuri Faier, the Bolshoi's chief ballet conductor, Cesare Pugni's original score was revised by the composer Reinhold Glière[149] and Tikhomirov set about re-focussing a work

---

147   As quoted by Souritz in *Soviet Choreographers of the 1920s*, p.199

148   Swift, *The Art of the Dance in the USSR*, p.38

149   Born in 1875 in Kiev, Glière studied at the Moscow Conservatoire between 1894 and 1900 after which he taught music, early pupils including the eleven-year-old Sergey Prokofiev. He was an enthusiastic supporter of the Soviet ideal and composed prolifically in a variety of genres as well as teaching at the Moscow Conservatoire. He was considered as the last of the great nationalist composers and was untouched by Stalin's purges of 1936

which had to a large extent become an exercise in dancing for dancing's sake, although he did revive Perrot's original 'Jealousy Waltz' *pas d'action*. He sought to focus on the populace of Paris and their quest for social justice: the ballet was "...entirely constructed on the idea...of expressing its search for truth, its search for light".[150] There was an emphasis on melodrama and it was noted how even the purely danced sections were well incorporated into the overall narrative. *Esmeralda* was, in truth, an amalgam, a mix of the 'pre-revolutionary old' and the 'Soviet new' but it was, despite any caveats, a success, performed twenty-two times in its first season and grossing the highest box office takings of any ballet. At the first performance in February 1926, Geltser danced Esmeralda, Tikhomirov was Captain Phoebus, Ivan Smoltsov[151] the poet Gringoire, Bulgakov appeared as the priest Claude Frollo and Vladimir Ryabtsev[152] was Quasimodo.

1926 – *Pulcinella*

In May 1926, Lopukhov chose Igor Stravinsky's score for *Pulcinella* which he had composed for Diaghilev's Ballets Russes and premièred in Paris in May 1920 with choreography by Léonide Massine. Taking unfinished fragments of music by Neapolitan eighteenth century composer Giovanni Pergolesi, Stravinsky conceived a score to accompany a *commedia dell'arte* narrative. It is an indication of the relatively porous nature of new Soviet state's borders in this period that Lopukhov knew about and was able to secure the music for ten performances of his own Leningrad version. He changed the narrative into an anti-bourgeois satire and insisted on absolute precision in the delivery of his movement: "Everything is strictly measured and carefully studied"[153] wrote the choreographer. The young dancer Boris Komarov replaced an ailing Leontiev at the première, Smeraldina was danced by Elizaveta Gerdt, the Turk by Olga Berg[154] and Pantalone by Matilda Kschessinskaya's brother,

---

and 1948. He died in Moscow in 1956.

150 Souritz, *Soviet Choreographers of the 1920s*, p.227

151 Born in Moscow in 1892, Smoltsov graduated into the Bolshoi in 1910 where he appeared until 1953. He became a principal dancer, performing the main *danseur noble* roles of the repertoire as well as certain character parts. He taught at the Bolshoi School from 1920 onwards and coached at the theatre from 1937. He revived *La Bayadère* for the Bolshoi in 1940 and was instrumental in recreating several works including *Chopiniana* when the company was evacuated during the war. He died in Moscow in 1968.

152 Born in St Petersburg in 1880, Ryabtsev graduated from the Bolshoi School into the company in 1898 firstly in the corps de ballet and then, having developed his acting talent, in character roles. He appeared at The Bat theatre of miniatures from 1908 onwards and taught facial expressions and character dance at the Bolshoi School from 1920 to 1930. He died in Moscow in 1945.

153 As quoted by Souritz, *Soviet Choreographers of the 1920s*, p.298

154 Born in St Petersburg in 1907, Berg graduated into GATOB in 1925 where she danced until 1945. A soloist with a dynamic technique, she was able to execute virtuoso

Joseph.[155] The ballet was light-hearted and extremely well received by critics and audience alike, but, given that hard currency was needed to secure the rights to further use of the score, it was dropped from the repertoire.

1927 – *The Ice Maiden*

In 1922, GATOB had staged *Solveig*, a ballet by Pavel Petrov[156] which was not considered a success and had run for only six performances. However, much work had been undertaken to bring it to the stage, not least that by Boris Asafiev on the music of Edvard Grieg, creating a score out of works by the Norwegian composer, and the construction of sets and costumes by Alexander Golovin.[157] Five years later, GATOB director Lopukhov used both, with some further musical revisions by Asafiev, for a new work, *The Ice Maiden*. Lopukhov wrote a new libretto based loosely on Hans Christian Andersen's 1861 fairy story and at the ballet's April première, cast Olga Mungalova in the title role with Pyotr Gusev as Asak. In his re-telling he combined classical dances with more experimental movement, including the famous 'ring' pose adopted by the flexible, long-limbed ballerina who, balanced and supported on her right leg reached back to touch the other extended behind her, thus creating a ring shape with her body. Lopukhov worked hard to find new combinations and found ready acceptance from the young dancers: "Fedor Vasilievich asked me if I could stand on Gusev's shoulder, and if so, then to do an arabesque standing on (it)" recalled Mungalova.[158]

Classified by the choreographer a "classical ballet in a 1927 inter-

---

steps usually only achieved by male dancers. From the age of 13 she was also a concert pianist and later an orchestral conductor. She worked as such at the Maly Theatre between 1949 and 1968. She died in St Petersburg in 1991.

155   Born in St Petersburg in 1868, Kschessinsky graduated into the Mariinsky in 1886 and was a lively performer who specialised in national dances. He was dismissed from the theatre in 1905 on account of having gone on strike but returned in 1914. He performed until 1928 and was much admired by Lopukhov who cast him in several of his works as a character dancer. Between 1917 and 1928 he taught at Petrograd's Art University and led his own ballet troupe between 1928 and 1930 (see 1928 – Kschessinsky's 'Leningrad Mobile Young Ballet Collective'). He died in 1942 during the Siege of Leningrad.

156   Born in St Petersburg in 1881 (or 1882), Petrov graduated into the Mariinsky in 1900 where he performed until 1922. Between 1918 and 1920 he staged a number of productions in the Petrograd Theatre of Miniatures and at the Maly Theatre, dances in operas, operettas and drama performances. From 1925 he worked in Lithuania, where he is considered the founder of professional ballet; he also founded a ballet studio in Kaunas. In the 1930s. he worked in France. He died in Paris in 1938.

157   Born in Moscow in 1863, Golovin initially studied architecture before turning to art. He moved to St Petersburg where he became a stage designer combining symbolism and modernism in his operatic and dramatic work for Diaghilev, Meyerhold and others; in 1910 he made the original designs for Fokine's *The Firebird*. After the revolution he worked increasingly in painting and illustration. He died in 1930 in Detskoe (now Tsarskoe) Selo.

158   As quoted by Souritz, *Soviet Choreographers of the 1920s*, p.303

pretation",[159] *The Ice Maiden* represented a clear synthesis of Petipa's *pas d'action*, Fokine's revisions, character dancing, a strong narrative and Lopukhov's own penchant for modern 'acrobatic' movement; it was also, tellingly, a full-length work at a time when the majority of new ballets were one-act pieces. What it lacked, however, was an unequivocally Soviet message, despite which it remained in the repertoire until 1937.

1927 – *The Red Poppy*

As Commissar for Enlightenment and a defender of the arts, Lunacharsky had to endure repeated attacks from the highest levels which in 1926 included a call to prioritise spreading literacy among the country's huge population rather than "search out old church monuments and develop the art of ballet".[160] As if answering his resolutely secular private prayers and perfectly timed to mark the tenth anniversary of the revolution, in June 1927 the Bolshoi premièred the first truly successful ballet of the Soviet era, *The Red Poppy*, a story conceived by the artist Mikhail Kurilko[161] and choreographed by Tikhomirov and company character dancer Lev Lashchilin.[162] Glière's score, originally intended for a ballet named *The Daughter of the Port* was re-purposed for the new project. Ideologically impeccable, *The Red Poppy (The Secret of the Chinese Tavern)* was the simple tale of the good inhabitants of a Chinese city, down-trodden by Western imperialists, throwing off the yoke of their oppression to create a new, free society. The heroine Tao-Hoa was a Chinese tea-house dancer who fell in love with the captain of a Russian ship and who sacrificed herself to assist the locals in a popular uprising aided by Russian sailors. Geltser created the highly dramatic role alongside Tikhomirov as the Russian sailor Krasnov although the choreographer seems to have insisted on a traditional divertissement in the middle second act which he named the 'The Dream of Tao-Hoa', evoking the *ballets féeries* of times past with dancing flowers, birds and butterflies. Alexey Bulgakov created the Captain of the Soviet Ship, Ivan Smoltsov the role of the vicious manager Li Shanfu and Asaf Messerer that of the Chinese Magician. It was

---

159   ibid, p.312

160   Swift, *The Art of the Dance in the USSR*, p.70

161   Born in 1880 in Kamenets-Podolsky, Ukraine, Kurilko graduated from the Imperial Academy of Arts in 1913 and became a theatre artist and set designer. He was Chief Artist at the Bolshoi Theatre between 1924 and 1928, a professor at the Moscow Architectural Institute from 1940 to 1956 and Head of the theatre and decoration workshop of the Moscow State Academic Art Institute between 1948 and 1960. He died in Malakhovka near Moscow in 1969.

162   Born in 1888 in Moscow, Lashchilin graduated into the Bolshoi company in 1906 where he remained until 1949. A character dancer, then choreographer and ballet master, he choreographed the first and third acts of *The Red Poppy* and co-created *The Footballer* with Igor Moiseyev in 1930. He died in Moscow in 1955.

an immediate success, totalling 69 performances at the Bolshoi in 1928 alone against the next most popular ballet, *Swan Lake*, with just eight, and went on to receive three hundred in the ten years after its creation. Despite some cavils expressed in some quarters concerning its lack of innovation, it clearly possessed a resonance with its audience; Chairman of the Soviet Government's Central Executive Committee Mikhail Kalinin[163] observed to a party congress:

> "I know that by nine o'clock, the curtain time for *The Red Poppy*, you'll all go. How can this be? Why is this so? You criticised it, wanted to sweep up and throw away everything in the Bolshoi Theatre, but you yourselves are going...Everyone is going to see *The Red Poppy*, yet they criticise the Bolshoi Theatre everywhere and see nothing positive in it. This is not normal. This is hypocrisy. If people are going...then it means that there is something of value there."[164]

The Red Poppy was a creation of crucial importance to the development of Soviet ballet. With it, the defenders of the art form could show that, even if tainted by its imperial past, ballet could now confidently move into its Soviet future, although some voices of dissent detected no material shift. Secondly, its very conservatism of characterisation and structure can be seen to be a victory for the traditionalists, of whom Geltser and Tikhomirov could be counted as among the staunchest. The tide of innovation represented by Goleizovsky had finally ebbed and what was left were the old ways which *The Red Poppy* showed could successfully serve the new social order. Mirroring the composite nature of the Moscow original, GATOB premièred its own version in early 1929 with choreography by Lopukhov (1st act), Ponomarev (2nd act) and Leontiev (3rd act), and featuring Lukom as Tao-Hoa, Dudko as the captain, Leontiev as Li Shanfu and *Alexey Ermolayev as the magician. In 1949, Lavrovsky and Zakharov created new versions for the Bolshoi and the Kirov respectively. Moscow saw *Galina Ulanova and Alexander Radunsky[165] lead the cast while Leningrad had *Tatiana Vecheslova and Mikhail Mikhailov.[166]

---

163 Born in the village of Verkhnyaya Troitsa, Tver Governorate in 1875, Kalinin joined the Bolshevik party in 1905 and became Petrograd's mayor in 1917. He became de facto head of state of Soviet Russia in 1919. An ally of Stalin, he remained in the politburo after Lenin's death, although wielding little real power. He died in Moscow in 1946.

164 Ezrahi, *Soviet Choreographers of the 1920s*, p.252

165 Born in Moscow in 1912, Radunsky graduated into the Bolshoi company in 1930 and became a much-admired character soloist. He choreographed Shchedrin's version of *The Little Humpbacked Horse* in 1960. He retired from dancing in 1962 and became the Chief Choreographer of the Red Army Song and Dance Ensemble. He died in Moscow in 1982.

166 Born in St Petersburg in 1903, Mikhailov graduated into GATOB in 1921 where he performed until 1959. In the early 1920s, he was a member of Balanchine's Young Ballet

The ballets continued to be revived and, from 1957 onwards, were renamed *The Red Flower*.

The birth of *drambalet*

As a ballet, *The Red Poppy* pointed the way forward for classical dancing in Soviet Russia in several ways: it signalled the beginning of the rise of the full-length ballet, as opposed to one-act, often experimental works based on contemporary themes. Its language was resolutely classical but it dealt with real people depicted in detailed dramatic settings. It was, in essence, the first Soviet 'choreodrama' which quickly also came to be termed 'drama-ballet' or *drambalet*. *The Red Poppy* set the tone and style in Soviet ballet for some thirty years.

In the late 1920s, clear differences could be seen between the Moscow and Leningrad ballet companies, their respective importance reversed by the geographical shift in political power. The Bolshoi was located in the capital, a stone's throw from the Kremlin, the seat of the Soviet regime; Leningrad was a full night's train ride away, the former capital, downgraded and not a little mistrusted. Lopukhov at GATOB had his own ideas about the future of ballet, as did Agrippina Vaganova who became his rival and successor as company director – neither afforded much if any consideration to purely political propaganda. They were, however, swimming against the political tide and a newly instituted artistic council at the Leningrad Academic Theatre succeeded, despite management opposition, in getting the company to stage its own *The Red Poppy* – it was performed 45 times in the 1929 season.

Dancers of the first Golden Age

Leningrad

Agrippina Vaganova was in essence a ballet traditionalist when it came to the training of dancers and was not a great supporter of many of Lopukhov's choreographic innovations. However, she sought to adapt and extend exercises the better to help dancers who were called upon to use more acrobatic movements in new ballets. In 1925 she wrote in the weekly Leningrad theatre, literature, film and art journal *Zhizn iskusstva* (Life of Art): "our dancers, educated according to the principles of contemporary classical training, are able to cope with *any* difficulties".[167] However, her focus was clearly to serve the state and its aims through the idiom of classical training and not by diluting it with external vocabularies: "Give us a Soviet theme" she observed, "and then we shall succeed in producing a highly artistic Soviet

---

group and progressed from dancing major roles at GATOB/the Kirov to character parts. From 1938 to 1953 he taught at the company and from 1947 to 1962 at the Leningrad Ballet School. He wrote several books on ballet. He died in Leningrad in 1979.

167   Roslavleva, *Era of the Russian Ballet*, p. 201

production even with the idiom of old classical ballet."[168]

From the outset, she worked tirelessly at the Leningrad Choreographic School. Her mission, whatever the arguments about innovation and traditionalism, was to produce superlative dancers as good as, if not better than, the pre-revolution Imperial ballet of which she herself had been part. In the mid-1920s, the first purely Soviet-trained ballerina emerged who, from the outset, showed that classical dance had survived all the upheavals: Marina Semyonova.

Born in St Petersburg in 1908, Semyonova entered the ex-Mariinsky school in 1919 and was trained by Vaganova from her arrival until her graduation performance at GATOB in 1925 for which her teacher revived three dances from *La Source*, an old Saint-Léon ballet, which she rechoreographed herself in order to show off her pupil's poise and steely technique. Semyonova made her debut in the former Mariinsky company as Aurora in *The Sleeping Beauty*, and was quickly seen as living proof of the new Russia's ability not only to maintain but also further the tradition of superlative classical dance training; in the words of the British journalist and critic Iris Morley,[169] she became a "symbolic triumph".[170] Semyonova, the first of the Soviet ballerinas, was in the eyes of many the greatest, "orthodoxy in its purest form".[171] She performed a wide variety of leading roles, the most notable of which was *Swan Lake*'s Odette-Odile in which she made a spectacular debut in early 1926 and which she would continue to dance for twenty-seven years until her retirement from the stage in 1953. Attaining the rank of ballerina just one year after joining GATOB, she was transferred to Moscow in 1930 at the age of twenty-two where she had a long, if not always comfortable, career, separated from her beloved Vaganova and often at odds with the more dramatically orientated repertoire in the capital. Nevertheless, she remained peerless in terms of the purity of her classical dancing. She taught in Moscow for a further four decades, coaching successive generations of Bolshoi ballerinas. She died in Moscow in 2010 at the age of 102.

Despite being born in St Petersburg in 1907, the year before Semyonova, Olga Jordan (or Iordan) graduated the year after her in 1926, and so ceded the title of 'first Soviet ballerina'. Her graduation performance was as Niriti in *Le Talisman* alongside Ermolayev as Vayou. She was a brilliant technician and became the company's leading classical ballerina after Semyonova's transfer

---

168 ibid.

169 Born in Carshalton, Surrey in 1910, Morley wrote a trio of historical novels during the Second World war before moving with her husband to Moscow in 1944 where she wrote as a journalist for *The Observer* and *The Yorkshire Post*. She became a committed Communist. She returned to the UK in 1947 and died in 1953.

170 Morley, *Soviet Ballet*, p.16

171 ibid, p.52

to Moscow in 1930. She created several roles, among which Jeanne in *The Flames of Paris* and Zarema in the *Fountain of Bakhchisarai*, as well as dancing all the major classical ballets. During the Great Patriotic War, she remained in Leningrad and led a small group of dancers throughout the long siege. She taught at the Leningrad Art University from 1950 until her transfer to Moscow in 1963 where she taught and coached with distinction at both the Bolshoi School and ballet company. She died in Leningrad in 1971.

Galina Ulanova was born in St Petersburg in 1910, the daughter of two Mariinsky dancers, Sergey Ulanov and Maria Romanova. She first trained with her mother and then entered the Petrograd Choreographic School in 1919, studying under Vaganova and graduating in 1928. Her graduation performance was as a corps de ballet member in *Chopiniana* and the Fée Dragée (Sugar Plum Fairy) in a divertissement from *The Nutcracker*; she was considered sweet but unremarkable. Far from possessing the technical accomplishment and 'steel toes' of Semyonova, she was challenged and, at times, defeated by some roles, but Ulanova was to become one of the greatest Soviet ballerinas. Her development took time – it was her assumption of Odette in *Swan Lake* in 1933 which proved the turning point and confirmed her unforced lyricism as her greatest strength. From then on, she became the most famous of the company's ballerinas, establishing herself as the supreme lyrical dancer, often compared with Marie Taglioni. In 1940, she created Juliet in Leonid Lavrovsky's *Romeo and Juliet* which, with that of Giselle, became her most notable role. In 1944, after wartime evacuation, she was moved to the Bolshoi Ballet and was awarded the rank of *prima ballerina assoluta* by the Soviet Government. She danced until 1962 and then taught at the Bolshoi for decades after. She died in Moscow in 1998.

Born in St Petersburg in 1910, Tatiana Vecheslova graduated into GATOB in 1928 – her debut performance was as Gulnara in *Le Corsaire* – and became a ballerina with a wide and varied performing repertoire. She was a gifted actress as well as the possessor of a formidable technique. She created many ballets and was the first interpreter of the title role in Vaganova's 1935 version of *Esmeralda*. She and her good friend Ulanova were said to be perfect foils as Maria and Zarema in *The Fountain of Bakhchisarai*. In 1948, they jointly celebrated the twentieth anniversary of their debuts. Vecheslova retired from the stage in 1953. She was Director of the Leningrad Choreographic School from 1952 to 1954 and returned as a teacher between 1969 to 1970. She was also a valued teacher and coach at the Kirov Ballet from 1955 to 1969 and again in 1970 and 1971. She was the author of several books and articles on ballet. She died in Leningrad in 1991.

Born in Kharkov, Ukraine in 1912, Natalia Dudinskaya entered the Petrograd Choreographic School in 1923, where she was trained under Vaganova, and graduated into GATOB in 1931 having already debuted there as Princess Florine in *The Sleeping Beauty* as a student; she appeared as Odette-Odile in *Swan Lake* some six months after joining the company. A dancer of stupendous technique, she shone particularly in the classical roles, of which Nikiya in Petipa's *La Bayadère* was her favourite, but was no less successful in modern Soviet repertory, in which *Laurencia* was her first of many created roles. It was she who chose the twenty-one-year-old *Rudolf Nureyev to partner her in *Laurencia* in 1958 in his first assumption of a major part. She retired from dancing in 1962. Dudinskaya began to teach the *classe de perfection*[172] at the Kirov in 1951, taught at the Vaganova Academy from 1964 onwards and was a répétiteur at the Kirov between 1963 and 1978. She was married to the dancer and director Konstantin Sergeyev. She died in St Petersburg in 2003.

Though born a little later than her colleagues, Alla Shelest can be considered as part of this first golden age. Born in 1919 in Smolensk she graduated into the Kirov Ballet in 1937 and rapidly became one of the company's most popular ballerinas. She combined a fine technique and uncommon fluency of movement with great dramatic expressivity in a wide range of major roles ranging from Nikiya in *La Bayadère* to her creation of Aegina in Leonid Yakobson's *Spartacus* in 1956. However, she was almost never in the first cast of ballets, prompting Fyodor Lopukhov to observe: "I don't know of any ballerina whose career was as ill-fated...She was mostly granted roles inferior to her remarkable potential."[173] She became *Yuri Grigorovich's first wife in 1950. She retired from the stage in 1963 and became Director of Kuibyshev Ballet from 1970 to 1973 and ballet mistress at the Kirov between 1977 and 1979. She died in St Petersburg in 1998.

Semyonova's status as the first 'Soviet' Russian ballerina was mirrored by a male dancer of exceptional virtuosity and theatrical intensity: Alexey Ermolayev. Born in St Petersburg in 1910, he came to dancing relatively late, and, after a brief period at Volynsky's School of Russian Ballet, was accepted into the Leningrad Choreographic School in 1924 at the age of fourteen. Placed immediately in the intermediate class, he took just two years to graduate. Such was his physical prowess that Ermolayev became the first in the line of Soviet heroic dancers, the product of an age in which acrobatics and greater athleticism introduced themselves into classical dancing. His motto was said to be "Jump and turn as high and as fast as possible",[174] and he constantly pushed himself to ever more dizzying feats of virtuosity. His graduation performance in 1926 was as Vayou, God of the Winds, in Petipa's *Le Talisman*, a role previously danced only by Nijinsky and

---

172 The *classe de perfection* was an advanced ballet class given for the highest-ranking dancers in a company.
173 As quoted by Smakov in *The Great Russian Dancers*, p.119
174 Smakov, *The Great Russian Dancers*, p.307

Vladimirov. The ballet commentator Yuri Slonimsky[175] – always a supporter – wrote "the young dancer, like a hurricane, swept aside the old canons and stereotypes"[176] but many saw his technical wizardry as a coarsening of the art form. Once in the company at GATOB, he was cast by Lopukhov as The Blue Bird in *The Sleeping Beauty* and made an enormous impact with his airborne dancing, however a debut in 1927 as Siegfried in *Swan Lake* was a fiasco, the *métier* and temperament of the *danseur noble* far from his own capabilities. Like Semyonova, he was transferred to Moscow in 1930 where, despite dancing some twenty major roles until his retirement from the stage in 1959, he was under-utilised. Thereafter, he coached and taught with the company but fell foul of the Grigorovich regime. He died in Moscow in 1975.

Vakhtang Chabukiani, born in 1910 in the Georgian capital Tiflis (renamed Tbilisi after the 1917 revolution), came to Leningrad in 1926 and enrolled in the evening classes at the Choreographic School at the late starting age of almost sixteen, joining regular day classes only two years after. Through his schooling under Viktor Semyonov, Vladimir Ponomarev and Alexander Shiryaev, he graduated one year later in 1929 and went on to change the possibilities for, and perceptions of, male dancing. Of slimmer, less powerful build than Ermolayev, he nevertheless found fame and admiration for his bravura dancing. Like his contemporary, Chabukiani sought to extend the boundaries of male virtuosity, and scored his first successes in virtuoso roles such as the Bluebird in *The Sleeping Beauty* and the Slave in the *Le Corsaire* pas de deux. He created the role of the Count in Vaganova's 1933 production of *Swan Lake* and also scored great personal success as Basilio in *Don Quixote*. His theatrical instincts proved second to none and the changes of emphasis he made in established roles brought the two elements, classical and character, far closer together than they had ever been, establishing a performing tradition which continues to this day. He returned to Georgia in 1941 where he was dancer, choreographer and later ballet company director at the capital's opera house until 1973. He died in Tbilisi in 1992.

Konstantin Sergeyev was born in St Petersburg in 1910, where, from 1924 onwards he first followed the evening courses at the Leningrad Ballet School, before graduating to GATOB in 1930 where he soon became a *danseur noble* of considerable technical polish and elegance; he was considered to be blessed with an exemplary ballet physique. As an artist he was a firm advocate of Stanislavsky's 'realism' and made a great impact in the socialist

---

175 Born in St Petersburg in 1902, Slonimsky started writing ballet criticism in 1919 and became one of the founders of the Young Ballet group in 1921. He taught ballet history throughout the 1930s and 40s, was an active librettist for numerous works and the author of many books. He worked with Lopukhov to establish the new Choreography Department at the Leningrad Ballet School. He wrote several ballet librettos among which Sergeyev's *Path of Thunder*. He died in Moscow in 1978.

176 Smakov, *The Great Russian Dancers*, p.307

realist ballets. He created Romeo in Lavrovsky's *Romeo and Juliet* and was the regular stage partner of both Ulanova and, later, his wife Natalia Dudinskaya. He moved into staging, revising and choreographing ballets while still the Kirov's *premier danseur*. Sergeyev was one of Soviet ballet's most influential and long-serving personalities. He was Artistic Director of the Kirov Ballet from 1951 to 1956 and again from 1960 to 1970, as well as Director of the Leningrad Choreographic School between 1938 and 1940 and again from 1973 to 1992. He was married first to Kirov ballerina Feya Balabina[177] and then to Natalia Dudinskaya. He died in St Petersburg in 1992.

Moscow

There remained the Bolshoi School in Moscow which came under increasing political pressure to emulate and match the achievements of the somewhat suspect former capital.

Moscow's ballet audiences first greeted and then acclaimed the sunny virtuosity of Olga Lepeshinskaya in 1933; her bravura dancing came to epitomise the ideal of the new 'Soviet' ballerina in the capital. Born in Kiev, Ukraine in 1916, she entered the school in 1925, demonstrating her talent by appearing on the Bolshoi stage just one year later as Cupid in *Don Quixote* and assuming major roles immediately on her entry into the main company. She was noted for a powerful jump and sparkling characterisation in *demi-caractère* roles, such as Lisa in Gorsky's *Vain Precautions*. A fervent champion of the Soviet ideal, she went on to become one of the Bolshoi's great figures, retiring from the stage in 1963 after a spell of temporary blindness following the death of her husband. She was not subsequently engaged by the Bolshoi to teach and spent ten years at East Berlin's Komische Oper as ballet mistress. She died in Moscow in 2008.

One early post-revolution male graduate was the dynamic Asaf Messerer. Born in Vilna (now Vilnius) in 1903, Messerer firstly studied privately with Gorsky and Mikhail Mordkin[178] before joining the senior class at the Bolshoi

---

177   Born in Rostov-on-Don in 1910, Balabina trained with Vaganova at the Leningrad Choreographic School. She danced with GATOB from 1931, making her debut as Tao-Hoa in *The Red Poppy* and became known as a technically brilliant ballerina with a lively stage presence until her retirement from dancing in 1956. She taught at the Leningrad Choreographic School from 1947 onwards and was its Artistic Director from 1962 to 1973. She died in Yerevan, Armenia in 1982.

178   Born in Moscow in 1881, Mordkin graduated into the Bolshoi Ballet in 1899 as a soloist and was made assistant ballet master only five years later. Noted for his intense dramatic stage persona and intelligence, he was the ideal vehicle for Gorsky's innovations and created the lead male roles in several of his productions: *Raymonda*, *Swan Lake*, *La Bayadère* and *Giselle*. He featured in Diaghilev's inaugural Paris season of the Ballets Russes, partnered Anna Pavlova and established his own company before returning to the Bolshoi in 1912. He danced and set ballets throughout Russia until 1923 when he left the country, settling in the USA in 1924. He created a new company and worked as a

School at its re-opening in 1920. After his graduation the next year and entry into the company, his energy and drive allowed him to set himself greater technical challenges and rework the traditional mime used on stage. He straddled the divide in roles between *danseur noble* (he danced Siegfried in *Swan Lake* and Désiré in *The Sleeping Beauty*) and *demi-caractère* (he was the Acrobat in *The Red Poppy*) and was a dancer for some thirty years until his retirement in 1954. He led the Bolshoi troupe evacuated to Kuibyshev during the Great Patriotic War. He started teaching at the Bolshoi School in 1923 and continued until 1960, becoming one of the most distinguished teachers of the Soviet era. He gave the *classe de perfection* at the Bolshoi from 1943 onwards. He choreographed several works including Act IV of *Swan Lake*, the showpiece *Ballet Class* (later known as *Class Concert*) and the spectacular *Spring Waters* pas de deux, and both taught and mounted productions abroad. He died in Moscow in 1992.

Born in Velikie Gulyaky near Kiev in 1905, Mikhail Gabovich graduated from the Bolshoi School into the company in 1924 where he rapidly established himself as the only Muscovite *danseur noble* of note at the time. With a fine technique and a strong, easy jump, he excelled in all the classical lead roles, although he revealed greater depths of dramatic talent in 1938 as Vladimir in *The Prisoner of the Caucasus*. During the War, he led the company in Moscow and continued to dance until 1952 when he sustained a serious injury in rehearsal. After Ulanova's transfer to Moscow in 1944, he and she established a stage partnership which was greatly admired. He taught at the Bolshoi School from 1951 onwards and was its director between 1954 and 1958. In 1952, he co-staged *The Sleeping Beauty* at the Bolshoi with Asaf Messerer. He died in Moscow in 1965.

The Quest for a Soviet Ballet

1927 was not only the year of the première of Tikhomirov's *The Red Poppy* but also of the first Five Year Plan for the Russian economy presented in December by Trotsky and Stalin to the Fifteenth Party Congress; it demanded huge changes in the country's economic system and also decreed that the arts had to play their part in the construction of socialism. Political change was about to make the pressures of the preceding four years seem lightweight. *Narkompros* introduced repertorial control over theatres, which included ballet, and in 1929 brought in the Repertoire Index which classified all stage works from A (ideologically recommended) to E (forbidden). *The Red Poppy* was classed an 'A' ballet, alongside *Chopiniana*; the three Tchaikovsky ballets received a 'B' (ideologically acceptable and permitted without hindrance) while *Giselle* and *Le Corsaire* were given a 'C' (ideologically acceptable but

---

teacher and choreographer, a pioneer in the establishment of ballet in the country. He died in Millbrook, New Jersey in 1944.

primitive); there were no 'D' graded works but banned 'E' grade works included Goleizovsky's *The Whirlwind* and Nikolai and Sergey Legat's 1903 *The Fairy Doll*.

Alongside this apparent absolute evaluative clarity, there was also a degree of philosophical questioning concerning what in reality actually comprised a 'Soviet' ballet, what subject matter would be suitable for such a work and should ballet incorporate other forms of dance were two strands of argument. Musicologist and theatre critic Ivan Sollertinsky[179] and theatre specialist Alexey Gvozdev[180] were at the forefront of the intellectual discussion about the dramatisation of classical dancing, not in itself a new debate, given Gorsky's theatre-based work in Moscow since the turn of the century. However, the experiments by Lopukhov and others in allegorical and even abstract dance, the inherent ornamental quality of classical ballet and the ever more emphatic demands for meaningful Soviet art gave their discussions added weight. An open forum into these areas was launched in the pages of the magazine *Zhizn iskusstva* during the summer of 1928, prompting letters from across the spectrum of opinions, from Vaganova's advocacy of pure classicism to true iconoclasts, one of whom wrote "classical ballet must be annihilated".[181] A commonly held view was that ballet needed to reflect the contemporary population, which fairies and swans simply did not do, and to depict their largely urban, industrialised lives. Voices were heard in favour of putting acrobatics, sports, social and folkloric dancing into the mix; Leonid Yakobson,[182] wanted gestures from everyday life included rather than the mannered mime of the past and he proposed jettisoning such works as *La Bayadère*, *Don Quixote* and *The Little Humpbacked Horse* as vulgar

---

179 Born in Vitebsk in 1902, Sollertinsky studied philology at the University of Petrograd and theatrical history at the Institute of Art History during the early 1920s and taught the history of music, literature, theatre, psychology and aesthetics at a variety of institutions thereafter. In 1934 he became artistic advisor for the Leningrad Philharmonic Orchestra and worked at the Kirov Theatre. He lectured and wrote extensively on music and was a close friend of Dmitry Shostakovich. He died suddenly in Novosibirsk in 1944.

180 Born in 1887 in St Petersburg, Gvozdev graduated from the history faculty of St Petersburg University and in 1916 took up the first of several teaching posts. His first article was a criticism of Vsevolod Meyerhold. He published extensively thereafter on theatre and in 1939 wrote "West European Theatre at the Turn of the 19th and 20th Centuries". He wrote the entry 'Ballet' in the Great Soviet Encyclopaedia. He died in Leningrad in 1939.

181 Swift, *The Art of the Dance in the USSR*, p.82

182 Born in St Petersburg in 1904, Yakobson graduated from the Leningrad School in 1926 and joined GATOB where he excelled in character roles. His first choreography was for *The Golden Age*. He was a ballet master at the Bolshoi between 1933 and 1942 and then at the Kirov until 1969. He produced numerous works which often provoked controversy. He formed his own company, 'Choreographic Miniatures' (later called Yakobson Ballet), in 1970. He died in Moscow in 1975.

and examples of abstract aesthetics. The classicists, rather on the back foot in the face of such debate, could at least point to the emergence of genuinely Soviet ballet training, but the imperative for new, ideologically acceptable works could simply not be resisted. Lunacharsky, although still a champion of excellence, made that particular political imperative clear in a speech at the Bolshoi in response to the increasingly strident calls for wholesale change:

> "In the new ballet, there must be sufficient attention to reality. This reality must be captivating, dealing with present stories, and not of silly fairy tales".[183]

1928 – Kschessinsky's 'Leningrad Mobile Young Ballet Collective'

An early example of the promotion of the culture of ballet was the state-sanctioned Mobile Ballet Collective led by Matilda Kschessinskaya's elder brother Joseph. Between 1928 and 1930, and comprising young dancers from GATOB, it travelled far from Leningrad; in 1928 it undertook its first tour to the Russian Far East, appearing in Khabarovsk and Vladivostok, building on the presence of individual dancers since the middle of the decade. Kschessinsky's ensemble performed a traditional repertoire comprising *Giselle*, *Swan Lake*, *Esmeralda*, *Le Corsaire*, *Chopiniana* and divertissements. The performances were led by the young future principals Konstantin Sergeyev and Feya Balabina and were warmly received by the audiences. The company returned in 1930 with much the same repertoire except for *Raymonda*, which replaced *Le Corsaire*, and Ivanov's *The Magic Flute*. However, the subject of ballet's relevance to Soviet life was raised – the unknown critic of the *Krasnoye Znamya* (Red Banner) Vladivostok newspaper wrote: "Before us is the most conservative of the arts, although, as an art, ballet is at its best, but it is still, in a way, a museum."[184] No ideological complaints about the modernity of *The Red Poppy* which was also brought on tour, but real disappointment that it was unrealistic and too prettified to count as real Soviet art. The limited numbers of dancers in the ensemble also raised some regrets.

1929 – Viktorina Kriger and Art Theatre Ballet

Moscow's Art Ballet was founded in 1929 by Bolshoi ballerina Viktorina Kriger as an ensemble designed to bring simplified versions of the major works to the people, certainly made its mark. Born in St Petersburg in 1893, Kriger graduated from the Bolshoi School in 1910, joining the company and rising to become a leading 'Gorsky' ballerina. She excelled in *demi-caractère* roles requiring real stage temperament such as Lisa in *Vain Precautions*,

---

183   Swift, *The Art of the Dance in the USSR*, p.85

184   12th July 1930, as quoted by Krylovskaya in 'Dancers of the Leningrad ballet in the Far East in the 1920s-1930s.'

Swanilda in *Coppélia* and Kitri in *Don Quixote*. She danced with Pavlova's company in 1921 and also toured the United States with Mikhail Mordkin's company between 1923 and 1925 when she returned to Russia to rejoin the Bolshoi. In 1927, she started to appear with small groups of dancers in chamber versions of Bolshoi repertoire ballets which she determined should embody Stanislavsky's realistic approach to the portrayal of character and motivation; 1927 saw a version of *Schéhérazade* entitled *In the Chains of the Harem*, and others followed.

In 1932, the ensemble was renamed the Art Theatre Ballet, the year of *La Carmagnole*, a popular work set during the French Revolution to a score by Crimean composer Vladimir Femilidi[185] and choreography by Pavel Virsky.[186] In 1933 the company was joined by GITIS graduates and staged a new version of *La Fille mal gardée*, retitled *The Rivals*, which maintained the original score but used Richard Sheridan's 1775 play as the basis for the narrative. Kriger scored a personal triumph in both works while the latter also revealed the talents of Maria Sorokina[187] who became a noted leading dancer of great dramatic talent and charm, and possessed an impeccable technique. After directing the Art Theatre Ballet, Kriger returned to the Bolshoi, creating the role of the Stepmother in Zakharov's 1945 *Cinderella* and was Director of the Bolshoi Theatre Museum from 1955 to 1963. She died in Moscow in 1978. In 1939 the Art Theatre Ballet was renamed the Stanislavsky and Nemirovich-Danchenko Music Theatre Ballet, which survives to this day.

1930 – *The Golden Age*

In the continuing quest for a truly Soviet ballet, a libretto competition was announced for the spring of 1929 by the arts journal *Zhizn iskusstva* which was won by *The Golden Age*. It responded to the criteria of a full-length ballet on a contemporary, revolutionary theme, eschewing all abstraction – no dancing for dancing's sake – and mysticism. The scenario was by Alexander

---

185 Born in 1905, Femilidi graduated from the Musical Drama Academy of Odessa and became one of the first Ukrainian composers to promote revolutionary ideals in his compositions. He wrote the operas *The Break* and *Battleship 'Potemkin'* for the opera house in Odessa in the late 1920s. He died in Crimea in 1931.

186 Born in Odessa, Crimea in 1905, Virsky trained at the Music and Drama Institute of Odessa and at GITIS in Moscow; his first piece of choreography was *La Carmagnole* in 1932. He staged several ballets around the USSR and was principal dancer and choreographer at the Kiev Ballet until 1936. In 1937 he organised the first Ukrainian Dance Company, which, although short-lived, he re-founded in 1951, achieving national and international profile and recognition. He died in Kiev in 1975.

187 Born in Moscow in 1911, Sorokina studied at GITIS, graduating in 1929. She danced with the Moscow Drama Ballet until 1932 when she joined the Moscow Art Ballet (later the Moscow Academic Musical Theatre [MAMT] or the Stanislavsky Nemirovich-Danchenko Ballet) for which her greatest success was in 1943 in the title role of Burmeister's *Lola*. She died at the age of thirty-seven in Moscow in 1948.

Ivanovsky[188] and a young Dmitry Shostakovich[189], then an up-and-coming composer very much favoured by the Soviet regime, was engaged to compose the music. The title referred to an exhibition in a capitalist city whose decadence is shown in scenes at a cabaret and in a music hall; a fight takes place between some fascists and a Soviet football team who are joined by the workers to celebrate cooperation between the proletariat and the joy of work. The sets and costumes were by the important stage designer Valentina Khodasevich.[190] With choreography by Vasily Vainonen[191](first act), Leonid Yakobson (second) and Vladimir Chesnakov (third), it premièred at GATOB in October 1930 with a starry cast including Ulanova as Komsomolskaya Pravda, Jordan the Diva, Mungalova a Western *Komsomol* member, Shavrov in the role of a Fascist and Shelest as the Angel of Peace. However popular it proved at first, it soon foundered not only because of its ridiculous storyline but, more crucially, in the face of sustained official criticism that it minimised the conflicts of class war. It did not last beyond its first season.

1930 – *The Footballer*

Igor Moiseyev, the Bolshoi dancer who went on to become one of the most important figures in the promotion and presentation of Russian folk dancing, created his first ballet in March 1930 in co-operation with Lev Lashchilin.

---

188   Born in 1881 in Kazan, Ivanovsky worked in musical theatre and opera from 1904 to 1921. In 1918, he made his first film and thereafter pursued a successful directorial career both on film and in the theatre throughout the 1920s and 30s. He died in Leningrad in 1967.

189   Born in St Petersburg in 1906, Shostakovich studied at the Petrograd Conservatoire before embarking on a career of musical composition. Over his life he composed in various forms, from string quartets to operas, symphonies to film scores. He had a complicated relationship with the Soviet state and often fell in and out of official favour. He is regarded as one of the twentieth century's major composers. He died in Moscow in 1975.

190   Born in Moscow in 1894, Khodasevich studied art in Moscow, Munich and Paris. Initially as portrait painter, she set about designing for mass theatrical events after the revolution and worked at the People's Comedy Theatre and the Moscow Arts Theatre. She lived in Europe between 1924 and 1928 before returning to Russia. Between 1932 and 1936 she was GATOB's chief stage designer. Among many ballets, she designed *The Rivals* for Moscow Art Ballet in 1933, *The Fountain of Bakhchisarai* (1934) and *Esmeralda* (1935) at the Kirov. She moved back to Moscow in 1953 and left design three years later in favour of literary work. She died in Moscow in 1970.

191   Born in 1901 in St Petersburg, Vainonen graduated from the ex-Imperial Theatre School in 1919 and joined the Petrograd company that year, remaining as a dancer until 1938 and becoming a house choreographer in 1935. He was a member of Balanchine's 'Young Ballet' for which he started to choreograph, making the acrobatic *Moszkowsky Waltz*, which is still performed; his version of *The Nutcracker* is considered one of the best. He went on to become both an important figure in Leningrad and also in Moscow where between 1946 and 1950 and also 1954 and1958, he worked at the Bolshoi Theatre. He died in Moscow in 1964.

The Footballer was a three-act work to music by Viktor Oransky[192] which contrasted melodies of revolutionary and workers' songs with jazz-influenced rhythms to show the consequences of four protagonists (the bourgeois Dandy and Dame and the proletarian Streetsweeper and Footballer) falling in love with a representative of the wrong class. The second act included the appearance of a tractor and featured dances representing harvest, oil, coal and water. Asaf Messerer scored a personal success in the role of the Footballer while Anastasia Abramova[193] danced the Sweeper. The work, although an attempt to depict a revolutionary theme, was ultimately deemed an unsuccessful amalgam of ballet and athletic movement; Lunacharsky made it clear that he did not approve of bringing sporting games onto the ballet stage.

1930 – The Bolshoi Theatre Commission

In November 1930, a meeting of the Politburo established the Commission of the Presidium of the Central Executive Committee for the management of the Bolshoi and artistic theatres of the USSR. In practical terms, this meant that the running of the Bolshoi and Moscow Arts theatres bypassed completely the Commissariat for Enlightenment and lay in the direct control of the Kremlin. The Bolshoi effectively became a state within a state, its employees ultimately enjoying privileges undreamt of by the populace: apartments, summer dachas, sanatoria and a clinic, two closed canteens, pioneer camps for their children, taxi allowances, closed distributors and salaries several times higher than those in other theatres. Stalin controlled everything. Ballet soloist Vera Vasilieva[194] overheard Bolshoi director Malinovskaya observe that her own role was in fact very insignificant and that, in fact, the Bolshoi was controlled by the Government Commission which, in turn, worked directly under Comrade Stalin.

---

192 Born in 1899 in Feodosia, Crimea, Oransky studied piano at the Moscow Conservatoire and subsequently worked at the Bolshoi School. His first ballet, *The Footballer* in 1930 prompted further theatrical commissions and his appointment as conductor at the Moscow Art Theatre for Music. He was also a prolific composer of film scores. He died in Moscow in 1953.

193 Born in Moscow on 1902, Abramova graduated into the Bolshoi in 1918 and became a leading ballerina who danced all the major roles throughout the 1920s. She was noted for her grace and femininity on stage, her refined technique and speed. She was the first Swanilda in Gorsky's 1924 production of *Coppélia* and she also worked extensively with Goleizovsky. She was dismissed from the company in 1948 and died in Moscow in 1985.

194 Born in Moscow in 1909, Vasilieva graduated into the Bolshoi in 1926 where she danced until 1950. She appeared in many works by Kasyan Goleizovsky whom she later married. After her retirement from dancing, she arranged concert programmes and ballets by her husband. She taught at the Bolshoi School between 1950 and 1962. She died in Moscow in 2009.

An application the following year by Leningrad's GATOB to come under similar governmental control was initially rejected. The establishment of ballet dancers as favoured servants of the state was, nevertheless, a notable decision, leading to their increasingly privileged social status within the USSR.

1930 – The Purge of the Moscow School

The extent to which the Soviet regime wished to showcase the Bolshoi Theatre and to determine its artistic direction was exemplified by the transfer to Moscow in 1930 of two of the finest examples of the Leningrad school of dance: Marina Semyonova and Alexey Ermolayev. They were the first of many dancers, teachers, choreographers and directors to make the journey, and included Pyotr Gusev in 1935 and Galina Ulanova in 1944. Lepeshinskaya's 1933 Bolshoi debut may have been cited as proof of the reinvigoration of the Moscow dance school, but the reality in the early 1930s was a cultural purge of a generation of established and talented dancers trained by or under Gorsky and who had, from the revolution onwards, exemplified his style. Several had also been enthusiastic participants in Goleizovsky's choreographic and scenic experimentalism during the 1920s which no longer had a place in Stalin's increasingly conservative artistic policy. The 'Leningradisation' of the Bolshoi meant that Moscow's star dancers of the 1920s were side-lined during the following decade.

Choreographer Igor Moiseyev ultimately left the company in 1937 and pursued his own path in folk dance while his then wife, company ballerina Nina Podgoretskaya[195] found herself excluded from being cast in major parts, the last of which was the title role of her husband's 1932 ballet *Salambo*. She remained a Bolshoi dancer until 1948 but rarely appeared on stage. Moiseyev recalled the hostility shown to himself and his wife by Rostislav Zakharov who was appointed director in 1936:

> "Zakharov treated me with extreme hostility, seeing me as a competitor, and used any methods to get me out of the theatre. He began by hitting my wife...who, after the arrival of Semyonova, became the second ballerina of the Bolshoi Theatre. Zakharov removed her from all performances, sneered at rehearsals. I called him a scoundrel in front of everyone, and this gave him reason to persecute me openly."[196]

---

195 Born in Lubny, Poltava region in 1902, Podgoretskaya trained under Tikhomirov and graduated as a soloist into the Bolshoi company in 1919. In 1922, she danced the title role in Gorsky's new production of *Raymonda* and went on to appear in all the major ballets and was noted for her beautiful arabesque and expansive jump. In 1937, she co-founded the USSR Folk Dance Ensemble with her husband Igor Moiseyev and danced with them after that date. She was formally dismissed from the Bolshoi in 1948. She died in Moscow in 1977.

196 Moiseyev as quoted on http://cyclowiki.org

Valentina Kudryavtseva was another much-admired Moscow principal dancer swept aside by the changes. She had come to prominence in 1919 while still a school student, cast by her teacher Gorsky as Clara in his new production of *The Nutcracker* at the Bolshoi. Throughout the 1920s, she danced the major roles of the repertoire to acclaim as well as appearing in experimental works with Goleizovsky's Chamber Studio. From 1930 onwards, she was increasingly side-lined, and appeared rarely and only in minor roles.

Lyubov Bank, the dancer who had worked so closely with Goleizovsky in the 1920s, was less unfortunate, continuing to dance a limited number of principal roles – she appeared as Zarema in Zakharov's 1936 Bolshoi staging of *The Fountain of Bakhchisarai* – but did not enjoy anything like the profile she had the previous decade. Likewise, Anastasia Abramova, having enjoyed considerable success after her 1922 debut as Lisa in *Vain Precautions* and also been involved in Goleizovsky's choreographic experiments, saw her roles at the Bolshoi dry up after 1930; she remained officially a member of the company until 1948 when she was dismissed.

Margarita Kandaurova[197] was a highly regarded Bolshoi ballerina of the 1920s whose stage exposure shrank as a result of Stalin's changes. She performed a wide classical repertoire, often partnered by Viktor Smoltsov.[198] Brother of fellow Bolshoi dancer Ivan, Smoltsov was a highly regarded principal dancer; in the words of Asaf Messerer "he was lyrical in the noblest and most sublime sense of the word. And at the same time, on stage, Viktor Smoltsov knew how to present a lady, and not himself."[199] His partnering abilities meant that he danced with all the company's ballerinas; he remained at the Bolshoi after 1930, albeit increasingly in character roles.

The 'Leningradisation' of the Bolshoi continued apace through the 1930s and it can be argued that Moscow pulled away once more only after the war, Stalin's death and with a revival of a distinct performing style.

---

197 Born in Moscow in 1895, Kandaurova graduated into the Bolshoi in 1912 and appeared throughout the 1910s and 20s across the repertoire, known for the beauty of her line and her effortless technique. She remained at the Bolshoi until 1941. She died in Moscow in 1990.

198 Born in Moscow in 1900, Smoltsov graduated into the Bolshoi in 1918, appearing in three contrasting roles in *The Little Humpbacked Horse*. With a fine classical technique and a gift for acting, he easily encompassed *danseur noble* and character parts. Between 1921 and 1923 he toured with Balashova in Europe, in 1922 he danced with Anna Pavlova in Paris and in 1929 appeared with Bank in Paris, Berlin and Riga. From 1925 onwards he taught at the Moscow Ballet School. Between 1934 and 1935, he was director, choreographer and teacher in Baku. He retired from the Bolshoi in 1960 and died in Moscow in 1976.

199 Танец. Мысль. Время (Dance. Think. Time)

Overtures to return

As Commissar for Enlightenment, Lunacharsky maintained an international perspective – he had, after all, lived for many years outside Russia, most importantly in Paris in the early 1910s. Certainly, he was keen for notable artists living abroad to return to Russia which was intended to bring validation to the Soviet regime. It required the permission of Stalin for Lunacharsky to travel abroad to make overtures to important individuals based in Berlin and Paris ideally to persuade them to return to Russia for good or at least to visit on a regular basis.

Sergey Diaghilev

A high-profile Russian in exile courted by the regime was founder of the Ballets Russes Sergey Diaghilev. The poet Vladimir Mayakovsky, whom Diaghilev had met in Berlin in 1922 and whom he had helped obtain a French visa, was in Paris in 1924 and attempted to persuade the impresario to return to Russia. He wrote two letters of introduction, one of which was to Lunacharsky in which he stated:

> "Of course, former Russians turned Parisian have tried to frighten S.P.[200] with Moscow. But his desire has proved stronger together with my assurances that in delicacy and grace we surpass the French and that we are more 'business-like' than the Americans."[201]

Diaghilev continued to keep his homeland in his mind and asked Prokofiev to compose the music for a new ballet about contemporary Russia. Diaghilev admired the artistic experimentation in Russia which had followed the fall of the ancien régime; constructivism was one of the movements which had arisen, a celebration of the era of the machine, and the new work he conceived was an attempt to align the Ballets Russes with it and its contemporaneity. He wrote:

"J'ai voulu évoquer la Russie d'aujourd'hui – une Russie qui vit, qui respire, qui possède un visage bien à elle. Je ne pouvais tout de même la représenter dans l'esprit d'avant la révolution!"[202] (I wished to represent the Russia of today – a Russia which lives, which breathes, which possesses an aspect all her own. All the same, I could not show her in a pre-revolutionary spirit!)

The concept was a dangerous one, not least because of the adverse reaction almost guaranteed from exiled Russians in Paris towards a work embodying any positive depiction of the Soviet regime as well the potential negative impression on the impresario's American backers. By 1925, the project had the working title, *Ursignol* (a made-up word comprising *URSS* (USSR

---

200   S.P. - Sergey Pavlovich, Diaghilev's first name and patronymic.
201   Buckle, *Diaghilev*, p.444
202   as quoted by Poarskaâ and Volodina, *L'Art des Ballets Russes*, p.253

in French) and *guignol*), and the impresario was at pains to emphasise the Soviet nature of the work. Later that year, Diaghilev sent a request to direct the ballet to the theatre director Vsevolod Meyerhold in Moscow with whom he had worked before the revolution; it was refused. Meyerhold was in Paris in 1926 and Diaghilev was still eager to meet him; this occurred when the theatre director attended a Ballets Russes rehearsal with Prokofiev, but the meeting, however cordial, came to nothing. Diaghilev had initially wanted Goleizovsky to create the movement but that too was not to be and so it was finally entrusted to Léonide Massine, company dancer, rising choreographer and Diaghilev's then favourite.

When Prokofiev returned from Soviet Russia in March 1927, Diaghilev questioned him closely about his experiences: "Diaghilev moved on to questions about Russia, where he very much wants to go" the composer observed in his diary.[203] Lunacharsky himself arrived in the French capital – he knew Diaghilev's work and had written favourably on the early seasons of the Ballets Russes and the impresario's artistic vision – so the two men met amicably. However, the commissar was less than complimentary about Diaghilev in a newspaper article written upon his return, stating that if he ever entered the USSR, he would certainly not be welcomed with open arms. Diaghilev had at one time even considered the possibility of a Ballets Russes tour to the Soviet Union, but the difficulties involved and the hostility from some Soviet quarters towards someone they saw as a capitalist lickspittle meant that neither he nor his company ever made the journey. The Ballets Russes never performed in Russia.

Sergey Prokofiev

In 1925, both Igor Stravinsky and Sergey Prokofiev received letters setting out the terms under which they could return to Russia. Stravinsky rejected outright the overture made to him, but Prokofiev was attracted to the idea and pursued it, receiving a further letter offering him full amnesty for 'all prior offences', freedom to travel both into and out of the RSFSR[204] and assuring him that his return would be welcomed by the musical world of Russia. In 1926 he accepted an invitation to appear in a series of homecoming concerts, although it was only in early 1927 that he made a two-month visit. He performed in both Leningrad and Moscow, oversaw the Leningrad première of his opera *The Love of Three Oranges* and entered into discussions with Meyerhold about a Moscow staging for his first opera *The Gambler*. Excited, flattered but not a little troubled by the dark side of

---

203 Scheijen, *Diaghilev. A Life*, p.412
204 The Russian Soviet Federative Socialist Republic (RSFSR), the official name of what was the largest and most populous of the Soviet socialist republics of the Soviet Union (USSR).

life in Soviet Russia, the composer returned to Paris and Lunacharsky kept up his charm offensive on behalf of the regime. Prokofiev was given Soviet citizenship but he nevertheless renewed his French *certificat d'identité* on his return to France.

Le Pas d'acier

Le Pas d'acier (the retitled *Ursignol*) premièred in Paris in May 1927 with choreography by Massine and was a success with both audience and critics. Over two scenes, the ballet celebrated the collective subordination of the individual to the common good both in the fields and the factory, and the choreography, settings and costumes emphasised the constructivist nature of the whole enterprise. The English critic Cyril Beaumont wrote positively of its performance in London that summer, stating that the second scene "gave a masterly impression of rhythmic power and beauty of machines".[205]

Prokofiev returned to Russia in 1929 with the prospect of seeing *Le Pas d'acier* mounted at the Bolshoi with new sets and choreography. Intended as a tribute to the constructivist art of the young USSR, the project nevertheless provoked the ire of Russian critics who resented the depiction of Soviet life by someone lacking any first-hand knowledge. A strange amalgam of the realistic and the fantastical, it fell between two artistic stools and as a proposal pleased no one in Russia, least of all the Russian Association of Proletarian Musicians, which ensured that its scheduling in 1930 for performance at the Bolshoi was indefinitely cancelled. It was not the first bruising encounter with the Soviet administration the composer endured.

Soviet dancers abroad

By the late 1920s, the emergence of a new Soviet dancer was an identifiable phenomenon, and one which gained external ratification with performances outside the USSR. The cultural borders between Russia and the rest of the world had never been definitively closed, so Viktor Smoltsov had toured Europe from 1921 to 1923 with fellow Bolshoi principal dancer Alexandra Balashova (who in 1922 chose not to return to Russia), appeared with Anna Pavlova in Paris in 1922 and with Lyubov Bank in Paris, Berlin and Riga in 1929. Asaf Messerer appeared in Latvia, Lithuania and Estonia in 1929, partnering Viktorina Kriger and then again in 1930 with a young Bolshoi soloist Tatiana Vasilieva; these last visits had been arranged by *Posredrabis*, an organisation that had permission to authorise performing contracts in the Baltic states. A third invitation was extended to Messerer for the end of 1930 and he decided to appear for a New Year's Day performance with his sister, Sulamith. An inspection of their programme indicates what was considered appropriate as a Soviet ballet calling-card. The *Don Quixote* pas de deux was

---

205 García-Márquez, *Massine. A Biography*, p.196

followed by several solos including two for Asaf from *The Red Poppy* – 'Dance with a Ribbon' and 'Little Chinese God' – and one for Sulamith, of her own choreography entitled *Dance with a Hoop* as well as two more duets, including Asaf's miniature, *Pierrot and Pierrette*, to Johann Strauss. He also danced another solo of his own, *The Soccer Player*, set to the music of Alexander Tsfasman.[206] An invitation from the Royal Opera, Stockholm followed to appear both in their programme and a production of *Coppélia*, as did a request from Copenhagen, where they were enthusiastically received. In the Swedish capital, much comment was made about their elegance and schooling, not least by the critic of the newspaper *Aftonbladet* who observed that "since the time of Fokine and (Vera) Fokina, we in Stockholm have not seen anything comparable to this performance. But above all, one must say that even Fokine was incapable of demonstrating anything approaching Asaf Messerer's fabulous technique."[207] With the support of a politburo member, Bolshoi director Elena Malinovskaya allowed the Messerer siblings to continue on a tour which eventually lasted some five months; they travelled to Paris where they appeared at the Théâtre des Champs Elysées to great acclaim. Prince Sergey Volkonsky[208] wrote fulsomely about the performance in Paris's Russian language newspaper *Posledniye Novosti*, although he did comment that there was a heavy accent on virtuosity, prompting Sulamith to remark many years later:

> "True, he criticized us slightly for the fact that at times, carried away by 'virtuosity,' we lessened the 'spirituality of the dance.' …. We were young and fascinated by technical innovation."[209]

The Messerers then travelled to Berlin, then under the fledgling Nazi government, to appear at the Kurfurstendam Theatre. In the magazine *Der Tanz*, Joseph Levitan wrote:

> "Their tour should affirm the knowledge that the future of the dance points to this path. The past and future of the art of the dance belong together, a contrast between ballet and the modern dance is ridiculous and the much-

---

206 Born in 1906 in the Alexandrovskoye Urban Settlement, Tsfasman studied at the Moscow Conservatoire and then became an important figure in Soviet jazz from the period of the mid-1920s until the late 1960s as a pianist, composer, conductor, arranger and publisher. He died in Moscow in 1971.

207 Messerer, 'Asaf and Sulamith Messerer's 1933 European Tour', p.207

208 Volkonsky was born in 1860 in Lääne-Harju Parish, Governorate of Estonia. He was Director of the Imperial Theatres between 1899 and 1902, where he employed Diaghilev as his assistant. He was forced out of post after disagreement with Kschessinska. In 1910 he studied and then taught Dalcroze eurythmics. He remained in Russia after the revolution but eventually emigrated and lived in Paris from 1926 onwards, becoming a notable theatre critic. He died in Hot Springs, Virginia, USA in 1937.

209 Messerer, 'Asaf and Sulamith Messerer's 1933 European Tour', p.211

praised new discoveries of modernism can also be found in a ballet work as long as this is fully alive."[210]

A further appearance in Paris led to interest from American impresarios but the Soviet authorities finally decided that the chances of losing the two dancers were increasing and it was made very clear that their immediate return to Russia was required. They complied.

In November 1933, Vakhtang Chabukiani and Tatiana Vecheslova appeared at the opera house in Riga. Their appearance caused a stir with the brilliant virtuosity of their technique, their acrobatic skill and the absence of bourgeois sentimentality:

"La tendance soviétique a rigoureusement éliminé de son art et de l'esprit de la danse tout ce qui peut rappeler la 'sentimentalité bourgeoise', comme elle a banni ces éléments dangereux de la vie privée des ses citoyens"[211] (the Soviet trend (in ballet) has rigorously eliminated from its art and the spirit of the dance everything that could evoke 'bourgeois sentimentality', just as it has banished the same dangerous elements from the private lives of its citizens).

Further examination of the new Russian style of dancing came from the Lithuanian dance critic Jacques Brams:

"Cette danse ne porte plus le sceau de noblesse et de finesse qui furent l'enchantement du ballet russe d'antan. Elle est devenue plus grossière, plus matérielle et elle ressort plus de l'athlétique que de la poésie...Cet élément de cirque ressort trop dans chacun de leurs numéros"[212] (This dancing no longer carries the seal of nobility and gentility which were the delights of the Russian ballet of yesteryear. It has become coarser, more material and it is more athletic than poetic. This element of the circus is too apparent in each of their pieces).

Despite Brams's reservations, their performance was a popular success which led directly to an invitation to dance in the United States following the country's recognition of the Soviet Union in 1933. Unlike the Messerers, they obtained permission and successfully appeared at Carnegie Hall, New York in January 1934 before a tour to Chicago, Detroit, Boston, Los Angeles and San Francisco to similarly enthusiastic receptions. Chabukiani and Vecheslova's engagement was the first example of cultural relations between the United States and Russia since the 1917 revolution. That did not mean to say that the visit was free from tension – it is alleged that Stalin stated that the director of GATOB would face the firing squad if Chabukiani did not return. American audiences were also worried about the consequences

---

210 ibid p.215
211 *Archives Internationales de la Danse* No.1, 1934, p.150
212 ibid.

of watching communist dancers, leading the ballet critic John Martin to observe reassuringly in *The New York Times*: "The political influence of Soviet dancing is nothing to be alarmed about. Its freedom and disarming spirit are extremely potent. The audience simply adored it and bravoed throughout the evening with sincerity. The performance is fittingly to be described as a riot!" In recognition of the Russian dancers' virtuosity, *The New York Post* observed that "Vecheslova and Chabukiani can leap higher and whirl faster than perhaps any other dancers alive" while the *New York Daily Mirror* stated that they were "...artists of the very first rank. One rarely sees such perfect co-ordination and control of the human body."[213]

France signed a non-aggression treaty with the Soviet Union in 1932, which had facilitated the Messerers' appearances in Paris the following year. In reaction to the growing unease in Paris about a resurgent Germany under Reichskanzler Hitler, a treaty of military assistance was signed between the two countries in 1935, which led to an invitation for a Russian dancer to appear at the Paris Opéra. Marina Semyonova, the first Soviet ballerina, was dispatched to appear as Giselle alongside the émigré Russian Serge Lifar as Albrecht, prompting enthusiasm among the paying audiences but observations from some critics concerning the emphasis she gave to Giselle's peasant status and the resulting lack of psychological insight. One wrote that her interpretation suffered from "insufferable realism".[214] It must be remembered that Paris' view of what the role of Giselle 'should' be was coloured by Olga Spessivtseva's transcendent interpretation at the Opéra where she had been an *étoile* from 1924 until 1932.

1931 – *The Bolt*

In April 1931 Fyodor Lopukhov fared even worse with *The Bolt* than *The Golden Age* had done the year before. Set to a libretto by Viktor Smirnov,[215] director of MKhAT-2,[216] and a score by Shostakovich, it was based on a real-life incident of sabotage at the Red October factory, it was the USSR's first 'industrial ballet' which attempted a satirical representation of the petite bourgeoisie who try to sabotage the 'socialist machine' by placing a bolt into its workings. The ballet provoked stinging criticism for the representation of

---

213   As quoted by a promotional flyer for the San Francisco leg of the concert tour.

214   Scheuer, *Dancing Times*, February 1936.

215   Born in 1896 in Pyzhovka, near Smolensk, Smirnov studied at Perm State University before moving to Moscow in 1921, subsequently becoming Director of MKhAT-2. *The Bolt* was his first commission as a librettist. Between 1930 and 1937 he worked in the export of Soviet films worldwide. In 1937, he became Director of VOKS, the All-Union Society for Cultural Relations with Foreign Countries and, during the War, was responsible for the evacuation of art and culture professionals from Moscow to the Asian republics. He died in Moscow in 1946.

216   The Second Moscow Academic Arts Theatre.

the members of the Soviet youth organisation *Komsomol* who discover the plan as primitively grotesque characters, and negative commentary from the theatre critic Mikhail Yankovsky:

> "*Bolt* is not simply a failure of one theatrical appearance...It is a failure witnessing the depravity of that method and which graphically points out that its path, up to the present, lies hopelessly far from the general path of Soviet theatre. It seems... that *Bolt* – is a last warning."[217]

Shostakovich was himself far from critical of Lopukhov, ascribing the failure of both *The Bolt* and *The Golden Age* to other factors: "I hasten to exclude all of the ballet master Lopukhov's work on *The Bolt*. His work was wonderful, but Lopukhov found himself in the thrall of the theatre and took on a libretto of poor quality, the result being a pasquinade."[218]

Pulled at its dress rehearsal, *The Bolt* cost Lopukhov the directorship of GATOB, which was given to Vaganova, and he was persuaded to take up the running of the newly-formed Maly troupe, homed in the former Mikhailovsky Theatre. No matter how good the dancers in Soviet Russia, the clock was clearly continuing to tick for classical dance: Anatoly Lunacharsky, ballet's saviour after the revolution, had also been persuaded to step down as Commissar for Enlightenment in late 1929; there was no one who would again fight as hard as he had done on its behalf.

The Maly Theatre

The Maly (or Small) Theatre, originally named the Mikhailovsky in imperial times, was established in 1833 to stage French drama for the St Petersburg court. In 1918 it was re-commissioned as the Lyric Theatre to show comic operas, experimental drama and danced divertissements given by a small group of in-house dancers. The following decade saw the re-naming of the theatre on several occasions: in 1920 it became The State Academic Theatre of Comic Opera, then in 1921 the Maly Petrograd State Academic Theatre and in 1926 The State Academic Maly Opera Theatre (Gosudarstvenny Akademichesky Maly Operny Teatr), known by the acronym MALEGOT. Following his enforced departure from GATOB in 1931, Fyodor Lopukhov was asked to head a new 'laboratory of ballet' to be based at the Maly and he decided, given the varying quality of the dancers he would have, not to attempt to replicate what GATOB was presenting in terms of repertoire but rather to focus on 'ballet comedy'. Thirty-nine female and twenty-five male dancers were selected at audition. The creation of a new company was not warmly greeted by some and both individual artists and the management received anonymous letters; several dancers signed the article 'How We

---

217   As quoted by Swift, *The Art of the Dance in the USSR*, p.90
218   Fay, *Shostakovich and His World*, p.155

Worked' published in the *Komsomol* youth newspaper *Smena* (Change) in June, 1933: "The idea of creating a ballet at MALEGOT for some reason immediately antagonised some employees of other theatres. This manifested itself in distrust of the abilities of our theatre's ballet ensemble. We were called 'kindergarten children' and 'dancer dropouts'."[219] The initial brief was to create new narratives to new music in order to express revolutionary struggle and the construction of socialism, however, it became clear that an untrained company needed to dance the classics as a technical base. Lopukhov therefore chose *Les Millions d'Arlequin* (or *Harlequinade*), originally created by Petipa in 1900, as the first ballet performed by the new ensemble, stating that it "largely satisfies educational, pedagogical and training needs; I had to place special emphasis on classical dance, as the best way of educating a ballet dancer".[220] He created his own version to Riccardo Drigo's[221] original score, restoring some musical sections cut for the initial performances at the Hermitage Theatre. The production opened in 1933 to great popular success: "We won the first battle for the ballet MALEGOT"[222] Lopukhov observed; Colombina was first danced by Valentina Rosenberg[223] and Pierrette by Galina Isayeva.[224] His success subsequently attracted some notable dancers who sought to escape the restrictions at

---

219 V. M. Rosenberg, G. I. Isayeva, D. M. Musatov, F. I. Chernyshenko in *Smena*, 23rd June 1933 as quoted by Serdyuk in 'Ballet of the Mikhailovsky Theatre: from the organisation of the troupe to the first performance'.

220 Lopukhov 'Before the curtain: *Harlequinade*' in *Red Gas*, 5th June 1933, as quoted by Serdyuk in ibid.

221 Born in Padua, Italy in 1846, Drigo studied at the Venice Conservatoire and embarked upon a conducting career in Italy; in 1878 he was invited to work in St Petersburg where he initially conducted Italian opera. In 1886 he became kapellmeister for the Imperial Ballet after which he began to compose. He created the score for *Le Talisman* and for several of Petipa's late works. He returned to Padua in 1919 where he died in 1930.

222 Lopukhov as quoted by Serdyuk in 'Ballet of the Mikhailovsky Theatre: from the organisation of the troupe to the first performance'.

223 Born in Petrograd in 1915, Rosenberg graduated in 1931 into the Maly company with whom she appeared until 1959. She featured in numerous new works including as Olga in *Youth* (1949) and the Chinese Beauty in *Seven Beauties* (1953). She died in Leningrad in 1977.

224 Born in Petrograd in 1915, Isayeva first trained in the evening classes of the Leningrad Choreographic School. Between 1931 and 1963 she danced at the Maly Theatre, creating several roles in new works. She possessed a lively stage personality. She was the ballet company's artistic director between 1954 and 1960. She was the artistic director of the department of new work at the artists' organisation Lenconcert from 1967 to 1991, the year of her death at an unrecorded location.

GATOB: Pyotr Gusev, Alexander Orlov[225] and Nikolai Zubkovsky[226] joined Lopukhov at the Maly. In 1934, Lopukhov made a successful new version of *Coppélia*, bridging the gap between classical and character dancing in a production of considerable verve and enjoyment which included a puppet interlude; Zinaida Vasilieva[227] danced Swanilda at the opening performance, partnered by Gusev as Franz.

1932 – Socialist Realism

There can have been few artistic policies as comprehensively damaging to the arts as socialist realism, a term said to have been coined by Josef Stalin himself on a visit to Maxim Gorky's Moscow apartment and first seen in the magazine *Literaturnaya Gazeta* (Literary Gazette) in May 1932. That the concept was put into practice so enthusiastically indicates the new-found importance given to political orthodoxy in the arts and a realisation that they were powerful tools in the drive for total communism. The definition of this, on the face of it, innocuous term hints at what lay ahead for Russian artists of all persuasions until the disintegration of the regime's political beliefs in the late 1980s. "A comprehensive and truthful portrayal of life in art...Socialist Realism implies an art imbued with communist ideology, that is to say, its very core is a deliberate purposeful struggle for the victory of communism, an evaluation of life in the light of communist ideals."[228] Socialist realism became the overarching Soviet artistic policy demanding the portrayal of working-class heroes who display loyalty, duty and a shared drive towards the common goal; ballet was not exempt. At the 1933 Party Congress the defining characteristics of socialist realism were laid out.

---

225 Born in 1889, Orlov graduated into the Mariinsky in 1908 where he danced until 1924. He took part in the Ballets Russes seasons of 1909-1911, creating the role of the Moor in Fokine's *Petrushka* alongside Nijinsky and Karsavina in 1911. In 1915 he appeared in operetta for the first time and thereafter appeared frequently in musical comedy, being a member of the Leningrad Musical Comedy Theatre from 1929 to 1934 and 1941 to 1959. He appeared with the Maly company from 1934 to 1941. He died in Leningrad in 1974.

226 Born in Smolensk in 1911, Zubkovsky graduated into GATOB in 1931 where he would remain as a virtuoso dancer of considerable stage presence until 1962. He performed a wide variety of roles including The Blue Bird in *The Sleeping Beauty* and the three male roles of Pierre, Philippe and Jerôme in *The Flames of Paris*. He also appeared frequently at the Maly Theatre; from 1962 he taught there and at the Vaganova School from 1965. He married two Kirov ballerinas; firstly Inna Izraileva (Zubkovskaya) and secondly Ninel Kurgapkina. He died in Leningrad in 1971.

227 Born in St Petersburg in 1913, Vasilieva graduated from the Leningrad School into the Maly company in 1933, creating the role of Zina in *The Bright Stream*, before transferring to the Bolshoi in Moscow in 1935 and then to Minsk in 1937 where she remained as a leading dancer known for her lyrical qualities until 1949. From 1950 to 1961, she was a founder choreographer and teacher at the Novosibirsk Ballet School, and then taught in Cairo, Egypt from 1962 to 1965. She died in Novosibirsk in 1999.

228 Swift, *The Art of the Dance in the USSR*, p.92

Artistic works had to be:
1. Proletarian, i.e., relevant to the workers and understandable to them.
2. Typical, i.e., show scenes of the everyday life of the people.
3. Realistic, i.e., be representational.
4. Partisan, i.e., supportive of the aims of the State and the Party.

1932 also saw the reorganisation of all artistic and literary groups into the Union of Soviet Writers and the Union of Soviet Composers. These two bodies enforced conformity across the artistic world, a conformity with socialist realism at its core. Almost overnight, modern dance ensembles found their state support and funding removed – the future was to be representational and easily understood. The practical effect on the aesthetics of classical dance was a return to the nineteenth century and the quest to make the stage picture as 'real' as possible – seas had to churn, winds blow and fires burn. The artistic experimentation given free rein in the years after the 1917 revolution finally came to an end.

This new orthodoxy was, paradoxically, a fillip for the defenders of pure, classical dance technique in their struggle against the modernisers who, as we have seen, were constantly threatening to do away with it all; if there was a shift scenically back to the nineteenth century, it was all the more difficult to argue for the elimination of the style of dancing which went with it. It was no coincidence that in 1931, classical ballet's strongest advocate, Agrippina Vaganova, was appointed the artistic director of the ballet company at GATOB in succession to the experimenter Fyodor Lopukhov.

The imperatives of socialist realism pushed back against anything abstract; scenic representation returned to the literal, the scenery painting style of the nineteenth-century was revived to create realistic depictions of setting and the visually avant-garde banished from Soviet theatre stages. And yet, despite the dogged defences of the 1920s, forces against dance *per se* continued to be at play, making the demand to make ballet more dramatic and to exclude movement for its own sake. Even Petipa's choreographic legacy came in for criticism, his greatest achievements, those sections of pure dancing in his ballets, were dismissed as mindless entertainment and rejected as examples of formalism. Socialist realist *drambalet* sought to answer categorically the fundamental question of whether dance was in itself expressive or merely ornamental.

Formalism

"Formalism in ballet, as in other arts, is self-sufficient form-creation, devoid of content. In the decadent bourgeois art of the 20th century Formalism develops as a result of the spiritual devastation and dehumanisation of the arts, creativity, loss of artistic ideals and society's goals. It is expressed in the rejection of the classical language and narrative dance, of historical dance forms and in the cultivation of ugly plastique, in meaningless combinations of movements, deliberately devoid of expressiveness. Formalism develops under the flag of deceit; its supporters argue that they seek to enrich the form. However, a form devoid of content disintegrates, loses its humanity and beauty. Formalism's tendencies are also characteristic of those productions that do not break with traditional dance vocabulary, but they reduce the meaning of art to a pure 'play of forms', to an empty combination of elements, to bare technique. Formalism in choreography is related to such phenomena of decadent modernist art as abstractionism in painting, the theatre of the absurd, etc."[229]

1932 – *Salambo*

Bolshoi choreographer Igor Moiseyev's last major undertaking at the theatre was his new production of *Salambo* in June 1932. Gorsky had premièred his version of Gustave Flaubert's 1862 novel *Salammbô* at the theatre in 1910 with a score by Andrey Arends.[230] The narrative, set in First Punic War Carthage concerned the doomed love of the mercenary soldier Mato for Salambo, the daughter of the general Hamilcar Barca. For his 1932 treatment, Moiseyev trimmed down Gorsky's five act structure and made Mato's revolutionary struggle the main focus. Additionally, Arends' score was supplemented with pieces by Alexander Glazunov, Vasily Nebolsin[231] and Alexander Tsfasman. In something of a last stand for innovators at the Bolshoi, the first cast featured Podgoretskaya as Salambo, Moiseyev himself as Mato, Asaf Messerer as the Lydian military leader and Goleizovsky in the role of Camon. The ballet did not survive in the repertoire.

1932 – *The Flames of Paris*

What was needed was a new ballet which would show that dance could be

---

229   Entry on 'formalism' in Энциклопедия балета, 1981 (Ballet Encyclopaedia).

230   Born in Moscow in 1855, Arends graduated from the Moscow Conservatoire in 1877 where he studied composition with Tchaikovsky. In 1883, he became a violinist in the Bolshoi Theatre, chief conductor at the Maly Theatre, Moscow in 1892 and conducted the first performance in Moscow of *The Sleeping Beauty* in 1899, and served as chief conductor of the Bolshoi Ballet from 1900 until 1924. Arends made orchestral arrangements of several Tchaikovsky piano works. He died in Moscow in 1924.

231   Born in Kharkov, Ukraine in 1898, Nebolsin graduated from the Music and Drama School of the Moscow Philharmonic Society in 1920 and joined the Bolshoi Theatre as a chorusmaster. He debuted as a conductor there in 1922. He also composed two ballets, two symphonies and other works. He taught conducting at the Moscow Conservatoire between 1941 and 1945. He died in Moscow in 1958.

both socialist and realist, and in that Leningrad, the somewhat mistrusted second city, stole a march on the more politically orthodox capital. To mark the fifteenth anniversary of the revolution, *The Flames of Paris* received its première (initially under the title *The Triumph of the Republic*) in November 1932 and was an immediate success, hailed by the influential ballet writer and librettist Yuri Slonimsky as "a new chapter in the history of Soviet choreographic art".[232] Ideologically irreproachable, it was set during the French Revolution and depicted the victory of the peasantry over the aristocracy of the ancien régime. Suitably rousing music was provided by Boris Asafiev, who included a period song of the revolution in each of the three acts: 'La Marseillaise', 'Ça Ira' and 'La Carmagnole'. Vladimir Dmitriev provided realistic end-of-eighteenth-century settings and the stirring choreography was by Vasily Vainonen, by then one of the most promising of Soviet choreographers. It offered much needed confirmation to the authorities that the Leningrad company was observing fully the demands of socialist realism. Such was its success that the ballet was mounted at the Bolshoi the following year, and it enjoyed continuing favour for decades after, audiences and authorities alike delighted by the positive heroism it presented. And yet, it was not, on closer inspection, particularly Russian or realist: it dealt with Paris, not Moscow; it was set in 1792 and not 1932 and had a 'romantic-heroic' theme. The Soviet critic Vladimir Golyubov wrote: "The thing is realistic therefore is worthy of praise; and so we had honest and clean spectacles which were all timely and topical but you could smell bureaucracy and mothballs miles away."[233] The first performance featured Olga Jordan as Jeanne, Natalia Dudinskaya was Mireille de Poitiers, Vakhtang Chabukiani appeared as Jérôme and Konstantin Sergeyev was Philippe. Moscow produced the ballet the following year with Anastasia Abramova as Jeanne, Marina Semyonova as Mireille de Poitiers, Alexey Ermolayev danced Jérôme and Chabukiani was Philippe. It was in Moscow that *The Flames of Paris* firmly established itself as a cornerstone of the repertoire, offering successive generations of dancers ample dancing and interpretative opportunities.

1933 – Vaganova's *Swan Lake*

Vaganova's struggles to maintain the choreographic glories of imperial Russia in such a difficult political climate continued. GATOB company director since 1931, she mounted her own production of *Swan Lake* in April 1933, stripping the story of its supernatural elements and tackling the ideologically suspect concept of women portraying swans. Siegfried became an East Prussian count who, unable to distinguish between reality and illusion falls in love with a real swan, Odette, thinking it to be an enchanted princess.

---

232   Swift, *The Art of the Dance in the USSR*, p.96
233   Morley, *Soviet Ballet*, p.17

Odile was the daughter of his neighbour Rothbart who attends a ball in the hope of making a suitable match; Rothbart shoots and kills the swan out of jealousy after his daughter's rejection by Siegfried, who stabs himself in his distress. Somehow, this managed to convince the regime, and the production was hailed as a success, lasting in the repertoire until Lopukhov, Vaganova's great rival, took over the company again during the next decade and replaced it with his own version. At the first performance, Ulanova danced Odette, Jordan was Odile and Sergeyev appeared as Prince Siegfried.

The new narrative and setting notwithstanding, Vaganova's production was a clear attempt to preserve the choreographic text of this work, one of the pillars of the Russian school of classical dance. It was she who sought to improve on the imperial schooling of her own formation; the publication in 1934 of *The Fundamentals of Classic Dance*, written in collaboration with Lyubov Blok,[234] was a significant moment. It is the fundamental explanation of what she formulated and still exists to this day as the Vaganova Technique.

Ballet Schools in the 1930s

The two ballet schools of Petrograd/Leningrad and Moscow, which, alongside the companies, had survived both the ideological questioning of their existence and the proposed watering-down of their classical ballet education with gymnastics during the 1920s, nevertheless underwent change and development throughout the following decade. The schools themselves expanded, with the Leningrad Choreographic School growing from 186 students in 1927 to 466 in 1933. The seven-year training programme was extended by two years, and the education of the pupils underwent expansion to include history, geography, music, literature, graphic arts and theatre in general. In Moscow, a class in 'choreodrama' taught by Igor Moiseyev was instituted which sought to apply Stanislavskian 'realism' to ballet.

1937 was an important year at both institutions: in Moscow the first graduates of a course which had been introduced for aspirant choreographers received their diplomas, while in Leningrad Vaganova and fellow-teacher Boris Shavrov established a ballet masters' department to produce not only ideologically observant but also pedagogically and technically competent teachers and coaches. The move to ensure political orthodoxy mirrored that in the companies and society at large; in 1938 a conference was held in Moscow for ballet teachers from Leningrad, Kiev, Minsk and Sverdlovsk which discussed a common approach not only in terms of physical training

---

234 Born in St Petersburg in 1881, the daughter of the chemist Dmitry Mendeleyev, Blok became an actress, choreographer and notable dance critic. Blok established the foundations of a new approach to the historical study of classical ballet. She was married to the poet Alexander Blok. She died in Leningrad in 1939.

but also the 'question of the ideological-political education of the students'.[235] In a manifestation of the continuing mistrust of the former imperial capital by Moscow, it was decided in 1939 that the Leningrad school needed to work harder and deliver more lectures and studies which would underpin the political understanding of its students – outside 'workers' from the State University and Art History Institute were drafted in to deliver the new material.

1934 – *The Fountain of Bakhchisarai*

Building on its choreographic successes and starting what was to become a feature of Soviet ballet – the use of Russian literary works as a basis for dance-making – GATOB followed *The Flames of Paris* with another huge success in September 1934, perhaps the first true *drambalet*, *The Fountain of Bakhchisarai*. Alexander Pushkin's[236] reputation and acceptability as a writer had undergone something of a rehabilitation after a nationwide congress of the Union of Soviet Writers early that year emphasised the importance of the nation's literary heritage. Russia's national poet was now an ideologically safe source for dance librettists, and many followed this first and longest-lasting essay in using his works as the basis of their ballets (it remains in the active repertoire of the current Mariinsky Ballet). Asafiev was again the composer and this time he sought material from Pushkin's own era and used not only a romance from the early 1800s by composer Alexander Gurilyov[237] to start and end the ballet but also one of John Field's[238] nocturnes as the heroine Maria's musical leitmotif. Director Sergey Radlov worked closely with choreographer Rostislav Zakharov[239] to produce a melodramatic work

---

235 Swift, *The Art of the Dance in the USSR*, p.212

236 Considered many to be Russia's greatest poet, Pushkin was born in Moscow in 1799 and by his mid-teens was writing successful verse. He produced plays and novels in addition to poems, the most famous of which, *Eugene Onegin*, was written as a serialised work between 1825 and 1833. He died in a duel with his brother-in-law in St Petersburg in 1837.

237 Born in Moscow in 1803 as a serf to the Count Orlov under whose service he trained as a musician, Gurilyov gained his freedom in 1831 and pursued a musical career as a composer of over 200 songs, many of which gained great popularity. He died in Moscow in 1858.

238 Born in Dublin, Ireland in 1792, Field studied piano under Clementi and became a famous concert pianist, considered the 'inventor' of the 'nocturne' style of piano music. He lived in Russia from 1802 to 1834. He died in Moscow in 1837 and is buried in the city's foreigners' German Cemetery.

239 Born in Astrakhan in 1907, Zakharov graduated from the Petrograd State Ballet School in 1925 before dancing first in Kharkov and then Kiev before returning to Leningrad to study all aspects of theatre production under Radlov; he joined GATOB in 1932 firstly as an assistant director of operas. He was director of the Bolshoi Ballet between 1936-9 and continued to choreograph profusely, applying the Stanislavsky method to emphasise the drama of his works and remained the company's principal choreographer until 1960. He created the first version of *Cinderella* to Prokofiev's music in 1945. He directed

in which acting and the conveyance of meaning were placed above actual dancing; the choreography was blandly solid and no more, but Zakharov's commitment to the precepts and goals of *drambalet* was unquestionable. He employed the Stanislavsky method so that his dancers would create realistic characters, an approach which represented a significant departure in their working practices; many dancers proved sceptical about the need to sit down and learn about the nature of their parts and the motivations for their actions before beginning to learn steps:

"Reading *The Fountain of Bakhchisarai*, the study of literature and lithographs relative to the period, all this material enabled the artists to imagine with great clarity of perception the life of their heroes and to comprehend their psychology in a much more profound manner",[240] explained the choreographer.

An exotic story of the abduction of a Polish countess by a Crimean Tatar and the jealousy provoked in his chief wife, a Georgian princess, *The Fountain of Bakhchisarai* nevertheless enjoyed both official and public sanction from the moment it was presented to the Leningrad audience. Galina Ulanova was the first Countess Maria, a role which was to become one of her finest and in which she allied an otherworldly quality with seemingly spontaneous naturalism in her movements. Alongside her as the imperious Zarema was the ballerina Olga Jordan, Konstantin Sergeyev appeared as the Polish nobleman Vaslav and Mikhail Dudko was Khan Girey. Critic Ivan Sollertinsky hailed the ballet as a "happy step forward" and observed sarcastically:

"Orthodox balletomanes are not delighted by *The Fountain of Bakhchisarai*: not enough dancing! There are no dizzying variations with thirty-two fouettés, no pearls of the Italian school technique, no lush parade of symmetrically dancing corps-de-ballet masses in white tunics."[241]

The ballet was staged at the Bolshoi in late 1936 with Vera Vasilieva as Zarema, Lyubov Bank as Maria, Mikhail Gabovich as Vaslav and Pyotr Gusev as Khan Girey and was later acquired by numerous ballet companies in the republics.

Leonid Lavrovsky

Fadetta, presented at GATOB as part of a school graduation performance in March 1934, was an early indication of the style of its choreographer Leonid Lavrovsky. He sought to infuse classical steps with genuine character in a ballet which took Georges Sand's 1849 novel *La Petite Fadette* as its basis

---

the Bolshoi Ballet School from 1945 to 1947 and taught widely thereafter, heading the choreographers' department at GITIS from 1946 to his death. He died in Moscow in 1984.

240 Zakharov as quoted by Roslavleva, *Era of the Russian Ballet*, p. 231
241 Volkov, *St Petersburg; A Cultural History*, p.502

and used music by Léo Delibes (principally from the ballet *Sylvia*) to fashion a 'poor versus rich' narrative. Its simple storyline of a young man, Andrey, defying his bourgeois family in order to marry a peasant girl Fadetta, was well received, and Lavrovsky revived the ballet during his directorships of first the MALEGOT company and then the Bolshoi. In the autumn of 1936 *Fadetta* opened at the Maly with Feya Balabina in the title role, Galina Kirillova[242] as Madelon, Sergey Dubinin[243] was André and René was danced by Nikolai Zubkovsky. Once Lavrovsky became director of the Bolshoi, he staged *Fadetta* at the Filial Theatre in the summer of 1952 with Lepeshinskaya as Fadetta, Valentina Lopukhina[244] as Madelon, Vladimir Preobrazhensky[245] danced André and René was Anatoly Kuznetsov.[246]

Lavrovsky followed *Fadetta* in May 1935 with *Katerina*, a work also initially created for a graduation performance of the Leningrad Choreographic School, which this time was subsequently acquired by the Kirov Ballet the following year. As Lopukhov had done with his own *A Serf Ballerina* in 1927, the choreographer turned to the history of Russia and the eighteenth-

---

242 Born in Ekaterinburg in 1916, Kirillova graduated from the Leningrad Choreographic School into the Maly in 1935 where she danced until 1942. She then moved to the Kirov as a principal dancer of great technical accomplishment and a striking stage presence. She danced until 1961 and taught at the Bolshoi School from the next year onwards. From 1972 to 1974, she was the head of the ballet troupe of the Shevchenko Theatre, Kiev and then the artistic director of the Kiev Choreographic School until her death in the city in 1986.

243 Born in St Petersburg in 1912, Dubinin graduated from the Leningrad Choreographic School into the Paliashvili Theatre company of Tbilisi in 1930 before moving to the Maly in 1933 where he danced until 1941. He died in an unknown location in 1943 while serving as a soldier.

244 Born in Petrograd in 1917, Lopukhina graduated into the Kirov in 1933. In 1936 she moved to the Bolshoi where she danced until 1959 in a variety of soloist roles. From 1959 onwards she worked as a teacher and coach in theatres in Yugoslavia, Finland and Poland. She died in Moscow in 1977.

245 Born in Moscow in 1912, Preobrazhensky graduated from the Leningrad Choreographic School in 1931 into GATOB where he danced until 1935. Having taught at Sverdlovsk, he danced as a principal dancer in Kiev from 1939 to 1943 when he transferred to the Bolshoi where he danced for another twenty years, becoming a favoured stage partner of Lepeshinskaya and being renowned for his sculptural physique. After his retirement from performance, he became the head of the dance section of Moscow's concert organisation. He died in Moscow in 1981.

246 Born in Moscow in 1918, Kuznetsov graduated into the Bolshoi in 1935 where he danced until 1960. He appeared in all the major male roles of the repertoire and was noted for his refined technique and elegance of style. From 1962 to 1967 he was the choreographer of the Uzbek Ballet Theatre, of the Frunze Ballet Theatre between 1967 and 1969 and then of the Cairo Ballet Company and artistic director of the Cairo Ballet School until 1973. From 1938 he was a teacher of folk-character dance at the Bolshoi School and taught classical dance at the Soviet Army's Alexandrov Red Banner Song and Dance Ensemble of the Soviet Army. He died in Dnepropetrovsk, Ukraine in 1976.

century phenomenon of theatrical serf companies. Painstaking preparatory research became Lavrovsky's trademark feature, and for *Katerina* he studied the dance styles of the period to ensure that the 'ballet within the ballet' was as authentic as possible. The music was a composite score of work by Anton Rubinstein and Adolphe Adam, the composer of *Giselle*. The suicide of the serf ballerina herself in order to escape the pursuits of the local governor ended the work in tragedy and indicated the dramatic path the choreographer would take in later works such as *Romeo and Juliet*. At its Kirov première, Katerina was danced by Olga Jordan and Vladimir by Boris Shavrov, the Governor was Leonid Leontiev and Olga Mungalova appeared as Yulinka.

1934 – Vainonen's *The Nutcracker*

Since Lopukhov's re-workings in the 1920s, GATOB had shown its readiness to re-imagine the classics, so, following on from Vaganova's *Swan Lake* in 1933, the company premièred a new version of *The Nutcracker*, originally created in 1892 under the auspices of Petipa but with choreography by Ivanov. For his new production, Vasily Vainonen followed the revisions made to the narrative by Alexander Gorsky at the Bolshoi in 1919, combining the roles of Clara (renamed Masha) and the Sugar Plum Fairy and altogether eliminating the Fairy's Cavalier in favour of the Nutcracker Prince who partnered her in the Act II Grand Pas. He augmented the role of the magician Drosselmeyer and emphasised that the fantasy divertissements were all part of Masha's dream. The February première was danced by Ulanova as Masha, Sergeyev as the Nutcracker Prince and Leontiev as Drosselmeyer. In 1939 the Bolshoi acquired this version with Semyonova, Ermolayev and Ryabtsev appearing on the first night; it remained in the repertoire until 1966. The Vainonen *Nutcracker* became the classic Kirov production of Soviet times; it remains in the Mariinsky's current repertoire. The 'Waltz of the Snowflakes' was incorporated by *Mikhail Baryshnikov into his own 1976 production for American Ballet Theatre.

1935 – Ballet to the Republics

By 1935, ballet's popularity was unquestioned, the debates of the early post-revolutionary years completely forgotten. The demands of socialist realism were unavoidable, but the popular appetite for the art form remained undiminished: the French illustrator Chas Laborde[247] arrived in Moscow in 1935 and filed a record of what he saw in *Rues et visages de Moscou*. In it he observed that when the auditorium lights dimmed on a ballet performance: "la foule s'anime, s'émeut, applaudit…L'amour de la danse n'est pas en

---

247   Born in Buenos Aires, Argentina in 1896, Laborde studied painting at the École Beaux-Arts de Paris and went on to become a prolific illustrator in newspapers and magazines as well as designing advertising posters and stage sets. He died in Paris in 1941.

Russie, affair de snobisme, d'époque, de régime."[248] (the crowd comes alive, is moved, applauds ... The love of dance is not in Russia, a matter of snobbery, of the times, of the regime)

And yet, appreciation of ballet still focussed on the old imperial centres of Moscow and Leningrad. In 1935, a decision was taken which would have some of the most far-reaching consequences for ballet in Russia since the revolution and whose effects are still felt. A cultural programme was instituted by which talented children would be sent from the Russian republics to Moscow or Leningrad to train at a ballet school with a view to their returning to their native region where they would subsequently form the nucleus of a national dance company. Parallel to this initiative which over the decades led to an unprecedented concentration of dancing talent in the two Choreographic Schools, the following year saw the institution of the national *dekada*, a ten-day festival in which a chosen republic would put on plays, ballets and opera based upon national, local and folk themes. This policy coincided with new constitutions for the republics comprising the USSR which enshrined respect for and encouragement given to indigenous and local cultures. The first *dekadi*, beginning in 1936, were patchy affairs, owing to the nascent local opera and ballet troupes, but, some fifteen years later, they had expanded into elaborate and impressive displays.

1935 – *Three Fat Men*

In February 1935, Igor Moiseyev premièred a children's ballet, *Three Fat Men*, at the Bolshoi. Based on the 1928 story by Yuri Olesha[249] and set to a score by Oransky, who had previously collaborated with the choreographer in 1930 on *The Footballer*, it was a fairy tale shot through with the ideals of justice and social rebellion against everything unrighteous and cruel. Sulamith Messerer created the circus girl Suok, Ermolayev the tightrope walker Tibul and Asaf Messerer the Balloon Seller who succeed in outwitting the people's oppressors and in liberating a revolutionary gunsmith held captive by the three fat men. It was revived in 1938 with Lepeshinskaya as Suok and received another forty-two performances before finally falling foul of criticisms over its lack of definition in the scenes of social uprising and the portrayal of the proletariat, which led to its disappearance from the repertoire.

---

248   Chas Laborde in *Rues et visages de Moscou, la chronique filmée du mois*, No.19, as quoted by Pollaud-Dulian

249   Born in 1899 in Elizavetgrad, Belarus, Olesha graduated in law from Odessa University but turned to writing. He moved to Moscow in 1922 and wrote for newspapers and periodicals. He wrote *Three Fat Men* in 1924 which was published four years later and subsequently made into a play and a film. Despite Olesha being considered a writer of talent, his plays did not achieve success. Between 1936 and 1956 his works were banned. He died in Moscow in 1960.

1935 – *Esmeralda*

In Leningrad, as part of her continuing policy of preserving the glories of the imperial past, Vaganova set about the revival of Petipa's 1886 *Esmeralda* (itself a new version of Perrot's 1844 ballet *Esmeralda*), tweaking the narrative to show the heroine railing against the morally corrupt Catholic Church, thereby ensuring its ideological acceptability. A popular work before the revolution – the title role was a favourite of Matilda Kschessinskaya and Vaganova herself had danced solos – the ballet had last been revived in 1923 for Olga Spessivtseva. The new production included elements of Vaganova's own choreography as well as her arrangement of the 'Pas de Diane' from Petipa's 1868 ballet *Le Roi Candaule,* known today as the standalone showpiece pas de deux *Diana and Actéon*. *Esmeralda* opened at GATOB in April with Vecheslova and Leontiev as Esmeralda and Gringoire, Phoebus was danced by Shavrov and Claude Frollo by Dudko; Ulanova and Chabukiani appeared as Diana and Actéon.

1935 – GATOB into Kirov

December 1st 1934 saw the murder of Sergey Kirov, First Secretary of the Leningrad Communist Party, probably on the orders of Stalin himself, an act which heralded 'The Great Terror', as the subsequent purges, witch hunts and persecutions came to be known. In 1935, GATOB was renamed the Kirov Theatre and companies in his honour, and both the city and the nation entered far darker political and social times, with ever-increasing control of the daily lives and thoughts of citizens. Kirov's disloyalty and subsequent elimination led to a clear concentration of political might in Moscow, and, for dance, the transfer almost as a matter of course of Leningrad's best dancers to the capital – Vaganova continued to produce fine artists who then found themselves on the train bound for Moscow. Additionally, the state's grip on artistic decisions tightened with the establishment in 1936 of the All-Union Committee for Affairs of the Arts in the Council of People's Commissars, an umbrella organisation to oversee all cultural activities from sculpture to the circus, from cinema to ballet. Plans, designs, scores and libretti needed to be presented well ahead of time for ratification; spontaneous creativity was most certainly not encouraged or, indeed, permitted.

On the final evening of 1935, the newly-named Kirov company premièred *Lost Illusions*, another full-evening collaboration between composer Boris Asafiev and choreographer Rostislav Zakharov. Based in part on a section from Honoré de Balzac's 1838 *Splendeurs et misères des courtisanes*, it sought to "unmask the imaginary freedom of creativity in the capitalistic world".[250] Balzac was highly esteemed by the Soviet regime for his realistic depictions of life and society and this work was chosen for the way it highlights the

---

250 Swift, *The Art of the Dance in the USSR*, p.99

monetary shackles placed on the artist in a bourgeois society. Adapting the story, adding parts of other Balzac works and completely new elements, Zakharov constructed a narrative in which a poor composer Lucien succeeds in getting his new ballet staged only with the monetary aid of the rich patron of his lover, the dancer Coralie. However, Lucien leaves her for her rival Florine who forces him to write inferior music for her instead. It was premièred with Ulanova as Coralie, Vecheslova as Florina and Sergeyev, later Shavrov, as Lucien. The creation of *Lost Illusions* could not have been timelier, given the political climate of the moment, its prescient title and focus on the relationship between the artist, the creative process and society.

With hindsight, it would have been possible to see the storm clouds gathering for the ballet world in early 1935 with the denunciation of the opera *Lady Macbeth of Mtsensk District* and the humiliation of its composer Dmitry Shostakovich. Hailed previously as a beacon of socialism, and an enthusiastic creator of music for dance, he was attacked in the Communist Party newspaper *Pravda* in the article 'Muddle instead of Music'. So intertwined were art and politics in Russia at the time that what occurred in one sphere would have immediate ramifications in the other; thus, the political move away from the internationalism of the 1917 revolutionaries in favour of an inward focus on the motherland could not but influence the artistic world. Folk music, dancing and arts of the republics of the USSR had been banned in the 1920s but the regime had changed its approach completely by the 1930s, actively encouraging expressions of local culture under its watchful guidance. This led to the establishment of folk-dance groups, such as Igor Moiseyev's eponymously-named ensemble formed in 1937, and also fostered a greater respect for local traditions. It was this shifting political and artistic phenomenon which contributed to one of the most momentous and frightening moments in the history of Soviet ballet: 'Ballet Fraud'.

1935 – *The Bright Stream*

Having repressed the independently-minded and sometimes rebellious Cossack people since the revolution, the Soviet regime reversed its policy in the mid-1930s and became anxious to court them in order to bolster control in the important but troublesome areas of southern Russia. The timing could not have been better therefore when in April 1935 director Fyodor Lopukhov brought a new work to the stage of the Maly Theatre: *The Bright (or Limpid) Stream* to music by Shostakovich was a celebration of life on a Kuban Cossack collective farm. It was a comedy with an improbable libretto involving the visit of town folk and the upsets they provoke. At the première, Zina was danced by Zinaida Vasilieva, Pyotr by Pyotr Gusev and the classical dancers were Feya Balabina and Nikolai Zubkovsky.

The ballet provoked much criticism from Agrippina Vaganova who was not impressed. She had proved herself an intelligent and thoughtful contributor to the debates surrounding the role of classical ballet in Soviet society and, after the première of *The Bright Stream*, she contributed an article entitled 'The New Ballet' to the newspaper *Izvestia*. In it, she praised the achievements of the dancers (most of whom she had herself trained) but also analysed the imperatives placed on the art form; the use of important themes, logical and well-thought-out narratives and the realistic portrayal of character. She wrote another piece, 'No Ballet Falsitudes' which specifically criticised *The Bright Stream* for its illogical plot-line and its misuse of the idiom of classical dancing:

> "(It) is changing its forms and means of expression before our eyes, depending on the subject, its dramatic purpose, the period shown etc. Is there not a colossal difference between classical dancing in *The Sleeping Beauty* and the dialogue between Maria and Zarema in *The Fountain of Bakhchisarai?* In order to create a good contemporary Soviet ballet, one needs another approach to classical dance. But the second error of *The Bright Stream* consists precisely in the fact that their kind of classical dance is indifferent to action, periods, subject, or anything else. Any of these divertissements may be shown in *The Bright Stream* or another ballet. An attempt to create a Soviet ballet with such classical dance is to discredit both the theme and classical dancing as a whole."[251]

1936 – Ballet Fraud

Popular reaction to *The Bright Stream* in Leningrad was, Vaganova's criticisms notwithstanding, extremely positive, and such was the ballet's reception that Lopukhov was transferred to the Bolshoi as company director and invited to stage it the following season. The Moscow première in November 1935 went well, with an enthusiastic audience reaction – there is no doubt that it was a cheery work – with Vasilieva and Gusev, having followed Lopukhov to the Bolshoi, reprising their created roles and Sulamith Messerer and Alexey Ermolayev appearing as the classical dancers. The critics were impressed, commenting on the successful portrayal of the joys of *kolkhoz* or collective farm life; a group of Don Cossacks, visiting the Bolshoi for an early performance, gave their approval and even Stalin attended and seemed pleased enough. The composer was also praised for his lively score which included sections from the unsuccessful *The Bolt* from some years before, so nothing could have prepared Lopukhov, Shostakovich or anyone at the Bolshoi for what followed: a long anonymously-written article in *Pravda* on 6th February 1936 entitled 'Baletnaya Falsh' (Ballet Fraud).

---

251   Roslavleva, *Era of the Russian Ballet*, p.237

'Ballet Fraud' was an all-out attack on ballet's ability to portray real life, published in the party newspaper and sanctioned at the highest level. It accused Lopukhov of mocking the peoples of the Soviet republics, of portraying them not as real people but as pre-revolutionary dolls and stating with chilling finality "The basic difficulty in Soviet ballet is that dolls are impossible here." Lopukhov was also criticised for not presenting genuine Cossack dances on the stage, but rather giving his audience 'tinsel peasants, coming off a pre-revolutionary sweet box'. Shostakovich was spared the opprobrium of 'Muddle instead of Music', but his music was deemed "characterless...the composer (having) the same devil-may-care attitude toward the folk songs of the Kuban".[252]

'Ballet Fraud' provoked total panic among the artistic community and led to innumerable attacks on ballets, operas and plays as commentators, guided by *Pravda*'s pronouncements on art and sensing the changed direction of the cultural wind, felt entitled to denounce any endeavour. For Lopukhov, who lost the directorship of the Bolshoi in favour of Rostislav Zakharov, it sealed a fall from grace which he described as follows in later writings: "the thirties were a turning point not only for my personal fate, but in the life of Soviet ballet".[253] This was echoed by the Bolshoi Ballet's chief conductor Yuri Faier, who later observed:

> "The publication of the article about *The Bright Stream* had serious consequences for the art of ballet as a whole...The desire of authors to find new possibilities of classical dance in the embodiment of today's reality were sacrificed to a one-sided narrow understanding of the plausibility of what was happening on stage...The demand that the art of ballet should be plausible was turned into a prohibition for searches for new artistic forms, for the diverse use of the means of dance expression."[254]

In music, contemporary foreign composers were no longer to be played, the tonal developments of the time rejected in favour of direct, simple music, preferably sourced from folk tunes. Asafiev dutifully criticised Shostakovich for having had recourse to 'Lumpen-Musik' for *The Bright Stream* and even Vaganova stated that the creators had strayed from 'the correct path' of art. Composers, writers and artists felt compelled to align themselves with the official party line as the general nervousness took hold while changes in personnel took place on orders from higher up in the party structure – one morning in 1937, on finding a note pinned to the door of her office, Vaganova discovered that she had resigned as Director of the Kirov Ballet. She, at least, was allowed to continue with her teaching – dancers seemed

---

252 As quoted by Swift, *The Art of the Dance in the USSR*, pp.109-111
253 ibid, p.112
254 Ezrahi, *Swans of the Kremlin*, p.62

to have been spared the worst of the violence of the purges – but even the Bolshoi's prima ballerina Marina Semyonova was put under temporary house arrest following the arrest and subsequent execution of her husband.

1936 has gone down as one of the most chilling times in Soviet dance history. That there had been a series of measures and policies which had sought to curtail artistic freedom since Stalin's ascent to power, there was no doubt, but 1936 was the launch of the 'Great Purge' or 'Terror' which would cut swathes through the artistic fraternity as much as any other walk of life. The establishment in January 1936 of the All-Union Committee for Affairs of the Arts in the Council of People's Commissars brought all aspects of cultural life under a single organisation. Under its aegis, all parts of any artistic endeavour had to be submitted for approval, from subject matter to the music used and the set and costume design. But what happened had been an unexpected assault on an art form which had done what it could to be deemed politically and ideologically acceptable. Every stage of the creative process was to be scrutinised, culminating in a closed-door run-through which may or may not lead to actual performance; dress rehearsals were attended by numerous observers from the official Committee, union representatives and external commentators. Artistic freedom was dead.

1937 – *Partisan Days*

For the twentieth anniversary of the revolution in 1937, Vainonen and Asafiev sought to replicate the success of *The Flames of Paris* with *Partisan Days* at the Kirov Theatre in May. After the criticisms levelled at *The Bright Stream*, it was a conscious and careful attempt to depict Cossacks 'authentically' in an ideologically impeccable story involving the routing of the White Guard by the Red Army. It was a significant development in the quest for a truly Soviet ballet as its characters were drawn from recent revolutionary history, notably the peasant heroine Nastia who leaves a forced marriage to a rich Cossack to join the partisans who finally ally themselves with their Red Army comrades in order to achieve victory. It was the first dance work about the post-revolutionary Civil War and the first Kirov ballet to be danced off-pointe, the whole enterprise in essence a daring and experimental amalgam of character and authentic Caucasian dance styles. The first Nastia was Nina Anisimova,[255] not a company ballerina, but rather a character dancer for whom Vainonen had created a concert number about a female partisan in 1933 which found its way into *Partisan Days*. Despite Chabukiani dancing

---

[255] Born in St Petersburg in 1909, Anisimova graduated to the Maly Theatre company in 1926 before joining GATOB the following year where she would perform until her retirement from the stage in 1957. She created the role of Thérèse in *The Flames of Paris*. From 1936 onwards she also choreographed, creating *Gayaneh* for the Kirov in 1942, and taught at the Leningrad Conservatoire from 1963 to 1974. She was married to the *Gayaneh's* librettist Konstantin Derzhavin. She died in Leningrad in 1979.

Kerim, one of the brave partisans, the ballet enjoyed only a moderate success, achieving seventeen performances, and was far from being another *The Flames of Paris* for its creators or the company. The structure was somewhat loose, so that after a successful first act wedding scene, matters became rather more disjointed as the action transferred to the adventures of the partisans in their struggles against the White Guard. The ballet was nevertheless important in its use of folk-dancing as integral to characterisation and narrative.

1938 – three ballets

The use of classic Russian literature continued to be a main feature of Soviet ballet throughout the decade, with Pushkin taking the lion's share – seven of Asafiev's ballet scores were inspired by the poet's work – alongside other writers. In April 1938, Leonid Lavrovsky premièred his version of *The Prisoner of the Caucasus* at the Maly Theatre to a score by Asafiev where he was in his third and last year as director of the ballet troupe. Based on Pushkin's 1821 poem which had been made into a ballet by Charles-Louis Didelot in 1823, it told the story of a Byronic Russian officer escaping his elitist existence to find love and liberty among the Circassian people of the Caucasus. The ballet contrasted the hedonistic aristocratic life of pre-revolution St Petersburgers involving dancing, skating and games with the free life of Caucasian mountain-dwellers, and Lavrovsky successfully married the two, bringing in authentic folk movement from the Caucasus, including examples of traditional male dancing *sur les pointes*. The première featured Sergey Dubinin as the Prisoner, Galina Kirillova as Princess Nina and Elena Chikvaidze[256] as Cherkeshenka, a Circassian woman. It proved to be a deftly conceived romantic dance drama, told with verve, and ultimately more successful than Zakharov's altered version in Moscow six days later. There, a starry cast was led by Marina Semyonova as the actress Polina, a role later taken by Olga Lepeshinskaya and Sulamith Messerer, Mikhail Gabovich was the Prisoner and Marianna Bogolyubskaya[257] danced Cherkeshenka.

Christmas Eve was based on the Nikolai Gogol's short story, previously used by Tchaikovsky in his 1876 opera *Vakula the Smith* (later revised as *Cherevichki*) and set to a score by Asafiev. It was commissioned by the Kirov

---

256 Born in 1910 in Tiflis, Georgia, Chikvaidze graduated into the Kirov from the Leningrad Choreographic School in 1929 where she remained until 1941. Between 1941 and 1943 she was a member of the company in Yerevan before joining the Bolshoi where she danced major roles until 1957. She taught at the Bolshoi School between 1954 and 1956. She was the wife of Leonid Lavrovsky and the mother of Mikhail Lavrovsky. She died in Moscow in 1996.

257 Born in Moscow in 1919, Bogolyubskaya graduated into the Bolshoi in 1937 where she danced until 1959 in a variety of roles which included Odette-Odile in *Swan Lake*. From 1966 she was research assistant at the Research Institute of Artistic Education of Children of the USSR Academy of Pedagogical Sciences. She was married to Mikhail Gabovich. She died in Moscow in 2013.

for performances in June 1938 to mark the bicentenary of the founding of the Imperial Theatre School and it told the fantastical tale of the blacksmith Vakula who flies on the Devil's back to St Petersburg to bring back a pair of the Tsarina's slippers as a gift for his love Oksana. Humorous and grotesque, switching between smithy, witch's cottage and imperial palace, it was a light-hearted success for its choreographer Vladimir Varkovitsky[258] who combined classical and folk dancing for the students in the officially approved fashion. Such was its popularity that it was transferred to the professional stage in late December: the Moscow Art Ballet staged its production with choreography by Lopukhov and *Vladimir Burmeister which featured Ivan Kurilov[259] as Vakula, Angelina Urusova as Oksana,[260] Maria Sorokina as Solokha, Vakula's mother, and Anatoly Tolsky[261] as the Devil.

Vakhtang Chabukiani's Georgian heritage remained an essential part of who he was both as a man and as an artist. An early indication of the direction his career would ultimately take – he returned to his native Tbilisi in 1941 where he devoted the next three decades to dance – was *The Heart of the Hills*, a truly Georgian ballet, premièred at the Kirov Theatre in June 1938 by the resident company. It was Chabukiani's first large-scale work as a choreographer; it had music by George Balanchine's brother Andrey (originally Andria) Balanchivadze,[262] which was widely admired – Shostakovich wrote "Some parts of the score make a stunning impression...I would say that everything is noble and profound, while the pathos of the

---

258   Born in Odessa, Crimea in 1916, Varkovitsky graduated into the Kirov company in 1936 and then moved to direct the Maly company between 1941 and 1943. He taught at the Bolshoi School from 1944 to 1953 and then in Yerevan, Armenia. He created numerous ballets, including *The Snow Maiden* for the Bolshoi School in 1946, as well as concert dances. He died in Moscow in 1974.

259   Born in Kiev, Ukraine in 1910, Kurilov studied dance privately and at the Drama Studio of the Kiev Theatre before becoming a performer first in Kiev and then in Odessa. In 1931 he joined the Art Theatre Ballet and the Stanislavsky company in 1939 where he remained until 1962. He worked extensively with choirs, folk ensembles, circuses and in cinema. He died in Moscow in 1992.

260   Born in Saratov in 1910, Urusova graduated from the Baku ballet school in 1927 and joined the company as a soloist. In 1929, she moved to the Saratov company and joined the Moscow Art Ballet in 1931 where she danced many roles until her death in Moscow in 1949. As a dancer, she was noted for her charm and innate musicality.

261   Born outside Moscow in 1911, Tolsky graduated from GITIS in 1930 and joined the Moscow Art Ballet the following year, remaining with the ensemble after its re-organisation in 1938 as the Stanislavsky Ballet until his retirement in 1965.

262   Born in St Petersburg in 1905, Balanchivadze graduated from the Tbilisi State Conservatoire in 1927 and the Leningrad Conservatoire in 1931, before returning to Georgia where he would survive Stalin's purges to become a major figure in the republic's musical life, notably as chairman and then first secretary of the Union of Georgian Composers. He died in Tbilisi in 1992.

ballet emerges from its high poetic qualities."[263] The designs were by Simon Virsaladze[264] who would go on in subsequent decades to dominate Soviet stage design. Chabukiani showed "the early outbreaks of revolutionary discontent among the Georgian peasants, spontaneously rising against their feudal oppressors",[265] artfully interweaving folk dance and classical steps, nowhere more effectively than in the 'Horumi' or traditional Georgian war dance. Manije, the self-sacrificing heroine, was first danced by Vecheslova while Chabukiani himself danced the hero Djardje who tries to save her and then leads an uprising against an oppressive local prince.

The Bolshoi, still seriously rattled by the 'Ballet Fraud' debacle of 1936 and anxious not to fall foul of the authorities, created few genuinely new ballets, preferring to import new and approved productions from Leningrad. In August 1938, Zakharov presented a new and expanded version of his version of *The Prisoner of the Caucasus* at Moscow's Green Theatre, a large open-air auditorium in Gorky Park. His re-staging magnified the effects for the giant park stage so that the Caucasians rode on and off on horseback, live cows and dogs appeared and there was even a real waterfall flowing at the back.

1939 – *Laurencia*

In an example of politics influencing art, the Civil War in Spain created the political need to produce a work which portrayed Spanish Republicans resisting Franco's fascism. Stealing a march on Moscow yet again, Leningrad presented *Laurencia*, a new ballet by Chabukiani in March 1939 to music by Alexander Krein.[266] Based on Lope de Vega's 1619 play *Fuenteovejuna*, it was a tale of popular, collective vengeance on a corrupt and licentious aristocrat which had seen previous but unsuccessful balletic treatments, including *The Comedians* at the Bolshoi in 1931 to music by Glière and choreography by Alexander Chekrygin.[267] *Laurencia* proved to be stirring stuff and immediately

---

263 As quoted by Roslavleva, *Era of the Russian Ballet*, p.243

264 Born in 1909 in Tiflis, Virsaladze studied both ballet and art and became chief designer for the Tbilisi opera house in 1932. He eventually became chief designer for the Kirov in 1945, working on Sergeyev's *Raymonda* (1948), *Swan Lake* (1950), and *The Sleeping Beauty* (1952) and Vainonen's *The Nutcracker* (1954). In 1962 he followed choreographer Yuri Grigorovich to the Bolshoi in Moscow where he designed all the choreographer's major ballets. He died in Tbilisi in 1989.

265 Chabukiani quoted in *The Art of the Dance in the USSR*, p.193

266 Born in Nizhny Novgorod in 1883, Krein entered the Moscow Conservatoire before becoming a prolific composer, often drawing on his own Jewish heritage for melody. In 1917, he became director of the artistic wing of *Muzo-Narkompros*, the music section of a newly formed ministry of arts and education. He went on to hold a variety of posts under the regime. He died in 1951 in Staraya Ruza.

267 Born in 1884, Chekrygin became a Mariinsky mime artist (he was a noted Carabosse in *The Sleeping Beauty*), notator, serving as one of Nicholas Sergeyev's assistants, and ballet

became popular following its première; Chabukiani's success was again in creating a synthesis of classical and folk dance which was entirely in keeping with the artistic demands of the regime. He melded together diverse styles to create a work of great impetus and force, the corps de ballet playing a major role in the narrative as the collective representation of the spirit of the village which rises up against tyranny. He danced the main role of Frondoso, giving himself and successive male dancers a part with considerable technical and acting demands, Natalia Dudinskaya was the first Laurencia and scored a personal triumph in the role, sealing her position as the Kirov's most brilliant ballerina, and Pascuala was created by Vecheslova. The Bolshoi acquired the ballet only in 1956 with Laurencia danced by *Maya Plisetskaya, Frondoso by Chabukiani and Pascuala by *Raisa Struchkova.

As the clouds of war gathered in Europe, the world of Soviet ballet enjoyed a veritable golden age of superlative dancers producing miracles of dancing despite a repressive political regime which had imposed an artistic approach which seemed at odds with the very nature of dance. Created in response to mounting border tensions between Soviet and Japanese forces in Manchuria, *Svetlana* was a tale of anti-Soviet attempted sabotage by 'eastern' forces set in the desolate *taiga*. It was given its first performance at the Bolshoi Filial Theatre in December 1939 and was an important work in being the first ballet to portray successfully a contemporary Soviet woman as a ballet heroine – the name Svetlana also happened to be that of Stalin's daughter. To music by Dmitry Klebanov,[268] its choreography was a joint effort between Alexander Radunsky, Lev Pospekhin[269] and Nikolai Popko,[270] three house choreographers who had together already created a successful children's ballet *The Little (or Baby) Stork* for the Bolshoi Ballet School at the Filial Theatre in June 1937 which had featured future Bolshoi ballerina Raisa Struchkova. They would go on to create *Crimson (or Scarlet) Sails* in 1942. *Svetlana* was given by a strong cast led by Lepeshinskaya in the title role alongside the twenty-year-old Yuri Kondratov[271] as Ilko.

---

master (he re-staged Fokine's *Le Pavillon d'Armide* alongside Lopukhov at GATOB in 1923). He died in Tashkent in 1942.

268 Born in Kharkov, Ukraine in 1907, Klebanov studied composition in his native city and was seen as a rising composer throughout the 1930s, with several well-received works. His first symphony *In Memoriam to the Martyrs of Babi Yar*, first given in 1945, was deemed anti-patriotic after which his career progressed no further. He died in 1987.

269 Born in Moscow in 1909, Pospekhin graduated into the Bolshoi company from the school in 1928, becoming a well-known character dancer as well as teaching expressive movement and dance at Stanislavsky's request at his Opera Studio. He became a company répétiteur after his retirement from the stage. He died in Moscow in 1984.

270 Born in Moscow in 1911, Popko graduated into the Bolshoi company in 1930, becoming a ballet master after his retirement from dancing. He died in Moscow in 1969.

271 Born in Moscow in 1921, Kondratov graduated from the Bolshoi School to the

1939 – *Happiness* / 1942 – *Gayaneh*

1939 also featured the performance of the first ballet score by a composer who would go on to dominate Soviet music: Aram Khachaturian.[272] A hugely promising musical artist whose First Symphony in 1935 had achieved considerable and widespread success, he travelled to Armenia, his ancestral homeland, to study traditional songs and music in response to a commission from a local politician to mark the republic's *dekada* that year. The result was *Happiness*, the first ever Armenian ballet, premièred in the state capital Yerevan in October with choreography by Ilya Arbatov.[273] It told the story of Armen, a brave young man from a collective farm enlisting into the Red Army to defend his homeland. Despite being wounded in action, he returns home to marry his sweetheart Karine, the ballet ending with mass dances by the Armenians who are joined by Georgian, Ukrainian and Russian guests in an "apotheosis-chorus of kolkhozniks (sic) and frontier guards praising the socialist motherland".[274] Such was its success, *Happiness* was re-premièred by the Armenian performers at the Bolshoi later that month to an equally positive reception – it ticked every box of artistic policy, avoided the pitfalls into which many works had fallen and was, in the words of the choreographer himself "a cantata in honour of Stalin. Hence the name of our ballet: *Happiness*".[275] This was not the end of *Happiness*, as its merits demanded a longer life, thus Konstantin Derzhavin[276] was entrusted with imposing a stronger plot-line which he did by giving Armen a sister Gayané, after whom the ballet would then be named, who escapes the clutches of an oppressive husband to find happiness with a Russian officer. *Gayaneh* (or *Gayané*) was premièred in Molotov (now Perm) by the Kirov company in late

---

company in 1940, rising to the rank of principal. Initially a regular partner of both Ulanova and Lepeshinskaya, he was perhaps best known for partnering Maya Plisetskaya throughout the 1950s. He became the Artistic Director of the Bolshoi Ballet School in 1959 on his retirement from the stage. He died in Moscow in 1967.

272 Born in Tiflis in 1903, Khachaturian moved to Moscow in 1921 and entered the Moscow Conservatoire in 1929. After graduation, he composed in a wide variety of genres, from symphonies to concerti and ballet music, all heavily influenced by Armenian rhythms and melodies. He was denounced in 1948 for formalism but later rehabilitated to become one of the USSR's most celebrated composers. He died in Moscow in 1978.

273 Born in Zagatala, Azerbaijan in 1894, Arbatov (original surname Yagubyan) studied with Maria Perini in Tbilisi and also with Mikhail Mordkin. Between 1928 and 1938 he danced principally at the Paliashvili Opera House, Tbilisi and staged many ballets as ballet master. From 1938 to 1958 he was chief choreographer at Yerevan's Opera and Ballet Theatre. He died in Tbilisi in 1967.

274 Swift, *The Art of the Dance in the USSR*, p.198

275 Morrison, *Bolshoi Confidential*, p.305

276 Born in Batumi, Georgia in 1903, Derzhavin became a literary and theatre critic, translator, and writer. He was married to the dancer Nina Anisimova who choreographed *Gayaneh* for the Kirov. He died in Leningrad in 1956.

1942 with choreography by Nina Anisimova and featured Dudinskaya in the title role, Sergeyev as Armen and Vecheslova as Nune. The augmented score and ballet now featured the 'Sabre Dance' which would become the work's most famous number.

There were many subsequent versions of the ballet which included those by Vasily Vainonen for the Bolshoi in 1957 (with Struchkova in the title role and Kondratov as Armen), by *Boris Eifman for the Maly in 1972, *Alexey Chichinadze's one-act creation for the Stanislavsky Ballet in the same year and Natalia Kasatkina[277] and Vladimir Vasilyov's[278] for Moscow Classical Ballet in 1977.

1940 – *The Tale of the Priest and his Workman Balda*

1940 began with a promising Maly Theatre debut. In early January Vladimir Varkovitsky premièred *The Tale of the Priest and his Workman Balda*, based on Pushkin's verse fairy-tale. He had studied on the Ballet Masters' Course instituted by Lopukhov at the Choreographic School in 1937 and begun to choreograph in the late 1930s. With a vibrant score by composer Mikhail Chulaki[279] and a libretto by Yuri Slonimsky, the ballet was a strongly-structured and entertaining work which combined successful comedy – featuring dancing kettles and samovars – with fluent classically-based movement. On the opening night the role of Pop was performed by Alexander Orlov, Balda by Nikolai Sokolov,[280] Kirillova danced Popovna and Zubkovsky the Demon. *The Tale of the Priest and his Workman Balda* was toured to Moscow where it garnered much praise.

---

277 Born in Moscow in 1934, Kasatkina graduated into the Bolshoi company in 1953 where she danced until 1976 as a noted character dancer. With her husband, fellow dancer Vladimir Vasilyov, she began to choreograph in the early 1960s; they assumed the co-directorship of Moscow's Young (later Moscow Classical) Ballet in 1977 which, since his death, she continues to lead.

278 Born in Moscow in 1931, Vasilyov graduated into the Bolshoi company in 1949. He also studied at GITIS, and in 1953 graduated from there in choreography. From the early 1960s, his choreographic output was alongside his wife Natalia Kasatkina. He died in Moscow in 2017.

279 Born in Simferopol, Crimea in 1908, Chulaki graduated from the Leningrad Conservatoire in 1931 where he subsequently taught, as well as at the Moscow Conservatoire where he taught composition to the young Mstislav Rostropovich. He was artistic director of the Leningrad Philharmonic before the war. He was director of the Bolshoi Theatre between 1955 and 1959 and Artistic Director from 1963 to 1970. He died in Moscow in 1989.

280 Born in Krasnodar in 1912, Sokolov trained at the Leningrad School and graduated into the Tbilisi dance company before moving to the Maly Theatre in 1931. He remained there until 1962 as a valued character dancer, creating numerous roles. The date and location of his death are unknown.

1940 – *Romeo and Juliet*

Drambalet as an artistic phenomenon can be seen as an extension of the nineteenth century traditions but with greater focus on narrative coherence and deeper psychological insight. As if to show what could be achieved, its apogee and a vindication of the whole artistic approach came into being on the eve of war: on 11th January 1940, the curtain rose at the Kirov on *Romeo and Juliet*, a new ballet by Leonid Lavrovsky to a score by Sergey Prokofiev. It had been a long time in the making, with the idea first floated as early as 1934 by Sergey Radlov who suggested Zakharov as a suitable choreographer. In 1936, Prokofiev was given the commission to write the score for a performance to mark the 200th anniversary of the Leningrad Choreographic School in 1938 and he worked intensively with his librettist Adrian Pyotrovsky[281] on converting the stage play. Numerous to-ings and fro-ings between Moscow and Leningrad and disagreements about the music ensued which allowed the composer to accept an offer from the State Theatre in Brno, Czechoslovakia to première his ballet in December 1938 with choreography by local dancer Ivo Psota (who also danced Romeo) for whom he had altered the originally planned happy ending. The Kirov overcame Prokofiev's reluctance to allow the unknown-to-him Leonid Lavrovsky to create his version and later, the objections of the first Juliet, Galina Ulanova, who said she found the music undanceable. The choreographer delivered what was ultimately the best of the *drambalet* form, melding vernacular gesture with classical dance steps and demonstrating crystal-clear, ideologically pure story-telling which focussed on two "young, strong, progressive people" struggling against "feudal traditions".[282]

At the first performance, Ulanova danced Juliet with startling simplicity (it would become one of her most successful roles); English critic Iris Morley observed that with "...smooth flowing steps, the semi-tones and nuances of changing moods made her the Juliet of one's dreams. Expressing herself not in gestures and dramatic mimicry but in the shades and colour-schemes of the dance, she achieved perfection."[283] Konstantin Sergeyev was "the perfect Romeo (with) that combination of dark romantic looks and sensitive and noble dancing;"[284] he was by then the company's leading male artist who would continue to play a major role in its life as dancer, choreographer,

---

281 Born in 1898 in an unknown location, Pyotrovsky became a pupil of Meyerhold and worked with him in the theatre section of *Narkompros* shortly after the revolution. He became a distinguished teacher and dramaturge and was artistic director of the Leningrad Film Studio. He was arrested in late 1937 as part of the Great Terror and is assumed to have been executed shortly after.

282 Homans, *Apollo's Angels*, p.359

283 Morley, *Soviet Ballet*, p.20

284 ibid.

teacher and, ultimately, company director. Robert Gerbek[285] danced Tybalt and Andrey Lopukhov[286] was Mercutio. *Romeo and Juliet* was an immediate success, not only on account of its superlative dancing, but also for Prokofiev's now rightly-fêted music, which had initially been the cause of so many misgivings, even his original concept had been somewhat distorted by Lavrovsky's demands for changes during the rehearsal period. The designs were by Pyotr Williams.[287] Choreographer and librettist were deemed to have succeeded in their attempt "to convert the whole play, act by act and scene by scene, into a ballet which using the dance medium would convey to the senses of the audience the poetry of the original".[288] The Bolshoi Ballet staged the production in 1946, when Ulanova, by then transferred from Leningrad to the capital, reprised her Juliet opposite Mikhail Gabovich as Romeo and alongside Ermolayev as Mercutio and Sergey Koren[289] as Tybalt. It became a mainstay of the repertoire and an international calling-card when the company began touring abroad in the mid-1950s.

1940/1941 – *Taras Bulba*

Romeo and Juliet was not quite the final gasp for Russian ballet before the collapse of the Nazi-Soviet pact and Hitler's invasion of the USSR in June 1941. In December 1940, Lopukhov had presented *Taras Bulba* at the Kirov to a score by Vasily Solovyov-Sedoy. [290] It followed the narrative of

---

285   Born in Krasnodar in 1907, Gerbek studied first at the Leningrad Choreographic School's evening classes and graduated into the Kirov company in 1930 where he performed until 1962. An outstanding character dancer, he performed a huge number of roles and created parts in many new ballets. From 1961 to 1971 he was the chief choreographer of the Leningrad Theatre of Musical Comedy. Between 1954 and 1992 he taught pas de deux, folk dance and acting intermittently at the Leningrad Choreographic School. He died in St Petersburg in 1994.

286   Born in St Petersburg in 1898, Lopukhov graduated into the Mariinsky in 1916 where he danced until 1945. He was a celebrated character dancer, known for the detail of his portrayals. From 1927 he taught character dance at the Leningrad Choreographic School and the Kirov; from 1930 also at the Maly. He was the brother of Fyodor Lopukhov and Lydia Lopokhova. He died in Leningrad in 1947.

287   Born in Moscow in 1902 to a naturalised American scientist father, Williams studied art and design, taking part in 1922 in the creation of an experimental Museum of Scenery Art. He worked as a scenery artist from 1929 onwards and in 1941 became the head artist of the Kirov Theatre. He died in Moscow in 1947.

288   Morley, *Soviet Ballet*, p.20

289   Born in St Petersburg in 1907, Koren began ballet in the Evening Courses of the Leningrad School and graduated into GATOB in 1930, rapidly becoming an outstanding character dancer. He moved to the Bolshoi in 1942 where he continued to dance until 1960 when he became ballet master. He created many roles including Mercutio in *Romeo and Juliet*. He died in Moscow in 1969.

290   Born in St Petersburg in 1907, Solovyov-Sedoy graduated from the Leningrad Conservatoire in 1936 and began composition, mostly songs and popular ballads, the

Nikolai Gogol's 1835 novel in which the eponymous Cossack leader and his Ukrainian friends fight against their Polish oppressors (the USSR had seized Polish-controlled portions of Ukraine and Belorussia under the terms of the 1939 Nazi-Soviet Pact). Mikhail Dudko created the title role, with Chabukiani and Koren as his sons Andrey and Ostap; Alla Shelest was Oksana and Dudinskaya created the role of the Pannochka, daughter of the Polish overlord. The Bolshoi mounted its own production in March 1941 with choreography by Zakharov; Lashchilin was Taras Bulba, Sergeyev and Gabovich Ostap and Andrey and Semyonova appeared as the Pannochka with Lepeshinskaya as Oksana. The Kirov returned to the ballet in June 1955 with Boris Fenster's[291] new version in which Dudinskaya and Shelest danced their original roles (some sources say that Lyubov Voyshnis[292] was the first Oksana), Sergeyev was Andrey and Askold Makarov[293] was Ostap; Mikhail Mikhailov appeared as Taras Bulba.

From the death of Lenin in 1924 until the outbreak of war with Germany, Stalin had secured and strengthened his power and his wishes were implemented with almost unimaginable ruthlessness. Ballet was, ultimately, just one more building block in the quest to build communist society – dancers, choreographers, composers and directors had to negotiate often rapidly changing political and social shifts, all in an atmosphere of fear and anxiety. Despite the oppressive times, ballet not only survived but flourished, entering a golden age of dancing. In 1941 when the USSR itself was under threat of destruction, Soviet ballet was to live or die with it.

---

best known of which was 'Moscow Nights'. He died in Leningrad in 1979.

291   Born in Petrograd in 1916, Fenster remained at the Maly Theatre after his graduation until 1953 when he moved to the Kirov, becoming its chief choreographer between 1956 and 1959 and where he remained until his death in 1960 during the première of his ballet *Maskerade*.

292   Born in Kemerovo, Siberia in 1923, Voyshnis graduated into the Kirov in 1942 where she performed until 1963. A strong and versatile dancer, she danced a wide range of roles which ranged from the purely classical to demi-caractère. She taught in Cairo from 1963 to 1964, at the Vaganova Academy between 1965 and 1966 and at the Kirov from 1964 to 1972, the year of her death in Leningrad.

293   Born in the Tver Governate in 1925, Makarov graduated into the Kirov in 1943 and rose to become a leading soloist, known for his strong and virile stage presence. His greatest roles – the title role in *Spartacus*, Ma Lie-Chen (*The Red Poppy*) and Ali-Batyr (*Shuraleh*) – all showed these qualities. He became director of Yakobson's Choreographic Miniatures ensemble the year after the founder's death in 1975 until his death in St Petersburg in 2000.

5

War and Thaw

1941-1956

Romeo and Juliet may have premièred in Leningrad on 11th January 1940, but in terms of world politics the Capulets and the Montagues were far from reconciled: on 22nd June 1941, the Nazi-Soviet pact was torn up by Hitler's 'Operation Barbarossa', a full-scale invasion of the Soviet Union. The German military advance was nothing short of spectacular with both Leningrad and Moscow rapidly coming under direct threat, and the effect on the world of Russian ballet immediate.

Wartime

Both major ballet companies were evacuated from their home cities: the Bolshoi was sent to Kuibyshev (now Samara) in south-western Russia, a few of its dancers to Sverdlovsk (now Ekaterinburg) in the Urals and its school to the Volga town of Vasilsursk near Nizhny Novgorod. The Kirov and its school went to Molotov (now Perm) in the Urals, although some dancers from both companies either remained in their home cities or returned for specific performances. The MALEGOT company was evacuated to the city of Chkalov (today Orenburg).

Kirov

In Leningrad, June 1941 at the Kirov proceeded at first much as planned. On 23rd June, an anniversary gala for the distinguished ballerina Elena Lukom was scheduled and went ahead:

Elena Mikhailovna (Lukom) had rehearsed so that this performance would be "icing on the cake of her career" wrote a company dancer, "she planned for it to be her last performance, a farewell and a triumphant end to her stage career. Unexpectedly war broke out and the triumphant garland was broken."[294]

The performing schedule that June included graduation performances by the ballet school which danced Boris Fenster's three-act *Bela* to a score by Vladimir Deshevov.[295] The school appeared on the twenty-sixth but not thereafter.

---

294   Sakhnovskaya, 'Remembering Again', p.34

295   Born in St Petersburg in 1889, Deshevov studied composition at the St Petersburg Conservatoire between 1908 and 1914. After the revolution, he helped organise musical activities for the Soviet state, in 1921 he founded a People's Conservatoire in Sevastopol and became its director. He taught in Leningrad music schools between 1923 and 1933. His most famous work was *Rails* for piano composed in 1926. He composed the score for the ballet *Red Whirlwind* in 1924. He died in Leningrad in 1955.

On 15 August 1941, the Kirov ballet company was informed at a meeting that it and the opera company were to be evacuated on two special trains. Dancer Marietta Frangopulo[296] remembered:

"About 1600 people from the theatre and as many as 2000 members of their families were to be evacuated...on 19 August at four in the afternoon at the Moskovsky railway station. There were so many carriages, the train stood at two platforms: 83 heated goods vans and three class wagons. The theatre is taking costumes, sheet music, lighting equipment and props. It's impossible to take the sets...a group of pupils and teachers from the Ballet School is leaving the city with the theatre."[297]

On 14 September, the ballet company gave its first performance in Molotov, *Swan Lake*, although only half the corps de ballet could fit onto the smaller stage. The lack of audience reaction dismayed the dancers – they were used to a loyal and knowledgeable following back in Leningrad:

"Our hopes were not justified" wrote Tatiana Vecheslova, "Even the brilliant dancing of Dudinskaya and Sergeyev did not produce the expected reaction. At the end of the final act, the curtain came down to utter silence. 'Does anyone need our ballet?' we thought."[298]

Reactions in the town to the company verged on the hostile, with the male dancers in particular accused of not doing their wartime duty; they subsequently took on work at the local hospital throughout the night after performances in order to prove their patriotism. The company's first performance in Molotov was indeed coolly received; not even *Swan Lake* with Dudinskaya as Odette, Balabina as Odile and Sergeyev as Siegfried could arouse any enthusiasm. Nevertheless, interest and support for the ballet and the opera steadily grew. The evacuated ballet company gave performances of the main classical repertoire while also appearing at munitions factories, hospitals and orphanages and for army units. In addition to Molotov, Kirov dancers appeared in Ufa, Sverdlovsk and Chelyabinsk. The evacuated company's most notable première was Nina Anisimova's *Gayaneh* in December 1942.

The Leningrad Choreographic School re-established itself with limited resources and in unfavourable conditions. At first, younger pupils were sent to the Volga city of Kostroma but, owing to the German advance, moved

---

296 Born in Yeysk, Kuban in 1901, Frangopulo graduated into State ex-Mariinsky company in 1919 where she danced until 1947; from 1940 she taught the history of ballet at the Leningrad Choreographic School. She published many articles and books on ballet and established both the Research Museum of the History of National Choreographic Education and the Museum of the Vaganova Academy which she directed from 1957 to 1979. She died in Leningrad in 1979.

297 Frangopulo, 'Moscow-Leningrad Iskusstvo', 1948, pp.55-56

298 Vecheslova, 'Leningrad-Moscow Isskustvo', pp.145-146

two months later to join the older students and the company in Molotov. The school was initially housed in the village of Platoshino and then relocated in four small houses in Polazna, 45 km from the city, which lacked any form of studio. Olga Salimbaeva, a teacher at the Molotov Opera and Ballet Theatre wrote: "The School children lived far, beyond the River Kama, I know the conditions were not very good, the food was so-so, the Perm (sic) people fed them, left food in their desks."[299] In the spring of 1942, Vaganova arrived from Leningrad and established a teaching schedule delivered in a former church. Subsequently, the junior classes were moved to a summer cottage in Nizhnyaya Kurya on the banks of the Kama and in December the senior classes into the city centre; when the school returned to Leningrad, the latter's premises then housed the Molotov (later Perm) Ballet School.

In Leningrad, ballerina Olga Jordan stayed on during the hostilities with a few colleagues, forming a ballet collective at the Kirov which gave its first performance in June 1942. Fortified by extra rations, the small group of thirty-three dancers, which also included Sergey Koren and Alla Shelest, performed scenes from *Don Quixote*, *Le Corsaire* and *La Bayadère* among other dances in the harshest of conditions – the Kirov theatre had itself been shelled in September 1941. Jordan's technical brilliance shone out, alongside the powerful dancing of the Forty-Second Red Army's Robert Gerbek and his wife Natalia Sakhnovskaya.[300] In December, Jordan staged a reduced version of *Esmeralda* at the re-opened Comedy Theatre on Nevsky Prospect in Leningrad, as the Kirov remained closed owing to bomb damage. Conditions were tough and reminiscent of the first winters after the 1917 revolution:

Jordan wrote in her diary:

> "The class is not heated, the corps de ballet and non-dancing characters did not remove their street clothes at the rehearsal; they danced, or rather they made the movements in fur coats, felt boots and gloves. They also did arabesques like that...We faced another difficult problem: footwear...they wore out quickly and the dancers had to repair them themselves. They were darned and patched with fragments of silk ribbon found at home... And yet not one performance was performed *en demi-pointe*, everyone danced *en pointe*. It was a struggle, but we danced. When rehearsals were moved to the stage we were faced with new difficulties. The orchestra pit – intended for plays – could not accommodate even the small orchestra we had at our disposal. We had to expand it, removing the first two rows of the stalls. On the stage along the footlights there was a concrete block for the iron curtain

---

299 As quoted in 'Kirov theater in evacuation'

300 Born in St Petersburg in 1908, Sakhnovskaya danced with the Kirov Ballet, rising to the rank of soloist. She also appeared in film. She died in Leningrad in 1990.

– we had to pin it together and fill up the cracks with boards."[301]

The production received thirty-one performances before the end of the war.

The dancers suffered alongside everyone in the city; the winter of 1941- 2 was particularly harsh and they envied their audiences who could keep their coats, hats and boots on throughout performances. There was also the constant threat of bombardment. Jordan later wrote of one of her dancers:

"Once Nadya Feodorova was fifteen minutes late for rehearsal, and as I was in charge of the ballet, I had to find out the reason. 'A bomb fell on the house next to ours and I was buried under earth and debris' she exclaimed."[302]

In the autumn of 1943, the Maly Theatre was re-opened to take ballet and opera performances away from the cramped Comedy Theatre; the stage was considerably larger, the auditorium contained 1,300 spectators and there was no shortage of audience members during the increasingly distressing siege of the city. The thirty-three dancers were sometimes supplemented in non-dancing roles by actors from other theatres. Jordan cobbled together a production of *The Little Humpbacked Horse*, the choreography adapted owing to an almost complete lack of men, but the reaction was positive from a grateful public.

At no point did ballet training stop completely in Leningrad: with the majority of the school evacuated, a skeleton staff of teachers taught a handful of pupils – fifteen children aged between 13 and 18 in October 1941 – who gave dance concerts for the city's population and defenders. At the height of the German blockade in December 1942, auditions were held to recruit new students from Leningrad's orphanages with teaching beginning the following month. By September, the new recruits performed at the Maly Theatre. Another twenty-three children were accepted in September 1943, of whom four eventually graduated into the Kirov company including Tatiana Legat[303] and Alexander Gribov.[304] As the tide of the war turned against the Germans and the conditions in Leningrad eased somewhat, several teachers from the School wrote to the city's soviet asking permission to recruit suitable nine-year-olds to train: "The walls of our school have always rung with happy

---

301   Jordan, 'Moscow-Leningrad. Iskusstvo', pp.505–506

302   Jordan, 'The Soviet Ballet', p.171

303   Born in Leningrad in 1934, Legat graduated into the Kirov in 1953 where she danced as a confident and expressive soloist until 1985. Between 1985 and 1990 she was assistant-ballet master at the Stanislavsky Ballet. In 1992 she worked as a coach at the Boston Ballet and since 2010 she has coached the corps de ballet at the Mikhailovsky Ballet, St Petersburg.

304   Born in Leningrad in 1934, Gribov graduated into the Kirov in 1952, becoming a leading dancer; he was noted for his portrayal of Danila in *The Stone Flower*. He created roles in Grigorovich's *Legend of Love* and Belsky's *Coast* (or *Shore*) *of Hope*. He died in 1998.

children's voices. We have given years of our life to training Soviet children and now we miss our familiar work."[305] A class was enrolled although, as children who had endured the privations and horrors of the siege "first of all, they had to be taught to smile"[306] observed Jordan.

The Siege of Leningrad was finally lifted in January 1944. The final performances by the Kirov in Molotov were painful for a population which by then had grown to love and admire the remarkable artists of the Kirov. Ulanova appeared as Giselle, prompting such overcrowding in the theatre that there were fears the balcony would give way under the weight. Frangopulo remembered:

> "On 29 May we again stood on the platform of Molotov Railway Station at which our train from Leningrad had arrived almost three years ago. Only instead of heated goods wagons there were carriages with carpets on the floors, clean curtains hanging in the windows and bed linen that was white as snow...On 2 June the first special train arrived, the second left on 5 June and the third on 9 June."[307]

Molotov (whose original name of Perm was only restored in 1957) thereafter created its own ballet tradition thanks to its wartime exposure to the Leningrad company.

The School returned to its building on Rossi Street in June and a few weeks later the students gave a performance at the Maly Theatre; auditions for the new academic year were held in August with 150 applicants for 50 places. Dudinskaya as Aurora and Sergeyev as Prince Désiré re-opened the Kirov Theatre in *The Sleeping Beauty* on 31 August 1944 at a performance for construction workers of the border force; they appeared for the general public the following evening. The Kirov Ballet had returned to Leningrad.

Maly

The Maly companies performed in Leningrad until the beginning of July 1941 and were then evacuated to the city of Chkalov by special train in late August 1941. The city's Operetta Theatre was put at their disposition, although, seating only 300, it was significantly smaller than their home stage. Conditions in the city were difficult, made all the more so by the influx of refugees from the conflict. *Coppélia*, *Fadetta*, *The Prisoner of the Caucasus* and *The Tale of the Priest and His Workman Balda* were considered ready for performance in the first season commencing in September while *The Nutcracker* and *Don Quixote* were identified as able to be revived. However, decisions about the repertoire continued to be referred to the Kirov management evacuated to Molotov; the

---

305   ibid. p.175
306   ibid. p.175
307   Frangopulo, 'Moscow-Leningrad Iskusstvo', 1948, pp.91-93

1939 - *Swan Lake*, Kirov. Galina Ulanova as Odette and Konstantin Sergeyev as Siegfried. Courtesy of *Dancing Times*

1940 - *Romeo and Juliet*, Kirov. Andrey Lopukhov as Mercutio. Courtesy of *Dancing Times*

1940 - *Romeo and Juliet*. Courtesy of *Dancing Times*

1940 - *Taras Bulba*, Kirov. Mikhail Dudko in the title role.

1941 - *Straussiana*, MALEGOT.

1941 - Leningrad Choreographic School in Platoshino near Perm.

1944 - Maly Opera and Ballet Theatre (MALEGOT).

1945 - Victory - 9th May celebrations outside the Bolshoi Theatre.

1945 - *Cinderella*, Bolshoi. Galina Ulanova in the title role. Courtesy of *Dancing Times*

1946 - *Cinderella*, Kirov - Natalia Dudinskaya in the title role and Konstantin Sergeyev as the Prince.

1947 - *The Sleeping Beauty*, Bolshoi. Galina Ulanova as Aurora, Mikhail Gabovich as the Prince, Cherkasov as the King and Evgenia Biber as the Queen. Courtesy of *Dancing Times*

1946 - *Heart of the Hills*, Kirov. Vakhtang Chabukiani as Djardje. Courtesy of *Dancing Times*

1947 - Elizaveta Gerdt (seated), Maya Plisetskaya, Vladimir Preobrazhensky in rehearsal at the Bolshoi.

1948 - *The Little Stork*, Bolshoi. Courtesy of *Dancing Times*

1948 - *La Bayadère*, Kirov. Vakhtang Chabukiani as Solor. Courtesy of *Dancing Times*

1949 - *Youth*, MALEGOT.

1948 - Agrippina Vaganova and her class, LHU. Courtesy of *Dancing Times*

1949 - *The Bronze Horseman*, Bolshoi. Raisa Struchkova and Alexey Ermolayev.

1950 - *Swan Lake* Act II at the Bolshoi. RIA Novosti archive, image #854874 Anatoliy Garanin CC-BY-SA 3.0

1953 - *Swan Lake*, MALEGOT. Violetta Bovt as Odile, Alexey Chichinadze as Siegfried and Alexander Klein as Rothbart.

1953 - *The Seven Beauties*, MALEGOT.

1951 - *La Bayadère* Act I, Kirov. Natalia Dudinskaya as Nikiya. Courtesy of *Dancing Times*

1950s - *Don Quixote*, Bolshoi. Maya Plisetskaya as Kitri. Courtesy of *Dancing Times*

1950s - *Moszkowsky Waltz*, Bolshoi. Raisa Struchkova and Alexander Lapauri. Courtesy of *Dancing Times*

left: 1954 - Raisa Struchkova as Aurora in *The Sleeping Beauty*, RIA Novosti archive, image #644728 Umnov CC-BY-SA 3.0

right: 1956 - Nikolai Fadeyechev as Siegfried in *Swan Lake*, RIA Novosti archive, image #672496 Umnov CC-BY-SA 3.0

result was the effective banning of performances of the 'classics' by the Maly ensemble for the duration of their time in Chkalov.

The first performance by MALEGOT in Chkalov took place on November 7th, 1941. *The Prisoner of the Caucasus* was not well received by local audiences unfamiliar with the art form and unable to understand why the dancers neither sang nor spoke. The company persevered: Lopukhov's production of *Coppélia* opened in January 1942 with Galina Isayeva as Swanilda and Nikolai Sokolov as Franz, followed by *Fadetta* in February with Isayeva again in the title role, Viktor Tulubiev[308] as René and Sokolov as André in a revival supervised by company ballerina Natalia Sheremetyevskaya[309] in the absence of a company director. The dancers of the company also performed extensively in concerts for the military.

In 1943, a change of management meant that in August the choreographer Boris Fenster was sent to Chkalov and Lopukhov arrived as company artistic director. Conditions for the dancers did not improve – a company musician wrote in his diary:

"March 20, 1944. Fenster, who is our company choreographer and assistant to Lopukhov, complained about the starvation situation of the ballet troupe. The ballet dancers are malnourished and exhausted. Fenster wants to petition that, in view of this situation, it is necessary to stop for ballet rehearsals in the morning and put off any new productions, so that they have enough strength to participate in evening performances. I think that he will not achieve this."[310]

MALEGOT returned to Leningrad in September 1944.

Bolshoi

Under the directorship of Asaf Messerer, the majority of the Bolshoi troupe arrived in Kuibyshev in October 1941 where they subsequently appeared in performance at the city's Palace of Culture. Those dancers who remained in the capital were put under the leadership of Mikhail Gabovich who was

---

308   Born in Petrograd in 1920, Tulubiev graduated from the Leningrad Choreographic School into the Maly in 1939 where he danced until 1963. A characterful dancer, he specialised in comic roles, although he performed an extensive repertoire with the ensemble. He taught at the Maly from 1963 to 1967, in Cairo between 1967 and 1969. and then at the Leningrad Art University between 1969 and 1985.

309   Born in Petrograd in 1917, Sheremetyevskaya graduated from the Leningrad Choreographic School into the Maly in 1935 where she remained as a dancer until 1944. She was a member of the USSR Folk Dance Ensemble from 1945 to 1949. Between 1964 and 1977 she worked in research at the Institute of Art History and was the author of numerous works on theatre and dance. She died in 2013.

310   Polomarenko, 'A Theatre in Evacuation', (From the Musician's Notes), p.207 as quoted by Serdyuk, 'Ballet of the Leningrad State Academic Maly Opera House in evacuation (1941-1944)'

determined to put on classical ballets to help boost morale among the Muscovites and the city's defenders – he himself operated a search spotlight during the German Luftwaffe airborne raids in 1941; it was at this time that a fifteen-year-old schoolgirl named Maya Plisetskaya was drafted in to dance two adult roles in *Swan Lake*. Despite much reduced numbers and resources available, as well as the threat of physical attack, Moscow continued to see ballet throughout the war performed not in the historic main auditorium but in the nearby Filial Theatre. In 1940 the capital saw 112 performances by the Bolshoi which dropped to 56 in 1941 but rose again to 126 by 1942, 120 the following year (the company swelled by returning dancers) and 144 in 1944. There was movement between the two 'branches': Olga Lepeshinskaya, the most ideologically pure of Soviet ballerinas, quickly returned to Moscow to dance, also making use of her famed marksmanship to protect her apartment block from attack from its roof, before joining the Bolshoi's 'front brigade' which performed for troops in the battlefield. The evacuated companies and schools continued to work wherever they were, bringing the art form to often bemused locals – in 1942 the Bolshoi troupe presented 89 performances in far-off Kuibyshev – and the quality of teaching remained high: future ballerinas and household names Maya Plisetskaya and Raisa Struchkova graduated during the war. Indeed, in 1942, at the height of hostilities and despite the threats the whole of the country was facing, the two Bolshoi ensembles contracted themselves and each other to produce two new works and give one thousand concerts. During its time in Kuibyshev, the Bolshoi Ballet staged five productions.

Of this war period, perhaps the best-known work was the "the worst Soviet ballet" Iris Morley had "ever seen".[311] *Crimson (or Red or Scarlet) Sails* was premièred by the Bolshoi company at the Palace of Culture, Kuibyshev in late December 1942 with a score by Vladimir Yurovsky[312] and choreography by the Radunsky, Pospekhin and Popko trio who had created *Svetlana* in 1939. It was an escapist fantasy, based on the popular 1922 children's book *Scarlet Sails* by Alexander Grin,[313] and summed up by Morley as an "acrobatic bore...full of every balletic cliché ever conceived in the eighteen-nineties".[314] The first performance in Kuibyshev saw Irina

---

311   Morley and Manchester, *The Rose and the Star*, p.89

312   Born in Tarashcha, Ukraine in 1915, Yurovsky became a successful film composer. His son Mikhail and his grandsons Vladimir and Dmitry are all conductors. He died in Moscow in 1972.

313   Born in 1880 in Vyatka as Alexander Grinevsky, he became a successful writer in the 1920s; his works contained an element of fantasy and took place in what was often referred to as 'Grinlandia' by fans. He died in Stary Krym, Crimea in 1932.

314   Morley and Manchester, *The Rose and the Star*, p.89

Tikhomirnova[315] as Assol, Vladimir Preobrazhensky as Grei and Asaf Messerer as Letika. The ballet was first given at the Bolshoi in late April of 1943 with Lepeshinskaya as Assol. What is notable is that the ideological spotlight had clearly turned away from ballet and the arts as the nation focussed on resisting and, ultimately, defeating the German invaders. The 'mysticism' of its subject matter would never have seen the light of day in peace-time and, indeed, by 1950, it had fallen foul of official condemnation and was permanently dropped from the repertoire.

The war years were as hard on the dance troupes as for the wider population, but the tide of the conflict eventually turned against the Germans, allowing the companies to return to their homes – the Bolshoi in the autumn of 1943 to a theatre which had narrowly avoided total destruction in 1941 and the Kirov to their war-beaten home in 1944. Iris Morley described her visit to the Kirov Theatre in the spring of 1944:

> "The theatre had been badly hit by shells and the whole of the heating system destroyed, which meant much more serious repairs than the destruction of the plush stalls or the crystal lustres. But unlike the rest of the city, it was in the centre of a hum of activity." She reported a dogged determination to re-open the theatre: " 'A priority over everything?' I asked, wanting to be quite sure. 'Yes, you see if we can't open on May 1st, I don't know what the people will say...It makes us feel when the theatre is open that life has begun again'."[316]

Stanislavsky

At the outbreak of war, the authorities merged the Stanislavsky Opera with the Moscow Art Ballet. The Stanislavsky and Nemirovich-Danchenko Musical Theatre companies were left in Moscow for the duration of the hostilities, intended to raise the morale of the population. The ensemble worked hard to deliver new ballets; Vladimir Burmeister both assumed the directorship and became chief choreographer in 1941 and set about the task with gusto, creating a series of high-quality productions. The light-hearted *Straussiana* opened in October 1941 as the battle for the city raged and *The Merry Wives of Windsor* premièred at the theatre in June 1942 to a score by Oransky, and featuring the great mime artist Ivan Kurilov as Sir John

---

315   Born in Moscow in 1917, Tikhomirnova graduated into the Bolshoi in 1936 where she performed until 1959, rising to the rank of principal and dancing a wide repertoire. She was the wife of Bolshoi dancer and teacher Asaf Messerer. In 1966, she co-founded the Young Ballet with Igor Moiseyev and was its director until 1970. She died in Moscow in 1984.

316   Morley, *Soviet Ballet*, pp..12-13

Falstaff, Alexander Tomsky[317] as Page and Maria Sorokina as Anne Page was an example of his talent with narrative. In June 1943, clearly inspired by the success of Chabukiani's Spanish-themed *Laurencia*, Burmeister premièred *Lola*, a three-act ballet of real dramatic impact set during the Peninsular War of 1808-1813 to music by Vasilenko which featured Sorokina scoring a great personal success in the title role. Burmeister created a version of *Schéhérazade* to Rimsky-Korsakov's score which opened in late December 1944 with Sorokina as Gulnara and Alexander Klein[318] as Sinbad and proved a popular success.

1944 – Change of directors at the Bolshoi and Kirov

In 1944, towards the end of hostilities and when the ballet companies had returned to their homes, Leonid Lavrovsky, director of the Kirov Ballet since 1938, was transferred to Moscow to lead the Bolshoi as part of a wholescale re-focussing of Russian ballet; star Kirov dancer Galina Ulanova also made the journey to the capital and remained there for the rest of her life. One of Lavrovsky's first decisions in Moscow was to mount a new production of *Giselle* to showcase her unique talent; the first performance saw her partnered by Alexey Ermolayev, himself a Leningrad transfer in 1930, as Albrecht. At the Kirov, Lavrovsky was replaced as director by none other than Fyodor Lopukhov. Lavrovsky remained at the Bolshoi for twenty years, Lopukhov at the Kirov for one.

1945 – Victory

It is hard to overestimate the effect that the Great Patriotic War with Germany, the painful struggle for survival and the victory over the invaders, had upon Soviet society as a whole. As part of that society, dancers were far from immune to this phenomenon, and it can be persuasively argued that their experiences of the conflict directly moulded the post-war generation of Soviet ballet: *Maya Plisetskaya *Nikolai Fadeyechev and Yuri Grigorovich,

---

317 Born in Moscow in 1905, Tomsky graduated from the evening courses of the Moscow Choreographic School in 1923. Between 1927 and 1929, he danced at the Moscow Operetta Theatre and then he worked in Sverdlovsk and Molotov before joining the Stanislavsky in 1941. In 1948, he joined the Bolshoi where he appeared until 1951. Some sources say he was the company's artistic director between 1957 and 1959, and he was company manager from 1964 to 1970. He was artistic director of the Stanislavsky from 1959 to 1964. He staged productions in many different cities of the USSR and abroad. He died in Milan in 1970.

318 Born in Volkovyshki (now Vilkaviškis), Lithuania in 1904, Klein graduated from the Bolshoi School and danced with Moscow's 'Young Ballet' for three years before moving to dance in Baku, Azerbaijan for a further two years before a year with the Leningrad People's Theatre. In 1931 he became a soloist of Moscow Art Ballet (later the Stanislavsky company) where he remained until 1965; from 1943 he was its deputy artistic director. He was a celebrated mime artist. He died in Moscow in 1971

amongst others, were all characterised by a genuine and fervent patriotism and 'an urgent exhilaration of dancing'. It must also be noted that, while the ballet schools continued with their dance training as before, *Andrey Zhdanov's 1946 decrees meant that the pupils' ideological indoctrination was noticeably intensified, so that 'right-thinking' ballet dancers were being produced as a matter of course.

1945 – *Cinderella* at the Bolshoi

Victory and peace came in May 1945, and with them Stalin's attention turned once more to the arts as vehicles for the promotion of Soviet values to which he now added the need to mark and celebrate both the stoicism and heroism of the Russian people during the Great Patriotic War; any attempts at modernity were to be stifled. The first notable post-war ballet première was *Cinderella* which opened at the Bolshoi in November of that year. It had had a difficult genesis – Prokofiev had started to work on it in 1940, but had left the score to complete his opera *War and Peace* (which received its stage première at the Maly Theatre in June 1946) before returning to it during the war and in 1943 publishing the first of several piano transcriptions from the score. The project had gained and lost choreographers during the war (Chabukiani, Goleizovsky and Sergeyev included) before Rostislav Zakharov, recently elevated to the post of company chief choreographer, was decided upon, someone guaranteed to focus on the proletarian heroine's triumph over adversity. As rehearsals progressed, an ailing Prokofiev (he had suffered a heart attack) was unable to prevent his score from being re-orchestrated to become brasher and more triumphant. The title role represented a real girl, downtrodden by circumstance and society who triumphed in the end; a poetic Ulanova performed the first night in November, partnered by Mikhail Gabovich as the Prince, and alternated thereafter with the more emphatic Lepeshinskaya partnered by Preobrazhensky. Maya Plisetskaya was the first Autumn Fairy.

1945 – Boris Fenster at the MALEGOT

At Leningrad's Maly Theatre, Boris Fenster became its chief choreographer in 1945, a post he held until 1953. He was unusual in that, having graduated from the Leningrad Choreographic School in 1936, he joined the Maly company where he remained, firstly as a soloist and then as an assistant ballet master to Lopukhov. He was very much influenced by the theatre's tradition of realistic acting and his ballets were characterised by their dramatic content. *The False Bridegroom* in March 1946 with a score by Mikhail Chulaki was a notable achievement. Based on Goldoni's *Il Servitore di due padroni* (*The Servant of Two Masters*) it gave ample opportunities for comedy and characterisation to a cast led by Nikolai Zubkovsky, a highly technically accomplished *demi-*

caractère dancer, who excelled as Trufaldino, the servant of the title.

1945 – *Raymonda*

Petipa's 1898 late masterpiece *Raymonda* had never slipped entirely from the repertoire, less on account of its preposterous storyline and more for Glazunov's sumptuous music and some outstanding choreography. In July 1945, newly-installed Bolshoi director Lavrovsky staged a production which included movement by Petipa, Gorsky's 1900 revisions and several numbers of his own. In 1938, the Kirov had staged a version by Vainonen which used a new scenario but Lavrovsky decided to return to the original for his production. Semyonova danced the title role with pure classicism and exceptional musicality, Gabovich was a dashing Jeanne de Brienne and Abderakhman was danced by Ermolayev.

1946 – *Mistress into Maid*

Rostislav Zakharov followed his *Cinderella* for the main stage of the Bolshoi with *Mistress into Maid*, a smaller-scale work for the Filial Theatre in March 1946. Using a Pushkin narrative had been a success for him with *The Fountain of Bakhchisarai*, so he returned to the author in the form of one of his five *Belkin Tales*, the short story *The Squire's Daughter* published in 1831. Set to a score by Asafiev, it was a three-act ballet which featured only six named characters and successfully told a light comic tale concerning rival landowners, the love between their children and a frightful English governess. On opening night Vladimir Preobrazhensky was Alexey, Marina Semyonova the object of his affections Lisa, and Lyubov Bank appeared as Miss Jackson. Semyonova observed "when I dance it, I feel a tenderness as if I held my little daughter in my arms".[319] The ballet was re-choreographed by Boris Fenster at the Maly in 1951.

1946 – *Cinderella* at the Kirov

Soon after the Moscow première of Zakharov's *Cinderella* in November 1945, the Kirov gave the first performances of Konstantin Sergeyev's Leningrad version in April 1946. The Kirov management, having first commissioned the score from the composer, had then cooled towards the project, allowing the Bolshoi to steal a march, but later changed its stance. The first night cast read as a roll-call of the finest company dancers of the time; Dudinskaya as Cinderella, Alla Shelest and Tatiana Vecheslova as her sisters Zyluka and Krivlyak, Sergeyev himself as the Prince and Sergeyev's first wife, Feya Balabina, dancing the Fairy Godmother. The choreographer married his second wife, Natalia Dudinskaya, after the ballet's première.

Reactions were very positive; Sergeyev had given his own role some impressive choreography and the audience responded to what was a feast of

---
[319] Quoted by Morley, *The Rose and the Star*, p.42

dancing throughout. Boris Erdman was the set designer. This first Sergeyev version remained in the repertoire for some ten years until his removal from the directorship of the company.

Sergeyev's *Cinderella* returned to the Kirov stage in June 1964 with new designs by Tatiana Bruni,[320] who had, by then, worked extensively with the company; they proved popular, mirroring the irony inherent in the music but also serving to create an atmosphere of festive theatricality. At this revival Cinderella was danced by Irina Kolpakova and the Prince by Vladilen Semyonov.[321] Sergeyev's version was last revived by the Mariinsky in 1996.

Cinderella proved attractive to many later Soviet choreographers: Alexey Chichinadze staged his own version at the Stanislavsky in 1971, *Oleg Vinogradov at the Maly in 1977 and *Vladimir Vasiliev at the Kremlin Ballet in 1991, in addition to several others around the republics.

1946 – The Choreographers' Course at GITIS

Recognising the need for the formal education and training for choreographers across the Soviet Union, Moscow's Lunacharsky State Institute for Theatre Arts – GITIS, established a four-year course in 1946. The first intake comprised twelve students from the RSFSR, Tajikistan, Uzbekistan, Turkmenia, Latvia, Estonia and Ukraine which was widened from the second year onwards to include applicants from the communist satellite states of Eastern Europe. Students generally needed to have had formal secondary-level dance training and at least two years' experience in a theatre or dance ensemble. From the outset the syllabus was ambitious in the range of skills it covered: the theory and practice of mounting a production, the theory and history of music as well as the composition of classical, folk and historical dances. The trainees worked extensively with young dancers from the Bolshoi and other dance troupes to develop their ideas and, ultimately, to stage full productions. From the outset, Rostislav Zakharov occupied the Chair of Choreography, a position he held until his death in 1984.

---

320 Born in St Petersburg in 1902, Bruni studied art and joined a travelling collective of artists in the early 1920s, working with Balanchine's Young Ballet group among others. She designed the costumes for Lopukhov's *The Bolt* and worked mainly in Leningrad until the war when she was evacuated to Molotov with the Kirov and designed many of their productions there. After the war she taught in the production department of the Ostrovsky Leningrad State Theatre Institute. She died in St Petersburg in 2001.

321 Born in Samara (later Kuibyshev) in 1932, Semyonov graduated from the Leningrad School into the Kirov in 1950 where he danced for a further twenty-two years, most of which as a principal. A lyrical dancer with an airy jump and an impeccable finish, he was considered a real stylist. He taught at the Vaganova Academy from 1963, was Acting Artistic Director of the Kirov from 1970 to 1973 and coached at the company until 1997. He is married to Irina Kolpakova.

Andrey Zhdanov

The prevailing artistic atmosphere was, however, worsening: in August 1946 denunciations of writers including that of the poet Anna Akhmatova began to appear, followed in later years by those of film makers and composers (Prokofiev, Shostakovich and Khachaturian were all denounced in 1948 for subversive tendencies). There was, perhaps surprisingly, no direct critique of the world of dance, but that did not stop the recently returned ballet troupes being anxious to affirm their ideological purity – when a dancer with the Kirov, Pyotr Gusev once declared in a company meeting that "ballet (was) a part of the ideological front".[322] Key to the setting of Soviet ballet's post-war direction was Andrey Zhdanov,[323] one of Stalin's intimates, who in mid-1946 was charged by the Great Leader with ensuring political orthodoxy in the arts. At the ballet schools there was an immediate intensification of ideological and political training whilst in the companies themselves, his mandates gave immediate rise to several works which evoked the heroism of the recent war. In the light of this new politico-cultural imperative, *drambalet* returned with a vengeance to portray in as realistic a way possible the struggles and sacrifices Soviet Russia had had to endure. "Realism is an intrinsic feature of Soviet ballet and of all Soviet art" wrote theatre critic Nikolai Volkov[324] in 1948, "... which lends to the ballet completeness, purpose and a monolithic quality. Soviet ballet abounds in human passions and thoughts".[325]

1946 – the emigration of Violetta Prokhorova

In a sequence of events reminiscent of Tamara Karsavina's departure from Russia in 1918, Bolshoi soloist Violetta Prokhorova[326] married a British Embassy employee and was granted permission to emigrate. She was a highly

---

322 Swift, *The Art of the Dance in the USSR*, p.129

323 Born in 1896 in Mariupol, Ukraine, Zhdanov joined the Bolshevik party in 1915 and rose through the ranks, assuming the running of Leningrad after Kirov's murder. A leading party ideologue, he played a major part in the terrors and purges of the 1930s. Stalin placed him in charge of post-war cultural policy which became known as the Zhdanov Doctrine or Zhdanovism which continued into the late 1950s, well after his death in Moscow in 1948.

324 Born in Penza in 1894, Volkov was a theatrical historian and dramatist who had worked on numerous ballets including *The Flames of Paris* and *The Fountain of Bakhchisarai*, becoming a leading voice in the push for stage realism. He died in 1965.

325 Volkov, *USSR Information Bulletin*, Vol.8, p.265

326 Born in Moscow in 1924, Prokhorova graduated as a soloist into the Bolshoi in 1942. Having danced with the Uzbek State Ballet for two years, she transferred to the Bolshoi in Kuibyshev and, on her return to Moscow appeared with the Stanislavsky Ballet in 1945. In the UK, she danced with the Sadler's Wells Ballet as a principal dancer, creating several notable roles and impressing with both her glamorous stage presence and strong Soviet technique. She retired from the stage in 1956. She was director of the Teatro San Carlo Ballet in Naples from 1985 to 1986. She died in Naples, Italy in 2021.

promising dancer who, during evacuation firstly to Tashkent and then with the Bolshoi in Kuibyshev, had danced several leading roles including Odette-Odile in *Swan Lake*. Her departure was unusual, given the strict post-war social and political regime. In February 1946, she danced as a guest artist with Sadler's Wells Ballet, appearing as Princess Florine in the Bluebird pas de deux on the second night of their new production of *The Sleeping Beauty* and she joined the company as a permanent member the following season under the name of Violetta Elvin. She brought considerable technical and interpretative strength to the ensemble.

1947 – Increasing political orthodoxy

In a further example of the reimposition of the need to promote Soviet values in ballet, a conference was held in Moscow in early 1947 which identified that, of the repertoires of twenty ballet companies, only *Gayaneh* was on a Soviet theme. "It is contended that the Soviet theatres must take an active part in the Communist education of the people and that the new ideas and the new features of modern life ought to be glorified and extolled in dance by all the means and possibilities available to this form of art" reported writer Lionel Bradley in the British magazine *Ballet*, adding "How this is to be done is not explained...all experience has shown that works of art which are conceived on purely propaganda lines, fail as works of art and thereby lose their propaganda value also."[327]

War-themed ballets

Two new ballets of the late 1940s exemplified the post-war cultural imperative: *Tatiana, or Daughter of the People*, depicting triumph over the Nazis in the Gulf of Finland, premièred at the Kirov in June 1947 with choreography by Vladimir Burmeister who also created *Shore (or Coast) of Happiness* at the Stanislavsky in November 1948 set to a score by Antonio Spadavecchia;[328] it depicted the heroism of young Communist Pioneers as they grew up and fought for the motherland

Ballets about the Great Patriotic War continued to be favoured throughout the 1950s. *We Stalingraders* was premièred at the Bolshoi in 1959 with choreography by Vladimir Varkovitsky; it depicted the spirit of defiance of the city which withstood a terrifying German siege during the war and opened with five Soviet men holding a red flag aloft. An unexpected source of dance evoking war was Leonid Yakobson, who was never in the mainstream of Soviet choreography. Typically, his creations approached the subject matter in unconventional ways. In 1958, as part of his *'Choreographic Miniatures'

---

327 Bradley, 'News from Abroad', *Ballet*, Vol.3, No.4, pp.42-43

328 Born in Odessa, Crimea in 1907 into a family of Italian descent, Spadavecchia graduated from the Moscow Conservatoire in 1937, studying with Prokofiev in 1944. He is noted for his 1957 opera *The Gadfly*. He died in Moscow in 1988.

programme for the Kirov, Yakobson created *Mother*, a three-minute solo for a loose-haired Olga Moiseyeva.[329] In terms of its weighty movement quality, it drew on the choreographer's time working with the Duncan School in Moscow a decade before and depicted a mother looking in vain for her missing child. The music was the same Scriabin piano étude used by Duncan for *Revolutionary Étude* in 1921, her solo in tribute to the Bolshevik fighters. Another Yakobson miniature on the subject of war that evening was *Stronger than Death*, featuring three Soviet prisoners who are due to be executed. It depicted their collective strength in extremis – as each is shot, he crumples but does not fall; ultimately, they are not vanquished by their enemy. The atmospheric music was written by Isaac Shvarts (Schwartz).[330]

1947 – *Doctor Aibolit*

The importance given to the cultural education of children in the USSR was always strong, and performances for young audiences of operas and ballets were a notable phenomenon of the entire Soviet era. September 1947 saw the opening in Novosibirsk of *Doctor Aibolit*, a new children's ballet which would, with different choreographies, spread across the Soviet Union and its satellite states. Based on the children's poems *Aybolit and Barmaley* by Korney Chukovsky,[331] as well as the author's novella *Doctor Aybolit* (itself inspired by Hugh Lofting's *Dr Doolittle*), the eponymous character, whose name in Russian can be translated as 'Ouch, it hurts!', travels to Africa to help the animals and foils an attempt to imprison them. Mikhail Moiseyev[332] choreographed the work and appeared in the title role in Novosibirsk; the

---

329   Born in Leningrad in 1928, Moiseyeva graduated into the Kirov in 1947, debuting as Nikiya in *La Bayadère* and was appointed to the rank of ballerina in 1953, dancing all the major roles and creating many, including Mekhmeneh Banu in Grigorovich's *Legend of Love*. A highly emotional artist, she sought to bring fresh interpretations to the classical roles. She performed with the company until 1973 when she retired to become ballet mistress and coach. She died in St Petersburg in 2021.

330   Born in 1923 in Romny, Ukraine, Shvarts became a child piano prodigy, performing with the Leningrad philharmonic at the age of twelve. His father was executed during the great purge and the family exiled. After the war, Shostakovich paid for Shvarts to attend the Rimsky-Korsakov Conservatoire in Leningrad from where he graduated in 1951. Thereafter, he became a noted film composer. He died in St Petersburg in 2007.

331   Born in St Petersburg in 1882, Chukovsky was a celebrated poet, publicist, literary critic, translator, children's writer and journalist. He remains the most published author of children's literature in the Soviet Union and Russia. He died in Moscow in 1969.

332   Born in Moscow in 1882, Mikhail Moiseyev graduated from the Bolshoi School in 1899 and from 1903 to 1910 danced at the Zimin Opera House, Moscow. In 1910 he toured abroad with the Anna Pavlova company. After the revolution he worked in a number of theatres including those in Odessa, Sverdlovsk, Novosibirsk and Yerevan, staging versions of the classics and was the head and teacher of ballet studios at several theatres and choreographic schools. He died in Moscow in 1955.

score was by Igor Morozov.[333] The ballet opened the following year in Moscow at the Stanislavsky with choreography by Nikolai Kholfin[334] and in Leningrad at the Maly Theatre in a version by Fenster. It became very popular and was performed extensively across the USSR thereafter.

1948 – *La Bayadère* returns to the Kirov

By the 1940s, Petipa's *La Bayadère* had fallen from the Kirov's active repertoire; in 1920, a revival was staged to showcase Olga Spessivtseva's extraordinary talents but the scenery of the final fourth act was lost during the middle of the decade (perhaps due to the flood of 1924) and the ballet had dropped from the schedules by the end of the 1920s. In 1941, Vladimir Ponomarev, by then director of the Kirov Ballet, set about its restoration, enlisting Chabukiani to contribute new dances to insert into Petipa's choreography. Dudinskaya danced Nikiya and Chabukiani, Solor. In 1948 the company returned to *La Bayadère* and augmented Ponomarev's production further – a notable addition was the virtuoso Golden Idol solo, choreographed and first performed by Nikolai Zubkovsky; Inna Zubkovskaya[335] was the first cast Nikiya. This version has remained in the Kirov repertoire to this day.

1949 – *The Bronze Horseman*

Not every ballet created directly after the end of the war featured heroes and heroines; the use of politically acceptable Russian classic literary sources was also revived. To mark the 150th anniversary of Pushkin's birth *The Bronze Horseman* premièred at the Kirov in March 1949 with music by Glière and choreography by Zakharov. It told the story of Pushkin's poem, depicting the tragic love story of Evgeny who loses his beloved Parasha in the historic 1824 flood of St Petersburg; driven mad by his loss, he rails against the famed statue

---

333 Born in Lugansk, Ukraine in 1913, Morozov graduated in composition from the Moscow Conservatoire in 1936. He successfully worked in a number of genres including film music; his score for *Doctor Aibolit* was celebrated for its musical characterisation of the animals. He died in Moscow in 1970.

334 Born in Moscow in 1903, Kholfin first studied ballet privately before joining GITIS from where he graduated in 1928. Between 1928 and 1932 he was an artist and choreographer of the Drambalet studio performing character roles. He was an artist and chief ballet master of the Moscow Art Ballet from 1932 to 1938 and then choreographer of the Stanislavsky Theatre between 1939 and 1958. He specialised in comic works and contributed greatly to the development of ballet in Kyrgyzstan and Turkmenistan. From 1960 to 1968 he was a ballet master at the Moscow Music Hall. He died in Moscow in 1979.

335 Born in Moscow in 1923, Zubkovskaya graduated from the Bolshoi School in 1941 and joined the Kirov while the company was in Perm during the war. Nicknamed the 'Black Pearl' on account of her striking dark looks, she danced all the major roles of the classical repertoire as well as in new works by Grigorovich and several by Yakobson. She became a noted teacher and coach after retirement from the stage in 1970. She died in St Petersburg in 2001.

of Peter the Great (the bronze horseman of the title). For the production, designer Mikhail Bobishov[336] observed every requirement of socialist realism, so the storm which provokes the flood visibly ruffled the dancers' hair and caused tethered boats to pitch, while the flood itself was reproduced on the Kirov stage by every trick of stagecraft. Dudinskaya was the first to dance Parasha and Sergeyev, Evgeny. After Leningrad in March, it premièred at the Bolshoi in June with Preobrazhensky as Evgeny, Lepeshinskaya as Parasha, Semyonova as the Queen of the Ball and the exciting soloist Georgy Farmanyants[337] as Harlequin in Act I. It became a popular and frequently performed work in the repertoires of both companies.

1949 – *Mirandolina*

Lighter fare was on offer from *Mirandolina*, based on Carlo Goldoni's comedy. A first version had been created in 1948 for the Moldovan music-drama theatre in Tiraspol, but real success came with Vainonen's production which opened at the Bolshoi's Filial Theatre in January 1949. The first performance featured Lepeshinskaya in the title role of the innkeeper's daughter who rejects the advances of three aristocratic suitors in favour of Yuri Kondratov's waiter Fabrizio; as the suitors, Ermolayev danced Ripafratta, Radunsky Count Albafiorita and Alexey Zhukov[338] was the Marquis of Forlipopoli. Vainonen supplied entertaining choreography to a score by Sergey Vasilenko which enjoyed considerable success because of its resolutely light atmosphere which provided an escape for the audiences from the challenges of post-war life:

> "Vainonen and Lepeshinskaya gave a holiday performance, which post-war Moscow enjoyed, forgetting about the hardships of devastation. Lepeshinskaya turned into an expansive Italian. Sly, cunning with her noble suitors and passionate with her beloved Fabrizio, she captivated the

---

336   Born in 1885 in Pogoreloye, Tver Governorate, Bobishov studied art both in Russia and abroad, becoming a theatre artist in St Petersburg in 1911; he went on to design for the major Russian stages. Between 1926 and 1964 he taught in the Repin Institute of Arts and several of his works are in the State Russian Museum. He died in Leningrad in 1964.

337   Born in 1921 in Bezhetsk, Tver Region, Farmanyants graduated in 1940 from the Bolshoi School into the company. Drafted into the army at the outbreak of war, he was quickly transferred to the NKVD Song and Dance Ensemble. On his return to the Bolshoi, he established himself as a brilliant soloist with a soaring jump and became an audience favourite both in Russia and on tour. He danced until 1962 and then between 1962 and 1984 was ballet master with the Song and Dance Ensemble of the Soviet Army. He died in Moscow in 1995.

338   Born in Moscow in 1908, Zhukov graduated into the Bolshoi in 1927 where he remained until 1951. He danced a variety of lead soloist and principal roles. He taught at the Bolshoi School from 1932 onwards, was the founder and director of the Cairo Ballet School from 1958 to 1963 and of the ballet school in Kampuchea (now Cambodia) between 1966 and 1967. He died in Phnom Penh in 1967.

audience. The audience roared with laughter, as rarely happened in ballet: it was real comedy! With a tambourine in her hand, Lepeshinskaya set off on a tarantella and the audience could hardly restrain themselves so as not to start dancing. Among the spectators there were many officers and soldiers who had passed through the hospitals: *Mirandolina* healed their war wounds."[339]

At the Bolshoi, 1949 also saw the première of a divertissement by Lavrovsky to Gounod's ballet music for his 1859 opera *Faust*; *Walpurgis Night* was twenty-five minutes of frolicking nymphs and fauns led by Bacchus, a Bacchante and a satyr which became a regular item on tours abroad in subsequent decades, providing show-off choreography for generations of Bolshoi star dancers.

1949 – *Youth*

At the Maly, director Boris Fenster scored a notable success in December 1949 with *Youth*, a new ballet loosely based by Slonimsky on Nikolai Ostrovsky's[340] novel *How the Steel was Tempered*. It was considered to have successfully portrayed the Russian Civil War with a detailed scenario in which three young town-dwellers in southern Russia are moved to join the youth movement in defence of the revolution. Fenster and his collaborators sought to depict modern soviet citizens and to infuse ballet movement with contemporary meaning:

> "In this performance I wanted to show a young man of our time, to penetrate into his spiritual world, which changes under the influence of events and feelings. I used classical and folk-character dances, and sometimes combined them, as best I could, broadly. For example, in the episode when the 'golden youth' tries to dance to the girl Dasha until she faints, I used the famous *fouetté* movement as a culmination, which in old ballets was just a demonstration of brilliance and spinning. Here it acquired a different meaning: a couple more turns and Dasha will fall and not be able to get up."[341]

The ballet was a personal success for two company ballerinas who both shone in terms of their vivid characterisations, Svetlana Sheina[342] as the

---

339 Zamostyanov, '*Mirandolina* for war veterans'

340 Born in Viliya, Volhynian Governorate in 1904, Ostrovsky joined the Bolsheviks in 1917 and fought in the civil war against the White army. He suffered from ill health and lost his sight in 1929. He began to work on his first novel *How the Steel Was Tempered* in 1930 and became a prolific writer thereafter. He died in 1936.

341 Fenster as quoted by Degen and Stupnikov in BelCanto.ru

342 Born in Odessa, Crimea in 1918, Sheina graduated from the Leningrad Choreographic School in 1938 and joined the Maly company where she danced throughout her

schoolgirl Lena and Galina Isayeva as Dasha the tomboy, as well as for the fine actor-dancer Viktor Tulubiev as their friend Petya. Such was the impression the ballet made on audiences that it was given 134 times at the Maly alone.

1950 – *Ali-Batyr/Shuraleh*

Ali-Batyr opened at the Kirov in May 1950, a full-length ballet by Leonid Yakobson on which he had worked while in Kazan in 1941 ahead of scheduled performances in Moscow during the Festival of Tartar Art. Those performances had never happened owing to the outbreak of war, so the choreographer took his earlier work as the basis of his post-war Leningrad commission. Shuraleh, a wood demon of Tartar folklore, enslaves the girl-bird Suimbike who finally escapes his spell only by a suicide pact with her beloved, the hunter Ali-Batyr. For the Kirov production, the Ministry of Culture insisted on a more optimistic ending so, in Leningrad, when Shuraleh's spell is broken, the couple are spared death and reunited in life. Yakobson's folk-dance inflections as well as his own non-classical leanings led to tensions with some dancers uncomfortable with what was being asked of them. At the première the character dancer and future choreographer Igor Belsky[343] danced the role of Shuraleh to great acclaim alongside Dudinskaya as Suimbike (later casts featured Gerbek as Shuraleh and both Shelest and Zubkovskaya as Suimbike) and Askold Makarov as Ali-Batyr (followed by Sergeyev and Boris Bregvadze[344]). The ballet was a popular success and was acquired in 1955 by the Bolshoi with the new title of *Shuraleh*. It was danced at its Moscow opening by Vladimir Levashov[345] as Shuraleh, Plisetskaya as

---

career, becoming a house choreographer between 1959 and 1976, when she moved to Poland to teach at the Teatr Weikl. She was married to Boris Fenster. She died in 2014 in an unknown location.

343   Born in Leningrad in 1925, Belsky graduated into the Kirov in 1943, becoming a much-valued character soloist. He started to choreograph with *Coast of Hope* for the Kirov in 1959. He was director of the Maly company between 1962 and 1973, producing versions of classics in addition to original choreography after which he took over control of the Kirov until 1977. He was chief choreographer at the Leningrad Music Hall from 1979 to 1992, and then artistic advisor of the Vaganova Academy from 1992 onwards. He died in St Petersburg in 1999.

344   Born in Saratov in 1926, Bregvadze trained and danced at first in his home town before spending 1946-7 at the Leningrad Choreographic School and then joining the Kirov where he danced for twenty years. He danced with a warm directness and portrayed fully-developed characters in lead roles across the repertoire. After retirement, he taught at the Vaganova School and in 1964 founded and led the Department of Choreography at the Krupskaya Institute of Culture, a post he held until 2011. He died in St Petersburg in 2012.

345   Born in Moscow in 1923, Levashov graduated from the Bolshoi School into the company in 1941, where he would remain as a character dancer until 1978. He was much admired for his expressivity and musicality. He created the roles of Drosselmeyer and Fairy Carabosse in Grigorovich's *The Nutcracker* and *The Sleeping Beauty*. He coached company dancers until 1985. He died in Moscow in 2005.

Suimbike and Kondratov appeared as Ali-Batyr. The ballet was subsequently staged in many republics in versions by local choreographers.

What occurred between the two premières is an example of the shifting sands of cultural policy under Stalin. After the Kirov opening, Yakobson was praised in both *Izvestia* and *Pravda* newspapers and the ballet was subsequently awarded the 1950 Stalin Prize in Literature and Arts. However, on his return to Leningrad after the award ceremony in Moscow, the internal Kirov Theatre newspaper carried an anonymous denunciation entitled 'We have a 'cosmopolitan' in our midst', clearly singling out the Jewish Yakobson (Jews were often accused of being rootless and therefore unpatriotic), despite no name being given. It was four years before he returned to work at the theatre. Yet Yakobson continued to work at the School, the Maly Theatre and other ensembles, so his fall from grace at the Kirov seems to have been the result of localised tensions or in-house rivalry.

In 1950, a victim of pervading Zhdanovism was the projected new Lavrovsky ballet at the Bolshoi, *Ruby Stars*, with a score by Balanchivadze. A love story set in the Caucasus during the war, it appeared on paper to tick every ideological box, but with such glaring mistakes as setting the beginning of the war in Georgia when in fact Russia had been attacked first, the production was definitively withdrawn at its dress rehearsal. It was never performed.

1951 – The death of Vaganova

In November of 1951, Agrippina Vaganova, widely held as the Soviet Union's greatest ballet teacher, died. Since the early days after the revolution, she had dedicated herself to the preservation of the St Petersburg school of classical dancing, facing off the innovators whom she deemed to seek its corruption and bending to the ideological pressures imposed by the regime. Her achievement was simply extraordinary – she had maintained and, arguably, strengthened the technique and standard of the school's graduates which, by the time of her death, numbered among the greatest in the world. Six years after her death, the school to which she had devoted herself was renamed the Vaganova Academy of Russian Ballet in her honour and carries her name to this day.

1951 – Sergeyev becomes director of the Kirov Ballet

In 1951, star dancer Konstantin Sergeyev became company director at the Kirov, a post he held, a hiatus in the mid-1950s notwithstanding, until 1970, bringing what the post-war generation of young dancers increasingly saw as a dead hand over the repertoire and casting. An entrenched traditionalist in some ways, he nevertheless became known for his revisions of the classical canon, bringing socialist realism to the fore and excising courtly gesture and mime. In his first major contribution to the repertoire as director, he staged a new production of *The Sleeping Beauty* in March 1952 which excised much of the surviving mime, streamlined some of the action and added two solos for Prince Désiré – he had created the Act III variation for himself as far back as 1942 when in Molotov. It proved very popular and remained in the Kirov repertoire until 1999. At the first performance, Dudinskaya danced Aurora, Sergeyev was Prince Désiré, Alla Shelest appeared as the Lilac Fairy and Boris Shavrov was the Fairy Carabosse.

Vladimir Burmeister

Vladimir Burmeister (or Bourmeister) emerges as one of the most interesting individuals of this period. Born in 1904 in Viciebsk, Belarus, he joined the Lermontov school in Moscow in 1920 and then trained at GITIS between 1925 and 1929 before joining Moscow's Art Theatre Ballet in 1930 where he became a noted character dancer. He started choreography in 1931 with his own version of *Le Corsaire* for the company. In 1941, he became the chief choreographer and artistic director of its successor the Stanislavsky and Nemirovich-Danchenko Music Theatre, stepping down briefly between 1960 and 1963 before continuing until 1970. He was a prolific dance-maker, creating a wide variety of works notable for their psychologically plausible characters and fully satisfying the demands of socialist realism. His still-important production of *Swan Lake* opened in 1953 using Tchaikovsky's score in close to its original 1877 form; Ivanov's second act was retained (and set by Pyotr Gusev) while Burmeister created new choreography for the first and fourth acts and radically revised the third. The opening night cast was led by *Violetta Bovt as Odette-Odile, Alexey Chichinadze as Prince Siegfried and Alexander Klein as Rothbart. Burmeister staged it for the Paris Opéra in 1960 and in 1961 became the first Soviet choreographer allowed to create new work in the West when he made *The Snow Maiden* for London Festival Ballet. He died in Moscow in 1971.

Violetta Bovt

The first Odette-Odile of Burmeister's *Swan Lake* for the Maly was the American-born Violetta Bovt who spent forty-two years with the Stanislavsky company, thirty-five as a dancer and the remaining seven as a teacher. Her parents moved to the Soviet Union a few years after her birth in Los Angeles in 1927. She graduated from the Bolshoi School in 1944 but, on account of her never having renounced American citizenship, she was not offered a permanent contract with either the Bolshoi or Kirov companies, although she subsequently danced as a guest artist with both. She was not permitted to dance in the United States. She joined the Stanislavsky company and became its reigning ballerina, appearing to great success in classical and contemporary ballets alike on account of her excellent technique and dramatic intensity; among many new ballets in which she appeared, she created the title role in Burmeister's *Joan of Arc* in 1957. During his four years with the company before his move to the Bolshoi, her regular stage partner was *Māris Liepa. In 1986, she left Russia and settled in Columbus, Ohio where she died in 1995.

Regeneration

In April 1952 Igor Moiseyev, founder of the USSR Folk Dance Ensemble, wrote an article bemoaning the lack of ballets on contemporary topics and criticised recent high-profile works such as *Cinderella* and *The Bronze Horseman* for dull choreography and an increasing reliance on stage effects to engage the audience:

> "We have justly criticised many old ballets because they do not combine the dance with healthy thought, but we cannot permit new ballets to have healthy thought un-combined with the dance... classical ballet...was dance plus fairy tale and not fairy tale minus dance".[346]

In April the following year, Galina Ulanova wrote the article 'The artist is answerable' in which she called for greater creativity; new ballets had reduced to a trickle at best – in the three years up to 1953, the Bolshoi produced none at all while the Kirov barely managed the one a year it was supposed to present.

1953 – the Death of Stalin

What had seemed unshakeable imperatives as the ballet companies moved into the 1950s were all called into question with the death of the Great Leader, Joseph Stalin, on 5th March 1953 which also saw the passing of Sergey Prokofiev, the Soviet Union's greatest dance composer who had suffered so greatly under the former's rule. Soviet ballet entered a new era.

News of Stalin's death sent people crying into the streets, such was the sense of loss felt by the population; one suspects that in the corridors of the Bolshoi and the Kirov something akin to sighs of relief could also be heard. State control had reduced the creation of new ballets to almost nothing and the entire form seemed in a state of paralysis – the dancers themselves may well have been of the first order, but artistic policy comprised mainly of not getting caught in the firing line, both metaphorical and actual. At the Kirov, the repertoire seemed preserved in aspic: almost half of performances in the 1954 season were of the 'classics' while the rest were either fairy-tales or Soviet *drambaleti*; only twenty per cent could be said in any way to reflect a 'Soviet outlook' on life. This stasis can be attributed to the long-drawn-out fear engendered by the 1936 'Ballet Fraud' storm which definitively put an end to the post-revolution period of experimentation.

---

346   Ezrahi, *Swans of the Kremlin*, p.104

1953 – *Native Fields*

One new work brought to the Kirov stage some two months after Stalin's death was *Native Fields* by *drambalet* stalwarts Alexey Andreyev[347] and Nina Stukolkina[348] with a score by Nikolai Chervinsky.[349] In many ways it came to exemplify the severe limitations of the form and the near stasis of Soviet ballet. Set on a collective farm and featuring on-stage tractors, the building of the Volga-Don canal and a dam to irrigate the Steppes, it had a short performance life despite its impeccable ideological credentials. Dudinskaya and Sergeyev as the couple Galya and Andrey led the unfortunate cast in what was widely seen as a nail in the coffin of *drambalet*: "Parodies of *Native Fields* were more popular than the performance itself. For many years, the name of the ballet became synonymous with the worst examples of the genre, and its director immortalized his name in history: 'Andreevschina'... served as the concept of the militant ideology of an exhausted form of drama ballet" observed ballet historian Larisa Abyzova.[350] The moribund nature of *drambalet* in the 1950s was summed up by the critic and academic Viktor Vanslov[351] in the observation that in the form "the expression of life in dance was replaced by the image of dances in life".[352]

1953 – *Seven Beauties*

In 1953 ex-Kirov director Pyotr Gusev brought *Seven Beauties* to the stage of the Maly Theatre, a work he had created the year before in Baku, Azerbaijan fully in line with the policy of fusing classical movement and the traditional dancing of the outlying Soviet republics. The superb symphonic score was by the Azerbaijani composer Kara Karayev[353] who had composed it in 1948

---

347   Born in Petrograd in 1920, Andreyev graduated into the Kirov in 1939 where he danced until 1959. He created the role of Ishmael in *Gayaneh*. He began to choreograph during the war and was Chief Choreographer in Minsk, Belarus from 1960 to 1964 and again from 1971 to 1973. He died in St Petersburg in 2004.

348   Born in 1905 in the village of Kuznechko, Tver Province, Stukolkina graduated into GATOB in 1922 where she remained until 1957 as a character dancer of note. She taught at the Kirov from 1950 to 1958 and then in Minsk between 1960 and 1964 and again from 1971 to 1973. She died in St Petersburg in 1999.

349   Born in Leningrad in 1925, Chervinsky became a prolific composer of film scores throughout the 1960s and 70s.

350   Abyzova, *Игорь Бельский. Симфония жизн»и* (*Igor Belsky and the Symphony of Life*), p.108

351   Born in Vyatka (now Kirov) in 1923, Vanslov graduated from the Moscow Conservatoire in 1940 and worked in a number of academic posts associated with the study of the performing arts. He wrote many books including *Grigorovich's ballets and problems of choreography* in 1968 and *What is Socialist Realism* in 1988.

352   Vanslov 'About music and ballet': *Monuments of Historical Thought*, 2007, p.332, as quoted by Rozanova in 'Drambalet – a view from the XXI century'.

353   Born in Baku, Azerbaijan in 1918, Karayev (or Garayev) studied locally before

to mark the eight hundredth anniversary of classical Persian poet Nizami Ganjavi. Gusev created a full-length dance-drama which was an early departure from the strictures of *drambalet*, focussing on expressing action through dance and not mime. The story was taken from Nizami's 1197 text and concerned the banishment of Shah Bahram by his own people for having betrayed both a hunter, Menzer, who had saved his life and his sister, Aisha, whom the Shah kills at the end of the ballet. The 'Vision of the Seven Beauties', side-lined somewhat in Gusev's reworking, nevertheless allowed for an entertaining divertissement. At the Maly, the first performance was given by Vera Stankevich[354] as Aisha, Yuri Litvinienko[355] as Menzer and Veniamin Zimin[356] as the Shah Bahram. As a new ballet it was deemed to affirm "the idea of the moral-ethical excellence of the people over the spineless government".[357] But over and above its perceived political message, Gusev successfully infused classical dancing with oriental steps and arm movements in what became a popular and long-lived work either in his original version or those by other choreographers around the republics.

1954 – *The Tale of the Stone Flower*

In Moscow, Bolshoi director Lavrovsky brought a new work to the stage in February 1954: *The Tale of the Stone Flower*, preliminary work having started as far back as 1949 with the composer Sergey Prokofiev and librettist Levon Atovmyan.[358] The story of the stone-carver Danila's quest to carve a perfect

---

moving to Moscow and taking part in the 1938 Azerbaijani Art *dekada* festival. He studied at the Moscow Conservatoire before returning to Baku in 1941 where he worked thereafter, becoming a leading composer and teacher. He died in Moscow in 1982.

354   Born in Petrograd in 1920, Stankevich graduated into the Maly in 1940; during the war she remained in Leningrad as part of Olga Jordan's ensemble. She danced at the Maly from 1944 to 1964 as a ballerina of noted dramatic projection. She taught at the Vaganova Academy from 1964 to 1983 and also at the Iraqi Ballet School, Baghdad between 1969 and 1971 and again from 1976 to 1978. From 1985 to 2007 she was a teacher-coach with the Classical Ballet Ensemble at the Novgorod Philharmonic. She died in St Petersburg in 2007.

355   Born in Burynovo (now Chernigov), Ukraine in 1914, Litvinenko first trained in Tbilisi before graduating from the Leningrad Choreographic School in 1940. He danced with MALEGOT between 1941 and 1957 in a number of *demi-caractère* roles. He taught at the Vaganova Academy between 1970 and 1976 and died in Leningrad in 1989.

356   Born in Leningrad in 1932, Zimin graduated into the Maly in 1952 where he danced until 1972 and was known as classical dancer with a strong technique and bright temperament. In 1967 he started to teach at the Leningrad Art University, between 1970 and 1972 at the ballet school in Baghdad and since 1972 he has been a classical dance teacher at the Opera Studio of the Leningrad Conservatoire.

357   Swift, *The Art of the Dance in the USSR*, p.192

358   Born in Askhabad (now Ashgabat), Turkmenistan in 1901, Atovmyan studied composition at Tbilisi University before moving to Moscow in 1929. He was assistant director of the Bolshoi Studio between 1934 and 1936. He worked on piano transcriptions

flower for his beloved Katerina from malachite taken from the realm of the Mistress of the Copper Mountain was well known. It came from a popular collection of short stories from the Ural Mountains which was published before the war under the collective title of *The Malachite Box* and in 1947 was made into the Soviet Union's first colour film. Lavrovsky's ballet was in many ways an exemplar of the deadening effect of official meddling in artistic projects, as it became bogged down by repeated demands to alter plot, music and choreography. Despite praise for Ulanova as Katerina and the presence of Plisetskaya as the Mistress of the Copper Mountain, Preobrazhensky as Danila and Ermolayev as Severyan the Bailiff, *The Tale of the Stone Flower* opened to lukewarm reviews and critical advice directed at the choreographer "to find choreographic expression of the central concept: the people's spirit as manifested in their work and their constant striving towards beauty and perfection".[359]

1954 – Paris

A little-known aborted foreign tour in 1954 meant that the Bolshoi's London visit in 1956 was the first major overseas season by a Russian ballet company. In May 1954, the fall of Diên Biên Phu in French Indochina to communist Viet Minh forces meant that forty-seven Russian dancers from both Moscow and Leningrad in Paris had to return to the Soviet Union as a result of French domestic political pressure and the fear that performances would be disrupted by demonstrations if they went ahead. Led by Ulanova, described by *Le Monde* newspaper as the 'Garbo of the Bolshoi', the mixed-company troupe had already landed and spent several days in the capital as part of a planned cultural exchange with the Comédie Française theatre company which was appearing in Russia. Paris had been particularly eager to see the forty-seven Russian dancers, the French ballet world excited by its first view of a tradition, a repertoire and artists they had only read about and perhaps seen on newsreel. It was not to be; the Russian tour was cancelled at the French government's behest and the ensemble departed France. On their return journey to Russia, the dancers stopped in East Berlin, the capital of the communist satellite German Democratic Republic, to give a hastily arranged three-week season housed in the Friedrichstadt-Palast located off the main Unter den Linden thoroughfare. It attracted ballet fans from all over Germany and further afield, the Berlin Wall not yet being in existence. The cream of Russian dance talent – among whom, Dudinskaya, Moiseyeva, Shelest, Struchkova and Ulanova, Kondratov, *Lapauri and Sergeyev – appeared in three programmes comprising whole acts from *Romeo and*

---

of many works including nearly all of Prokofiev's symphonies, ballets and operas. He died in Moscow in 1973.

359   Morrison, *Bolshoi Confidential*, p.325

Juliet, *The Bronze Horseman*, *The Fountain of Bakhchisarai* and *Laurencia* plus scenes from *Shuraleh*, *Cinderella* (in Sergeyev's version) and the Grand Pas from *Raymonda*. Additionally, audiences saw individual pieces including the Krakoviak from *Ivan Susanin*, the *Don Quixote* pas de deux, excerpts from *Swan Lake*, *The Flames of Paris*, *Gayaneh* as well as the show-piece duets *Moszkowsky Waltz* and *Spring Waters* and the solo *The Dying Swan*. In *Dancing Times*, Kurt Peters criticised the "so-called 'realistic realism'" of many of the works he saw, but of the dancing he wrote "I have never seen such leaps, lifts and arabesques, such precise and delicate movement together with magnificent aplomb."[360]

However happy German dance-goers were as a result, the aborted Paris season made very clear that artistic visits and exchanges between the communist East and the 'free' West could and would never be just that – political considerations and imperatives would always dominate such projects; dancers were also representatives of their respective governments and regimes. This was the new reality for ballet dancers, whatever the political hue of their home nation. There were certainly many in society who believed in the fraternity of art and the transcendence of politics by higher cultural ideals but the reality of Cold War politics meant that such beliefs were never the sole or indeed main motivations for sending dancers or companies into 'enemy' territory.

1955 – The return of Lopukhov

Stalin's death brought about what came to be termed 'The Thaw', a relative relaxation of the strictures upon Russian society in general and the arts in particular at the behest of the new leader Nikita Khrushchev. Importantly for ballet, the death of the Great Father allowed for the rehabilitation of the innovative classicist Fyodor Lopukhov who had led the Kirov company in the twenties and again, briefly, in the mid-1940s, and had founded the Maly ballet troupe in the 1930s. But it was not his generation which would bring dynamism and impetus to the Soviet Union's increasingly moribund world of ballet; younger artists would seize the limited opportunities they were given.

Not that it seemed like it at the time. *Drambalet* was the form still approved by the authorities and any tendency to abstract movement (i.e. without a dramatic or narrative purpose) was condemned under the umbrella term of 'formalism'. Ballet had, it was generally believed, been saved from the fripperies of pre-revolutionary society through socialist realism; choreographer Rostislav Zakharov's 1954 manifesto *The Art of the Choreographer* identified folk art and Stanislavsky's theatrical realism as the foundations of Soviet dance. At the Kirov, director-dancer Konstantin Sergeyev and his wife prima ballerina Natalia Dudinskaya reigned supreme, so it was a matter of some surprise that in February 1955 a letter by three

---

360 Peters, *Dancing Times*, July 1954.

company dancers appeared in the newspaper *Pravda*, accusing the pair of dominating the performing schedule and stifling new ideas. This episode can be seen in the wider context of the Soviet leadership's post-war promotion of the cult of youth and a more general desire to revitalise the rigid and formulaic cultural approach of Stalinism. Whatever the extent to which this attack on Sergeyev was orchestrated, nothing can deny its consequences: in March Deputy Minister of Culture Vladimir Kemenov[361] instructed the Kirov Artistic Council to 'renew' itself with a view to kick-starting creativity at the theatre and implementing a reinvigorated policy of producing ballets on Soviet themes. The meeting at which all this and more was said was nothing less than a humiliation for Sergeyev and his directorship and ended with the abolition of his post of chief choreographer and the re-composition of the artistic council which was to be chaired by none other than ex-company director Fyodor Lopukhov.

In the historical sweep of Soviet ballet Lopukhov stood for innovation rather than stasis and was something of a torch-bearer for those who saw dance existing on its own terms and as a physical manifestation of music. *Drambalet* and the dominance of narrative had pushed him aside, but he had survived both their heyday and Stalin's purges, and in 1955 he was once again in a position of influence at his old company and able to strike back for what was termed 'choreographic symphonism'. He saw himself very much in a line with Fokine, Ivanov and Petipa, which continued through him on to Balanchine. Under Lopukhov's influence, matters started to move with some speed: initially, it was the 'radical' choreographer Leonid Yakobson whom he brought to the fore, observing that he possessed "a dance vocabulary that bonds classical and folk techniques in a way that seems natural".[362] However important his influence, his tenure as director of the Kirov only lasted a year when his former deputy at MALEGOT, Boris Fenster, became Chief Choreographer, a post he held until 1959.

1956 – Yakobson's *Spartacus*

A Kirov soloist in the late 1920s and early 30s, Leonid Yakobson, once described as 'like a bomb going off' as much because of his yearning for a new artistic order in dance as for his explosive stage presence, was drawn by many styles, from acrobatics to Duncan and expressionist movement. It was Lopukhov who brought him back to the Kirov and in 1955 commissioned

---

361 Born in 1908 in Ekaterinoslav (now Dnepropetrovsk), Ukraine, Kemenov graduated in art history from Moscow State University in 1930 and taught at GITIS from 1933 to 1938. He was director of the Tretyakov Gallery, Moscow between 1938 and 1940 and was deputy minister of Culture from 1954 to 1956, after which he was the USSR representative to UNESCO for two years. He wrote extensively on art and aesthetics. He served as Vice President of the Academy of Arts for 22 years from 1966. He died in Moscow in 1988.

362 Ross, *Like a Bomb Going Off*, p.157

Spartacus, a full-length ballet for the main stage, despite resistance from within the theatre concerning Yakobson's awkward temperament and his working and artistic styles. *Spartacus* was to become a key work in the history of post-war Soviet ballet, undergoing three incarnations: Yakobson's for the Kirov in 1956 (revised for the Bolshoi in 1962), Igor Moiseyev's for the Bolshoi in 1958 and finally Yuri Grigorovich's in 1968. Central to its importance was the subject matter, the historical figure of Spartacus who between 74-71 BC led a slaves' revolt against their Roman oppressors which was ultimately crushed by the general Crassus. It was perfect material for a society established and defined by revolution – Lenin had referred to Spartacus as "one of the most outstanding heroes of one of the most important slave rebellions".[363] A ballet of this revolutionary story was first discussed during the war but it was only in 1951 that Khachaturian began to write the score in association with the librettist Nikolai Volkov who studied both Plutarch and Appian's accounts of the historical uprising and reworked them, introducing newly created characters of his own invention, such as Crassus' mistress Aegina. Yakobson studied images of Roman life from vases, reliefs and carvings in his research for the ballet and even took some dancers to see the Pergamon Altar in the basement of the Hermitage where it had been transported having been looted from Berlin at the end of the war. *Spartacus* represented the choreographer's artistic credo – Lopukhov reported approvingly the observation "this is not ballet"[364] overheard repeatedly during intervals in performances, commenting that the same had been said of Fokine's works. In a radical approach, Yakobson dispensed with pointe shoes altogether, deeming them unrealistic in the context of Ancient Rome and, in favouring 'plastique' movement, turned his back on purely classical dancing in a series of episodes from the life of the hero rather than a continuous narrative. It premièred in late December 1956 to great popular success; scenically large and ponderous (the American critic Walter Terry who saw it in its revised version during the Bolshoi's 1962 American tour, observed that it "out De Milled De Mille"[365] in a reference to the early film-maker who shot on a monumental scale), Yakobson's *Spartacus* contained much that was new, not least an overt sexuality and a new freedom of movement style. The opulent sets and costumes were by Valentina Khodasevich. On first night, the title role was taken by Askold Makarov, a tall and athletic company dancer who looked suitably heroic opposite Inna Zubkovskaya as Phrygia, Robert Gerbek as Crassus and the striking Aegina of Alla Shelest.

---

363   ibid, p.243
364   ibid. p.251
365   Swift, *The Art of the Dance in the USSR* p.141

6
Cold War Dances
1956 - 1962

1956 – The First Bolshoi Tour

In contrast to Stalin's domestic focus, Khrushchev thought on a global scale, and the first Bolshoi tour to the UK was born out of his outward-looking policy in international relations and a rethinking of the Soviet Union's position on the world stage. In April 1956 he accepted Prime Minister Anthony Eden's invitation to visit the United Kingdom, one of the few concrete results of which was agreement for a ballet exchange between the two countries. In the increasingly febrile context of the Cold War, the Bolshoi Ballet's visit to London can be interpreted as part of a wider Soviet charm offensive designed to show the USSR and what it represented in a more favourable light. Western overtures had been made during Stalin's rule, with Covent Garden's General Director David Webster inviting the Bolshoi to London as early as 1946, Ulanova was offered some guest performances at the theatre in 1952 and a request for the company to come to the USA was allegedly rebuffed by the Great Father himself with the retort that, much as he would like to agree, he was having troubles on the Manchurian border and the company was needed there.

Much has been written about the run-up to and the Bolshoi season at Covent Garden itself from a Western perspective, but little is said about their effect on the Russian ballet world. It is important to note that the first-ever company tour was made by the Bolshoi and not the Leningrad-based Kirov which in dance terms could lay claim to greater purity of style. The Bolshoi had become the Soviet state's preferred company, its ascendency over Leningrad's former imperial ensemble a post-revolution phenomenon. It was therefore Moscow's ballet company which was entrusted with the first foreign tours.

Earlier appearances abroad

In 1956, the artists of the Bolshoi were not the first Soviet Russian dancers to venture abroad; there had been a long-standing tradition even under the tsars to send performers outside Russia which dated back to the very beginning of the nineteenth century and extended to the early pre-First World War Ballets Russes seasons in the West. After the revolution, cultural borders initially remained relatively porous – Bolshoi ballerina Viktorina Kriger toured Europe and North American between 1920 and 1922 and was in the USA again in 1935 with a folk-dance ensemble. A French-Russian treaty in 1932 allowed Asaf and Sulamith Messerer to dance in Paris to much acclaim and Marina Semyonova travelled to the French capital in 1935 to dance in *Giselle* at the Opéra. The USSR having been given diplomatic recognition by the USA in 1933, Vakhtang Chabukiani and Tatiana Vecheslova were given permission to tour the States in 1934, and there was a steady trickle of mostly politically and socially motivated Western performers and groups who travelled to the USSR, including the modern dancer Anna Sokolow.[366] Several Russian dancers danced as guest artists mainly in satellite countries and other communist states; Galina Ulanova appeared in Vienna in 1945, Asaf Messerer and Irina Tikhomirnova in 1951. Stalin's death allowed for more opportunities for artistic travel so, from 1953 onwards, the UK began to see more Russian performers, including wife and husband Raisa Struchkova and Alexander Lapauri[367] who danced in London during 1954 British-Soviet Friendship month.

1956 – Paris

In the early summer of 1956, the Stanislavsky Nemirovich-Danchenko company appeared in Paris, presenting Burmeister's *Swan Lake*, "although not so brilliantly danced (as the Bolshoi version), even better dramatically",[368] an evening of excerpts from the company repertoire and *Shore of Happiness*. Augmenting their ranks were the young dancers *Alla Osipenko and Svyatoslav Kuznetsov,[369] 'on loan' from the Kirov. The company's performances prompted both public enthusiasm and outraged reactions from the French critics for whom this was the first exposure to a world of

---

366 Born in Hartford, Connecticut in 1910, Sokolow trained under Martha Graham with whose company she danced until 1938. She formed the first of several companies of her own in 1934 which lasted until the late 1960s. She dealt with social issues and uncompromising contemporary subjects. In later years she taught at the Julliard School. She died in New York in 2000.

367 Born in Moscow in 1926, Lapauri graduated into the Bolshoi company in 1944 and became one of its leading *premiers danseurs*, allying strong technique, musicality, presence and great expressivity. He taught at the Bolshoi school from 1946 onwards and co-choreographed two ballets, *Song of the Woods* (1960) and *Lieutenant Kijé* (1963). He danced often and successfully with his wife, ballerina Raisa Struchkova. He died in a car crash in Moscow in 1975.

368 Clarke, *The Ballet Annual*, Vol 12, p.102

369 Born in Leningrad in 1930, Kuznetsov graduated into the Kirov in 1950 where he danced until 1970. Known for his beautiful line and soft jump, he excelled in lyrical works, although he appeared successfully in main roles across the whole repertoire. From 1971 to 1973 he was the chief choreographer of the Leningrad Theatre of Musical Comedy and between 1972 and 1992 he taught at the Leningrad Institute of Theatre, Music and Cinematography, rising to become Dean of the Faculty of Dramatic Art. He died in Rome in 1992.

ballet which had not known Diaghilev, Massine or Lifar. The subsequent rebuttals from their Soviet counterparts bemoaned a fundamental lack of understanding in France that the essential purpose of a ballet was the ideological concept behind it.

1956 – London

It was the Bolshoi Ballet's four-week London visit which became fixed as a turning point in east-west cultural relations and the first major western showcase for Soviet Russian dance. In its run-up there were many moments of genuine fear that it would not take place, worries which lasted until the Covent Garden curtains rose on the first night of *Romeo and Juliet* on 3rd October with Galina Ulanova and her partner *Yuri Zhdanov in the title roles, Sergei Koren as Mercutio and Alexander Lapauri as Paris. In August, a Russian shot-putter Nina Ponomareva was arrested for shop-lifting five hats from the C&A shop on Oxford Street, London, sending the Soviet administration and the press into a frenzy, calling into question the entire Bolshoi tour on the grounds of the dangers of being 'subjected to outrages and other forms of persecution'.

The atmosphere in Moscow was tense in the months ahead of the journey to the UK with much speculation about who would and would not be allowed to travel. Certainly, only dancers of whom the state could be entirely sure would be sent; there was no place for 'tourists' who would be more susceptible to seduction by western fripperies. Ahead of the company's departure for London, much ideological examination of the dancers took place, resulting in Maya Plisetskaya, one of the three ballerinas who were to carry the tour, being refused permission to travel only two months beforehand. This left Galina Ulanova and Raisa Struchkova to shoulder the burden of the twenty-five-performance season, with exhausting and injurious consequences on Ulanova who, despite her fragile health, had to take on even more in addition to her existing lion's share of performances. But, to the Soviet authorities the personal consequences to a comrade were as nothing to the potential damage from a renegade artist such as Plisetskaya, who came from a family deemed tainted by ideological impurity[370] and was herself outspoken and somewhat careless in her choice of the company she kept. No matter that London was expecting her, that she was a box-office draw and that she was a truly magnificent dancer, she remained in Russia and was only allowed to travel abroad three years later. Plisetskaya was characteristically not prepared to take such a slap lying down and gleefully engaged in a revival of the 1937

---

370 Plisetskaya's father, Mikhail Plisetsky, a Soviet official, was arrested in 1937 and executed the following year, while her mother, the actress Rachel Messerer, was arrested in 1938, imprisoned for a few years, then held in a camp together with her infant son, Azary. Maya was adopted by her aunt, Bolshoi ballerina Sulamith Messerer, and Azary by his uncle Asaf Messerer.

production of *Swan Lake* for the so-called 'disenfranchised' section of the Bolshoi company which remained in the USSR, a production which became the talk of Moscow. With input from her uncle Asaf Messerer, from Marina Semyonova who oversaw the 'white' Act II and IV acts, and from Anatoly Kuznetsov working on Acts I and III, she triumphed as Odette-Odile. She was also absent from the Bolshoi's Paris tour in 1958 and only allowed onto the foreign travel list to New York the following year after she had showed sufficient contrition.

Ultimately, despite numerous last-minute concerns – it was rumoured just two days before opening night that Ulanova would not come – too much rested on the London visit for it not to take place and for both Covent Garden and the Soviet administration it was financially too important to fail. Ulanova came, as did another 150 Bolshoi dancers, and their first night passed into legend. The company brought *Swan Lake* and *Giselle*, and two *drambaleti*, *Romeo and Juliet* and *The Fountain of Bakhchisarai*. Company dancer Ekaterina Sheveleva recorded: "English newspapers could not avoid writing of the exceptional triumph of the Bolshoi artists in London," adding that "...the press passed over in silence the concluding performance...with its more than half-hour ovation".[371] On 21st October, the BBC aired a recording of the second act of *Swan Lake* with Ulanova as Odette and Nikolai Fadeyechev as Siegfried to an audience of some 9.5 million; the Bolshoi had made a national impact. By the time the season closed on 29th October, Ulanova had danced Juliet on six occasions, Giselle and the second act of *Swan Lake* in a total of thirteen appearances (it must be remembered that at the time Russian principal dancers performed on average about four times a month); she was also forty-six years of age. On her return to Russia, she was hailed as a 'Hero of Labour' but, exhausted, was too unwell to attend a celebratory event held in her honour.

The success in London of the Bolshoi was unquestioned, although a clash between the post-Diaghilev western and Soviet Russian views of ballet was bound to occur. The strength and technical mastery of the Russians "leave us standing" in the words of the monthly magazine *Dancing Times*, "(they) carry everything before them",[372] even if there were doubts raised about some of the 'old-fashioned' quality of the productions (something of an Achilles heel for the Russians, given the domestic demands for scenic realism), the paucity of choreographic invention – Noel Goodwin in the *Daily Express* wrote the review 'Incredible! Superb! But is it new?'[373] – and the excision of small steps (*petite batterie*) and gestures. The company's return to Russia was greeted with unabashed cultural triumphalism from the regime with

---

371 Swift, *The Art of the Dance in the USSR*, p.260
372 Clarke, 'The Bolshoi Ballet: The Four Ballets' in *Dancing Times*, Vol.48, No.554
373 Goodwin, The Daily Express, 4th October 1956

the Bolshoi portrayed as the bringer of socialist truth to a misguided West. Deputy Minister of Culture Vasily Pakhomov stated that Western ballet had developed as "...a method to distract the attention of the spectator from the unsightly capitalist reality surrounding him".[374] The superiority of Russian art became a politico-artistic trope over the decades following the Bolshoi visit and is one which still exists in some form today; certainly, the quotation from Pushkin's *Eugene Onegin* 'the soulful flight of the Russian Terpsichore' was repeated again and again from this time to emphasise the unique quality of Soviet Russian dancing.

On a political level, the Bolshoi tour to London was also a triumph, a triumph for the Soviet cultural project; the Bolshoi had been confirmed in itself and received external validation for its artistic policy after decades of isolation. That is not to say that the reservations expressed by foreign observers were not taken to heart, even in official circles – a party meeting of the ballet company elicited the comment "...we don't have the right to close our eyes to just criticism".[375] Addressing criticisms of an under-reliance on the power of pure movement, Pakhomov commented that: "The language of ballet is dance, and it must be allotted a fitting place in choreographic productions. After all, it's not a secret that quite often ballets emerge here where pantomime occupies a significantly bigger place than dance."[376] Artistic soul-searching and agenda-pursuing took place, with some arguing for the reinstatement of the elements of mime and danced divertissements excised during the cultural purges of the 1930s. On a personal level, those Soviet dancers who travelled abroad had the chance not only to see performances by foreign ensembles but also to share class with their dancers and thus were exposed to influences from outside their cultural world. In a discussion with Culture Minister Ekaterina Furtseva,[377] attended by the photographer Albert Kahn in 1961, Ulanova observed that "our trips abroad and our contacts with Western countries have shown us that they've learned from the Russian ballet school; but at the same time we've seen that there are things we can learn from them".[378] Even if in 1956 the artists of the Bolshoi had not seen many British dancers in performance, they had been struck by

---

374   Ezrahi, *Swans of the Kremlin*, p.161

375   ibid p.163

376   ibid.

377   Born in 1910 in Vyshny Volochyok, Tver Province, Furtseva joined the Communist youth movement *Komsomol* in 1924 and rose up through the party structure thereafter. She graduated in chemical engineering in Moscow in 1938 and continued to work on party committees. Under Khrushchev, she became a member of the seven-strong ruling Presidium of the Central Committee of the Communist Party in 1956. Her fall from favour began in 1959 – she was made Minister of Culture in 1960, a post she held until her death. She died suddenly at her dacha in 1974.

378   Kahn, *Days with Ulanova*, p. 99.

the pluralism, experimentation and general artistic freedom enjoyed by their counterparts, although in subsequent years something of a view developed in Russia that Western dancers were cold and detached. In London, there had been no opportunity for the Russian dancers to see performances of the Sadler's Wells Ballet, but company director Leonid Lavrovsky had seen a rehearsal by Festival Ballet and been scathing in his judgment. Of a new work he saw, he observed "this isn't even Duncan, but some tenth school of the twenty-fifth student of Duncan. Something has been collected from all movements."[379] The dismissal of the choreographic developments in the West after the artistic schism brought about by the Russian revolution was something to which the regime would repeatedly return in subsequent years, but in the light of western company visits to Russia, with decreasing certainty. All this being said, in 1956 there was something of a collective sigh of relief in Russia that its own vision of ballet had been validated. The Bolshoi's spectacular London success was also confirmation for both sides of the Iron Curtain of the worth of the developing phenomenon of company visits, tours and seasons abroad and, for the Soviet regime, of not only a powerful propaganda weapon but also a lucrative source of foreign currency.

1957 – MALEGOT and Boyarsky

By the end of the 1950s, Leningrad's MALEGOT, where the ballet company continued to present its own distinct repertoire, began to see more of a focus on the revival of classical ballets with the express purpose of improving technical standards. The first of these was the third act Grand Pas from Petipa's *Paquita* in 1957, staged by Konstantin Boyarsky, a choreographer who came to specialise in the restitution of 'lost' or forgotten ballets. Born in Petrograd in 1915, he graduated into the Kirov in 1935 where he remained as a dancer until the outbreak of war in 1941, dancing a variety of roles including Ivan the Fool in *The Little Humpbacked Horse* and Jean in *The Flames of Paris*. During that time, he also graduated both from the *régisseur* faculty of the Leningrad Theatre Institute and Lopukhov's three-year choreographers' course at the Choreographic School. Having been a dancer and choreographer at the Leningrad Musical Comedy Theatre from 1945 to 1956, he joined the Maly where he remained until 1967, becoming a major creative force. In 1961 he brought Fokine's *Petrushka*[380] to the Russian stage for the first time since 1920, as well as creating many original works of his own. He was noted for the directness and clarity of his choreographic vision. Maly dancer, fellow choreographer and later company director Nikolai Boyarchikov[381] recalled:

---

379 Ezrahi, *Swans of the Kremlin* p.165
380 See entry '1961 – *Petrushka*'
381 Born in Leningrad in 1935, Boyarchikov started to dance with the evacuated Leningrad School in Perm before returning to continue his studies in the city after the

"Boyarsky wrote quickly, easily and very musically: he didn't just put dance and music together, he used the logic of the musical themes or the rhythmic pulse. He wanted to create something new; he had original ideas. Boyarsky was wonderfully skilled at duets, able to feel the subtle nuances of a relationship."[382]

In 1959, Boyarsky was responsible for engaging the ex-Kirov principal Semyon Kaplan[383] to teach the *classe de perfection* at the Maly Theatre which improved the overall standard of dancing within the company and developed the virtuosity of the young dancer Valery Panov.[384] After the Maly, Boyarsky became the artistic director of the Leningrad Ice Ballet until his death in the city in 1974.

1957 – Grigorovich and *The Stone Flower*

Spearheading change within the Kirov was Yuri Grigorovich, a Lopukhov protégé, and sometime company dancer. Born in Leningrad in 1927, he graduated from the Choreographic School into the Kirov in 1946, excelling in *demi-caractère* parts until he finally ended his dancing career in 1962. He began to create movement firstly with students, choreographing Glinka's *Valse-Fantaisie* for the School's 1956 graduation performance, and received his first major commission in 1957 from the Kirov. He provided a new take on Lavrovsky's less-than-well received 1954 Bolshoi production of *The Tale of the Stone Flower*, a project first intended for Konstantin Sergeyev, but then assigned to him given the latter's paucity of invention. Grigorovich, buzzing with new ideas, took both Lavrovsky's concept and Prokofiev's score and

---

war. He graduated in 1954 to the Maly where he performed until 1971 in character parts. He was chief choreographer at Perm Ballet until 1977 when he returned to the Maly firstly as choreographer before becoming director, a post he held until 2007. In 2001 he became director of the Ballet Master Training Faculty at the Vaganova Academy. He died in 2020.

382   Mikhailovsky Theatre website. '100th anniversary of choreographer Konstantin Boyarsky'.

383   Born in St Petersburg in 1912, Kaplan graduated into the Kirov in 1930 where he danced until 1959 in the full range of the repertoire, from the classics to new work. After Chabukiani's departure from Leningrad he was considered the company's finest Solor in *La Bayadère*, a role he carefully coached long after he had stopped performing it. He taught at the Leningrad Choreographic School with interruptions from 1936 to 1970, at the Maly from 1959 to 1964 and also at the Kirov. He died in Leningrad in 1983.

384   Born in Vitebsk, Belorussia in 1938, Panov graduated into the Maly in 1957 where he danced until 1963 when he transferred to the Kirov. A dynamic dancer who excelled in created roles including Sergeyev's Hamlet and in Kasatkina and Vasilyov's *Creation of the World*, in 1972 he applied with his wife Galina for exit visas to emigrate to Israel, their plight becoming an international cause célèbre. In 1974 they were permitted to leave Russia. Panov was guest choreographer and principal dancer with the Berlin Opera Ballet between 1977 and 1983 and artistic director of the Royal Ballet of Flanders from 1984 to 1986.

injected them with new life. He intended the work to represent something genuinely new, describing it as a 'youth production' and dedicated it to the 1957 Sixth International Youth Festival. *The Stone Flower* opened at the Kirov in April; as a ballet it was far from perfect, but it represented a milestone in the development of Soviet ballet with a new level of expressivity brought to what was a typical tale of the workers triumphant. Led by Alexander Gribov as the stone-cutter Danila, the excellent company character artist Anatoly Gridin[385] as the Bailiff Severyan and two new-generation dancers, Irina Kolpakova as Katerina and Alla Osipenko as the Mistress of the Copper Mountain, it brought fresh choreographic air to the stale atmosphere of the repertoire. The ballet was eagerly acquired by the Bolshoi two years after its Leningrad première, when Maya Plisetskaya danced the Mistress of the Copper Mountain, *Marina Kondratieva appeared as Katerina, Nikolai Fadeyechev was Danila and Vladimir Levashov,[386] Severyan. The somewhat untidy narrative progression apart, it represented something of a return to dance for dance's sake, containing large sections of pure movement. It did not jettison *drambalet* completely, but its flavour was decidedly new, emphasised by Simon Virsaladze's radical settings, the first of many collaborations between choreographer and designer.

Drambalet called into question

Reaction to *The Stone Flower* was mixed, with champions and detractors of both *drambalet* and 'choreographic symphonism' having their say and even the company divided between traditionalists and modernisers. Future company ballerina Gabriela Komleva[387] wrote:

> "*The Stone Flower* revealed the dissatisfaction of a part of the company with the repertoire... A split appeared within the company: some thirsted for novelty, the usual suited the rest."[388]

---

385 Born in Novosibirsk in 1929, Gridin studied ballet locally and performed with the Novosibirsk company between 1945 and 1950 before moving to the Leningrad Choreographic School from where he graduated in 1952. He appeared at the Kirov until 1982 in a variety of character roles across the repertoire which he invested with great detail and depth. He worked especially fruitfully with Grigorovich and Yakobson. He was ballet master at the Teatr Weikl, Warsaw from 1975 to 1977, taught choreography in Leipzig between 1982 and 1983 and then coached at the Kirov from 1984 to 1989.

386 Born in Moscow in 1923, Levashov graduated into the Bolshoi in 1941 and appeared with the company until 1978 as a character artist of considerable refinement and distinction. In 1966 he was the first Drosselmeyer in Grigorovich's *The Nutcracker*. He coached and taught at the Bolshoi from 1978 to 1985. He died in Moscow in 2005.

387 Born in Leningrad in 1938, Komleva graduated into the Kirov company in 1957 where she remained until 1988, performing all the major roles of the repertoire. From 1971 to 1978, she taught at the Vaganova Academy and then moved into staging ballets around the world. She taught at the Kirov from 1979.

388 As quoted by Ezrahi, *Swans of the Kremlin*, p.130

The two sides lined up against each other in many forums, including the 1960 All-Union Choreographic Conference held in Moscow at which Konstantin Sergeyev launched an attack on the innovators and mounted a defence of *drambalet*, arguing against the so-called "theory of the world of agitated feeling."[389] Rostislav Zakharov, also a *drambalet* conservative, summed up the two sides as he saw them:

> "Two currents were outlined in the discussion: one defends realism in the art of dance, the other – anti-realistic tendencies adversarial to these concepts. After all, the most agitated feelings, if they are separated from ideas, lead to a completely incorrect abstract conception – 'the world of feelings' in general."[390]

The debate raged on, prompting Ulanova to write in *Izvestia* that the new guard deserved encouragement: "It is easiest to stick a label on somebody. For example, Igor Belsky is sick with abstractionism, Yuri Grigorovich is a modernist. That's it."[391] Despite negative commentary, Grigorovich continued to create striking new work, following *The Stone Flower* with *The Legend of Love* in 1961 and laying the beginnings of a career which led to the directorship of the Bolshoi in 1964 and the post of Chief Choreographer. On Grigorovich's side, Lopukhov stated that he had "restored symphonic chronicling, in which actions, conditions, moods, lyrical thoughts, and patterns of nature all come together in a complex picture".

In 1957, commentator Yuri Slonimsky acknowledged the earlier period of artistic stagnation in ballet and the failure of the quest for contemporary themes which could work in the medium of dance. Crucially, he rejected much of the fundamental reasoning which underpinned *drambalet*: "our fault lay in the applying to the ballet the same measure of realism as to a stage play or motion picture, in spite of the fact that realism in each of these arts is expressed in its own specific way".[392] He continued: "To dress the artists up in costumes of to-day and have them act against a background of contemporary urban or rural scenery does not solve the problem of the contemporary in dance... The dogmatic approach to realism had often drained our ballets on present-day themes of their dance content."[393]

The Stone Flower represented a significant shift in Soviet ballet and ushered in a period of renewed experimentation which itself reflected developments in the arts and society at large. It signalled the revival of 'symphonic' or abstract ballet which would often take the form of a single short act. Alongside

---

389   As quoted in *Soviet Ballet*, 'Dancing the heritage of humanism'.
390   ibid.
391   Quoted by Ezrahi, The *Swans of the Kremlin*, p.134
392   *The Ballet Annual*, Vol. 12 p.92
393   ibid pp.92-93

the multiplication of structure, Soviet ballet also saw a broadening of its vocabulary with a resurgence of interest in the revival of choreographic traditions, the use of small stage forces and the incorporation of modern dance movements. The hegemony of narrative ballet was being eroded by an increasing spread of allegorical and metaphorical works which themselves evoked some of the ballets of the 1920s and a broadening of themes deemed suitable for dance. This new period lasted into the 1980s, expanding even further, it can be argued, with the opening up of Soviet ballet and society under the reforms of Mikhail Gorbachev.

1957 – *Othello*

Vakhtang Chabukiani had, since his return to his native Georgia in 1941, built up the ballet company based in the capital Tbilisi. In late 1957, he created *Othello* to music by Alexey Machavariani[394] which Moscow was able to see a few months later as part of the capital's Georgian cultural festival. Chabukiani himself took the part of the Moor of Venice to great success and provided the superb roles of Desdemona and Iago for the ensemble's ballerina Vera Tsignadze[395] and second *premier danseur* Zurab Kikaleishvili.[396] The ballet was taken into the repertoire of the Kirov in early 1960 with Chabukiani and subsequently company principal Boris Bregvadze as Othello, Alla Osipenko and Irina Kolpakova alternating as Desdemona and Svyatoslav Kuznetsov as a pantherine Iago. It was both an example of the continuing Russian fascination with, and respect for, the work of William Shakespeare, as well as a clear shift away from overtly political narrative.

1957 – Foreign Guests

In the spirit of the Thaw and Cold War cultural politics, 1957 also saw performances in the USSR by foreign guest artists. Having recently left The Royal Ballet, Beryl Grey[397] became one of the first Western dancers since

---

394 Born in Gori, Georgia in 1913, Aleksandre (Alexey) Machavariani graduated from the Tbilisi Conservatoire in 1936 and became a successful composer of string quartets, seven symphonies, a violin concerto and several stage-works. He was the artistic director of the Georgian State Symphony Orchestra between 1956 and 1958 and directed the Composers' Union of Georgia from 1962 until 1968. He died in Tbilisi in 1995.

395 Born in Baku, Azerbaijan in 1924, Tsignadze graduated from the Baku Choreographic School in 1943, joining the Georgian National Opera Theatre in 1946 where she rapidly developed a strong stage presence allied to a secure technique. She died in Tbilisi in 2016.

396 Born in Batumi, Georgia in 1924, Kikaleishvili trained in Tbilisi and Moscow before joining the Georgian National Opera theatre in 1942, dancing major roles in both classical and new ballets. He was also a prolific choreographer who worked across the USSR and abroad.

397 Born in London in 1927, Grey (born Groom) was an early pupil of Ninette de Valois, joining the Sadler's Wells Ballet in 1941. A tall, strong and elegant dancer, she danced

the revolution to appear with the Bolshoi Ballet. In December she danced Odette-Odile in *Swan Lake* in Moscow, having received coaching from Marina Semyonova and Asaf Messerer. Her Siegfried was the Bolshoi's Yuri Kondratov after her chosen partner, Chabukiani, injured himself in rehearsal. After her performance, the British ambassador gave a reception at his embassy which was the first occasion that anyone from the Bolshoi had accepted an invitation to enter. Grey and Kondratov subsequently repeated their performance in Kiev and then appeared in *Giselle* in Tbilisi and Leningrad where she watched the Kirov dancers closely, observing subsequently that they "lacked the spontaneity of the Bolshoi artists and their beautiful arms".[398] At the same time as Grey, Paris Opéra ballet *étoiles* Liane Daydé[399] and Michel Renault[400] were also guesting in *Giselle* in both Leningrad and Moscow. Another foreign visitor to Russia was the Cuban ballerina Alicia Alonso[401] who appeared in Moscow in 1957 and in Riga and Leningrad the year after.

Appearances by foreign guest artists continued piecemeal thereafter. Invitations were extended in August 1960 to the South African-born ballerina Nadia Nerina[402] to dance with the Bolshoi and the Kirov. A bright and vivacious virtuoso dancer who had so successfully created the role of

---

with the company (later The Royal Ballet) until 1957 when she became a freelance artist. In 1964 she guested in China with the Peking and Shanghai companies. From 1968 to 1979 she was director of London Festival Ballet and has staged numerous works around the globe. She was made a DBE in 1988.

398   Grey, *For the Love of Dance*, chap 67.

399   Born in Paris in 1932, Daydé graduated into the Paris Opéra Ballet in 1945, becoming an *étoile* in 1950. A small, brilliant dancer, she was a valued and versatile artist. In 1960 she left Paris to become an international freelance artist. After retirement from dancing, she went into teaching and then became director of the dance department of the Conservatoire à rayonnement régional de Paris.

400   Born in Paris in 1927, Renault graduated into the Paris Opéra Ballet in 1944, becoming an *étoile* in 1946. A dancer of immense strength and versatility, he shone throughout the repertoire in a wide variety of roles. He left the Opéra in 1959 and worked as a freelance choreographer. He taught at L'École de Danse de l'Opéra de Paris between 1982 and 1990. He died in Paris in 1993.

401   Born in Havana in 1920, Alonso trained locally and then in the School of American Ballet, New York. She started to dance in musicals before joining Ballet Caravan in 1939. Renowned for her interpretation of Giselle and her stage partnership with Igor Youskevitch, she created the brilliant ballerina role in Balanchine's *Theme and Variations*. She returned to Cuba in 1948 to found Ballet Alicia Alonso which became the Ballet Nacional de Cuba after Fidel Castro's 1959 revolution. She remained as its director and that of the school until her death in Havana in 2019.

402   Born in Cape Town in 1927, Nerina trained locally and moved to London in 1945 completing a year at the Sadler's Wells Ballet School before joining the Sadler's Wells Theatre Ballet and then the Sadler's Wells Ballet in 1947 as a soloist. She became a principal dancer in 1952, dancing a varied repertoire and creating numerous new works – she was a particular favourite of Frederick Ashton and distinguished herself in his ballets. She retired from dancing in 1969. She died in 2008 in Beaulieu-sur-Mer near Nice.

Lise in Frederick Ashton's *La Fille mal gardée* at Covent Garden in January of that year, she appeared in Moscow in December 1960 in *Swan Lake*, partnered by Fadeyechev and then in Leningrad in January 1961 in *Giselle* partnered by Sergeyev. Nerina delighted Russian audiences with her vibrant interpretations and they warmly welcomed her again on the first tour to the USSR that summer by The Royal Ballet.[403]

1957 – the Bolshoi in Japan

The success of the Bolshoi's tour to London prompted several more visits abroad. Subsequent to the joint declaration on peaceful cooperation signed by the USSR and Japan in 1956, the company visited Tokyo and Osaka the following year, the first visit by a ballet company from Russia since 1916 when three concert performances were given by the Mariinsky company. Olga Lepeshinskaya and her stage partner Vladimir Preobrazhensky led a fifty-strong ensemble on a six-week tour to Japan in late August of 1957. The ballerina contributed three articles to the magazine *Sovietskaya Zhenshchina* (Soviet Woman) in 1958, giving her impressions of the visit during which she noted the genuine enthusiasm of the Japanese audiences and "the friendship of people who have deep common interests".[404] During the tour, the dancers performed in stadia as well as conventional theatres to some 60,000 people. Since 1957, the Bolshoi Ballet has visited Japan seventeen times to date.

1957 – The Ministry of Culture Decree

Leonid Yakobson's 1956 *Spartacus* had been the first major ballet work created under what amounted to a new cultural regime, prompted in February 1956 by the so-called 'Secret Speech'. It was delivered by the new leader Nikita Khrushchev and did nothing less than denounce Stalin to the Central Committee of the Communist Party. While a perceptible thaw in the arts had already started since the death of the Great Father, the official sanction for greater freedom thus given was the starting gun for the cautious innovations of the late 1950s.

An additional spur was given by a Ministry of Culture decree issued on the last day of 1957 entitled 'On measures for the further development of Soviet ballet art'. The political background for this signal change in the regime's cultural policy was Khrushchev's move away from Stalinism and towards the demands of new, Cold War politics. In the years after the revolution, Russia's ballet had been re-purposed from imperial plaything to proletarian art form, but the 1950s and 60s heralded a two-fold approach, the first domestic, the second international.

---

403   The Sadler's Wells Ballet company was granted a Royal Charter on 31st October 1956 re-naming it The Royal Ballet.

404   Sapanzha, 'The first tour of the Soviet ballet of the Bolshoi Theater of the USSR in Japan (1957)': Memories by Olga Lepeshinskaya', p.70

In domestic terms, ballet was a powerful propaganda tool, touching the lives of those who saw it. That exposure had grown immeasurably since tsarist times when St Petersburg and Moscow (with Warsaw as a quasi-colonial add-on) were the only places to see performances. From the mid-1930s onwards, a conscious policy was enacted of exporting ballet to the whole of the USSR by means of training dancers in Moscow and Leningrad so that they could return to their home republics, as well as the sending of teachers and choreographers to work with local dancers and troupes. By 1947 the pre-revolutionary ballet axis of the Soviet and old imperial capitals and their schools had been joined by some twenty-nine more opera and ballet theatres and thirteen additional ballet schools.

The international dimension took the form of ballet's use as a propaganda tool in the rivalry across the Iron Curtain and a demonstration of the superiority of the Soviet experiment in producing world-class art and culture. This was an aspect which would colour the relationship between ballet and the regime until almost the end of the Soviet Union. A show-off performance of *Swan Lake* at the Bolshoi Theatre for high-ranking visitors, and international tours presenting the cream of the country's dancing talent were both powerful weapons in the country's jockeying for cultural supremacy which, in itself, formed part of the wider propaganda war between East and West. Historian David Caute observes:

> "With the ostensible goal of promoting understanding between peoples of rival nations and the clandestine ambition to secure the sympathies of the citizens of their foe, the Soviet government utilized members of both the Kirov and the Bolshoi as cultural representatives on the other side of the Iron Curtain."[405]

The decree opened with an emphasis on Soviet ballet's long and illustrious heritage going back into imperial times and the preservation of its best aspects while taking the art form forward. It was in that context of continuity that it proceeded to outline the need to create new Soviet ballets which would engage and delight on the same level as the great classics of the past. Thus, a focus on creativity was made in order to produce new masterpieces. This was not in itself original; the post-revolutionary Commissar for Enlightenment, Anatoly Lunacharsky, had said more or less the same in the 1920s and used the argument of creating the new from the old as a weapon with which to defend ballet as an art form in the face of forceful arguments for iconoclasm and the establishment of a cultural *tabula rasa* in order to create a fully proletarian culture.

The 1957 decree emphasised the need to disseminate examples of good works across the republics and was strong in its support of filming ballets to

---

405 Caute, *The Dancer Defects: The Struggle for Cultural Supremacy during the Cold War*, p. 3

be shown to as wide an audience as possible; the Kirov's *The Sleeping Beauty* and the Bolshoi's *The Red Poppy* were specifically mentioned. It also insisted on the production of more publications on ballet as well as an increase in more detailed criticisms in newspapers and journals. This was a wholescale attempt to increase the profile of the art form throughout the USSR and further afield and would characterise the state's approach for decades to follow.

1957 – *The Path of Thunder*

Post-Stalinist Russia, fully engaged in a propaganda war with the United States and the West, sought actively to extend its influence around the world, emphasising its egalitarian and proletarian credentials in countries emerging from colonial rule. One area of focus was Africa and both the promulgation of communist thought and the support for indigenous art forms became political targets for the regime. As with previous reactions to international developments, the world of ballet did not stand immune to such policies; Sergeyev's *The Path of Thunder* premièred at the Kirov on the same day as the decree was issued. Set to a score by Karayev which included African hymns and rhythms, it was a version of South African author Peter Abrahams' 1948 novel depicting a young mixed-race man, Lenny, and Sari, a white landowner's daughter under the menacing shadow of enforced segregation. The narrative was much simplified by the librettist Slonimsky who reduced it to a struggle between good native Africans and bad colonials. Sergeyev himself took the role of Lenny and Dudinskaya, that of Sari, with Belsky as Mako. The ballet was subsequently acquired by several companies including the Bolshoi in 1959 with Lepeshinskaya and Kondratov taking the lead roles.

'Revolutionary' ballets at MALEGOT

February 1958 saw the première of *Gavroche*, a three-act ballet choreographed by Vladimir Varkovitsky based on the street urchin character in Victor Hugo's 1862 novel *Les Misérables*. With a score by Boris Bitov[406] and Evgeny Kornblit;[407] it featured company ballerina Galina Isayeva in the title role. It was the first of several ballets (and operas) presented by the theatre well-into the 1960s which portrayed popular discontent through

---

406 Born in St Petersburg in 1904, Bitov graduated in composition from the Leningrad Conservatoire in 1941. He created several ballet scores including *Twelve Months* in 1954 which he co-wrote with Kornblit. He died in Leningrad in 1979.

407 Born in St Petersburg in 1908, Kornblit graduated in conducting from the Leningrad Conservatoire in 1936 and worked in the city's musical theatre until 1941. In 1944 he took up the post of conductor at the Maly Theatre where he also composed several original scores for the ballet company over more than twenty years as well as arranging and orchestrating others including the Grand Pas from *Paquita* for Boyarsky with the Maly company in 1957. He died in Leningrad in 1969.

historical revolutionary uprisings. *Stronger than Love* opened in 1961, based on Boris Lavrenyev's 1924 *The Forty-First*, a tragic romance between Maria, a Red Army sniper, and Lieutenant Govorukha-Otrok of the White Army; it featured choreography by Varkovitsky and a score by Alemdar Karamanov.[408] After the success of *Leningrad Symphony* in 1961, Igor Belsky returned to Shostakovich in 1966 with *Eleventh Symphony*, seeking to evoke the revolution to which the score's 'The Year 1905' subtitle refers.

1958 – Moiseyev's *Spartacus*

The Bolshoi Ballet, increasingly emboldened in its desire to create original work, turned to Khachaturian's score and, instead of acquiring Yakobson's 1956 ballet for the Kirov, commissioned Igor Moiseyev to create his own original version. The choreographer, known for his work in folk-dance with his eponymously-named ensemble, used his knowledge in a treatment which had undeniable highlights, notably the gladiators' combats at the Circus Maximus. However, the production was fatally static and the hero-figure of the slave leader was poorly drawn. Lavrovsky expressed his disappointment: "For me, this is not a production – it is a piece with no developed figures, with no build-up of the action."[409] Plisetskaya, who created the role of Aegina, was less critical and described her choreography as "uncommonly beautiful" and the crowd scenes as "...practically Hollywood on the Soviet Sverdlov Square".[410] She approved of her daring duets with Nikolai Fadeyechev as Harmodius but concurred that the title role of Spartacus was weak, owing to the technical limitations of Dmitry Begak,[411] the dancer chosen for the role on account of his heroic size: "Moiseyev created Spartacus' part within the limitations of Begak's dancing capabilities. And he miscalculated. In the opera you have to sing. In the ballet you have to dance. There's no other way..."[412] Natalia Ryzhenko[413] was the first Phrygia. Despite its cost – estimated at a

---

408   Born in Simferopol, Crimea in 1934, Karamanov studied at the Moscow Conservatoire from 1953 onwards, composing ten symphonies during his studies. During the early 1960s, he formed part of the Soviet Union's avant-garde before becoming a fervent Christian and turning his attention to spiritual works as well as another fourteen symphonies. He died in Simferopol in 2007.

409   Ezrahi, *Swans of the Kremlin*, p.207.

410   Plisetskaya, *I, Maya Plisetskaya*, p.174.

411   Born in 1935, Begak graduated into the Bolshoi company where he became a soloist. Later he became chief ballet master of the All-Russian Creative Workshop of Variety Art and between 1975 and 1976 was the choreographer of the USSR national rhythmic gymnastics team.

412   Plisetskaya, *I, Maya Plisetskaya*, p.174

413   Born in Moscow in 1938, Ryzhenko graduated into the Bolshoi in 1956 where she danced until 1977 as a respected soloist. In 1968 she co-choreographed her first work, a television version of *Romeo and Juliet* with Smirnov-Golvanov and went on to create numerous works for both screen and stage, mostly with the Stanislavsky Ballet. From

million roubles – Moiseyev's *Spartacus* lasted just nine performances and was then dropped from the repertoire.

1958 – the Paris Opéra Ballet in Moscow

If the Bolshoi visit to Covent Garden in October 1956 had been a landmark event in the history of ballet, what followed after the dancers were safely back in Moscow was nothing short of a cultural upheaval. The effect on western ballet of 1956 and subsequent visits was huge; for the Russians, witnessing dancers from other schools and traditions, with other artistic motivations and messages, was revelatory.

The agreed reciprocal tour by The Sadler's Wells/Royal Ballet to Moscow after the Bolshoi's London season was cancelled on advice from the British government because of both the Soviet invasion of Hungary in November 1956 and the Suez Crisis. It prompted a furious reaction from Mikhail Chulaki, the director of the Bolshoi Theatre who blamed Suez on "Anglo-French and Israeli aggressive agitation" and referred to material concerning "the brutalities of the White Terror in Hungary".[414] But the gates of cultural exchange had been definitively opened and when the political temperature had dropped, tours resumed, the first being a visit in 1958 by the Paris Opéra Ballet to Moscow and the Bolshoi to Paris.

What was perhaps under-appreciated by the Western ballet companies visiting the Soviet Union was the ideological unacceptability of much of what they intended to present to Russian audiences, from the actual nature of their ballets, often guilty of the artistic 'formalism' proscribed in the USSR, to both the absence of a political message and the presence of undesirable sexual content. An entry in *Bolshaya Sovietskaya Entsiklopediya* (The Big Soviet Encyclopaedia) sums up the official opinion of Western ballets which, with the arrival of foreign companies in Russia, were being shown to Soviet citizens:

> "They express a hideous picture of the decay of reactionary bourgeois culture. Just as in the other forms of bourgeois art, the present ballet of capitalistic countries serves the reactionary aims of imperialism. In it are preached submissiveness to fate (*Dante Sonata* – London) ...death as a 'higher rest' (*Le Jeune Homme et la Mort* – Paris); insanity (*Night Shadow* – USA)"[415]

During the Paris Opéra visit, criticism of the works performed mounted, with Serge Lifar's poetic *Les Mirages* targeted for its portrayal of human

---

1977 to 1989 she was choreographer at the Odessa State Opera and Ballet Theatre. She died in Moscow in 2010.

414 Swift, *The Art of the Dance in the USSR*, p.261
415 As cited by Swift, *The Art of the Dance in the USSR*, p.262

solitude 'in the midst of deceptions'. Its focus on the loneliness of existence ran contrary to accepted Soviet ideology which rejected anything that could be interpreted as society denying the individual his true identity; a tenet of communism was that it is society which gives humankind its superior existence. Thus, the wholesale rejection of any 'Freudian' aspect in dance – as in all art forms, for that matter – was a cornerstone of Soviet political and cultural philosophy. Excessive introspection was one of the main reasons for the moral decay of the West according to accepted thought and was considered a way to subjugate the proletariat. As early as in 1949, an article by Bolshoi Theatre director Alexander Solodovnikov[416] appeared in the periodical *Sovietskaya Muzika* (Soviet Music) which deplored the 'formalistic decadent tendencies' in Ninette de Valois'[417] *The Rake's Progress*. In 1950, ballet commentator Vera Krasovskaya[418] penned the article 'Corruption of the Art of Ballet in the West' which stated unequivocally that the repertoire of Western companies was designed to promulgate a 'reactionary and cosmopolitan ideology, the cult of death, of criminality and of depravity' and used corrupt authors as the basis for their ballets, Proust, Freud and Sartre, among others. However, the tours both from and to Russia continued despite what could be termed such 'cultural misunderstandings'.

Nevertheless, the visit by the Paris Opéra Ballet carried great symbolic weight. Russian ballet was rooted in the arrival of a succession of French *maîtres de ballet* during the nineteenth century and the early twentieth century saw the successes of Diaghilev's Ballets Russes in the West and in France in particular. The revolution had almost severed the link between the two countries, so this first exchange between them carried great historical significance. Added to which was the piquancy of a French company led by a Russian émigré, Serge Lifar, who, having escaped in early 1923, had always retained his stateless Nansen passport but insisted that he was "russe

---

416   Born in Chernigov Province in 1904, Solodovnikov was initially a factory worker before taking evening courses and graduating in philosophy, literature and history. From 1937 onwards he was a party official in several arts organisations and was made director of the Bolshoi Theatre in 1948 before being removed in 1951 after the scandal of German Zhukovsky's opera *From the Whole Heart*. In 1953 he returned to favour, serving as director of the Moscow Art Theatre from 1955 to 1963. He died in Moscow in 1990.

417   Born Edris Stannus in Ireland in 1898, Ninette de Valois trained with Edouard Espinosa and Enrico Cecchetti in London before joining Diaghilev's Ballets Russes in 1923. In 1926 she formed the Vic-Wells ballet which grew to become The Royal Ballet. She was also an accomplished choreographer. She stood down as company director in 1963 and continued to teach and coach. She died in London in 2001.

418   Born in Petrograd in 1915, Krasovskaya (or Krassovska) graduated into GATOB in 1933 where she danced until 1941. She then worked at the Leningrad Theatre Institute becoming a distinguished ballet writer and historian, writing the four volume *The History of Russian Ballet* between 1958 and 1972 as well as many other books, including one on Nijinsky. She died in St Petersburg in 1999.

toujours" ('still' or 'forever' Russian).[419] In contrast to the Bolshoi repertoire in Paris of eleven performances of four full-evening works (*Giselle*, *Swan Lake*, *Romeo and Juliet* and *Mirandolina*), the French ensemble offered twelve ballets in four programmes over a three week season of sixteen performances, the only full-length work being *Giselle*. Two plotless ballets scored the greatest success, Harald Lander's[420] *Études* and Lifar's *Suite en blanc*, while *Divertissement*, a pot-pourri of Russian repertoire extracts, fell flat in Moscow with both audience and critics.

1958 – The Cairo Ballet School

There is no clearer indication of the value of dance in the sphere of international politics than the establishment of the Cairo Ballet School by Leonid Lavrovsky in 1958. Following the declaration of the Egyptian Republic and the Suez Crisis with France and United Kingdom in 1956, the fledgling country's government turned to other international powers. The Soviet Union was only too glad to respond to Culture Minister Tharwat Okasha's approach for assistance in establishing and staffing a dance school; Egyptian dancers were also to be trained in Russia. In late 1959, the Kirov Ballet spent two months in Egypt and Soviet dance teachers ran the school until 1973. The first Egyptian ballet performance, a staging of *The Fountain of Bakhchisarai*, took place in 1966.

1958 – 'Choreographic Miniatures' at the Kirov

The end of 1958 saw something quite extraordinary come to the stage of the Kirov: an evening comprising only short or 'miniature' works. The choreographer of all twelve[421] which received their première on the opening night and featured the cream of company talent was Leonid Yakobson. It was a radical departure both from the established three-act ballets and one-act ideological pieces which made up the majority of the repertoire and was an indication of the direction ballet in the Soviet Union would take in the future. That the evening was commissioned at all is surprising, given the political imperatives in post-Stalin times – twelve generally unrelated small-scale works which placed free-form dance alongside classical and folk-inspired movement, tragedy next to lighter fare, the music of Debussy,

---

419   Poudru, 'Les tournées du Ballet de l'Opéra de Paris au temps de Lifar (1930-1958)'

420   Born Alfred Stevnsborg in Copenhagen in 1905, Lander studied under Hans Beck in Copenhagen and became a principal dancer with the Royal Danish Ballet in 1929. He was the company director from 1932 to 1951 and oversaw a renaissance in the dancing of Bournonville by the company as well as choreographing several ballets of his own, the most famous of which was *Études*. He became director of the Paris Opéra Ballet in 1951 and of the company's school between 1956-1957 and again from 1959 to 1963. He staged ballets around the world until his death in Copenhagen in 1971.

421   *Last Song, Skaters, Troika, Encounter, Stronger the Death, Snow Maiden, Prometheus, Mother, Toady, Eternal Spring, The Kiss, Eternal Idol.*

Prokofiev and Ravel with that of Shvarts, Boris Kravchenko,[422] and Vladimir Tsïtovich.[423] The works ranged from *Snow Maiden* featuring Irina Kolpakova to the free plastique of *Toady* created on a young Konstantin Rassadin.[424] The most notable section was the 'Rodin Triptych' which closed the programme; based on three sculptures by the renowned French artist, the dance works sought to portray three stages of human love to orchestrations of Debussy's *Suite bergamasque*. Clad in flesh-coloured body stockings, the dancers depicted the changing nature of love and desire with age. Some viewers considered their apparent nakedness pornographic, despite the last-minute addition of flimsy over-tunics, but the triptych and the entire evening were considered a great success, garnering a further 72 performances. In the triptych, Ninel Petrova[425] and Anatoly Nisnevich[426] appeared in *Eternal Spring*, Alla Osipenko and Vsevolod Ukhov[427] in *The Kiss* and Alla Shelest and Igor Chernishev[428] in *Eternal Idol*.

---

422   Born in Leningrad in 1929, Kravchenko graduated from the city's conservatoire and established himself as a versatile composer. He was best known for his music in 1972 for the puppet opera *The Tale of the Priest and of His Workman Balda*. He taught composition at the Leningrad Conservatoire from 1967 to 1971. He died in Leningrad in 1979.

423   Born in Leningrad in 1931, Tsïtovich graduated from the city conservatoire in 1957 and embarked on a career in composition. At times heavily influenced by the music of Bela Bartók, he created music in a wide variety of genres from symphonies and concerti to vocal music and instrumental solos. He died in St Petersburg in 2012.

424   Born in Leningrad in 1937, Rassadin graduated into the Kirov in 1956 where he established himself as a character dancer. Closely involved with Yakobson, he appeared in several of his works as well as in the standard repertoire. Having graduated from the Choreographic Department of the Leningrad Conservatoire in 1979 he retired from dancing and became chief choreographer of the Leningrad Ice Ballet. Between 1967 and 1972 he taught character dance at the Leningrad Art University and from 1979 to 1984 in the choreographer department of the Leningrad Conservatoire.

425   Born in Leningrad in 1924, Petrova graduated in 1944 from the Leningrad Choreographic School as Juliet in a performance of Yakobson's *Romeo and Juliet*. She joined the Kirov where she danced until 1969, her strength being her lyricism and sense of drama; she danced a wide repertoire. She taught at the school between 1969 and 1971 and from 1976 to 2001 was the main teacher-coach of the Choreographic Miniatures company. Since 1977 she has been an Associate Professor of the ballet department of the Leningrad Conservatoire.

426   Born in Lomonosov near Leningrad in 1937, Nisnevich graduated into the Kirov in 1956 where he remained until 1976. An elegant performer, he danced many major roles. He also appeared with Georgy Aleksidze's Chamber Ballet. From 1963 onwards he was a teacher at the Leningrad Choreographic School and from 1978 was also a teacher and coach at the Maly Theatre. He died in 2012 in St. Petersburg.

427   Born in Leningrad in 1925, Ukhov graduated into the Kirov Ballet in 1944 where he remained until 1970, known as a fine lyrical dancer with a sense of drama. He taught movement and plastic arts at the directing department of the Leningrad Conservatoire. Between 1970 and 1976 he was head of the Kirov ballet. He died in Leningrad in 1991.

428   Born in Leningrad in 1937, Chernishev graduated in 1956 into the Kirov as a

Dancers of the second Golden Age

Whatever the debates over artistic policy, the dearth of first-rate choreographers and the restrictions imposed by the need to promote the Soviet way of life, there was no doubting the quality of training at the Vaganova, Bolshoi and, increasingly, other ballet schools and their extraordinary output of equally extraordinary dancers. The 1960s saw a blossoming of dance talent in Soviet Russia, the groundwork for which had been laid long before. In the post-war period, many of the teachers of young ballet students came from a rich and illustrious past and had, often against immense odds, survived revolution, terror and war to maintain something of an unbroken line back through Stalin's purges, the early, tumultuous days of the Soviet state and into the imperial era. *Natalia Makarova pays tribute to her teachers at the Vaganova Academy, most notably Mikhail Mikhailov and Nikolai Ivanovsky[429] whom, she states, Stalin's purges had 'passed over' and who gave their students an understanding of social graces and simplicity of manners which are vital to an understanding of roles in the classical ballet canon. More pre-revolution dancers had survived than might have been expected, and the part they played in imbuing their pupils with a sense of continuity and tradition should not be under-estimated – Elizaveta Gerdt, daughter of the imperial era *danseur noble* Pavel joined the Mariinsky troupe in 1910, and, after a distinguished dancing career, became one of the most distinguished teachers at the Bolshoi Ballet School where until 1960 she taught the likes of Maya Plisetskaya, Raisa Struchkova and Ekaterina Maximova.

But, as Natalia Makarova states, the late-1950s and early-1960s also represented a time of change when several of these revered teachers retired and she personally did not rate their replacements. What is undeniable however is the talent which was nurtured at the ballet schools was no less impressive than in earlier times. In Leningrad, the name of *Alexander

---

soloist where he danced a variety of major roles until 1969. He began to choreograph in the late 1960s. In 1969, Chernishev moved to Odessa, Crimea as director of the ballet troupe where he created many more works ranging from reworkings of the classics to a plotless work using Brahms' *Variations on a Theme by Haydn* in 1974. He became chief choreographer of the Moldavian Opera and Ballet Theatre in 1975 and then was at the Kuibyshev (now Samara) Opera and Ballet Theatre between 1976 and 1995, after which he went to Moscow to teach in a variety of institutions. He died in Moscow in 2007.

429   Born in St Petersburg in 1893, Ivanovsky graduated into the Mariinsky in 1911 where he remained as a dancer until 1942. Noted for his character dancing, he appeared with Diaghilev's Ballet Russes between 1912 and 1914 and at the Petrograd Theatre of Miniatures from 1914 and 1915. He took part in the première of Lopukhov's *Dance Symphony*. At the Leningrad Choreographic School, he taught ballet history and everyday dance from 1925 to 1928 and 1935 to 1940 and was its director between 1940 and 1952 and again from 1954 to 1961. From 1946 until his death in Leningrad in 1961, he headed the department of dance teachers at the Leningrad Conservatoire.

Pushkin is still remembered; a dancer with the Kirov from 1925 until 1953, he went on to become one of the finest teachers of male dancers, training such stars as Rudolf Nureyev and Mikhail Baryshnikov. In the companies themselves, the dancers were coached in their roles by many of the great names of pre-war Soviet ballet – Natalia Dudinskaya taught the *classe de perfection* at the Kirov, Marina Semyonova and Asaf Messerer at the Bolshoi and Vakhtang Chabukiani ran the ballet company of the Paliashvili Georgian Theatre in Tbilisi.

Bolshoi

If Maria Semyonova, Galina Ulanova and Olga Lepeshinskaya represented the first golden generation of Soviet ballerinas, by the 1960s, the second was in its prime, from Maya Plisetskaya, a dazzling technician and spellbinding actress to the dynamic Nina Timofeyeva, the ethereal Marina Kondratieva and the heart-warming Raisa Struchkova. Two outstanding younger Moscow ballerinas, the joyous Ekaterina Maximova, coached by Ulanova, and the intensely lyrical Natalia Bessmertnova, coached by Semyonova, would take over their mantle as the decade progressed and the company moved towards the 1970s.

Maya Plisetskaya was born in 1925, the niece of Asaf and Sulamith Messerer and a member of a distinguished artistic family. In 1943, she graduated from the Bolshoi Ballet School into the company and, in succession to Ulanova, became its greatest and best-known ballerina, receiving the rank of *prima ballerina assoluta* from the Soviet government upon Ulanova's retirement in 1962. She dominated the company and its repertoire for decades until her official company farewell in 1990. She had uncommon technical and dramatic abilities which she brought to blazing interpretations across the repertoire. She was known particularly for her Odette-Odile in *Swan Lake*, Kitri in *Don Quixote*, The Dying Swan and Carmen. From the 1960s onwards, she travelled and performed extensively abroad, always in an atmosphere of glamour. She led several dance companies during the 1980s. She died in Munich in 2015.

Born in Moscow in 1925, Raisa Struchkova graduated into the Bolshoi from its school in 1944, having studied with Elizaveta Gerdt, and rapidly rose to the rank of ballerina after her breakthrough assumption of the title role in *Cinderella*. She allied a strong technique with a warm stage personality and was one of the company's most popular artists, appearing in a wide repertoire from the classics to the Soviet ballets – her Maria in *The Fountain of Bakhchisarai* was especially praised. She enjoyed a strong stage partnership with her husband Alexander Lapauri; they were famed for show-stopping virtuosic duets such as *Moszkowsky Waltz* and *Spring Waters*. After her retirement from the stage in 1978, she continued to coach at the Bolshoi and was the founding editor of the dance magazine *Sovietsky Balet* (Soviet Ballet). She died in Moscow in 2005.

Born in Leningrad in 1934, Marina Kondratieva graduated in 1952 from the Bolshoi Ballet School into the company, establishing herself as a strong, versatile and expressive artist and quickly attaining principal status. She danced the full classical and Soviet repertoire, being the first Bolshoi Katerina in Grigorovich's *The Stone Flower* and the creator of The Muse in Lavrovsky's *Paganini*. Kondratieva established a fruitful stage partnership with Māris Liepa with whom she excelled as Juliet and Giselle. On her retirement from the stage in 1980, she has taught and coached at the Bolshoi Ballet. She taught at GITIS from 1980 to 1989 and at the Bolshoi Ballet School from 1990 to 2000. Since 1988 she has choreographed and staged works worldwide.

Nina Timofeyeva was born in Leningrad in 1935, graduating in 1953 from the school into the Kirov Ballet. However, despite having already danced Odette-Odile in *Swan Lake* and Masha in *The Nutcracker*, she transferred to Moscow three years later at Lopukhov's suggestion, joining the Bolshoi's 1956 London season. She rose rapidly through the ranks to become one of the company's most celebrated principals. A fearsome technician, achieved through determined hard work, she also developed a strong stage personality; one of her most notable roles was the complex Queen Mekhmeneh Banu in *The Legend of Love*. She appeared on stage with the company until 1988 and then coached until the disintegration of the Soviet Union in 1991 when she moved to Israel where she died in 2014.

Born in Moscow in 1939, Ekaterina Maximova graduated into the Bolshoi company in 1958 and rapidly established herself as an audience favourite with an elegant technique and a charming, feminine stage presence. She danced the full range of the repertoire and established a strong and complementary stage partnership with her husband Vladimir Vasiliev. In 1959, she danced Katerina in *The Stone Flower*, which elicited much attention and led to her preparation for *Giselle* with Ulanova who then became her regular coach. In 1964, it was her assumption of the title role in *Cinderella* which announced her as a ballerina of note. Her career at the Bolshoi began to wane with the onset of the Vasiliev-Grigorovich split; she performed extensively abroad. She died in Moscow in 2009.

Natalia Bessmertnova was born in Moscow in 1941 and graduated into the Bolshoi from its school in 1961, appearing in the Mazurka and Waltz in *Chopiniana* just two weeks after joining. She was in many ways atypical as a Bolshoi dancer, embodying 'Romantic' feminine ethereality; her Giselle was tinged with a degree of mysticism. With a delicate physique, she was nevertheless a strong technician and possessed a high, floating jump. Often ill-served by the company's repertoire, she found certain of the brasher roles outside her scope, but brought much to any part that called for introspection.

In 1964, she created Leili in Goleizovsky's *Leili and Majnun* and also many leading roles in her husband, Yuri Grigorovich's ballets. She retired from the stage in 1994 and died in Moscow in 2008.

During this period, the Bolshoi's reigning *premier danseur* was Nikolai Fadeyechev who regularly partnered Plisetskaya and greatly influenced an upcoming generation of male dancers not least of whom Vladimir Vasiliev. Very much one of kind, Vasiliev was himself an heroic, dynamic virtuoso who went on to dominate the repertoire, defining the Bolshoi style of male dancing for over a generation. Bessmertnova was often paired with another exceptional male dancer, Mikhail Lavrovsky, son of Leonid, noted for his charm, elegance and refinement who joined the company in 1961 and rapidly rose through the ranks. The company's third star male dancer was Māris Liepa, a Latvian who, after graduating from the Bolshoi Ballet School in 1955, had danced elsewhere before joining the company as a principal in 1960. Brilliant, elegant but initially considered inexpressive, he came into his own in his created role of Crassus in the Grigorovich *Spartacus* which revealed another side to him as an artist. Adding to the roster the energetic and forceful Yuri Vladimirov and we see a company which could field male artists of exceptional merit and interest. These were dancers whom Grigorovich used time and time again in his creations for the Bolshoi which throughout the late 1960s and the 1970s reshaped and redefined the company.

Nikolai Fadeyechev was born in Moscow in 1933 and in 1952 graduated from the Bolshoi Choreographic School into the company, where he would dance for some twenty-five years. He was one of the Bolshoi's key male principals, appearing with distinction and refinement in all the classical ballets, notably *Giselle* and *The Sleeping Beauty*. He partnered all the company ballerinas but established a firm stage bond with Plisetskaya with whom he appeared in many ballets, not least *Swan Lake* in which he first partnered her in 1964. He was the first Moscow Danila in *The Stone Flower* and Prince Ivan in *The Firebird*. He retired from the stage in 1977 and thereafter continued to teach and coach with distinction at the Bolshoi until his death in Moscow in 2020.

Māris Liepa was born in Riga, Latvia in 1936 where he initially trained before joining the Bolshoi School for two years and graduating in 1955. Having initially returned to his native Latvia to dance, he was noticed by Plisetskaya and invited by her on a tour to Budapest in 1956. After four years with the Stanislavsky Ballet, he joined the Bolshoi in 1960, debuting as Basilio in *Don Quixote* with Plisetskaya as Kitri. His performances in *Le Corsaire, Swan Lake* and *La Bayadère* were particularly celebrated, and he was awarded the Lenin Prize for the role of Crassus in *Spartacus*. He also danced with Boris Eifman during the 1970s and left the Bolshoi in 1982. He taught from 1963 onwards and was the Artistic Director of Sofia National Opera between 1983 and 1985. Liepa died in Moscow in 1989.

Born in Moscow in 1940, Vladimir Vasiliev graduated into the Bolshoi Ballet in 1958, first making an impact as the jealous villain Gianciotto in Alexey Chichinadze's *Francesca da Rimini* and seemingly destined for a career in character roles despite Ulanova choosing him to partner her for one of her last appearances in *Chopiniana*. Danila in *The Stone Flower* and Ivan the Fool in *The Little Humpbacked Horse* did nothing to change the course of his career until he came under the tutelage of Alexey Ermolayev who encouraged him to find his own way into, and then to extend further, the major roles of the repertoire among which Basilio in *Don Quixote* and Frondoso in *Laurencia*. During only his second year in the company, he was made a principal dancer at the age of nineteen. In 1964, his psychologically intelligent and nuanced Albrecht in *Giselle* was considered as radical as Baryshnikov's at the Kirov would be some ten years later, while his intense Majnun in Goleizovsky's *Leili and Majnun* was a searing portrayal of doomed love. Of stunning technical virtuosity – Lopukhov deemed him superior to both Chabukiani and Ermolayev – he was "an unprecedented phenomenon with whom no one can be compared, including Nijinsky".[430] He was one of Soviet ballet's greatest ever dancers. He became Director of the Bolshoi Theatre in 1995 before being removed from post in 2000.

Born in Tbilisi in 1941, Mikhail Lavrovsky graduated in 1961 from the Bolshoi Ballet School into the company. It was with Yuri Grigorovich's arrival in 1964 (replacing Mikhail's father Leonid as director) that his career took off; Struchkova chose him to partner her in *Cinderella* and he scored early successes as The Prince in *The Nutcracker* and Ferhad in *The Legend of Love*. He danced a broad repertoire, projecting an open, virile stage personality, and often partnering Natalia Bessmertnova. One of his greatest achievements was as Spartacus in Grigorovich's version, a role which he invested with true tragic depth. From 1977 onwards Lavrovsky was principal dancer and guest choreographer with the Tbilisi Ballet, becoming artistic director of the Paliashvili Theatre between 1983 and 1985. He was director of the Stanislavsky Ballet between 2005 and 2008.

Yuri Vladimirov was born in Kosterovo, outside Moscow in 1942 and, after training at the Bolshoi School, graduated into the company in 1962 where he quickly established himself as an energetic and forceful soloist excelling in created roles requiring elemental power and explosive energy. He worked fruitfully with Bolshoi choreographers Natalia Kasatkina and Vladimir Vasilyov on *Heroic Poem (Geologists)* and *Le Sacre du Printemps* and created the title role in Grigorovich's *Ivan the Terrible*. He retired from dancing in 1987 and went on to teach and coach soloists within the Bolshoi company.

---

430   Smakov, *The Great Russian Dancers*, p.325

Kirov

Leningrad's Kirov Ballet did not boast such dance titans as the Bolshoi, partly because of the continuing favour shown by the Soviet regime to the Moscow company, partly because the company continued under the increasingly dead artistic hand of Konstantin Sergeyev until 1970; there was no Grigorovich, no *Spartacus* to re-invigorate the troupe. Yet the Kirov remained the acknowledged guardian of classical dance in Russia. The reigning prima ballerina continued to be Natalia Dudinskaya, while Ninel Kurgapkina established herself as a technically brilliant stalwart of the company. Alla Osipenko, who joined the company in 1950, described later by Mikhail Baryshnikov as "the most modernistic, most neoclassical classical ballerina" and the virtuoso Alla Sizova were the main female dancers on the company's first overseas visits in 1961. They shouldered the bulk of performances alongside arguably the finest of them all, Irina Kolpakova, who was, with Osipenko, in the last cohort of Vaganova's pupils, both graduating a few months before their teacher's death in November 1951. For a quarter of a century Kolpakova embodied the legendary stylistic purity of the company and its traditions. Younger dancers of interest emerged in the 1960s, the most notable of whom in hindsight was Natalia Makarova who joined the company in 1958, made her debut as Giselle in London three years later, but who initially struggled with her technique. Her evident artistry and hard work paid off, making her the darling of the 1964 American tour – she debuted in Chicago as Cinderella in Sergeyev's version of the ballet – and paving the way for further roles, even if these were, owing to the ossified repertoire, limited. For the duration of 1960s the Kirov's reigning male dancer was the prodigiously talented Yuri Soloviev who graduated in 1958 and went on to demonstrate dancing of exceptional quality even if he possessed a passive, phlegmatic character which would never fire his roles with an interpretative spark. His apparent suicide in 1977 was a shock to the Soviet and wider ballet world.

Ninel Kurgapkina was born in Leningrad in 1929, and, following training at the Leningrad Choreographic School as one of Vaganova's last pupils, graduated into the Kirov in 1947. Despite a somewhat sturdy physical frame, she rose to be a famed company ballerina, combining a joyful stage personality with great technical accomplishment and danced all the major roles of the repertoire. She was an acclaimed Aurora in *The Sleeping Beauty* and Gamzatti in *La Bayadère*, while Kitri in *Don Quixote* and Jeanne in *The Flames of Paris* allowed her to display her brilliant technique. Having retired from the stage at the age of fifty-two, she taught at the Vaganova Academy from 1982 to 1990 and was a much-sought-after coach at the Kirov. She died in St Petersburg in 2009.

Born in Leningrad in 1932, Alla Osipenko graduated from the Leningrad Choreographic School into the Kirov in 1950, becoming a principal dancer in 1954 with her debut as Odette/Odile in *Swan Lake*. Her range was broad, encompassing all the major classical roles and new works; she was particularly admired in adagio movement. In 1952, her breakthrough moment was her debut as The Lilac Fairy in *The Sleeping Beauty*, illuminating the abstract nature of classical dance with a sculptural appeal and subtle eroticism. She was much sought after by choreographers and created The Mistress of the Copper Mountain in *The Stone Flower* and the title role in Igor Chernishev's *Antony and Cleopatra*. From 1971-73, she worked with Yakobson's 'Choreographic Miniatures' company, then with Boris Eifman from 1977 to 1982, always searching for new movement and ideas. She emigrated to the USA in the 1990s but returned to Russia in 2000.

Irina Kolpakova was born in Leningrad in 1933, and graduated into the Kirov from the Leningrad Choreographic School in 1951 in the last class to be taught by Vaganova. She danced her first major role, the title role in *Cinderella*, in 1955, followed shortly after by Aurora in *The Sleeping Beauty*, rising thereafter to become the company's prima ballerina. She created several roles in new ballets including Katerina in *The Stone Flower*, Shyrien in *The Legend of Love*, and leading parts in *Coast of Hope* and Kasatkina and Vasilyov's *Creation of the World*. She excelled in the classical repertoire, notably as Giselle, Aurora (*The Sleeping Beauty*) and Raymonda and was celebrated for her clean, pure line and unforced grace on stage. She has coached at the Kirov since 1971 and at American Ballet Theatre since 1989.

Alla Sizova was born in Moscow in 1939 and studied at the Leningrad Choreographic School, a classmate of Rudolf Nureyev with whom she danced the *Le Corsaire* pas de deux in a graduation performance. In 1958, she joined the company as a soloist and was made a principal shortly after. Her first major role was as Masha in *The Nutcracker* to which she added a further fourteen major roles within three seasons. Known for her high jumps and accomplished technique, she was nicknamed 'Flying Sizova' and, after Nureyev's defection, established a successful dance partnership with Yuri Soloviev. She combined superb musicality with great sensitivity, and was a particularly admired Aurora in *The Sleeping Beauty*. She retired from performing in 1988 and then taught at the Vaganova Academy and in the United States. She died in St Petersburg in 2014.

Natalia Makarova was born in Leningrad in 1940 and graduated into the Kirov Ballet in 1958. An unremarkable technician at first, she nevertheless demonstrated individuality from her earliest appearances, making a much-noted debut as Giselle in 1959. It was as a lyrical dancer that she was most admired, a quality that was evident in her performances on tour in the West. She was eager to explore new choreography and stood out in Yakobson's ill-fated *The Bedbug*. Stifled by the atmosphere at the Kirov throughout the Sixties, she defected in 1970, establishing herself in the West as a glamorous performer of intense artistry with the major world companies. Her technique became strong and her repertoire wide. Since the mid-1970s, she has staged numerous ballets around the world.

Under Sergeyev as director, the Kirov did not develop a second generation of 'star' male dancers in the way achieved by the Bolshoi, despite a roster of highly accomplished performers. A male dancer of the first rank to emerge from the new generation was Nikita Dolgushin, although his time at the Kirov would be relatively short owing to disagreements with the company management, while both Rudolf Nureyev and Yuri Soloviev were rising company stars. Nureyev too did not remain long with the company, becoming the first notable Soviet ballet defector; the focus then fell, perhaps disproportionately, on the virtuoso Soloviev.

Nikita Dolgushin was born in Leningrad in 1938 and graduated from the Leningrad Choreographic School in 1959, performing a concert version of Act II of *Giselle* with Natalia Makarova. His elevation was limited and he was not particularly swift in movement but these seeming limitations spurred him to develop rare artistic sensibility and intelligence. In 1960 as Albrecht in *Giselle*, his interpretation departed from Sergeyev's accepted portrayal of a cruel aristocrat and showed a tortured, almost Hamlet-like figure. He left the Kirov in 1961 after disagreements with the director and danced in Novosibirsk for five years where he met and collaborated with the young choreographer and future Kirov director Oleg Vinogradov. He danced in the experimental Muscovite company, The Young Ballet, returning briefly to the Kirov in 1968 before moving to the Maly troupe with which he danced extensively until 1983. He also staged many ballets there, including a celebrated 'original' version of *Giselle* in 1973 which remains in the repertory of the Mikhailovsky (former Maly) company. He died in St Petersburg in 2012.

Born in Siberia in 1938, Rudolf Nureyev studied in Leningrad, finishing his training in the class of Alexander Pushkin. His graduation performance comprised the *Diana and Actéon* and *Le Corsaire* pas de deux and a solo from *Gayaneh*, all received to great acclaim. He entered the Kirov Ballet as a soloist in 1958. He possessed a strong and forceful stage persona from the start but was never considered a technically 'neat' dancer. Despite his personal and on-stage haughtiness, he successfully danced with the company's leading ballerinas. After his 1961 defection, he went on to become a global ballet super-star, dancing with every major ballet company and establishing a now-legendary stage partnership with Margot Fonteyn. He worked with all the important choreographers in a variety of styles and himself began to stage and choreograph ballets. He assumed the directorship of the Paris

Opéra Ballet in 1983, heralding a golden age for the company until his death in the French capital in 1993.

Born in Leningrad in 1940, Yuri Soloviev trained at the Leningrad Choreographic School from which he graduated into the Kirov company in 1958. He was blessed with phenomenal elevation and perfectly-honed classical purity; Nureyev admired him greatly and later observed "You think I'm good? You want to see Soloviev!"[431] He was an exceptional Bluebird in *The Sleeping Beauty* at his graduation performance and also danced Acteon in the showpiece *Diana and Actéon* pas de deux and in a duet from *Esmeralda*. Soloist roles followed and he went on to dance all the major roles of the classical canon, as well as in several new ballets, although his relatively short stature and limited acting abilities meant that he was not considered to have attained the interpretative heights of some dancers. His contemporary Natalia Makarova observed, however, that he had never been developed as an artist: "No one nurtured Soloviev's soul or fostered his mind; no one ever produced a ballet to tap his inner world. This was a Stradivarius which played beautifully but never sang."[432] Soloviev died in 1977 in mysterious circumstances in an apparent suicide in his dacha outside Leningrad.

1959 – *Coast of Hope*

In April 1959, Igor Belsky, the dancer who in 1950 had scored such as success in the title role of Yakobson's *Shuraleh*, and by then a budding 'Lopukhov' choreographer, premièred *Coast* (or *Shore*) *of Hope* at the Kirov. To music by the young composer Andrey Petrov,[433] it concerned two fishing villages, one happily Soviet, the other not, the shipwreck of a Soviet fisherman on the wrong side of the water and his final restoration to his home 'shore'. It was in many ways a standard tale of Russian loyalty to the motherland, but in its metaphorical rather than literal approach to narrative, it was a choreographic experiment which was more a 'dance poem' than straight story-telling. In explaining his view of choreography and belief in the primacy of dance, Belsky wrote:

> "I am firmly convinced that ballet is an independent art form capable of conveying content through its own purely choreographic means – dance is the most important of these, while dance *recitative*, or, in other words, mime firmly wedded to music, complements it...The main principal of my choreography in this ballet (is)...everything is to be conveyed through

---

431   As quoted by Kavanagh, *Rudolf Nureyev*, p.52
432   Makarova, *A Dance Autobiography*, p.72
433   Born in Leningrad in 1930, Petrov studied composition at the Leningrad Conservatoire before embarking on a successful career in a variety of genres. He became best-known for his film scores but worked in ballet; in 1971, he composed the score for *Creation of the World* at the Kirov. He died in St Petersburg in 2006.

dance that is *never* used in *divertissement* form."[434]

The ballet was notable also for its uncluttered stage: the first act featured a blue cyclorama dominated by two suspended sails fluttering in the breeze. *Coast of Hope* was a clear example of Soviet ballet both wanting and being permitted to pull away from the strictures of choreodrama and socialist realism. The first performance was led by Makarov as Rybak the Fisherman, Osipenko as His Beloved and Tatiana Legat as the Lonely Girl.

It was enthusiastically received by audience and critics alike. Yuri Slonimsky observed: "The ballet *Coast of Hope* announced the emergence of not only a talented choreographer, but also an artist with a different understanding of the nature of ballet realism, actively fighting for the embodiment of the Soviet theme in the art of choreography,"[435] while Lopukhov wrote "For the first time in the life of a Soviet ballet, a romantic poem about the warm and loyal heart of a Soviet man whose love for the Motherland is stronger than a storm, stronger than death, appeared and fell in love with the public."[436]

1959 – the Bolshoi in New York

The April 1959 Bolshoi season in New York and the return visit to Moscow the following year by American Ballet Theatre can be seen as pivotal moments in the development of American-Soviet cultural relations. The Russians' reception at the Metropolitan Opera House[437] was every bit as enthusiastic as it had been in London three years before – *Giselle* and *Romeo and Juliet* were the hits, while Grigorovich's *The Stone Flower* found far less favour. What struck viewers, as it had in London, was the sheer virtuosity of the dancers whose physical attack contrasted sharply with their less showy counterparts in the West. The productions too were on a monumental scale. Khrushchev knew that ballet was, indeed, a strong propaganda tool in the ideological struggle between Russia and the United States; at a formal dinner he asked:

> "Which country has the best ballet? Yours? You do not even have a permanent opera and ballet theatre. Your theatres thrive on what is given them by rich people. In our country it is the state that gives it money. And the best ballet is in the Soviet Union. It is our pride."[438]

An artist of whom Khrushchev could now be proud on tour was Maya

---

434 Rene, 'New Choreographer in Leningrad', *Dance and Dancers*, March 1961. pp.14-15, 34.

435 As quoted by Degen and Stupnikov in www.belcanto.ru

436 ibid.

437 Opened in 1883, New York City's Metropolitan Opera House (the 'Old Met') was located on 39th and Broadway until it was replaced in 1966 by a new theatre (the 'New Met') in the Lincoln Center for the Performing Arts in the Upper West Side.

438 Homans, *Apollo's Angels*, p.373

Plisetskaya for whom the New York season was her first taste of the West. An unexpected late addition to the roster of dancers, she caused a stir on her arrival in Manhattan, appearing on the cover of *Newsweek* in costume as *The Stone Flower*'s Mistress of the Copper Mountain and electrifying audiences with her dynamic performances. Other dancers who made a mark were Ekaterina Maximova and Vladimir Vasiliev who "burst upon New York City in 1959, the greatest of the passionate young dancers who, with Moscow's more established stars, made the Bolshoi Ballet's American debut a total triumph".[439] The forty-nine-year-old Ulanova also made the journey to New York and repeated her London successes. While praise was heaped upon the company's dancers, there was much criticism of the old-fashioned quality of the choreography; Grigorovich may have been seen as an innovator in the Soviet Union, but for American observers there was little difference between him and Lavrovsky: "what is new in Russia has become almost routine in New York",[440] commented New York critic Miles Kastendieck. The inclusion of *The Stone Flower* in the repertoire was nevertheless an attempt by the Bolshoi to present contemporary Soviet ballet – its première had taken place only weeks prior to the beginning of the American tour.

There is no doubt that the years after Stalin's death and the onset of Khrushchev's 'thaw' brought about a shift for the arts in general and ballet in particular, but not without a fundamental questioning of what it could as well as should portray. In 1976, ballet historian Vera Krasovskaya wrote:

"The 1950s marked a new age for the Soviet ballet. The aesthetics of the dance symphony began to take a practical shape, inspired by the crisis in dance drama. The latter had a big effect on ballet, but that effect was as good as it was bad. The lessons learned from the classic literature were good; it was from there that dance drama took its plots. Ideal dance drama had to be real and natural, with a definite conflict, logical actions and deeply-motivated characters. This implied a special choice of expressive means, the best one being pantomime, a form in which description prevails over expression...(However,) the neglect of drama in music and of dance as a means to express that drama was bad. Onstage realism permitted no imagery, so in dance drama, dance was no longer to be abstract, ambiguous or metaphorical. Its structural forms were (therefore) ignored and its functions restricted."[441]

---

439   *The New York Times*, May 16th 1990, Section C, p.13
440   Kastendieck, 'Brilliance by Bolshoi', *New York Journal American*, May 5, 1959.as quoted by Searcy, *Ballet in the Cold War: A Soviet-American Exchange*, p.42
441   Krasovskaya, *The Middle of the Century*, p.218

1960 – *The Little Humpbacked Horse*

In March 1960 the Bolshoi essayed a new version of a ballet which, in Arthur Saint-Léon's 1864 original creation, dated back to St Petersburg's Bolshoi Theatre. C-rated in the 1929 Repertoire Index, it had never really fallen from favour despite its fairy-tale narrative: the hero Ivanushka defeats the wicked Khan to win the hand of the Tsar Maiden and is helped through a series of impossible tasks by the magical little humpbacked horse. Gorsky had created his own version in Moscow in 1901 which he revised in 1914 with Geltser appearing to great acclaim as the Tsar Maiden. In 1945 Lopukhov created a production 'after Gorsky' at the Kirov which saw Shelest as the Tsar Maiden. and in 1948 the Bolshoi mounted a similar revival by Tamara Nikitina,[442] Lev Pospekhin and Alexander Radunsky featuring Sofia Golovkina[443] and Radunsky himself as the Khan.

In 1960, Radunsky was asked to create a brand-new version of the ballet for the Bolshoi; a new score commissioned from *Rodion Shchedrin replacing Pugni's original music. The first performance saw Vladimir Vasiliev as Ivanushka, Rimma Karelskaya[444] (in later performances Plisetskaya) as the Tsar Maiden, Radunsky as the Khan and Alla Shcherbinina[445] as the Little Humpbacked Horse. It was an immediate success and a film with the original cast (except for Plisetskaya replacing Karelskaya) was made and distributed internationally. In 1963, Lopukhov created his own version of the ballet to Shchedrin's score for MALEGOT.

1960-1964 – 'old guard' ballets

By the beginning of the new decade, even the 'old guard' of established Soviet choreographers were not immune to the changes in public taste. This shift

---

442 Born in Moscow in 1904, Nikitina graduated into the Bolshoi in 1920 where she danced as a soloist until 1946 and then became a company teacher and coach until 1978. She died in Moscow in 1993.

443 Born in Moscow in 1915, Golovkina graduated into the Bolshoi in 1933 and established herself as a dynamic virtuoso dancer who appeared in a wide range of leading roles, retiring from the stage in 1959. From 1960 to 2001 she was in a directorial capacity at the Bolshoi Ballet School. She oversaw the move of the school to new premises in 1967. She died in Moscow in 2004.

444 Born in 1927 in Kaluga, Karelskaya graduated into the Bolshoi in 1947 where she would appear until 1973. She performed many leading roles, including a well-received Odette-Odile in *Swan Lake* during the company's 1958 Paris tour. From 1974 to 2007 she was a teacher and coach at the theatre. She died in Moscow in 2014.

445 Born in Moscow in 1934 to a family of dancers, Shcherbinina appeared with the Bolshoi aged seven and was evacuated with her parents to Kuibyshev during the war. She entered the Bolshoi School in 1943 and graduated into the company, rising to soloist level. During the early 1970s she was a staunch defender of Prokofiev and Shostakovich's music at party meetings which led to her forced retirement in 1974. In 1981 she left the USSR and moved to Canada, where she taught at the Royal Ballet of Winnipeg until 1996.

had begun following a degree of ideological relaxation from the regime and seasons in Russia by foreign companies which demonstrated that plotless works could be expressive. There was a growing desire to see action expressed through dance alone.

In April 1960, Leonid Lavrovsky created *Paganini* at the Bolshoi to Sergey Rachmaninov's *Rhapsody on a theme by Paganini*, music previously used by Fokine in his 1939 ballet for the Colonel de Basil company and later in 1980 by Frederick Ashton for *Rhapsody* for The Royal Ballet at Covent Garden. To a libretto of his own devising, Lavrovsky sought to create an impressionistic evocation of the famous violinist's emotional conflicts in a series of scenes without establishing a clear narrative. It was also a one-act work, a form generally absent from the performing repertoire of the company at the time, but one which Lavrovsky and the audience had seen successfully used by visiting ensembles from abroad. It featured Yaroslav Sekh[446] as Paganini and Marina Kondratieva as his Muse. He followed it with *Night City* in 1961, imposing a new libretto to Bela Bartók's music for *The Miraculous Mandarin* which conveyed a dark tale of underworld thuggery and violence, a surprising storyline to have made it past the censor. The role of The Girl was powerfully taken by Nina Timofeyeva, allowing her to reveal unknown dramatic talents; The Youth who attempts to defend her against thugs was created by Māris Liepa. However powerful the depiction of the characters, the subject matter made some viewers uneasy – Liepa later spoke about the criticism that the work received:

> "Critics immediately condemned *Night City*, blaming Lavrovsky for deviating from the libretto of Bartók's *Miraculous Mandarin*. These were unfair attacks, since the choreographer remained faithful to the music and idea. He only elevated from 'passion is stronger than death' to 'love is stronger than death' and therefore replaced the (character of the) Mandarin Youth. Lavrovsky had every right to such a reading of the ballet, given the theatre in which the ballet was staged, our morality and ethical principles. At that time, our 'morality' was stronger than copyright!"[447]

Another Lavrovsky work, *Life (or Pages of Life)* also opened at the Bolshoi in 1961 to music by Balanchine's brother Andrey; it featured Struchkova and later Timofeyeva as Tamara, Zhdanov and then Liepa as Georgy and Vladimir Vasiliev as Andrey. Lavrovsky, the weightiest name in *drambalet*,

---

446 Born in Gonyatichi, Ukraine in 1930, Sekh studied at the ballet studio of the Lvov Theatre between 1946 and 1948 before joining the Bolshoi School from where he joined the company in 1951 and where he danced as a soloist until 1974. In 1971 he graduated from the ballet department of GITIS and between 1971 and 1975 was a teacher-coach in ballet companies in Finland and Yugoslavia and in Czechoslovakia in 1982. He taught at GITIS since 1975 and was appointed a professor in 1989. He died in late 2020.

447 As quoted by Degen and Stupnikov on Belcanto.ru

signalled a shift in his own view of dance in an article published in 1963. Whilst not going so far as to advocate abstraction in dance, he admitted that 'meaning' could satisfy the imperative for dramatic 'content': "can a man dance without any reason, make the slightest move, without an inner compulsion? This does not mean that every dance should express action, but it should by all means express man's inner state."[448] Lavrovsky turned to creating plotless works to symphonic music with *Boléro* and *La Valse* in 1964, both set to Ravel's music.

Konstantin Sergeyev at the Kirov continued to strive to create a successful Soviet ballet, making *Distant Planet* in April 1963 which was, despite official policy on meaningful Soviet narrative, a rather abstract and ultimately unsuccessful fantasy concerning Man danced by Yuri Soloviev as a weightless cosmonaut, Earth, a role taken by Kaleria Fedicheva[449] and Gabriela Komleva's Planet. The score was composed by Boris Maisel.[450] In June 1964 Sergeyev essayed a second version of *Cinderella* in which character was further embedded in the movement rather than developed solely by mime; it featured Irina Kolpakova in the title role, which was later taken successfully by Alla Sizova, and the elegant Vladilen Semyonov, later the virtuoso Soloviev, as The Prince.

The beginning of the 1960s saw the return to the Bolshoi of one of Soviet ballet's great experimenters, Kasyan Goleizovsky. In October 1962, he was invited to stage the ten-part *Scriabiniana* (Balanchine had seen a dance suite by him to that name in Petrograd in 1922) and in 1964 was commissioned to create *Leili and Majnun*, based on a classic Azerbaijani tragic love story, for the main stage. It had music by Sergey Balasanian[451] and featured Natalia Bessmertnova as Leili who in the ballet became a visual metaphor for oriental sensuality and Vladimir Vasiliev as Kais – called Majnun or 'possessed' – who dominated the action as her doomed lover. It was Goleizovsky's last

---

448   Roslavleva, *Era of the Russian Ballet*, p.275

449   Born in Ust-Ijori, near Leningrad in 1936, Fedicheva graduated into the Kirov in 1955, dancing her first Odette-Odile in *Swan Lake* in 1961. Physically beautiful, she lacked the lyricism of the great ballerinas but scored particular success in contemporary works, creating roles in many throughout her career in the company. After her emigration to the United States in 1975, she taught at her husband's dance school and staged ballets until her death in Maribor, Slovenia in 1994.

450   Born in St Petersburg in 1907, Maisel studied at the Leningrad Conservatoire and became a prolific composer in a variety of forms including nine symphonies, concerti, song cycles and, in addition to *Distant Planet*, another ballet, *The Snow Queen*, in 1940. He died in Moscow in 1986.

451   Born in Askhabad, Turkmenistan in 1902, Balasanian studied in Tbilisi and at the Moscow Conservatoire before becoming a composer. In 1939, he wrote the first Tajik opera *The Uprising at Vosse*, concerning a late nineteenth-century popular rebellion. He was instrumental in organising a national music theatre there between 1936 and 1949. He taught at the Moscow Conservatoire from 1965 onwards. He died in Moscow in 1982.

work at the Bolshoi; he died in 1970.

In 1963 Fyodor Lopukhov, the other great innovator of the 1920s, created *Pictures at an Exhibition* for the Stanislavsky company to Modest Mussorgsky's score. It proved to be a work of great depth, with a genesis which could be traced back to the choreographer's creation of the 'Gnome' section in 1927: "I have revised some of the details", he wrote, "but not the fundamentals, conceived thirty-five years ago."[452] For the Stanislavsky, he expanded his vision to encompass all ten sections of the score, bringing a breadth of movement quality to each. Section Two, 'The Old Castle', was given purely classical steps and featured a romantic pas de deux while he set Section Eight, 'Catacombs', in Greek mythology, using semi-acrobatic movements to depict Hades, God of the Underworld and the three Furies. The most admired section was the fourth, 'Bydlo' or 'Cattle' which showed four peasants on their knees, attempting to rise in growing revolt with the swell of the music, but returning to their original positions at the end, weighed down by their lowly class and the oppression of society by religious superstition.

1960 – American Ballet Theatre in Russia

ABT's six-week visit in the autumn of 1960 was Russia's first opportunity to see the ballet mettle of their ideological foe, even if they were, as the Soviet leader had so pointedly observed (and which was echoed throughout their visit by the Soviet press), a company without a permanent home and beginning to be overshadowed by Balanchine's New York City Ballet. The company was not accorded an engagement at the Bolshoi Theatre, having to make do with appearances at the Stanislavsky Theatre before travelling on to Tbilisi, Leningrad (not the Kirov but the Theatre of the Cultural Cooperative Centre) and Kiev. They finally returned to Moscow to appear again at the Stanislavsky and at the Lenin Palace of Sports. Russia was not to see some of the jewels of the company's repertoire which had fallen foul of the Soviet censor: Eugene Loring's *Billy the Kid* (celebrating a murderous outlaw) and Agnes de Mille's *Fall River Legend* (which 'revealed the morasses of abnormal psychology') were dropped, although Rafael Zaakov, vice-president of *Gosconcert*,[453] insisted that, given ABT's relative technical weaknesses, the works had been voluntarily removed by the Americans at Soviet suggestion so as not to compromise the overall success of the company's tour. The Russians were given three mixed bill programmes which included two Petipa pas de deux (*Don Quixote* and *Swan Lake* Act III), Fokine's *Les Sylphides*, Balanchine's *Theme and Variations*, Jerome

---

452 Lopukhov quoted by Roslavleva, *Era of the Russian Ballet*, p.266

453 The State Concert Association of the USSR (Gosconcert) was formed in 1956 to oversee trips, visits and tours by Soviet Russian artists.

Robbins'[454] *Fancy Free*, Agnes de Mille's *Rodeo*, Tudor's *Lilac Garden* ('a so-called psychological ballet' in which 'a feeling of tragic doom predominates'), David Lichine's *Graduation Ball* and three now near-forgotten works – William Dollar's *Le Combat* which garnered much positive comment for its anti-war message, Fokine's penultimate ballet *Bluebeard*, completed some ten months before his death in August 1942, which solicited much interest and admiration for its theatrical effect and Birgit Cullberg's *The Lady from the Sea*. The reaction of the Russian audiences was distinctly mixed, with *Theme and Variations*, the ballet which opened the season, universally disliked: Soviet dance critic Natalia Roslavleva[455] quoted an unnamed Bolshoi dancer who observed: "each *note* was adequately matched by the choreography, but the *music* was not danced".[456] Seymour Topping of *The New York Times* reported on a performance at the Stanislavsky Theatre:

> "The Russians were alternately delighted and puzzled with the cowboy ballet *Rodeo*. The critics found the Americans generally did not perform with the authority or classicism of their own Bolshoi and Stanislavsky ballet companies. Only Erik Bruhn and Maria Tallchief (in the 'pas de deux' of *Swan Lake*) evoked the bravos and cadenced clapping the Russians award as their highest accolade."[457]

It was not ABT's repertoire which ultimately troubled the Soviets, nor indeed the dancers of ABT whose "corps de ballet in classical creations was mostly on the short and plump side;" the company's dance schooling was judged not to be "...harmoniously developed. While the footwork was quite good, the upper part of the body looked rigid and undeveloped."[458] It was the presence of a male dancer every bit as good as any Russian, the Danish Erik Bruhn[459] which came as a revelation; the Bolshoi's Mikhail Gabovich found

---

454   Born in New York in 1918, Robbins studied dance with Eugene Loring and Antony Tudor and danced in musicals before joining Ballet Theatre in 1940, his first choreographic work was *Fancy Free* in 1944. He joined New York City Ballet in 1949 and became its associate director. He left in 1959 before returning in 1969 as ballet master. Alongside those of Balanchine, his ballets form the core of the company's repertoire. He died in New York in 1998.

455   Born in Moscow in 1907, Roslavleva graduated from GITIS in 1930. She became a highly respected ballet critic and historian, producing numerous publications including *Era of the Russian Ballet*. She sometimes wrote under the pseudonym Natalia Rene. She died in Moscow in 1977.

456   Roslavleva, 'Soviet Reactions to the American Ballet Theatre', *Dancing Times*, October 1960

457   As quoted by Caute, *The Dancer Defects: The Struggle for Cultural Supremacy during the Cold War*, p.483

458   Roslavleva, 'Soviet Reactions to the American Ballet Theatre', *Dancing Times*, October 1960

459   Born in Copenhagen, Denmark in 1928, Bruhn graduated into the Royal Danish

him "outstanding for his truly noble and manly but elegant style of classical dancing".[460] With his aristocratic demeanour and technical perfection, he offered the Russians 'a glimpse at their own lost past'.[461]

1961 – *Petrushka*

Fokine's *Petrushka* had not been performed on the Soviet ballet stage since Leontiev's 1920 version for the GATOB stage. Interest in the choreographer had grown with the publication of his letters and memoirs and Lopukhov was approached by MALEGOT concerning a revival of the ballet, which he rejected. Pyotr Gusev's suggestion of Konstantin Boyarsky was taken up and in March 1961 he staged a production at the Maly which sought to return the Ballets Russes masterpiece to the repertoire and brought great personal success to Valery Panov in the title role and Maria Mazun[462] as the Ballerina. The only person living in Russia to have danced the title role, Leonid Petrov,[463] had no memory of Petrushka's solo in the scene inside the puppets' tent, so Boyarsky composed his own, although Panov's virtuoso steps led to the communication of the full and correct notation by Joan and Rudolf Benesh[464] in the UK via the USSR-Great Britain Friendship Society. Such was *Petrushka*'s success that Boyarsky was invited in 1964 to stage it for the Bolshoi appearing at the Kremlin Palace of Congresses with Vladimir Vasiliev in the title role and Ekaterina Maximova as the Ballerina, and again for the main theatre in 1982 with Mikhail Tsivin[465] and Ludmilla Semenyaka.

Ballet in 1947 and quickly became recognised as one of the world's finest dancers, renowned for his noble stage bearing and immaculate technique. He later received plaudits for his clear and intelligent stagings of the classics. He died in Toronto, Canada in 1986.

460   As quoted by Roslavleva, 'Soviet Reactions to the American Ballet Theatre', *Dancing Times*, October 1960

461   Homans, *Apollo's Angels*, p.374

462   Born in 1924 in the village of Zakharovo, Tver region, Mazun graduated into the Maly company from the Leningrad Choreographic School in 1943 where she danced until 1963. She was considered as a versatile ballerina, as comfortable in lyrical as in dramatic roles. She died in 1997.

463   Born in St Petersburg in 1898, Petrov graduated into the ex-Mariinsky in 1919 where he danced until 1937. He danced a variety of soloist roles and created the part of the Counter-revolutionary in Lopukhov's 1924 *Red Whirlwind*. He taught at the Choreographic School from 1922 onwards. He died in Leningrad in 1963.

464   Husband and wife team who devised the Benesh notation system for recording dance. Rudolf, an engineer (born London, 1916, died London, 1975) and Joan, a dancer (born Liverpool 1920, died Skelmersdale, Lancashire, 2014) started in 1955 and began teaching the system in 1956 at the Royal Academy of Dancing. In 1962, they founded the Institute of Choreology which later became the Benesh Institute. The system is now used by almost every major ballet company worldwide.

465   Born in Moscow in 1949, Tsivin graduated into the Bolshoi in 1967 and rose to soloist level. He danced as a member of the company until 1988 but continued to appear as a guest artist until 1992. In 1983 he graduated from the ballet master department of

Boyarsky's work on *Petrushka* can be seen as the beginnings of the USSR's reclamation of the Ballets Russes repertoire, a phenomenon which gathered pace in subsequent decades.

The revival of *Petrushka* by Boyarsky was also important on a musical level. Igor Stravinsky's music had been officially banned following Andrey Zhdanov's further 1948 decree but had not been played for some considerable time before that. By 1961, such had been the relaxation by the regime that performance of the full score was now permitted, eliciting favourable comments from the composer and then deputy chairman of the board of the Leningrad branch of the Union of Soviet Composers Valerian Bogdanov-Berezovsky:[466]

> "It is well known what a significant role this outstanding work of Russian music played both in the work of the composer himself and in the world of choreographic art. Therefore, the great interest that aroused the performance is natural. It is invariably performed to a full auditorium, meanwhile the Leningrad press is still silent about this significant event in theatrical life – a direct consequence of the prejudice against some major phenomena of modern artistic culture that developed during the period of the personality cult."[467]

Boyarsky followed the success of *Petrushka* and the composer's music with an all-Stravinsky evening in the spring of 1962 which comprised *Orpheus* in its first production in the USSR with choreography by Boyarsky, a revival of *Petrushka* and his staging of Fokine's *The Firebird*. In 1962 Lopukhov and Sergeyev revived the Fokine ballets *Le Carnaval* and *Une Nuit d'Égypte* (known in the West as *Cléopâtre*) respectively at the Kirov.

1961 – *The Legend of Love*

In the early 1960s, Yuri Grigorovich's ascent to his long-unassailable directorship of the Bolshoi Ballet was far from a foregone conclusion. His earliest choreographic success in Leningrad was *The Stone Flower* in 1957 which was considered strong enough to open the 1961 Kirov London season. In March 1961 he presented his second full-length ballet, *The Legend of Love*, a melodramatic orientalist tale which, nevertheless, showed his

---

GITIS and was Director of the Vivaldi Orchestra between 1994 and 1996. He was director of the Bolshoi company between 1998 and 2002.

466   Born in Pargolovo, St Petersburg in 1903, Bogdanov-Berezovsky graduated in composition from the Leningrad Conservatoire in 1927 and became an associate of Asafiev. In 1940 he began to teach the history of Soviet music at the Leningrad Conservatoire and wrote his opera *Leningradtsy* during the siege. He oversaw repertoire at the Maly Theatre from 1951 to 1961. In the 1960s, his compositions became more dramatic in tone. He died in Moscow in 1971.

467   Bogdanov-Berezovsky, 'The History of *Petrushka*', *Izvestia*, January 1962

development of through-danced action and an expansive use of the corps de ballet; the score was composed by Arif Melikov.[468] The narrative was based on Turkish poet Nazym Hikmet's verse, concerning a love triangle of Queen Mekhmeneh-Banu, her sister Shyrien who both love the stone-cutter Ferhad, who in turn loves only Shyrien. When the lovers flee, Ferhad ultimately sacrifices himself to spare the Queen's vengeance on her country. Grigorovich constructed the ballet with care, and provided a powerful trio in each act for the protagonists. On opening night, Zubkovskaya was Mekhmeneh-Banu (some sources say Moiseyeva), Kolpakova appeared as Shyrien and Gribov danced Ferhad (replacing Nureyev who had walked out of a rehearsal and been removed from the cast). The ballet initially came in for serious criticism, notably for its perceived eroticism and reliance on acrobatic lifts; the Kirov's Principal Conductor Alexander Klimov[469] referred to it in a 1963 article in the periodical *Soviet Art* as having exhibited "a tendency to the imitation of models of bourgeois art, the striving for 'novelty' that has nothing in common with genuine innovation".[470] Official reaction notwithstanding, *The Legend of Love* became a firm audience favourite and enjoyed frequent revivals and stagings elsewhere. It was not subtle story-telling, but Grigorovich succeeded in making his dances musical, the narrative understandable with nothing extraneous or purely decorative. It was acquired by the Bolshoi in April 1965, a little after Grigorovich took up his appointment as company choreographer, with Plisetskaya as the spitfire Queen, Bessmertnova as Shyrien and Liepa as Ferhad.

1961 – *Seventh Symphony / Leningrad Symphony*

Igor Belsky achieved his greatest choreographic success in April 1961 at the Kirov with *Seventh Symphony* (the ballet was renamed *Leningrad Symphony* in the following year) which he set to the first movement of Shostakovich's Seventh Symphony. As a dance work, it was an abstract evocation of Leningrad's heroic resistance to the Nazi siege during the war, as far from *drambalet*'s principles as could be, but fully understandable to its audience, many of whom had themselves lived through unspeakable privations.

468   Born in Baku, Azerbaijan in 1933, Melikov graduated from the Baku Conservatoire in 1958. His first success was *The Legend of Love*, which made his name, after which he composed more ballets, symphonies and film scores. He died in Baku in 2019.

469   Born in Kostanay, Kazakhstan in 1898, Klimov graduated from the Kiev Higher Institute of Music and Drama in 1928. After several posts around the Ukraine, he directed the Ukrainian Symphony Orchestra and the orchestra of the Tajik Opera House. After the end of the war, Klimov became a conductor of the Odessa Opera House and a professor at the Odessa Conservatoire and was director of the Kiev Conservatoire from 1948 to 1954. Between 1954 and 1961 he headed the Kiev Opera and Ballet Theatre and was principal Conductor of the Kirov Theatre orchestra from 1961 to 1967. He died in Leningrad in 1974.

470   Ezrahi, *Swans of the Kremlin*, p.198

It depicted the girls and boys of the city who learn to defend it through adversity and months of sacrifice and was led in the first cast by Yuri Soloviev as The Youth and Alla Sizova as The Girl. It was a surprise success, due in no small part to Belsky's novel approach in depicting Soviet heroism. The ballet critic Arkady Sokolov-Kaminsky[471] observed:

> "In a completely new and excitingly interesting way...Belsky solved the heroic theme in his *Leningrad Symphony*. For him, the main thing was to show the heroic character as ordinary and familiar; ordinary as the only possible struggle in this situation for the freedom of the Motherland, for the future, for common happiness. The heroic, therefore, is portrayed as inherent to the nature of Soviet man, as an integral feature of his spirit."[472]

In the light of its unquestionable success, Belsky left the Kirov the next year to take up the directorship of MALEGOT where he stayed for some eleven years, continuing to choreograph, but never replicating the success of *Leningrad Symphony*. He returned to the Kirov in 1973 as company director and in May 1974 created his last work for the company, *Icarus*, featuring Yuri Soloviev in the title role alongside Irina Kolpakova as the Dream Bird.

1961 – Rudolf Nureyev

The Danish *danseur noble* Erik Bruhn was the inspiration for the young Rudolf Nureyev, a notoriously temperamental rising star at the Kirov; he watched him again and again on pirated film, but was denied the opportunity to see him dance with ABT in Leningrad in 1960; he was sent to East Germany on a gruelling bus tour in the company of circus performers – Nureyev believed it was so that he would not be influenced by Western dance styles. Part of the reason perhaps for Nureyev's defection to the West in 1961 was that, apart from Soloviev, there was no other male dancer whom he admired in Russia. Simply speaking, Bruhn was a Western dancer, dancing in the West and Nureyev wanted to learn from him. Nureyev had also got something of a taste for a forbidden world when he was included in a group of dancers who attended the Seventh World Communist Youth Festival held in Vienna in July 1959. During that stay, he tried to expose himself artistically to as much as possible and managed to meet the French choreographer Roland Petit,[473]

---

471 Born in Leningrad in 1937, Sokolov-Kaminsky graduated from the Leningrad State Institute of Theatre, Music and Cinematography in 1967, having already begun ballet criticism. Between 1971 and 1992 he worked as a researcher at the Russian State Institute of Performing Arts and has been on the editorial board of the *Soviet Ballet* magazine since 1990. He has taught at many institutions, most notably at the Leningrad Conservatoire where in 1988 he instituted the History and Theory of Choreographic Art course. He is married to Kirov ballerina Gabriela Komleva.

472 As quoted by Degen and Stupnikov in www.belcanto.ru

473 Born in Villemomble in 1924, Petit graduated into the Paris Opéra Ballet in 1940

whose *Cyrano de Bergerac* made a great impression on him; the year before he had travelled without permission to Moscow to see Alicia Alonso's Cuban troupe perform Balanchine's *Apollo* and was, in his own words "agog".[474]

1961 – The Kirov in Paris

The Kirov Ballet had not been allowed to tour abroad in the same way as the Bolshoi, but in 1961, visits to Paris and London were finally permitted and arranged, coinciding with another factor which contributed to Nureyev's defection, the return of Konstantin Sergeyev as company director, an individual for whom the young Tartar dancer had almost complete contempt. The Kirov's French producers insisted on Nureyev's inclusion on the list of dancers travelling in May to Paris for a month-long season, but he and they knew that removal could happen at any moment – ballerinas Alla Shelest and Ninel Kurgapkina were dropped in the run-up to departure, the latter allegedly for wearing trousers on a previous company tour to Dresden. Nureyev was not trusted by the authorities – he had refused to join the communist youth organisation *Komsomol* and had, suspiciously, learned some English. However, their nervousness at letting him go was offset by the excitement abroad that his presence would undoubtedly generate; he was a rising star noted for his dynamic on-stage persona, and popular with the public. He boarded the flight to Paris for the start of a month-long season.

The company was scheduled to perform at the Opéra's Palais Garnier and the large Palais des Sports and it opened with *The Sleeping Beauty* which did not please many Parisian critics with what they perceived its fussy and old-fashioned aesthetic: Patrick Thévenon in *Paris-Presse L'intransigeant* observed of the production that: "C'est sans doute l'œuvre la plus poussiéreuse que l'on puisse voir à l'heure actuelle"[475] (It is perhaps the dustiest work you can see at present). There was, however, general admiration for the purity of the dancers' style; in the magazine *Arts*, J. Bourgeois wrote: "C'est une joie complète d'admirer des placements corrects dont la justification même reside dans le résultat esthétique incomparable"[476] (It is an utter joy to admire perfect placement whose sole justification lies in an incomparable aesthetic effect). Central to the company's growing success were the appearances by Nureyev who garnered wild enthusiasm at his eleven performances.

---

but left four years later. In 1945, he established the Ballets des Champs-Elysées with himself as leading dancer and chief choreographer. Early successes included *Le Jeune Homme et la Mort* (1946) and *Carmen* (1949). His choreography was grounded in classical ballet, but he was also a theatre showman and happily included other influences. He went on to produce ballets, shows and revues, often showcasing his wife, the dancer Zizi Jeanmaire. He died in Geneva in 2011.

474   Kavanagh, *Rudolf Nureyev*, p.107
475   Thévenon, *Paris-Presse L'intransigeant*, 18th May 1961.
476   Bourgeois, *Arts*, 31st May 1961

Defection

The details of Nureyev's defection have been retold countless times but it is useful to examine this event from the Soviet perspective. Fears about Nureyev and his behaviour proved to be entirely justified, as, once in Paris, he went out of his way to speak to and befriend French dancers and, giving his KGB minders the slip, to expose himself to everything the French capital had to offer. There were conflicting currents among the Russians, with Minister of Culture Furtseva allegedly wishing Nureyev to dance the first night of *The Sleeping Beauty* and company director Sergeyev deciding to give it to Vladilen Semyonov who partnered his wife Irina Kolpakova. Despite the ecstatic ovation which greeted his tour debut as Solor in the 'Kingdom of the Shades' from *La Bayadère*, dancing opposite Olga Moiseyeva as Nikiya, Nureyev's intolerable behaviour off-stage finally persuaded the authorities to act: the order was sent to Sergeyev that the young rebel was to return to Russia before the end of the tour. Such had been Nureyev's success – he had received the prestigious Prix Nijinski from Serge Lifar – that Sergeyev, the Kirov and the Soviet ambassador all attempted to make the case for him to remain. It was to no avail. On 16th June, as the dancers of the company prepared themselves at Le Bourget airport to board their plane for London, Nureyev was informed that Khrushchev wished to see him dance and that he would now take another aircraft bound for Moscow; he was also told that his mother was unwell. Flanked by KGB guards, Nureyev was led away to an airport bar to wait a further two hours for his flight. It was then that he got up, walked six steps towards two officials who he had been told by a friend would be standing nearby and stated that he wished to stay in France. The most famous Russian ballet dancer of the moment had defected.

It is all too easy to think that Rudolf Nureyev's 'Great Leap to Freedom' – in his own words 'six steps exactly' – represented one of the most important moments in twentieth century ballet. Nothing could be further from the truth from the Russian perspective. The Soviet authorities had been thwarted, and their ideologically wayward twenty-three-year-old star had slipped from their grasp, but it was hardly as if the Kirov Ballet collapsed as a result, despite Serge Lifar's pronouncement that Nureyev's decision to remain in France was a disaster for Leningrad ballet. Far from it.

1961 – The Kirov in London

The company continued with their scheduled visit to the United Kingdom, appearing in London to great acclaim and fielding a stable of notable dancers, from Alla Osipenko, Alla Sizova, Inna Zubkovskaya and Irina Kolpakova to Vladilen Semyonov and Yuri Soloviev, a dancer in 1961 "on the brink of greatness" according to critic Clive Barnes and, on his return to London five years later, "a dancer...incomparable and unsurpassed"[477] in the words of Richard Buckle in the *Sunday Times*.

The enthusiasm for the company was different from that for the Bolshoi some six years prior: "If the Bolshoi is the blazing sun...then the Leningrad State Kirov Ballet, I think, resembles the moon...The initial impact is less powerful; the cumulative effect of its beguiling magic is little short of bewitching"[478] observed English dance critic Mary Clarke. The Kirov's purity of schooling was praised time and again: "...there is all the time in the world for a développé to unfold and for an arabesque to reach right out, out, out towards infinity".[479] The company performed *The Stone Flower*, *The Sleeping Beauty*, *Giselle*, *Swan Lake* and a gala programme comprising the 'Kingdom of the Shades from *La Bayadère*, the Rose Waltz from Vainonen's *The Nutcracker* and *The Flames of Paris* pas de deux, Yakobson's *Fantasia* pas de deux, a solo from his *The Snow Maiden*, the comic *Gossiping Women* and an extract from *Taras Bulba*.

In *The Times*, Clement Crisp observed of the company:

"Theirs is a style that does not at first reveal itself fully to the spectator, and one of the joys of this season has been the gradual discovery of the richness of the Kirov school. It is an essentially classical art of ease, assurance and harmony, where nothing appears excessive or strained and nothing is skimped."[480]

After their departure, the veteran English ballet critic Arnold Haskell concluded "...the Kirov ballet has safeguarded its great classical dance tradition and even enhanced it".[481]

The news of Nureyev's defection in Paris was not well received by his fellow Kirov dancers, the ballet audiences in Leningrad or Russian society at large. The reaction in Russia was one of fury and incomprehension in equal measure with many simply unable to understand how someone in his position could betray his country; how could 'someone with our training and our background do such a thing?' Alla Osipenko is alleged to have asked, despite being his friend. The KGB became very nervous in London, so when Osipenko accepted gifts at her birthday party held by a balletomane British diplomat, she was not only denounced the next day before the assembled company but also locked into her hotel every night after the performance. She was not allowed to take part in further foreign tours for six years.

---

477   *The Sunday Times*, 18th September 1966
478   Clarke, 'The Season Reviewed', *Dancing Times*, Vol 51., pp.662
479   ibid.
480   *The Times*, 7th July 1961
481   Haskell, *The Ballet Annual*, 1962, p.36

Reaction

On their return to Leningrad, the Kirov dancers were summoned and debriefed by the KGB as to the official line on Nureyev's defection – he would be excised from all company records. In 1962 Nureyev was tried and sentenced to prison in absentia and both his image and records of him were systematically erased from all sources in the public domain; it was only in 1987 that he was officially rehabilitated. His defection to the West did have an effect on those who would, in later years, follow him, and there was contact between him and Soviet dancers on tour outside the USSR, but in terms of the nature and direction of Soviet ballet, he was to be forgotten.

Not all in the West greeted Nureyev's defection with pleasure: Haskell wrote of him as a "crazy mixed-up dancer (who) may be forgiven but not those who exploited him",[482] expressed worry that his 'leap to freedom' would sour relations between the Soviet Union and stated that "the star needs the company more than the company needs the star".[483]

1961 – The Royal Ballet in Russia

By the early 1960s, the policy of cultural diplomacy was fully espoused on both sides of the Iron Curtain, and ballet company tours into the 'enemy camp' were well established. So, while the Kirov Ballet was performing in London in June and July, The Royal Ballet embarked on a month-long visit to the USSR, first appearing in Leningrad and then Moscow. Their visit was enthusiastically received in both cities, with much favourable commentary for Frederick Ashton's *Ondine* (if not for Hans-Werner Henze's score) and *La Fille mal gardée*, "a perfect recreation of Dauberval's masterpiece as seen by a contemporary eye, and a thoroughly British ballet"[484] which also prompted ex-Bolshoi principal dancer Mikhail Gabovich to observe that it deserved to be mounted by other companies. It was noted with pleasure that Ashton had made several uses in the ballet of a favourite Soviet lift, the *stulchik* (rather more vulgarly termed in English a 'bum lift'). John Cranko's *The Lady and the Fool* and Ninette de Valois' *The Rake's Progress* were praised, even if the latter's final madhouse scene was considered by Gabovich as too pathological, whereas less favourable comments were drawn by the company's stylistic approach to Fokine's *The Firebird*. Natalia Goncharova's[485] 1926 re-designs

482   Haskell, 'A Sorry Affair', *Dancing Times*, Vol.51, p.676
483   ibid.
484   'The Royal Ballet in the USSR', *Ballet Annual*, No.16, p.41
485   Born in Nagaevo, Tula Governorate in 1881, Goncharova studied art at the Moscow Institute but was expelled with her fellow painter and future partner Mikhail Larionov in 1910 because of her avant-garde style. She became a leading exponent of Futurism and Rayonism and was a member of 'Der Blaue Reiter' group from its founding in 1911. She became involved with the Ballets Russes, designing *Le Coq d'Or* in 1914 and, after her move to Paris in 1921, *Les Noces* (1923) and completed the redesign of *The Firebird* in 1926. She

in particular were not welcomed, although dance commentator Roslavleva did write that "...we are extremely grateful to The Royal Ballet for having preserved and brought to us this masterpiece of Fokine which had never been shown in Russia".[486] In Leningrad *Les Patineurs* was seen and praised by the then 89-year-old Adelina Giuri,[487] a former Bolshoi ballerina who had danced in the skating divertissement of the 1892 London production of Giacomo Meyerbeer's *Le Prophète* – from which music had been taken for Ashton's ballet – and who herself had been a notable Moscow Aurora in 1899. *The Sleeping Beauty* provoked much enthusiasm in both cities, although criticisms were made of the later 'Diaghilev additions' which de Valois had incorporated, and of the preservation of certain elements, such as mime and courtly pageantry, which Soviet productions had long excised.

The company's dancers were closely watched and analysed, with "considerable progress" noted in the development of their "own classical style and school"; Marina Semyonova observed that the dancers' arms were "better than those of the French" and rather cryptically said that the company dancers would "get rid of the defects (in their dancing) once they are shown them". The great teacher Asaf Messerer was satisfied with the company's "solid foundation" but expressed "a desire for better épaulement and stronger backs".[488] Nadia Nerina was enthusiastically welcomed back to Russia and scored a personal triumph as Lise in *La Fille mal gardée* while the critic Natalia Roslavleva voiced great admiration for Margot Fonteyn who made "...us realise from the very first encounter that she belongs to the numbered ranks of the greatest ballerinas of our time".[489]

1961 – The Kirov in New York

After Nureyev's June defection in Paris and the company's London season, the Kirov continued on to New York and a residency at the Metropolitan Opera House. Historically, their visit has been overshadowed by those by the Bolshoi in 1959 and again in 1962, but was significant in that it brought another view of Soviet ballet to the American audiences and critics, that of what came to be considered as the more refined Leningrad style. *Giselle*, *The Sleeping Beauty* and *Swan Lake* were the full-length works performed as well as the 'Kingdom of the Shades' from *La Bayadère* and excerpts from

died in Paris in 1962.

486   ibid, p.46

487   Born in Cairo in 1872, Giuri first trained in Milan and finished her dance education in Moscow. She was engaged by the Bolshoi and was prized for her flawless line and crystalline brilliance. She danced much of the repertoire including the title role in *Raymonda* (alongside Vasily Tikhomirov). She took Russian citizenship in 1946 and died in Moscow in 1963.

488   'The Royal Ballet in the USSR', *Ballet Annual* No.16, p.146

489   ibid, p.41

Taras Bulba, *Le Corsaire* and *The Flames of Paris*. The season also included the first performances outside the Soviet Union of Igor Belsky's *Leningrad Symphony* which was moderately successful but nevertheless welcomed as a "praiseworthy step towards a broader conception of choreography in the Soviet theatre".[490] Soloviev and Sizova were the most popular dancers of the season and Irina Kolpakova was hailed as an exquisite Aurora and Giselle.

1962 – Kirov troubles

Sergeyev and Dudinskaya's perceived stranglehold on the Kirov and its repertoire provoked growing resentment and frustration among the younger generation of dancers who felt their development limited, their opportunities curtailed and their performances often under-rehearsed. Early 1962 saw the publication of two letters signed by company members criticising the director: the first was signed by senior dancers including Askold Makarov and Nikolai Zubkovsky; the second by younger artists such as Kolpakova, Kurgapkina, Moiseyeva, Osipenko, Shelest and Sizova.

1962 – Yakobson's second *Spartacus*

Following Moiseyev's failure with *Spartacus* in 1958, the Bolshoi despatched Lavrovsky, Ulanova and Semyonova to Leningrad to see Yakobson's version, which continued to enjoy not inconsiderable local success. Their positive opinions received, the choreographer was invited to stage a version for Moscow, reusing as many of the previous production's costumes as possible. Yakobson proposed a refocussing of his Leningrad ballet, bringing very much to the fore Spartacus' own heroism in the context of the highlighted depravity of the Romans. In practice, the feast at Crassus's palace proved to be by far the most successful scene of the ballet, thereby taking the focus away from the story of Spartacus himself. The production opened in Moscow in April with Dmitry Begak as Spartacus (as in the Moiseyev version), Plisetskaya as Phrygia, Natalia Ryzhenko as Aegina and Alexander Radunsky as Crassus, but it was not a success and received censure for the overtly erotic nature of some of its content. Despite considerable misgivings in some quarters, it was included in the company's repertoire for its American tour which took place while Balanchine and NYCB were in Russia. It opened in New York to destructive reviews.

1962 – The Bolshoi's second USA tour

Taking place during the growing political tensions of the Cuban Missile Crisis, the Bolshoi Ballet's second North American tour began in September 1962. Over three months, the company visited nine US cities plus Canada, offering three full-length ballets, *Spartacus*, *Giselle* and *Swan Lake*, the last of which was particularly anticipated given no North American company

490 Moore, 'The Kirov Ballet in New York', *Dancing Times*, Vol.52., p.84

presented a credible version of the complete work at the time. In addition, the 'Kingdom of the Shades' from *La Bayadère*, Fokine's *Chopiniana*, the fourth act from Anisimova's *Gayaneh*, Lavrovsky's *Paganini* and *Walpurgis Night* and Asaf Messerer's *Ballet Class* (originally created for the Bolshoi Ballet School in the late 1950s and known later as *Class Concert*) appeared variously in mixed programmes. A new feature of the American critical response to the Bolshoi on this occasion was an unfavourable comparison between the Leningrad and Moscow companies, especially regarding their respective versions of *Swan Lake*. *Ballet Class* however, proved extremely popular wherever it was performed, given the stunning virtuosity of the company's finest dancers.

1962 – The return of Stravinsky

In September 1962, Igor Stravinsky made a three-week visit to the USSR, some forty-eight years after his departure for the West – he had first sought exile in Switzerland and subsequently took French and then later American citizenship. His attitude towards the Soviet ideal was in essence hostile, mirrored by the regime's opinion of him and his music; even before the revolution, his compositions for Diaghilev's Ballets Russes were criticised, a young Prokofiev allegedly calling *Petrushka* "rotten rubbish".[491] The regime's hostility intensified after Stalin's rise to power and his imposition of cultural orthodoxy; in 1948, the composer's music was banned in its entirety throughout the Soviet Union. However, Stravinsky had established himself internationally as a composer of the first rank who had a particular affinity to ballet thanks to the artistic understanding between himself and George Balanchine. In the post-Stalin era, official opinion towards him softened and in 1962 he was invited to Russia just before the arrival of Balanchine and New York City Ballet; while the ballet company was in Moscow, Stravinsky was finishing his visit to Leningrad. He attended four concerts of his own music in the capital, conducting some works himself and, at the Palace of Congresses, watched the Maly Ballet's triple-bill comprising *Petrushka*, *The Firebird* and *Orpheus* which had premièred in Leningrad in the spring.

1962 – Balanchine and New York City Ballet in Russia

A major event for the Russian ballet world was the eight-week visit by New York City Ballet in the autumn of 1962. Not only was the company the undisputed dance flagship of the United States, but it had been founded and forged into a great ensemble by George Balanchine, the émigré Russian dancer-choreographer who had chosen life in the West after the social and cultural upheavals of the Russian revolution. The stakes could not have been higher nor the tensions and expectations on both sides any more pronounced

---

491 Cross, 'Telling Tales: The Myths of Stravinsky'

than on 9th October 1962 when the curtains of the Bolshoi Theatre opened on NYCB's first performance.

Balanchine had not been to the country of his birth for thirty-eight years, and is said to have found the whole experience traumatic, from his reunion with members of his family to the constant reminders that Russia was his true 'home' and, indeed, the home of ballet. On his arrival at Moscow's Sheremetyevo airport, he is said to have retorted to an official newspaper interviewer: "Thank you, but America is now the home of the classical ballet. Russia is home of the old romantic ballet."[492] It was NYCB's repertoire which was an artistic shock to the Russians – eighteen one-act works, of which sixteen by Balanchine, were presented in five programmes. When Balanchine and his old St Petersburg classmate Leonid Lavrovsky had met in New York during the Bolshoi's 1959 visit, the Soviet ballet master had observed: "You know, in the Soviet Union, work such as yours would be condemned as mere formalism, as inhuman."[493] In 1962, Balanchine knew full well the effect his choreography would have on Russian audiences. The NYCB Russian season opened with *Serenade* set to Tchaikovsky's 'Serenade for Strings' and one of his first ballets created in the United States which represented Balanchine's artistic credo and exemplified his dance aesthetic. The American dance critic John Martin, who accompanied the company to Russia, observed that "the response was a perplexed and fairly indifferent one". Jerome Robbins' jazzy *Interplay* to a score by Morton Gould was followed by Balanchine's spare *Agon* to Stravinsky which, perhaps surprisingly given its uncompromising modernity, "brought forth the first sign of enthusiasm." The evening concluded with the all-American *Western Symphony* which prompted "the greatest ovation".[494] Momentum gathered as the tour progressed, with ever-more enthusiastic receptions from the audience who clamoured for tickets to see such diverse works as *Donizetti Variations* and the stark and challenging *Episodes* and demanded to see Russian ballet's 'prodigal son' appear on stage with repeated chants of 'Bal-an-chine!'. The enthusiasm was genuine. Martin also commented on the nature of a Russian audience: "(It) is altogether an honest one. It applauds furiously when it is moved to do so, and sits in absolute silence when it is not so moved."[495]

Official and critical reactions were confused, as the repertoire presented the antithesis of everything Soviet ballet stood for – these were one-act works which had no story, no set and, in some cases, precious little costume. There was unequivocal acknowledgement of a brilliant virtuosic company who, in the words of choreographer Rostislav Zakharov possessed " ...an exacting

---

492 Taper, *Balanchine – A Biography* p.280
493 ibid., p.275
494 Buckle, *George Balanchine – Ballet Master*, pp.233-4
495 ibid., p.233

attitude toward their art",[496] but Balanchine's ballets did not escape censure – the composer Aram Khachaturian wrote in *Izvestia* that his ballets adhered to " ...the principle of plotlessness. This principle is foreign to Soviet artists and spectators. Without an idea, without a subject, there cannot be true emotional art."[497] It seems, though, that despite some strident voices, one of whom described Balanchine as a fanatic who had sacrificed classical ballet to his own vanity, audiences and critics alike were won over. *Symphony in C* (created in 1948 as *Le Palais de Cristal* for the Paris Opéra Ballet) was a particular success: "life-affirming" in the words of ballet critic Yuri Golovashenko, "a true festival of dancing ...agile and light, diversified and wonderfully harmonious".[498] Balanchine was said by one observer to have bettered Petipa.

The divide between American and Russian understanding of ballet at the time is shown by the reports compiled after several Russian dancers and teachers from the Bolshoi attended Balanchine's morning classes. The Russian teachers were amazed by what was achieved with the dancers and there was much admiration expressed for the American's precise footwork however, the upper body and arms were felt to be too inexpressive.

A telling episode took place when Balanchine learned that *Scriabiniana*, a new work by Kasyan Goleizovsky, his choreographic inspiration in the 1920s, was in rehearsal in the city. Having attended a rehearsal, however, he was said to have been so disappointed by what he saw – the same ideas he had seen some forty years before – that he could not bring himself to call upon the old man while in the capital.

The company's appearances in Leningrad provoked enthusiastic reactions, with the discerning audience and critics clearly appreciating un-Soviet plotless ballets. The early Sixties were a period in Soviet cultural life when the whole principle of socialist realism in the arts was beginning to be challenged, and, in many ways, NYCB's repertoire showed a way forward to many at the vanguard of what would become an aesthetic revolution; "they were" wrote Martin "hit very hard by it". Mikhail Gabovich wrote a thoughtful piece on the company and Balanchine's choreography, according much praise but insisting that the Soviet 'language' of ballet occupied an equally valid place in the art form.

One afternoon Balanchine met with the choreographers of Leningrad at their request in the city's Ballet Museum, a building which carried for him the memories of his childhood and youth. In their discussions, he emphatically rejected narrative work, shocking the older members of his audience, but galvanising the younger ones to the extent that they asked

496   ibid., p.280
497   ibid.
498   Taper, *Balanchine – A Biography*, p.281

for another opportunity to meet two days later. Long after the return of Balanchine and his company to New York City, his words resonated with the new generation of Russian dance-makers. The effect of NYCB's visit went far beyond American trumpeting of their own ballet superiority and Russian attempts to claim Balanchine as their own; at the Communist Party Congress of 1963 real concern was expressed that the Soviet Union might well be overtaken by America in the field of classical ballet, hitherto one of their strongest cards in the game of cultural diplomacy.

Ballet around the USSR

The ballet world in Soviet Russia had, by the beginning of the 1960s, expanded considerably since the days before the Russian revolution when only the two Imperial companies existed as permanent professional troupes. In the 1959-60 season there were 33 dance companies in existence.[499] The nationwide policy of expansion instituted in 1935 meant that talented youngsters from the republics were being sent to Moscow and Leningrad to train in classical ballet then generally returned to their native lands there to continue their work as dancers, choreographers and, ultimately, directors. Thereby, 'national' ballet traditions took root.

The London-published *Ballet Annual* of 1962 contains 'A Checklist of Soviet Ballet 1959-60' which provides a snapshot of the companies of the Soviet Union (see Appendix A). What emerges is a clear picture of repertoire under the communist regime: there was a wholesale export of successful works from the two major ensembles to the republics of the USSR, with a core of ballets common to many: *The Fountain of Bakhchisarai* was performed by eighteen out of the thirty-three companies, *Giselle* by twenty-one and *Swan Lake* performed by all but one. In addition, local works based on domestic stories or historical events featured in the repertoire of many companies but did not translate to other ensembles: *Kambar and Nazym*, a 1959 ballet based on the Kazakh epic *Kambar batyr* with choreography by Dauren Abirov[500] and a score by Vasily Velikanov[501] was performed only at the Abay Kazakh

---

499   John Percival. *Ballet Annual* No. 16. See appendix A.

500   Born in 1923 in Karakemer Korday District, Kazakhstan, Abirov graduated from the local ballet school in Alma-Ata in 1942, and the choreographers' department of GITIS in 1952, becoming director-choreographer of the Abay Kazakh Theatre in 1958 where he created both numerous original works and new versions of existing ballets. He also staged dances in operas, plays and films. In 1976 he became chief choreographer of the Kazakh Concert. He died in Alma-Ata in 2001.

501   Born in St Petersburg in 1898, Velikanov graduated from the Leningrad Conservatoire in 1930. From 1936-1937 he took part in a musical and ethnographic expedition to Kazakhstan where he studied folk song after which he settled in Alma-Ata and worked at the Abay Kazakh Theatre. He was an important figure in establishing classical music in the region and composed in a variety of genres, from symphonic, chamber and instrumental works to songs, romances and film music. He taught locally

Theatre in Alma-Ata. The centralised, monitored and approved structure for bringing a ballet to the stage, developed under Stalin in the 1930s and designed to ensure ideologically correct works, remained in place well into the 1960s, as did the focus on meaningful, narrative ballets and the censorship of anything that could be interpreted as abstraction or 'dance for dance's sake'.

Under the terms of the 1939 Soviet-German Molotov–Ribbentrop Pact, the three Baltic states of Latvia, Lithuania and Estonia were occupied by Russia in June 1940; Nazi Germany took control from 1941 to 1944 after when Soviet Russian rule was re-imposed. In Latvia, Voldemārs Komisārs,[502] one of Mikhail Mordkin's pupils, had established a ballet troupe at the opera house in Riga in 1919 whose first performance was *La Fille mal gardée* in 1921 in a production staged by Nikolai Sergeyev. Later, aided by both Russian émigrés and Soviet guest teachers, the company was performing several large-scale works by the mid-1920s, many staged by ballerina Alexandra Fedorova.[503] The Riga Ballet School was established in 1932 and by World War II it numbered 120 pupils. In 1945, subsequent to the second Russian occupation, ballet was taken up again with artistic policy implemented as everywhere else throughout the Soviet Union. In 1955, Latvia's *dekada* was marked in dance terms by the creation of two new works: *Amulet of Freedom* with choreography by ballet master Eugeni Changa[504] to a score by Ādolfs Skulte,[505] and *Laima* with choreography by ballerina Elena Tangieva-

---

from 1951 onwards. He died in Alma-Ata in 1969.

502 Born in Riga in 1899, Komisārs trained at the Moscow Ballet School before returning to his native Latvia. He joined the Latvian Army against the Bolsheviks during the Russian Civil War. In 1921, he invited Olga Spessivtseva to perform in Riga and later the ballet masters Nicholas Sergeyev and Alexander Fyodorov to work with the company. He died in Riga in 1931.

503 Born in St Petersburg in 1884, Fedorova graduated into the Mariinsky in 1902, becoming a first soloist in 1906. Between 1914 and 1917, she appeared as prima ballerina at the Troitsky Miniature Theatre, owned by her husband Alexander Fokine, the elder brother of choreographer Mikhail. She moved to Riga in 1922 and was engaged as a dancer and teacher; she also staged several ballets. In 1937 she emigrated to the USA and settled in New York. She was a choreographer and teacher with the Ballet Russe de Monte Carlo in 1940; the company performed her revival of *The Nutcracker* for many seasons. She ran her own ballet school until 1965 and died in New Jersey in 1972.

504 Born in Pskov in 1920, Changa graduated from Riga Ballet School in 1940 and in 1950 from the choreographer department of GITIS. He danced as a soloist at the Riga Theatre from 1940 to 1946 and was its house choreographer between 1950 and 1961. He created numerous works, several of which were of Latvian folk tales. In 1968 he became the choreographer of Moscow's Ballet on Ice, a post he held until 1977. He died in 1999.

505 Born in Kiev in 1909, Skulte began to study composition at the Latvian Conservatoire in 1930 and was its director from 1948 to 1955 and 1957 to 1972. He composed in a variety of genres from orchestral and vocal music to opera, ballet and film. He died in Riga in 2000.

Birzniek[506] and a score by Anatols Liepiņš.[507] Both depicted the struggle of the population against their historic oppressors, the Teutonic Knights, and "the great, strong friendship of the Latvian people and Russian people".[508] The first casts of both featured a young Latvian dancer Māris Liepa who would later become a star dancer of the Bolshoi.

Following the declaration of an independent Lithuania in 1920, an opera company was established in the country's second city, Kaunas. Initially, the dance troupe appeared only in opera productions but in 1925 it presented its first ballet, *Coppélia*, under the instruction of ex-Mariinsky dancer Pavel Petrov who went on to stage several works from the classical repertoire as well as his own *Lithuanian Rhapsody* in 1928. In 1935, the company toured abroad to Monte-Carlo and at London's Alhambra Theatre where it presented *Giselle*, *Coppélia*, *Swan Lake* and *Raymonda*. Petrov also established a ballet school in Kaunas in 1925. Having been under Nazi occupation between 1941 and 1944, when Soviet rule was re-established half the ballet company had fled to the West. In 1948, the company was moved to the capital Vilnius and Lopukhov was sent from Leningrad to mount his production of *Swan Lake*. Mikhail Moiseyev headed the company between 1951 and 1954 when he was replaced by the Moscow-trained choreographer Vytautas Grivickas.[509] The company participated in the 1954 *dekada* of Lithuanian culture for which Vilnius-born Bolshoi dancer-choreographer-teacher Asaf Messerer created *On the Seashore* in Moscow to a score by Julius Juzeliūnas.[510] Positive and brimming with folk aesthetic, the story centred on love, jealousy and betrayal in a Baltic fishing collective. Reviews were extremely positive and praised the creators for having "raised the ballet's ideological level and

---

506 Born in Pavlovsk in 1907, Tangieva-Birzniek trained under Vaganova and graduated into GATOB in 1924 where she danced for three years. From 1927 to 1937 she was the prima ballerina of the Riga Theatre; in 1935 she staged *Le Corsaire*. From 1945 to 1951 and 1956 to 1965 she was its chief choreographer staging more than twenty ballets. She died in Riga in 1965.

507 Born in Moscow in 1907, Liepiņš (known also as Anatoly Lepin) graduated from the Moscow Conservatoire in 1936. Between 1945 and 1950 he lived in Riga, the author of the anthem of the Latvian SSR. He composed an opera, eight operettas, three piano concerti and the music for twenty films. He died in Moscow in 1984.

508 Swift, *The Art of Dance in the USSR*, p.175

509 Born in 1925 in Beinorava, Lithuania, Grivickas graduated from the Lithuanian State Theatre's Ballet Studio in 1944, and joined the company where he danced until 1947. He then trained at Moscow's GITIS until 1953 and was Senior Choreographer in Vilnius from 1954 to 1971. He was also a respected educator and ballet historian. He died in Vilnius in 1990.

510 Born in Bauska, Latvia in 1916, Juzeliūnas studied composition in Kaunas and then at the Leningrad Conservatoire, returning to Lithuania in 1952 to become one of Lithuania's most illustrious composers, a music teacher, a musicologist and activist in public affairs. He died in Vilnius in 2001.

educated the working people in the spirit of political vigilance".[511] Further productions were mounted in Latvia and Estonia. 1954 also saw the first Lithuanian children sent for dance training in Leningrad.

In Estonia, ballet began during the first decade of the twentieth century and throughout its subsequent history was dominated by female directors and choreographers; in 1925 Rahel Olbrei[512] founded the Estonian Theatre Ballet Company with locally-trained dancers and led it until 1944, putting on productions of the classics in Tallinn, notably *The Nutcracker* in 1936 and *Swan Lake* in 1940. She choreographed the first Estonian ballet *Kratt* in 1944, based on a goblin figure from Estonian mythology to a score entirely based on national folk tunes by Eduard Tubin.[513] The ballet's fourth performance on 9th March was interrupted by a Soviet Russian air attack which destroyed the opera house. Under Soviet rule, repertoire followed official lines, although further national works were encouraged: *Kalevipoeg*, created in 1948 by Helmi Tohvelman[514] to a folk tune-based score by Eugen Kapp,[515] was taken from local myth, but the title role was made into a people's hero who defeats the old world of superstition represented by the sorcerer Sorts to create a bright and optimistic future based on work and creativity. Thereafter, Estonia came increasingly into the Soviet sphere and Russian guest-choreographers such as Fenster and Burmeister often made the journey to Tallinn. During the mid-1960s, Mai Murdmaa[516] emerged as a choreographer of distinction,

---

511   Swift, *The Art of the Dance in the USSR*, p.173

512   Born in Tallinn in 1898, Olbrei trained locally between 1918 and 1922 before studying with Mary Wigman in Germany between 1922 and 1923. Working at the Estonian Theatre primarily in arranging dances for opera productions, she worked on pure dance performances from 1936 onwards. After the Russian bombing, she fled first to Sweden and ultimately to Canada where she was unable to find theatrical work. She died in Canada in 1984.

513   Born in 1905 in Tartu, Governorate of Livonia, Tubin studied music and established himself as a composer initially using Estonian folk rhythms and melodies before becoming less 'national' in style after his exile to Sweden after the second Soviet occupation of 1944. He composed numerous symphonies, concerti, chamber works and both operas and ballets. He died in Stockholm in 1982.

514   Born in Väätsa, Estonia in 1900, Tohvelman trained locally and with Mary Wigman in Dresden. On her return to Estonia, she worked in several theatre companies in Tallinn as a dancer and choreographer and taught dance at the Tallinn Conservatoire between 1957 and 1981. She died in Tallinn in 1983.

515   Born in 1908 in the Volga city of Astrakhan, Kapp graduated in music from the Tallinn Conservatoire in 1931 where he became a professor in 1947 and its rector between 1948 to 1965. His style was melodic and harmonious; his best-known works were several operas on Estonian themes. His music was much favoured by the authorities – he won his third Stalin prize for *Kalevipoeg*. He died in Tallinn in 1996.

516   Born in Tallinn in 1938, Murdmaa graduated from the Tallinn Ballet School in 1956 and danced with the Estonian Ballet until 1960. She studied at the Moscow Choreographic School, graduating in 1964 to become a prolific choreographer. Her first

taking over the company in 1965, and producing a dizzying array of intelligent works from *Medea* to a score by the American Samuel Barber in 1965 to *The Prodigal Son* set to Prokofiev in 1973. Hers was a Balanchine-like approach with music as the only point of departure for movement which she allied with the experimentation of Goleizovsky.

In 1933, the first season of the newly-formed Belorussian Theatre of Opera and Ballet in the capital Minsk included a production of *The Red Poppy*, although some ballet had existed since 1920 when the National Drama Theatre was established. A ballet studio was also established for local children. A new theatre was built, subsequently named 'Bolshoi', which opened in 1939 with a production of *The Fountain of Bakhchisarai*, choreographed by Goleizovsky. The following year, the first Belorussian ballet was premièred: *The Nightingale* was co-choreographed by Bolshoi principal Alexey Ermolayev and Fyodor Lopukhov to a score by Mikhail Kroshner[517] and with a libretto by Yuri Slonimsky. It told the story of serfs Simon and his beloved Zosya whose love is thwarted by the local landowner who provokes a popular uprising by the local population with his extortions and demands, the title coming from Simon's ability to imitate the song of a nightingale. The ballet was successfully shown in Moscow later that year as part of the Belorussian *dekada* festival. The role of Zosya was created by the distinguished ballerina Zinaida Vasilieva. The Belorussian Ballet School was established in 1945. In 1973, Valentin Elizariev[518] became ballet master in chief of the Minsk Ballet and, over subsequent decades, created a repertoire comprising his versions of the classics and original creations, including his 1980 production of *Spartacus* which was preferred in some quarters to that by Grigorovich.

The Ukraine possesses a rich tradition of folklore and amateur dancing; the first appearance of ballet dated back to 1816. A resident dance company was established at Kiev's Russian Opera House in 1897 and a ballet studio opened in 1918; both were nationalised in 1919, subsequently undergoing numerous name changes. Mikhail Mordkin was a regular visitor to the city with a small dance troupe and was hired by the experimental Kiev Young Theatre between 1916 and 1919. In the early years after the revolution and as part of a general flowering of artistic experimentation in the city, the main

---

work was *Ballet Symphony* in 1963 to music by Estonian composer Eino Tamberg (1930-2010). She worked with the Moscow Young Ballet and was Chief Ballet Mistress of the Estonian Ballet between 1974 and 2001.

517   Born in Kiev in 1900, Kroshner graduated from the Minsk Conservatoire in 1937 and worked as an accompanist at the opera house between 1933 and 1939. Many of his compositions were based on Belorussian melodies. He died in Minsk in 1942.

518   Born in Baku, Azerbaijan in 1947, Elizariev graduated from the Vaganova Academy in 1967, and the Leningrad Conservatoire's choreographers' course in 1973 upon which he took up his post in Minsk at the age of twenty-six. He has remained at the opera house in a variety of management posts since then.

company gained a reputation for avant-garde dance productions before they were curtailed by Moscow. The opera houses of both Odessa and Kharkov also gave small-scale dance performances but in 1925 the latter staged its first full-length work, *Swan Lake*. *The Red Poppy* was the first Soviet ballet given in Kiev in 1928, while the first Ukrainian-themed ballet, *Pan Koniowski*, was created in Kharkov, the then capital, in 1931 with choreography by Vasily Litvinenko[519] and a score by Mikhail Verikovsky.[520] It was the story taken from a popular song about the rejection of advances made by a local count towards a peasant girl which then becomes concerned with an uprising against the aristocrat. Following the move of the capital from Kharkov to Kiev, the company grew to some eighty dancers who performed many of the successful Soviet ballets, while 1932 saw the establishment of the Dnepropetrovsk Opera and Ballet Theatre which was joined with the Odessa company in 1941 when both were evacuated to Krasnoyarsk. In 1938, the Kiev Choreographic School was founded out of a merger of the opera house's ballet studio and the school previously established in 1935. During the war, the ensemble was evacuated to Ufa in Bashkortostan and then to Irkutsk in Siberia where it combined with the dancers of the Kharkov Theatre. In 1954, Vakhtang Vronsky[521] became chief choreographer of the Kiev Ballet, a post he held until 1969, and the repertoire broadened with further Ukrainian-themed works, including the short-lived *Black Gold* from 1957, an ideologically impeccable ballet about coal mining in the Donbass region.

Ballet came to the Volga city of Saratov in 1928, when a group of Vronsky's ex-students arrived at the city's opera house from Baku under the leadership of ballet master Sergey Kevorkov[522] as part of the Soviet state's policy of spreading culture throughout the republics. As they established themselves, their repertoire expanded to include all the major works from Leningrad and

---

519   Born in 1899 in Savelyevka, Samara, Litvinienko graduated from the Tbilisi Conservatoire and began to work in theatre, starting to choreograph in 1926 with *Swan Lake* in Kiev. He died in Moscow in 1967.

520   Born in 1896 in Kremenets, Verikovsky graduated from the Kiev Conservatoire and became a house conductor at the Kiev and Kharkov opera houses between 1926 and 1935. In 1946 he became a professor at the Kiev Conservatoire. He composed seven operas and in a variety of musical forms. He died in Kiev in 1962.

521   Born in Tiflis, Georgia in 1905, Vronsky (born Nadiradze) trained in the city's Choreographic Studio before performing at the dance theatre in Rostov. In 1926 he joined the Azerbaijani Theatre of Opera and Ballet where he worked until 1940, after which he moved to Odessa and then in 1954 to Kiev as Principal Choreographer where he worked until 1969. He died in Kiev in 1988.

522   Born 1886 in Elizavetpol (now Ganja), Azerbaijan of Armenian origin, Kevorkov trained in St Petersburg before moving to Baku in 1920 as ballet master at the Akhundov Theatre. In 1923, he founded the city's Ballet Studio. He died in Kislovdsk in 1951.

Moscow. However, the appointment of Valentin Adashevski[523] as Chief Ballet Master in 1951 – a post he would hold until 1968 – signalled an upturn in local creativity, not least with Lyubov Serebrovskaya's[524] production of *Swan Lake* using Tchaikovsky's complete 1877 original score which, despite the fact it lacked choreography of distinction, represented an early manifestation of the late twentieth-century trend of turning towards a creative artist's original intentions. The first ballets with local themes and storylines began to be created, from Adashevski's setting in 1951 of composer Farhid (Färit) Yarullin's[525] 'Shuraleh', the score and story used by Yakobson at the Kirov in 1950, to Ashot Asaturyan's[526] treatment of Khachaturian's *Gayaneh* in 1972.

In 1923, a ballet studio was established in Azerbaijan's capital Baku by the People's Educational Commissariat, becoming the Baku School of Choreography in 1929 which by 1933 numbered some 157 students who benefitted from input from Moscow dancers and teachers including Ermolayev. An early graduate was Qamar Almaszade,[527] who became the first acknowledged ballerina of the Muslim world and who in 1940 co-choreographed the first Azerbaijani ballet *The Maiden's Tower* at the Akhundov Theatre, Baku, alongside Vakhtang Vronsky and her teacher and mentor Sergey Kevorkov. She danced the central role of Gyulyanak, the daughter of the despotic Dzhangurkhan who, having banished her at birth

---

523   Born in Kiev in 1910, Adashevski graduated from the city's choreographic studio in 1928 and became a soloist first in Kharkov between 1929 and 1937 and then in Saratov, dancing a range of leading roles. Between 1960 and 1968, he was also the Director of the Saratov Ballet School. He died in Saratov in 1968.

524   Born in Moscow in 1913, Serebrovskaya studied at the ballet studio in Simferopol and graduated from the State Association of Music, Variety and Circus Enterprises in Moscow in 1931. From 1931 to 1950 she created ballets in Tbilisi, Sverdlovsk, Saratov and Moscow. In 1955 she graduated from the ballet department of GITIS and became house choreographer in Saratov. Between 1958 and 1965 she was the main choreographer of the Gorky Theatre, Leningrad and then the Tajik Opera and Ballet from 1965 to 1973. She died in 2004.

525   Born in Kazan, Tatarstan in 1914, Yarullin graduated from the Moscow Conservatoire and began to compose. His most notable work was the score for the ballet Şüräle (*Shuraleh*). He was killed in military action near Vitebsk in 1943.

526   Trained at the Tbilisi Ballet School under Chabukiani, Asaturyan danced in Georgia and Uzbekistan before training under Lopukhov at the Choreography Department of the Leningrad Conservatoire. He was principal choreographer in Saratov from 1968 to 1973, Yerevan from 1973 to 1990 and Kharkov from then until 1997. Asaturyan died in Yerevan in 1999.

527   Born in Baku in 1915, Almaszade trained locally before going to Moscow in 1932 to study at the Bolshoi School and then on to Leningrad where she studied choreography under Maria Romanova-Ulanova (Galina Ulanova's mother). She returned in 1936 where she founded the Azerbaijan State Folk Song and Dance Ensemble the following year. She later directed the Baku School of Choreography where she continued to teach until the 1990s after her retirement from the stage in the 1950s. She died in Baku in 2006.

from his court, later demands her for his own harem. Her lover Polat is seized and Gyulyanak finally throws herself from a high tower on the edge of the Caspian Sea, thinking the Khan is attempting to seize her and never knowing the footsteps she hears approaching are those of Polat. The score was by the noted Azerbaijani composer Afrasiyab Badalbeyli.[528] Almaszade continued to dance and choreograph for the ballet company which she eventually directed.

A permanent ballet ensemble was created in Tiflis (later Tbilisi), Georgia with the opening of the Paliashvili Opera House in 1896 which saw guest performances by principal dancers of both Moscow and St Petersburg in subsequent years. The Red Army invaded the country in 1921 and established Soviet control after which the ballet company began to perform state approved works. It was the rise of Vakhtang Chabukiani in the 1930s as one of the Soviet Union's star dancers that brought a focus on Georgian ballet. In 1936 Chabukiani created the first major ballet on a Georgian theme *Mzechabuki* (later revised as *Heart of the Hills* which premièred at the Kirov in 1938) to music by Andrey Balanchivadze, and then *Maltakva* two years later, a tale drawn from Georgian contemporary life to a score by Shalva Taktakishvili.[529] In 1941, Chabukiani was appointed principal dancer and ballet master in Tbilisi; he remained as the latter until 1972, creating numerous works of his own as well as overseeing productions of the classics. An opera ballet school was created in 1921, becoming the State Choreographic School in 1925. Georgy Aleksidze,[530] who succeeded Chabukiani as company director, led a shift away from expansive, full-length works towards one-act, often small-scale and plotless ballets with a greater focus on neo-classical movement. He also explored musical compositions from previous centuries; in 1973, *Variations on a Theme by Mozart* to Fryderyk Chopin represented a clear departure from his predecessor's approach. He left Tbilisi in 1985 to work in Perm and Leningrad, before taking up the directorial reins once more from 1985 to 2004.

---

528 Born in Baku in 1907, Badalbeyli studied locally and then graduated from the Leningrad Conservatoire in 1938. He wrote libretti and composed scores for a variety of theatrical productions throughout his life and published several historical studies. He began working as a conductor at the Azerbaijan State Opera and Ballet Theatre in 1930 where he remained until his death in 1976.

529 Born in Kvemo-Khviti, Georgia in 1900, Taktakishvili graduated in 1928 from the Tbilisi Conservatoire after which he founded the music school in Batumi before going on to hold various musical posts in Georgia. He composed several operas, arrangements of folk songs and orchestral and instrumental pieces. He died in Tbilisi in 1965.

530 Born in Tbilisi in 1941, Aleksidze trained at the Moscow Ballet School before returning to his home city as a dancer in 1961. He also studied under Lopukhov at Leningrad's Choreographic Faculty of the Leningrad Conservatoire before making his first work, *Oresteia*, a duet for Kaleria Fedicheva and Yuri Soloviev, for the newly formed Chamber Ballet in 1966. He was chief choreographer with Perm Ballet between 1980 and 1983. He died in Tbilisi in 2008.

A ballet studio was established in the Urals city of Perm in 1925 and the following year saw its first performances of *Giselle* and *Coppélia*; further expansion of repertoire took place thereafter. The source of Perm's distinguished place in Soviet ballet and beyond derives from the wartime evacuation of the Kirov Ballet to the city, named Molotov between 1940 and 1957. In 1945, a school was established under ex-dancer Ekaterina Heidenreich[531] which, thanks to enduring links with the Leningrad School, developed quickly into one of the Soviet union's premier dance academies, producing young dancers of exceptional talent; in 1973, student Nadezhda Pavlova[532] won the Grand Prix at the Moscow International Ballet Competition and went on to become a principal dancer of the Bolshoi Ballet. The company was drawn almost exclusively from the graduates of its own school, and the State Choreographic School, considered second only to those of Moscow and Leningrad. The theatre was accorded 'Academic' status in 1969.

Many centres of ballet were established during the era of Soviet control, spreading the art form to all the republics of the USSR. In Siberia, the Novosibirsk Theatre of Opera and Ballet (NOVAT) was opened in 1945 with an auditorium which was, and is, two and half times larger than that of the Bolshoi. At first, a dance ensemble comprised amateur performers, who were strengthened by dancers transferred from the Bolshoi; Vasily Vainonen served as director between 1950 and 1952. In 1957, the ballet company embarked on its first international tour to the People's Republic of China, which resulted two years later in the première of *The Magic Lotus Lantern*, staged by two Chinese choreographers, Li Tshen Len and Wan Si Sun. A school was established in 1956 with a view to feeding dancers for the resident company, with the first graduating year taking place in 1965; the school became one of Russia's premier dance academies. In 1964, NOVAT was accorded 'Academic' status, joining the Bolshoi, Kirov and Maly Theatres, and in the 1960s became something of a magnet for dancers

---

531 Born in Kiev in 1897, Heidenreich graduated into the Mariinsky in 1915 where she danced until 1935 as a valued soloist. She taught at the Leningrad Choreographic School from 1925 to 1941 but was arrested after a denunciation and sentenced to a forced labour camp in the Urals. Released owing to ill health and exiled from Leningrad and Kiev, she remained in Molotov and became the ballet school's first director, remaining in post until 1956. Subsequently rehabilitated, she re-staged *Chopiniana* at the Bolshoi in 1958. She died in Leningrad in 1982.

532 Born in Cheboksary, Chuvashia in 1956, Pavlova graduated from the Perm Ballet School into the ballet company in 1974 where she rapidly established herself as a strong, characterful and technically accomplished soloist. In March 1975, she danced Giselle at the Bolshoi and was invited to join the company by director Leonid Lavrovsky; she performed a full repertoire, often partnered by her husband Vyacheslav Gordeyev and was the first Sylph in the company's 1996 *La Sylphide*. She retired from the Bolshoi in 2000, but had led several small ensembles and had studied choreography at GITIS. Since 2009, she has taught at the Moscow Classical Ballet and the Bolshoi.

and choreographers. Kirov star Nikita Dolgushin appeared between 1961 and 1966 and future Kirov director Oleg Vinogradov,[533] having studied choreography in Leningrad, served an apprenticeship under the guidance of Pyotr Gusev, the artistic director between 1963 to 1966. Before leaving Novosibirsk, Dolgushin appeared as Romeo in Vinogradov's *Romeo and Juliet*, a production which caused controversy with major revisions to the score by the choreographer and a bold fusion of movement styles. In his time with the company, Gusev strengthened artistic and technical standards and staged his own versions of the classics as well as his own original choreography.

By the 1960s, the policy of disseminating classical ballet across the Soviet Union had borne considerable fruit. Not only were dozens of companies active around the republics, many with their own training schools, but Leningrad and Moscow benefitted considerably from the arrival of talent young artists from across the union. The two major ballet companies themselves saw many such dancers and choreographers bring their talents to their service.

---

533 Born in Leningrad in 1937, Vinogradov graduated from the Vaganova Academy in 1958 and joined the Novosibirsk Ballet where he soon developed an interest in, and talent for, choreography. Pyotr Gusev encouraged him with small-scale commissions until he deemed him ready for full-length works, *Cinderella* in 1964, followed by *Romeo and Juliet* in 1965. Both were considered experimental and unorthodox in their concept and staging. In 1967, he was invited to Moscow to create *Asel*, after which many commissions followed. In 1973, he became director of the Maly company where he staged many revivals and new works before moving to the Kirov where he remained in post until 1997.

7
The Time of Troubles[534]
1962-1977

Shifting sands – dance to the fore

On the surface, the Soviet ballet world seemed to continue into the 1960s much as it had before, characterised by the continuing search for a choreographer of note to produce a genuinely popular Soviet masterpiece. New work had been an Achilles heel since the revolution, with the ideological demands of the administration leading to the creation of new ballets which, with few exceptions, repeatedly failed to catch the audience's imagination, and 'approved' choreographers proving to be rather better party members than makers of interesting dance. The early sixties did, however, prove to be a time of change. The arrival of foreign companies and exposure to their repertoire had an effect on the domestic Russian view of what ballet was and was for. In 1963, Mikhail Chulaki, the newly re-appointed Director of the Bolshoi Theatre, and thus a mouthpiece for official cultural policy, made comments at an all-union meeting convened to discuss the challenges for Soviet choreography. One of his most notable observations concerned the paucity of actual dance contained in new ballets and the dominance of explanatory gesture. It was, in essence, a repudiation of 'choreodrama' or *drambalet* and an exhortation for dance-makers to focus more on movement.

1962 – *The Young Lady and the Hooligan*

Konstantin Boyarsky, director of Leningrad's Maly company, scored a major success in late December 1962 with his one-act ballet *The Young Lady and the Hooligan*, based on Mayakovsky's 1918 silent film, itself derived from Italian novelist Edmondo De Amicis' *La maestrina degli operai*. A tale of the transformative power of love – a 'hooligan' falls in love with a young village schoolmistress but loses his life in a revenge attack – it thrilled audiences with its narrative-through-dance approach and Valery Panov's electrifying performances as the Hooligan. On opening night Larisa Klimova[535] danced

---

534 Russia endured 15 chaotic years, known as the Time of Troubles, between 1598 and 1613 which ended with the election of Mikhail Romanov as the first tsar of a dynasty which lasted until the 1917 revolution.

535 Born in Leningrad in 1937, Klimova graduated into the Maly in 1956 and appeared in major roles in numerous new works. She was a classical lyrical dancer, with an attractive stage personality. In 1971, she joined the Perm company where she danced until 1977. She returned to teach at the Maly in 1978.

c.1950 - *Swan Lake*, Act III, Bolshoi. Alexey Ermolayev as Siegfried and Galina Ulanova as Odile. Courtesy of *Dancing Times*

1955 - *Amulet of Freedom*, Latvian Opera and Ballet Theatre.

above: 1951 - Ekaterina Maximova, Vladimir Vasiliev and Alla Mankevich at the Bolshoi Ballet School.

left: 1950 - *The Sleeping Beauty*. Irina Kolpakova as Aurora.

c. 1956 - Rudolf Nureyev with Alexander Pushkin, Natalia Kamkova and Alla Sizova, LHU.

c. 1957 - *The Stone Flower*, Kirov. Alla Shelest as Katerina. Courtesy of *Dancing Times*

above: 1956 - Poster for the Bolshoi *Romeo and Juliet* at Covent Garden.

left: 1954 - Galina Ulanova and Yury Zhdanov in *Romeo And Juliet* RIA Novosti archive, image #11591 Umnov CC-BY-SA 3.0

1956 - *Romeo and Juliet*, the ball scene, Bolshoi. Courtesy of *Dancing Times*

1957 - *Gayaneh*, Sabre Dance, Bolshoi. Courtesy of *Dancing Times*

left: 1958 - *Swan Lake*, MALEGOT. Māris Liepa as Siegfried and Violetta Bovt as Odette.

right: 1959 - *The Stone Flower*, Bolshoi. Maya Plisetskaya as the Mistress of the Copper Mountain and Nikolai Fadeyechev as Danila.

1959 - *Coast of Hope*, Kirov. Alla Osipenko and Askold Makarov. Courtesy of *Dancing Times*

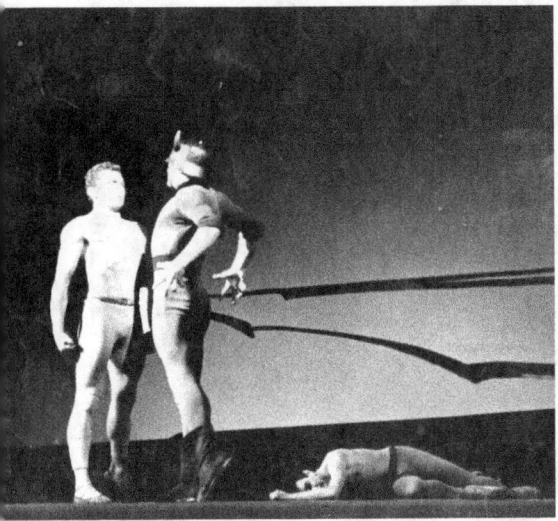

1961 - *Leningrad Symphony*, Kirov. Courtesy of Dancing Times

Yuri Faier - 1958 caricature.

1960 - *The Little Humpbacked Horse*, Bolshoi. Alexander Radunsky as the Khan and Rimma Karelskaya as the Tsar Maiden.

1961 - *Chopiniana*, Bolshoi. Galina Ulanova. Courtesy of *Dancing Times*

Opposite page, top left: 1962 - Mikhail Baryshnikov aged 14 at LHU.
top right: 1961 - Rudolf Nureyev as Solor in *La Bayadère*, Act III in Paris.
middle left: Māris Liepa teaching at the Bolshoi Ballet School.
middle right: 1962 - George Balanchine and Vakhtang Chabukiani.
below: 1960 - Arrival of the Bolshoi Ballet at Schiphol airport, Amsterdam (Nina Timofeyeva extreme left).

1962 - *Spartacus*, Bolshoi. Shamil Yagudin (right) as a Gladiator. Courtesy of *Dancing Times*

1962 - *Spartacus*, Kirov. Courtesy of *Dancing Times*

1962 - *Spartacus*, Bolshoi. Mikhail Lavrovsky as a Slave. Courtesy of *Dancing Times*

above: *The Fountain of Bakhchisarai*, Bolshoi. Alexander Lapauri as Khan Girey in 1954. Courtesy of *Dancing Times*

left: *Gayaneh*, Bolshoi. Nikolai Fadeyechev as Armen, late 1950s.

1962 - *The Bedbug*, Kirov. Dmitry Vovk and Elena Selivanova.

1964 - *Cinderella*, Kirov. Natalia Makarova as an Ugly Sister, Courtesy of *Dancing Times*

1963 - Ekaterina Maximova as Maria in *The Fountain of Bakhchisarai* - RIA Novosti archive, image #521299 V. Blioh CC-BY-SA 3.0

1966 - Vladimir Vasiliev as the Prince in Yuri Grigorovich's *The Nutcracker*. RIA Novosti archive, image #709789 Alexander Makarov CC-BY-SA 3.0

1966 - *Giselle*, Act I, Kirov. Yuri Soloviev as Albrecht. Courtesy of *Dancing Times*

1965 - *The Legend of Love*, Kirov. Alla Osipenko and Vladilen Semyonov. Courtesy of *Dancing Times*

1966 - *The Rite of Spring*, Bolshoi. Nina Sorokina and Yuri Vladimirov. Courtesy of *Dancing Times*

1967 - *Carmen Suite*, Bolshoi. Maya Plisetskaya as Carmen and Nikolai Fadeyechev as Don José.

1967 - Leonid Lavrovsky in a rehearsal of *Paganini* with Yaroslav Sekh in the title role. Courtesy of *Dancing Times*

1961 - *The Nutcracker*, Novosibirsk Ballet. Nikita Dolgushin as the Prince. Courtesy of *Dancing Times*

1968 - Kirov Mens' Class including Soloviev (second from right). Courtesy of *Dancing Times*

the Young Lady and Veniamin Zimin[536] was the original Hooligan. The music was by Shostakovich, an amalgam of numbers from his three scores from the 1930s for *The Bolt*, *The Golden Age* and *The Bright Stream* as well as fragments from his film music. In its subject matter and its choice of score, *The Young Lady and the Hooligan* was an example of where Soviet ballet was moving in the new decade; it would never have received official sanction only a few years before. It was staged soon after in numerous republics as well as engendering several versions by other choreographers; it received some 236 performances at the Maly alone, being last performed there in 1987. It was filmed in 1970 and was acquired and revived by the Mariinsky company in 2001.

1962 – the Choreographers' Course at the Leningrad Conservatoire

In 1962, the Leningrad Conservatoire established a department of choreography running a four-year course under Fyodor Lopukhov to train and develop aspirant dance-makers. The curriculum was divided into eight areas: the art of the choreographer, the study of the classical heritage, character dance, historical and contemporary dance, ballet technique, the analysis of musical scores, the theory of music and the history and dramaturgy of ballet. The first graduating class in 1966 included Georgy Aleksidze and Nikolai Boyarchikov. Pyotr Gusev assumed the directorship of the department in 1966 and continued Lopukhov's policy of inviting in notable choreographers, including Sergeyev and Yakobson, to work with the students.

1962 – *Vanina Vanini*

In Moscow, husband and wife Bolshoi character dancers Natalia Kasatkina and Vladimir Vasilyov began to choreograph, initially in their spare time, for fellow company members and to explore the new ideas and approaches which were beginning to make themselves felt in Soviet ballet. Their first staged work was *Vanina Vanini* in May 1962, based on Stendhal's 1829 short story, which received no little praise: Ulanova wrote in the *Gazette of the Bolshoi Theatre* that it was "new and fresh" and "danceable".[537] The score was commissioned from the young 'underground' composer Nikolai Karetnikov.[538] The dance idiom was unashamedly modern, devoid of props

---

536   Born in Leningrad in 1932, Zimin graduated in 1952 from the Leningrad Choreographic School into the Maly company where he danced for twenty years. With a lively stage presence and strong technique, he excelled in created roles as well as in the classics. He taught at the Leningrad Choreographic School from 1967 onwards, worked at the Baghdad Ballet School between 1970 and 1972 after which he taught classical dance at the Leningrad Opera Studio.

537   Roslavleva, *Era of the Russian Ballet*, p.297

538   Born in Moscow in 1930, Karetnikov graduated from the Moscow Conservatoire in 1953. After incurring the displeasure of the regime with his scores for the ballets *Vanina*

and focussed more on ideas than storyline; on opening night, the ballet featured Elena Ryabinkina[539] as Vanina and Vladimir Tikhonov[540] as Pietro.

1962 – *The Bedbug*

In something of a difficult position when it came to fulfilling the pressure from the regime to create new ballets as part of its declared financial and artistic plans, the Kirov continued its search for choreographers. Despite his awkward reputation, Leonid Yakobson was commissioned in 1962 by Konstantin Sergeyev to create *The Bedbug*, a project he had been pressing to work on for five years. When challenged, Sergeyev insisted that the ballet would affirm the concept of the 'New Man of Communist society' by rejecting the bourgeois world depicted in Vladimir Mayakovsky's original 1928 satirical play, but it was a project seemingly doomed to fail. There was vocal resistance from some company dancers unused to the choreographer's challenging knock-kneed, anti-classical movements, his strange aesthetics and own quarrelsome and confrontational character. A few dancers were positive, notably the young Natalia Makarova who described herself in her later memoirs as 'fabulously lucky' to have appeared as Zoya in the production, praising Yakobson for seeing beyond her type-casting as a Romantic-style dancer. Performed to a score by Oleg Karavaichuk[541] (under the pseudonym F. Otkazov) and Georgy Firtich,[542] *The Bedbug* was premièred in June 1962 and met with almost universal incomprehension, despite a few dissenting voices who saw something worthwhile in precisely what alienated the majority of viewers.

Vanini and *Heroic Poem (Geologists)*, he led a double artistic life: officially, he composed incidental music for theatre, film and television, but in secret he worked on several large-scale works, including two operas. He died in Moscow in 1994.

539   Born in Sverdlovsk in 1941, Ryabinkina graduated into the Bolshoi in 1959, having already made her debut as Odette in *Swan Lake* while still a student. She rose to the rank of ballerina and danced all the major classical roles as well as demonstrating an affinity with Goleizovsky's choreography. Since 1985, she has taught at the Bolshoi School.

540   Born in 1935 in Chisinau, Moldova, Tikhonov graduated from the Leningrad Choreographic School in 1954. After serving in the army from 1957 to 1960, he became a soloist at the Moldovan Opera and Ballet Theatre in Chisinau. He danced with the Bolshoi from 1960 to 1979 and was known for the beauty of his line and his unforced technique. During the 1980s he was the artistic director of the Moscow Ballet on Ice ensemble. He died in Moscow in 2000.

541   Born in Kiev in 1927, Karavaichuk graduated from the Leningrad Conservatoire in 1951 and worked extensively in film thereafter. After official censure and the banning of his work, he led a secluded life and became increasingly eccentric. After rehabilitation and *perestroika*, he continued to shun commercial activity and only participated in avant-garde performances. He died in St Petersburg in 2016.

542   Born in Pskov in 1938, Firtich graduated from the St Petersburg Conservatoire in 1962 and began to write music for cinema. In 1973, he composed the music for the musical *An Unusual Adventure on the Volga Steamer*. He also wrote symphonies, concerti and other genres. He died in St Petersburg in 2016.

The Poet was danced by Askold Makarov, Prisypkin by Konstantin Rassadin and Nonna Yastrebova[543] was the first Elsevira. The work was last revived in its two-act form in 1965 but in 1974 was reduced by Yakobson to a single act using music by Shostakovich composed for Meyerhold's 1929 production of the play for his own Choreographic Miniatures company.

1964 – *Heroic Poem (Geologists)*

Premièred in January 1964, *Heroic Poem (Geologists)* was another work for the Bolshoi by Kasatkina and Vasilyov with a score by Karetnikov, and became a real success, especially with the younger audience. It concerned three young, contemporary scientists trapped by a forest fire in the *taiga*; a young man loses his life fighting the flames while a second is badly burnt. The girl, a city-dweller, finds hidden reserves to save his life in the inhospitable environment. There were no props, the dance idiom was decidedly 'modern', including acrobatic lifts, and resolutely non-narrative. Nina Sorokina,[544] a young company dancer, made a real mark as the Girl, while the heroic youth was danced by Yuri Vladimirov. The *demi-caractère* dancer Vladimir Koshlev,[545] as the injured young man who finds reserves of strength to survive, made up the trio. As a ballet, it struck a definite chord with the young generation at the time and marked a clear shift in the Moscow ballet aesthetic.

Grigorovich and the Bolshoi

Yuri Grigorovich enjoyed considerable official favour – he once observed of Culture Minister Furtseva "she loved me"[546] – and showed himself adept at understanding and playing the political and cultural system in which he worked. In March 1964 he staged *The Legend of Love* at the Bolshoi which he had premièred at the Kirov three years previously. In doing so gained the support – later to be withdrawn – of reigning ballerina Maya Plisetskaya

---

543 Born in Petrograd in 1923, Yastrebova graduated into the Kirov in 1941 where she danced until 1964. A versatile classical dancer, she performed several leading roles as well as creating a number of parts. She was considered one of the best Kitris in *Don Quixote* in post-war Leningrad and also a charming Aurora in *The Sleeping Beauty*. A dedicated teacher of children after retirement, she headed the children's ballet studio at the Leningrad Palace of Pioneers. She died in St Petersburg in 2012.

544 Born in Elektrostal, east of Moscow, in 1942, Sorokina graduated into the company from the Bolshoi School in 1961 where she continued to dance until 1980, and then moved into coaching until 1988. She was a much-admired and loved virtuoso dancer who encompassed all the major classical ballets as well as creating roles in new works which included Vasiliev's *Icarus*. She died in Moscow in 2011.

545 Born in Moscow in 1938, Koshlev graduated into the Bolshoi in 1956 where he danced until 1978 in a variety of soloist and *demi-caractère* roles. Between 1978 to 1989 he taught classical dance at the Moscow State Academic College and has been a teacher and coach at the Kremlin Ballet Theatre since 1992.

546 Morrison, *Bolshoi Confidential*, p.351

who, alongside Māris Liepa as Ferhad, triumphed in the role of Queen Mekhmeneh-Banu at the Moscow première. In the early 1960s, the Bolshoi troupe was strong and full of young rising talent, but it seriously lacked anything genuinely fresh in its repertoire, leading to a disparity between the potential inherent in the members of the ensemble and the opportunities they had to develop it.

Company director Leonid Lavrovsky's attempts to create new work were often much criticised by Mikhail Chulaki, Director of the Bolshoi Theatre from 1955 to 1959 and again from 1963 until 1970, who engineered his removal in 1964. Far from leaving the Bolshoi in disgrace, he took up the directorship of the company's school; his departure left the way free for Grigorovich to be made ballet master-in-chief two years later, a post he occupied for almost 30 years, the longest tenure of any company director during the Soviet period.

1964 – *The Firebird*

Another consequence of the renewed interest in Fokine was a recreation by the Bolshoi of *The Firebird* at the Kremlin Palace of Congresses in the early summer of 1964. Based on Boyarsky's 1962 version at the Maly, its selling point was the restoration of Alexander Golovin's original 1910 décor and costumes after the discovery of the designs in Leningrad; The Royal Ballet's version, which the company had included on its Russian tour, used Natalia Goncharova's 1926 redesign. The restoration of the original visual concept was widely welcomed and an example of Russian ballet claiming the Ballets Russes heritage which it had rejected for so long. Maya Plisetskaya made a great impression with her fierce interpretation of the title role, partnered by Nikolai Fadeyechev's noble Tsarevich and opposite Vladimir Levashov as the Immortal Kostchei.

1964 – The Varna Ballet Competition

In the summer of 1964, the first professional international ballet competition was established in the seaside town of Varna, Bulgaria being at that time a Russian satellite state. Under the Bulgarian founder, musician and administrator Emil Dimitrov, it was designed to highlight the achievements in ballet of artists from the Soviet Union and its eastern bloc allies. However, the determination from the start was that it would also develop an international profile and so the jury was to comprise distinguished figures drawn from across the world. In 1964, Galina Ulanova sat as the first President of the Jury which included Cuban prima ballerina Alicia Alonso, Serge Lifar, Fyodor Lopukhov and Arnold Haskell amongst others. The list of the winners of that first competition was a roll-call of the finest Soviet dancers of the time: Vladimir Vasiliev received the Grand Prix Varna while Alla Sizova, Ekaterina

Maximova, Nikita Dolgushin and Sergey Vikulov[547] all won First Prizes. The only non-Russian in that category was the Bulgarian Vera Kirova.[548] The Varna competition was an indication of Soviet Russia's desire to showcase the achievements of its dancers and those of its allies by other means than simply foreign company tours. It also became a means by which to compare artists from different performing traditions. The second year of the competition in 1965 featured a similarly stellar jury which included Erik Bruhn. In 1970, the only First Prize of the Fifth Varna Competition was given to the American dancer Eva Evdokimova,[549] the first Western competitor to receive the gold medal. In subsequent years increasing numbers of competitors from outside the Eastern Bloc participated and began to be awarded prizes.

1964 – The accession of Brezhnev

Nikita Khrushchev, whose assumption of the post of General Secretary of the Communist Party after Stalin's death had begun the cultural thaw, was ousted from power in September 1964 and replaced by Leonid Brezhnev.[550] Initially in partnership with Alexey Kosygin[551] as the new Premier, Brezhnev asserted himself in a backlash against the former's policies surrounding the Prague Spring of 1968, even though Kosygin remained nominally in office until 1980. The Brezhnev period, later referred to as the 'Era of Stagnation', was one of an entrenchment of beliefs and, in cultural terms, the active promulgation of Soviet values within the framework of socialist realism.

---

547   Born in Leningrad in 1937, Vikulov graduated into the Kirov in 1956 and established himself as a lyrical dancer and a secure partner with a large, easy jump and a noble stage manner. He danced all the major roles in the repertoire before retiring from the stage in 1988. He graduated from the Leningrad Conservatoire choreographic department in 1977 and staged several ballets thereafter. Since 1998 he has coached at the Mariinsky Theatre.

548   Born in Sofia, Bulgaria in 1940, Kirova studied in her home city and joined the Ballet of the Opera of Sofia in 1958, rising to the rank of ballerina in 1961. From 1979 to 1982 she was the director of the Sofia Opera and Ballet.

549   Born in Geneva in 1948, Evdokimova began her ballet training in Munich and then was at London's Royal Ballet School between 1959 and 1965. In 1966 she became the first non-Dane to join the Royal Danish Ballet where she danced until 1969 when she moved to the Berlin Opera Ballet, attaining the rank of ballerina in 1973. She danced with several companies including London Festival Ballet where she was the first Aurora in Rudolf Nureyev's 1975 production of *The Sleeping Beauty*. After retirement, she taught and coached at Boston Ballet. She died in New York in 2009.

550   Born in Kamianske, Ukraine in 1906, Brezhnev joined *Komsomol* in 1923 and became an official party member in 1929. He rose to the rank of major general during the war and rose to join the Politburo by 1957. He became First Secretary of the Communist Party in 1964. He died outside Moscow in 1982.

551   Born in St Petersburg in 1904, Kosygin worked his way up the Communist party hierarchy from 1930 onwards, reaching the Politburo under Stalin in 1953. He served as Premier from 1964 to 1980, the year of his death in Moscow.

The tenets of that concept had however been constructed in a very different political, social and cultural world, and this period became characterised by tentative artistic experimentation, often as a result of cultural forces and movements external to the Soviet Union and despite official repression of the avant-garde.

1964 – *The Twelve*

Despite the failure of *The Bedbug*, other works by Yakobson followed at the Kirov, as he continued to explore and push at the boundaries of acceptability. *The Twelve* was his treatment of Alexander Blok's 1918 poem about twelve revolutionary Bolshevik soldiers who evoke Christ's apostles, and His appearance to them in a snowstorm. After its December opening, it was banned from performance with the words "What are you up to? Are you mocking us, Leonid Veniaminovich?"[552] Offence had been taken at the meek, even fearful red Army soldiers as they faced their uncertain future at the ballet's conclusion; such lack of confidence in the Soviet vision was not to be countenanced. Typically, Yakobson refused to change the ending. The music was commissioned from a Shostakovich protégé, Boris Tishchenko,[553] who provided an edgy, restless, experimental fifty-minute score. At the première, the character dancer Nonna Zvonareva[554] danced Katka and Petrukha was Igor Chernishev. The banning of *The Twelve* must also be seen in the context of the prevailing artistic and political climate – the early 1960s were a time of general artistic questioning of the Soviet ideal through such works as Solzhenitsyn's *One Day in the Life of Ivan Denisovich* and Shostakovich's Thirteenth Symphony, both published in 1962. This 'unpatriotic' movement in Soviet artistic circles provoked a political backlash, with targeted official denunciations and condemnations.

1965 – *Le Sacre du Printemps (The Rite of Spring)*

Choreographers Kasatkina and Vasilyov scored yet another success in June of 1965 with *Le Sacre du Printemps* which opened at the Bolshoi in a triple bill with Lavrovsky's *Paganini* and Poulenc's one-act opera monologue *La Voix Humaine*. The ballet combined the grotesque and the acrobatic with classical

---

552 Homans, *Apollo's Angels*, p.367

553 Born in Leningrad in 1939, Tishchenko studied first at the city's Musical College and then Conservatoire. He became a prolific composer in many forms, from two cello concertos to a setting of Anna Akhmatova's poem-cycle 'Requiem', chamber music and, in addition to *The Twelve*, another ballet score, *Yaroslavna* (*The Eclipse*). He died in St Petersburg in 2010.

554 Born in Leningrad in 1934, Zvonareva graduated in 1952 from the school into the Maly company where she danced until 1960. She then transferred to the Kirov where she performed in character roles for twenty-two years. She was the first Lezginka in Vinogradov's 1968 *Goryanka*. She retired from the stage in 1982.

dance to portray a rebellious individual set against inhuman paganism. In the first Russian treatment of Stravinsky's brutal score, the couple wrote their own scenario which they set in the second millennium BC. Kasatkina herself created the role of The Possessed, who chooses a victim for sacrifice, and delivered a performance of immense power. As the young shepherd who is infatuated with Nina Sorokina's Chosen Girl, Yuri Vladimirov scored a great success as the Shepherd, performing with a blazing physicality and impetuous bravado; the role lifted "him above even the high standard of the splendid Soviet dancers".[555]

1966 – The Young Ballet

In 1966, a new Moscow dance company was formed by the USSR Ministry of Culture under the artistic direction of Igor Moiseyev and Irina Tikhomirnova. Its formation represented a signal shift in official policy and was a recognition of the growing trend for smaller-scale dance pieces. The ensemble gave its first performances in 1968 and went on to present a repertoire of excerpts from classical ballets and new choreographic miniatures made by such choreographers as Vinogradov, Goleizovsky, Messerer and Moiseyev himself. In 1971, it was renamed the Classical Ballet Concert Ensemble of the USSR under the direction of Yuri Zhdanov[556] who continued the same artistic policy. From 1977 onwards it was led by the choreographer couple Kasatkina and Vasilyov, changing its name in 1986 to the Moscow Classical Ballet, by which it is known around the world but, since 1992, it has officially been the 'State Academic Theatre Classical Ballet of N. Kasatkina and V. Vasilyov'.

1966 – Grigorovich's *The Nutcracker*

Early in Grigorovich's tenure as Bolshoi director, he choreographed a new version of *The Nutcracker* drawing heavily on Vainonen's 1934 Kirov production which he knew from his time as a dancer with the company. His own version focussed on the girl Masha and The Nutcracker Prince with whom she danced the Act II Grand Pas and was characterised by extensive use of the *corps de ballet*. Mime was completely excised. The first cast was led by Ekaterina Maximova as Masha and Vladimir Vasiliev as The Prince who succeeded in transcending "Grigorovich's rather blatant and one-

---

555   Kun, 'The Bolshoi's Rite of Spring', *Dancing Times*, February 1966

556   Born in Moscow in 1925, Zhdanov graduated into the Bolshoi in 1944 where he performed until 1967 in major roles of the repertoire, partnering Ulanova between 1951 and 1960. He created the part of Andrey in Lavrovsky's *Pages of Life* in 1961. In 1964 he graduated from the ballet master department of GITIS and between 1971 and 1976 was director of the Classical Ballet Concert Ensemble of the USSR. From 1978 to 1979 he taught and coached at the National Theatre, Prague and between 1982 and 1986 taught at GITIS. He died in Moscow in 1986.

dimensional choreography"[557] in order to interpret Tchaikovsky's radiant score. Grigorovich's version remains in the repertoire of the Bolshoi Ballet.

1967 – *Asel*

The year 1967 held great importance for the USSR: it was the fiftieth anniversary of the revolution and, as such, a cause for celebration of a half-century of the Soviet ideal made real. All areas of society and the arts were to contribute to the celebrations, not least of which would be ballet. The Bolshoi decided upon two dance productions, the first being a third attempt at the story of Spartacus to be presented at the Kremlin Palace of Congresses; originally scheduled for the spring of 1966, it was put back until the following year. The second new production was *Asel*, a version of Chingiz Aitmatov's[558] story *My Little Poplar in a Red Scarf*, with music by Vladimir Vlasov[559] and choreography by Oleg Vinogradov, a young dance-maker who had been nurtured and encouraged at the Novosibirsk Ballet by Pyotr Gusev. This was the first major stage commission for Vinogradov who went on to become one of Soviet ballet's major players over subsequent decades. The narrative was an adaptation of the original story and concerned the girl Asel who falls in love with and marries Ilyas, a driver at a motor-transport depot, only to be betrayed by him for another woman, Kadicha. Finding new love with a war veteran, Baytemir, she has to choose between the two men when Ilyas returns to her; Asel chooses Baytemir. *Asel*'s narrative was resolutely non-linear and comprised scenes of the protagonists' memories. It premièred in February to a positive reception and featured Nina Timofeyeva in the title role, Nikolai Fadeyechev as Ilyas, Yaroslav Sekh as Baytemir and Elena Ryabinkina as Kadicha.

1967 – *Carmen Suite*

Maya Plisetskaya, by now trusted and, indeed, fêted by the regime – she had received the Lenin Prize in 1964 – had long been looking for a new vehicle for her talents. In 1966, the Cuban Ballet performed in Moscow as part of their Russian tour (they also visited Leningrad, Volgograd, Kiev and Tbilisi) and impressed audiences with their un-stereotypical 'Spanishness'.

---

557   Vasiliev quoted by Smakov, *The Great Russian Dancers*, p.329

558   Born in 1928 in Sheker Village, Kyrgyzstan, Aitmatov studied at the Maxim Gorky Literature Institute, Moscow from 1956 to 1958. For the next eight years he worked for *Pravda* which published his first stories. He went on to write novels, short stories and worked in films. His best-known work was *Jamila* which appeared in 1958. He died in Nuremberg, Germany in 2008.

559   Born in Moscow in 1903, Vlasov graduated from the Moscow Conservatoire in 1931. He founded the Music and Drama Theatre in the Kyrgyzstan capital Frunze (now Bishkek) in 1936 where he remained as artistic director until 1942 after when he took up the same post at the Moscow Philharmonic Orchestra. He was a composer of symphonies, cello works and orchestral works. He died in Moscow in 1986.

Having alighted upon Prosper Mérimée's story of Carmen, she approached Alberto, Alicia Alonso's choreographer brother-in-law, to make a version of the story which was to feature a rumbustious arrangement of Bizet's score by her husband Rodion Shchedrin.[560] Alonso subsequently spent six months in Moscow as a guest choreographer and his *Carmen Suite* premièred at the Bolshoi in April 1967, despite a degree of official nervousness about its unashamed eroticism, and became a huge success for Plisetskaya as Carmen who wound her legs seductively around Fadeyechev's Don José. The ballet was also given in Havana with Alicia Alonso in the title role opposite Plisetskaya's brother, Azary Plisetsky.[561] The ballet was designed by their cousin, Boris Messerer.[562]

1967 – *The Land of Miracles*

An allegory of war in a folkloric context, *The Land of Miracles* was originally conceived by Yakobson in 1944, but finally came to the Kirov stage in 1967. Set to a strongly rhythmical score by Shvarts, it garnered genuine audience enthusiasm with what the director and critic Boris Lvov-Anokhin[563] called "its daring methods of radical plastic grotesque".[564] The ballet, a simple allegory about the power of the moral hero in the face of evil, gave Makarova another fine dramatic role as Beauty Maiden (for which she was named best Soviet ballerina of the year) and provided the young virtuoso Valery Panov who danced the part of Bright Falcon with "the pinnacle of his dancing

---

560 Born in Moscow in 1932, Shchedrin graduated from the Moscow Conservatoire and became a prolific composer of tuneful, tonal music in a variety of forms, from symphonies, concertos and operas as well as several ballets, most of which featured his wife Maya Plisetskaya. He continues to compose.

561 Born in Moscow in 1931, Plisetsky studied first at the Moscow Conservatoire's central school of music before moving to the Bolshoi School from where he graduated in 1957 into the company. In 1963, he was sent to Cuba and danced as Alicia Alonso's regular stage partner and began to set and choreograph ballets and helped establish the Cuban National Ballet School in Havana. His first work of many was *La Avanzada* in 1963, an evocation of the Siege of Stalingrad. He returned to the Bolshoi in 1973 and danced there until 1978 when he became a teacher at Maurice Béjart's Ballet du XXe Siècle and Mudra School in Brussels and then in Lausanne from 1991 onwards. He continues to teach and set ballets around the world.

562 Born in Moscow in 1933, the son of Bolshoi star Asaf, Messerer graduated from Moscow's Architectural Institute in 1956 before gravitating to the theatre where he rapidly established himself as a theatre artist and set designer of distinction. He first worked at the Bolshoi in 1963 with a new production of Prokofiev's *Lieutenant Kijé*. He worked extensively in theatre both in Russia and, later abroad as well as in film.

563 Born in Moscow in 1926, Lvov-Anokhin graduated from the Ostrovsky Leningrad State Theatre Institute and became a noted director and writer for film. He died in Moscow in 2000.

564 Ross, *Like a Bomb Going Off*, p.326

career in the USSR".[565] After its première in late July 1967 it proved so popular that the Kirov moved the production to the larger stage of the House of Culture in order to satisfy the demand for tickets.

1967 – the Bolshoi Ballet School moves to new buildings

Having occupied the same site since 1865, the Bolshoi School moved into a purpose-built complex in September 1967. The new Frunzenskaya Street buildings hugely increased the school's capacity and facilities: the old building had been constructed for 80 students and held 360 by the early 1960s whereas the new premises were designed for 600, with boarding for 300, some 20 ballet studios and its own theatre. Sofia Golovkina, the school's long-serving director, oversaw the project and the successful move. The school remains in these premises.

Mikhail Baryshnikov

In 1967, an immensely talented nineteen-year-old Latvian dancer joined the Kirov Ballet as a soloist. A pupil of Alexander Pushkin, he gave every indication of outshining an earlier protégé, the now officially excised Rudolf Nureyev – he was Mikhail Baryshnikov. Born in Riga, Latvia in 1948, Baryshnikov trained locally before entering the Vaganova Academy in 1960. His graduation performance in 1967 exceeded all expectations with the display of an impeccable technique allied to puckish charm in the *Le Corsaire* pas de deux variation. He was a dancer impossible to characterise, and therefore difficult to cast – many roles simply did not suit his talents – and it was only the *demi-caractère* virtuosity of Basilio in *Don Quixote* and the part of the Soviet student in *Goryanka*, a 1968 ballet by Oleg Vinogradov which made full use of his technical wizardry, that were deemed to show him at his best. 1969 brought considerable interest from nonconformist choreographers and little from the Kirov management: Leonid Yakobson created *Vestris* on him, a solo combining immense technical demands with intense theatricality, which Baryshnikov performed at the 1969 Moscow International Ballet Competition and contributed to his securing the Gold Medal. It is still performed to this day. In December of the same year, former Kirov dancer Igor Chernishev created a one-act version of *Romeo and Juliet* which was banned. Drawn to Baryshnikov's abilities, the choreographer cast him as Mercutio. Natalia Makarova, who had previously danced with Baryshnikov in *Goryanka*, was cast as Juliet, but at the dress rehearsal the ballet caused a scandal – Dudinskaya and Sergeyev accused it of formalism, eroticism and imitating Western movement and it was subsequently banned. Baryshnikov made his mark during the Kirov Ballet's 1970 London appearances: *Financial Times* dance critic Clement Crisp observed: "he has a

---

565 ibid., p.323

superbly easy technique – fluent and never forced – and beautiful placing; night after night...he performed marvels of truly beautiful dancing with an engaging and unaffected air of enjoying himself thoroughly".[566] His notable portrayal of Adam in Kasatkina and Vasilyov's *Creation of the World* in 1971 led to his debut as Albrecht in *Giselle* the following year, a modern interpretation showing his character's innocence and genuine love for Giselle which was considered by many to have superseded Sergeyev's. "*Giselle* was important to me because the Kirov didn't really believe I could do it,"[567] he observed after his defection in June 1974. By 1973, he was accorded a gala performance focused on him alone by a management still rattled by Makarova's defection in 1970 and anxious to keep a star dancer.

1968 – Goryanka

Oleg Vinogradov was invited by the Kirov to create a new work for the spring of 1968. He chose Dagestan poet Rasul Gazmatov's[568] homonymous poem as his narrative and to a score commissioned from Murad Kazhlayev,[569] the choreographer used memories and impressions of his travels in the republic to create a work which infused ballet with regional folk-dance movement. It told the story of the refusal by mountain girl Asiyat to enter into an arranged marriage with local boy Osman. She flees and is encouraged to believe in another existence by 'modern' women. She begins a new life in the city and begins her studies; one day Osman appears and kills her to avenge the dishonour she has brought upon him. *Goryanka* was warmly received and featured in subsequent seasons; at the first performance Gabriela Komleva danced Asiyat and Valery Panov was Osman. It was revived at the Kirov in 1984 in a new version by the choreographer entitled *Asiyat*; the title role was danced by Elena Evteyeva,[570] Osman by *Konstantin Zaklinsky and *Farukh Ruzimatov was the Young Man.

---

566 Crisp, 'Kirov Dancers in London', *Dancing Times*, September 1970

567 Baryshnikov in Gottlieb, *Reading Dance*, p.271

568 Born in the Khunzakhsky District of the Soviet Republic of Dagestan in 1923, Gazmatov followed his father a well-known mountain bard, in writing poems on local themes from the age of eleven. He died in Moscow in 2003.

569 Born in Baku in 1931 to an ethnic Dagestan Lak family, Kazhlayev graduated from the city's music conservatoire and quickly became a major figure in Dagestan's cultural life becoming chief conductor of the Radio Symphonic Orchestra between 1957 to 1958, artistic director of the Dagestan Philharmonic Hall in 1963 and the secretary of the republic's Union of Composers from 1968. He worked extensively with poet Rasul Gamzatov. In 2010, he established the Dagestan Musical School for Gifted Children.

570 Born in Leningrad in 1947, Evteyeva graduated into the Kirov in 1966 where she remained until 1993. She rose to the rank of principal, performing an extensive repertoire which included all the major classical roles. She created Masha in Chernishev's version of *The Nutcracker* in Odessa in 1969. From 1993 to 1999 she taught at the Vaganova Academy and from 1993 has taught and coached at the Mariinsky.

1968 – Grigorovich's *Spartacus*

Grigorovich's career high-point came not long after his arrival in Moscow with his 1968 production of *Spartacus*. It was the third attempt successfully to create a dance work about the ideologically attractive leader of the slave revolt against Rome and using Aram Khachaturian's commissioned score. Grigorovich succeeded where Yakobson (at the Kirov in 1956 and the Bolshoi in 1962) and Igor Moiseyev at the Bolshoi in 1958 had failed. By the mid-1960s there was a real desire in the Bolshoi's management to revitalise the repertoire; they had been considering reviving *Coppélia* or even asking Frederick Ashton to stage *La Fille mal gardée*, but nevertheless decided to prioritise political necessity over purely artistic considerations given the upcoming fiftieth anniversary of the Russian revolution in 1967. The regime made it clear that it wished for a suitably revolutionary ballet to commemorate that important date, so by 1965 it was decided that *Spartacus* should be tried again with a première fixed for the spring of 1966. Grigorovich, who according to ballerina Ekaterina Maximova was initially unwilling to stage this particular commission, was also aware of the potential for his own career if successful and subsequently set about the project with gusto. He cut and reordered the composer's score (much against his wishes), refocussed the narrative to create conflict and contrast between the hero Spartacus and anti-hero Crassus, and made it a mimeless, through-danced work. The delayed première took place on 9th April 1968 featuring Vladimir Vasiliev as Spartacus, Ekaterina Maximova as Phrygia, Māris Liepa as Crassus and Nina Timofeyeva as Aegina. It was an immediate triumph and provided the Soviet regime with the much and long wished-for heroic ballet which broadcasted the revolutionary message loud and clear. That it has survived over fifty years and the regime itself shows that it possesses greater qualities than its Western critics allow. However impressive the effect of Grigorovich's often simplistic choreography, its success lay and continues to lie in the dancers who inhabit the main roles; the second cast of Mikhail Lavrovsky, Natalia Bessmertnova, Boris Akimov[571] and Svetlana Adyrkhaeva[572] brought their

---

571 Born in Vienna, Austria in 1946, Akimov graduated from the Bolshoi School in 1965 and joined the company with whom he danced until 1989 after which time he taught and coached, becoming its director between 2000 and 2003. His early appearances were in *Heroic Poem (Geologists)* and *Asel* after which he began to dance many of the principal roles of the repertoire, notably in Yuri Grigorovich's productions. He remains a highly valued teacher around the world.

572 Born in Khumalag, North-Ossetia in 1938, Adyrkhaeva graduated in 1955 from the Leningrad Choreographic School and joined the Chelyabinsk Theatre where she made her debut as Odette-Odile. She danced in Odessa from 1958 to 1960 before joining the Bolshoi where she appeared until 1988. Noted for her beautiful line and strong technique, she danced principal roles across the repertoire – Grigorovich's Aegina and Mekhmeneh Banu were favourite parts. In 1980 she graduated from GITIS and between 1995-2001

own qualities and subtle changes of focus and emphasis to their equally valid performances. It remains in the repertoire to this day.

Igor Chernishev

In August 1968, Kirov dancer Igor Chernishev presented *Antony and Cleopatra* at the Maly Theatre, his first full-length choreographic work. To a score by Eduard Lazarev,[573] and with Valentina Mukhanova[574] as the Egyptian queen and Vasily Ostrovsky[575] as her Roman lover – Alla Osipenko and John Markovsky[576] were the second cast – it caused a flurry with the vigour and passion of its depiction of doomed love, using of a variety of styles which combined the vocabulary of classical dance with more exaggerated and even grotesque movements. It was performed 120 times at the Maly. Chernishev's dance style placed him directly in the tradition of Lopukhov's early experiments in the 1920s and also Yakobson's; it was no coincidence that, as a dancer, he had been chosen to take part in the 1958 'Choreographic Miniatures' programme Yakobson had put on at the Kirov. In 1969, he created his ill-fated and short-lived one-act *Romeo and Juliet* for the Kirov, using Hector Berlioz's *symphonie dramatique* which was to have featured Natalia Makarova and Vadim Gulyayev;[577] she described it as a "dramatic

---

taught classical dance at the Dance Academy of the Natalia Nesterova New Humanitarian University.

573   Born in Sverdlovsk in 1935, Lazarev graduated from the Moscow Conservatoire to become a composer in a variety of genres, including both opera and ballet – his eight-act score for *The Master and Margarita* was completed in 1983. He died in Moscow in 2008.

574   Born in Leningrad in 1945, Mukhanova graduated from the Vaganova Academy in 1964 and joined the Maly company, rapidly attaining the rank of ballerina. She was a strong classical dancer with an intense stage personality. She excelled in newly-created dramatic roles. She retired from performing in 1982 after which she embarked on a teaching career outside Russia.

575   Born in Poltava, Ukraine in 1946, Ostrovsky graduated from the Vaganova Academy in 1966. After a year with the Mariinsky, he transferred to the Maly where he danced until 1990, performing in both romantic and comedy roles. After a few years staging ballets around Russia, he emigrated to Rosario, Argentina in 1994 where, with his wife Tatiana Fesenko, he founded a ballet school at the El Circulo Theatre.

576   Born in Yakutsk in 1944, Markovsky trained at the Riga Ballet School before entering the company. In 1964, he resumed training at the Vaganova Academy before graduating the year after and joining the Kirov. A tall dancer, he was much sought after as a stage partner. He left the Kirov with his wife Osipenko and danced with Yakobson's Choreographic Miniatures. From 1973 onwards, he toured Russia with her for the Leningrad Concert Organisation, and then with Boris Eifman's Theatre of Contemporary Ballet.

577   Born in Lomonosov, Leningrad in 1947, Gulyayev graduated into the Kirov in 1966 where he danced until 1989. His first notable role was Adam in *Creation of the World*, and he went on to dance the full repertoire as a senior soloist. He has coached at the Kirov since his retirement from the stage and has worked as a choreographer in Ekaterinburg.

flow of robust, active choreography".[578] His approach was always to seek the unexpected and unusual and he represented a genuinely individual creative force in Soviet ballet in this period.

1969 – Grigorovich's *Swan Lake*

In Moscow, buoyed by the roaring success of *Spartacus*, Yuri Grigorovich set about a wholescale remodelling of the Bolshoi repertoire by presenting his own versions of the classics which would grow to dominate the schedules. His controversial *Swan Lake*, premièred in late 1969, was something of a watershed, marking the end of his early creative period after which his ballets became increasingly repetitive and formulaic. For many in both company and audience who were brought up on the Gorsky/Messerer version, this new *Swan Lake*, influenced directly by the writings of E. T. A. Hoffmann, was hard to take. Von Rothbart became Prince Siegfried's shady double, and brought to the fore the exciting young dancer Boris Akimov, later Bolshoi company director and a distinguished teacher, in the enhanced role of the evil sorcerer. Odette-Odile was danced by Natalia Bessmertnova and the Prince by Nikolai Fadeyechev. Dance was all, mime and the Act III national dances excised, which provoked extensive discussion and polemic on both sides of the argument. The tenets of *drambalet* and realism were comprehensively rejected in favour of a form of danced-through reverie. Fyodor Lopukhov, ever the promoter of the primacy of dance as movement, defended his former protégé's work, but Grigorovich had to change his proposed depiction of the prince's ultimate disillusionment at the destruction of his dreams in order to ensure that the curtain would rise on the production – Culture Minister Furtseva had insisted on a bright and positive ending.

It was at this time that company prima ballerina Maya Plisetskaya started to shed her initial enthusiasm for Grigorovich. She believed that his early ballets *The Stone Flower* and *Legend of Love* were his finest: "They are the peak of his work. All his subsequent works – this is my opinion – went downhill. Fast."[579] She observed tartly of his reworkings of the classics: "He changed the good old classical ballets, adding just a light retouching but not forgetting to add his name. And then he took on Petipa, Perrot, Ivanov, Gorsky."[580]

Yakobson's 'Choreographic Miniatures'

Leonid Yakobson was never the balletic pariah as some have tried to portray – his commissions and his role as house choreographer at the Kirov give lie to that assertion – but he was a maverick, whose experimentations and fundamental questionings of the classical dance idiom and what it could and

---

578   Makarova, *A Dance Autobiography*, p.81
579   Plisetskaya, *I, Maya Plisetskaya*, p.360.
580   ibid., p.361.

should portray meant that he would never be a mainstream dance-maker. Some considered him a genius and many more thought him an important artistic voice in the world of Soviet dance; Mikhail Baryshnikov, for whom he created the notable *Vestris* solo in 1969, observed of him: "He was an extraordinarily gifted choreographer and a very free-minded and free-spirited man."[581] Yakobson believed that to be able to express contemporary ideas and concerns, dance needed a new idiom and to reject socialist realist ballets which featured on-stage tractors: "form and content in ballet must not be allowed to come to that catastrophic confrontation that we have witnessed so dolefully in our own time".[582]

In 1967, after years of petitioning, Yakobson finally persuaded the Leningrad authorities to allow the establishment of the first independent ballet company in the USSR since the 1920s. However, it was the more mainstream Pyotr Gusev who was initially appointed as the new Chamber Ballet's artistic director. Soon afterwards, however, Yakobson assumed control of the ensemble he had always wanted and announced his vision in December 1969 for the renamed 'Choreographic Miniatures'. His speech revealed a man at the forefront of thinking, far more in tune with developments in dance in the West than any of his contemporaries:

> "In the Kirov Theatre, ballet artists have magnificently developed feet and legs, but that is only half of the person needed to perform classical ballet. To do modern works they modernise only the top half of the artist, the torso, hands and arms. This sometimes would enrage me. How can you allow the feet of the artist to do classical while the top is doing something else?"[583]

1969 – The Moscow International Ballet Competition

In 1969 it was decided to establish an event similar to the Varna Ballet Competition in the Soviet Union itself – Moscow was chosen as the location for a new competition to be held every four years. Part of the ongoing Soviet cultural offensive, it was the latest in a series of competitions whose main purpose was to trumpet Russian achievements in the arts, the first of which, the Tchaikovsky Piano Competition, had begun in 1956. The first jury of The Moscow International Ballet Competition had Galina Ulanova as Chairman and included Vakhtang Chabukiani, Maya Plisetskaya and Konstantin Sergeyev as well as international members among whom were the *prime ballerine* Alicia Alonso and Yvette Chauviré.[584] In 1973 Yuri Grigorovich

---

581   As quoted by Ross, *Like a Bomb Going Off*, p.13.
582   ibid., p.330.
583   ibid., p.337-8.
584   Born in Paris in 1917, Chauviré graduated in 1936 from the school as a *première*

became the permanent Chairman of the Jury which slowly began to include ballet luminaries from outside Russia and the Eastern Bloc. During the period of the USSR (until 1991), the Grand Prix has been won only twice, on both occasions by Russian dancers: Nadezhda Pavlova at the second 1973 competition and *Irek Mukhamedov at the fourth in 1981; Mikhail Baryshnikov won a Gold Medal at the first competition in 1969 alongside Nina Sorokina and Yuri Vladimirov. Between 1969 and 2009, seventy percent of medal winners were Russian. Grigorovich continues to chair the jury.

Alexander Pushkin

With the exception of Agrippina Vaganova, few, if any, teachers in the history of Soviet ballet are regarded with such awe as Alexander Pushkin, a remarkable pedagogue whose approach and style created a stable of outstanding male dancers at the Kirov: Vladilen Semyonov, Askold Makarov, Rudolf Nureyev, Valery Panov and Mikhail Baryshnikov (Yuri Soloviev studied initially with Pushkin but for the last four years of his training worked exclusively with the distinguished Vaganova teacher Boris Shavrov in his parallel class). Born in Mikulino, Tver province in 1907, Pushkin trained initially under Nikolai Legat and then under Vladimir Ponomarev at the Petrograd, then Leningrad Choreographic School, graduating into GATOB in 1925. He danced with the company until 1953 but had begun to teach in 1932 at the School where his particular assemblage of dance combinations both strengthened the musculature and extended the technical capabilities of his students. His students revered him. A man of famously few words – it was said the only observations he made were 'don't fall' and 'get up' – he focussed on the individuality inherent in every male dancer and sought to capitalise on their particular attributes; he was, in the words of Baryshnikov "an extraordinarily patient and extraordinarily kind person".[585] He died in Leningrad in March 1970.

Ballet Conductors

The role of conductor in ballet performances is often overlooked. Not only is the conductor the only musician to see the action on stage and thus to be able to coordinate the orchestra in its pit with the dancing, but he/she has to rehearse the musical ensemble in often difficult and complicated scores, many

---

danseuse into the Paris Opéra Ballet where director Serge Lifar acted as her mentor. She was made an *étoile* five years later and remained with the company until 1972, becoming their senior ballerina. She was a beautiful and elegant dancer, as comfortable in new works as the classics. From 1963 to 1968 she was the director of the Paris Opéra Ballet School. She died in Paris in 2016.

585   Acocella, 'The Reluctant Prodigal', *The Guardian*, February 1998

being commissions. In the creative stages of a new ballet, a music director also has input into structure and form. In the history of Soviet ballet, some conductors emerge as crucial to the art form as well as being distinguished musicians in their own right. Many Russian conductors appeared in dance performances, but in the Soviet period, two emerge as real ballet specialists.

An individual of huge importance in the twentieth century history of the Bolshoi Ballet, Yuri Faier (or Fayer) was its permanent conductor for some forty years. Born into a Jewish family in Kiev in 1890, he graduated from the city's music conservatoire in 1906 but was unable to take up his place at the Moscow Conservatoire until he converted to Russian Orthodoxy. He worked as an accompanist and conductor at Riga's opera house between 1914 and 1915. He was engaged as an orchestral violinist at the Bolshoi in 1916 and in 1919 stepped in as conductor when the scheduled Andrey Arends fell ill shortly before a performance of *Coppélia*. He was promptly engaged as assistant chief ballet conductor.

In 1923, he became the theatre's chief ballet conductor, a post he would hold until 1963. He was exceptionally sympathetic to the needs of the dancers, having studied the rules of choreography the better to understand the needs of dance-makers and performers. He collaborated with numerous composers and choreographers to bring new works to the Bolshoi stage. He conducted over 400 performances of *Swan Lake* alone and was the conductor at the first performances of both *Romeo and Juliet* in 1940 and *Cinderella* in 1945. For many, he was the face of Bolshoi ballet music, conducting the orchestra on the company's foreign tours from 1956 onwards; he travelled to the United Kingdom, France, Belgium, Germany, Hungary, China and the United States.

Bolshoi ballerina Marina Semyonova wrote of Faier: "And even my impromptu changes always met with an instant response in him – this is his uniqueness. And what a person he was! Kindness, kindness, warmth itself. I loved him very much."[586] He retired in 1963 and died in Moscow in 1971.

Viktor Fedotov was born in 1933 in Novoalexandrovka (now Serebryansk) in the autonomous Tartar Republic and showed musical talent from a very early age. He graduated from the orchestral faculty of the Leningrad Conservatoire in 1956 and then in 1963 from the conducting faculty. That year he won a conducting competition at the Kirov Theatre and was offered a contract. His ability to conduct scores from memory received the approval of ballet company director Konstantin Sergeyev who felt he could then watch the stage more. He had a natural affinity with ballet and was said to be able to understand a dancer and his or her musical needs simply by looking at their body. He conducted the premières of many ballets at the Kirov, including

---

586 As quoted by the Bolshoi Theatre website: https://www.bolshoi.ru/persons/people/1362/

Belsky's *Leningrad Symphony*, and accompanied the ballet company on several foreign tours. He was much loved by the dancers who felt the active support he gave them from the pit.

Equally at home as an opera conductor, he was the Kirov's chief conductor between 1974 and 1976 and was appointed a professor of the Leningrad Conservatoire in 1977. He started to conduct abroad in the mid-1960s and was a regular guest with The Royal Ballet at Covent Garden until 1997; *Financial Times* critic Clement Crisp once called him the 'prince' of ballet conductors. He died in Moscow in 2001.

1970 – Makarova's defection

The late summer of 1970 saw the third Kirov visit to London (the second having taken place in 1966) with Natalia Makarova again as part of the troupe and scheduled to dance in *Giselle* and *Chopiniana*. It was during the season that one evening after dinner with friends she took the decision to ask for asylum. She has stated that the banning the previous year of Chernishev's *Romeo and Juliet* in which she was due to create the role of Juliet contributed to her decision, as did the artistic sterility of the Kirov company under Sergeyev.

Having decided to remain in the West, she initially received letters from her now ex-colleagues and friends in the Kirov imploring her to return: company director Sergeyev wrote several times, at first in a spirit of disbelief and then, as it became clear that Makarova was not minded to return, with increasing desperation: "shake yourself free of this delusion" he wrote in his third letter, "...when someone is torn from his native roots, he perishes".[587] Ballerina Alla Osipenko also focussed on the emotional wrench of defection: "Your soul is Russian...it will not survive what you are doing."[588] Tatiana Vecheslova, Makarova's dance coach back at the Kirov Theatre, also wrote: "Your not returning home is monstrous. Do you really think any foreigner could respect you?"[589] But Makarova knew she had made the right decision:

> "Russia could not offer me any more than what was already given" she observed seven years after the event, "Although I stood in heavy debt to the Kirov, nothing there could inspire me any longer. My imagination was in a stupor, my technique did not progress; my intuition prompted me to run away from the void looming ahead."[590]

Makarova's first appearance in the West as a 'free' dancer was as Giselle that autumn in New York with American Ballet Theatre.

---

587 Makarova, *A Dance Biography*, p.91
588 ibid.
589 ibid.
590 Smakov, *The Great Russian Dancers*, p.50

1970 – Investigation and the 'fall' of Sergeyev

A direct consequence of the Makarova's defection to the West was the dismissal from the Kirov of its director and ex-*premier danseur* Konstantin Sergeyev. A survivor in the tricky world of Soviet Russian cultural politics, he had negotiated the multiple twists and turns and even a period out in the 'cold' in the second half of the 1950s. Makarova's betrayal of the USSR required that someone be deemed responsible and it was Sergeyev who was chosen. By the beginning of the new decade, he appeared increasingly old-fashioned and out of touch with contemporary cultural trends which included the move towards 'symphonism' and abstraction in ballet.

A State Security Committee investigation report observed of Makarova: "the theatre staff knew that Makarova was morally unstable in terms of her personal qualities, she repeatedly expressed dissatisfaction with her position. However, on the part of the theatre administration, these facts were not given appropriate importance."[591] The name and image of Makarova were also promptly excised from all literature and company records.

Criticism was severe for Sergeyev and his wife, prima ballerina Dudinskaya. They were censured for their leadership of the troupe:

> "The selection of candidates for touring trips abroad was carried out not for creative reasons, but on the principle of the attitude of one or another artist to the artistic directors of the ballet Sergeyev and Dudinskaya, whose personal behaviour was not an example for the collective. During foreign tours Sergeyev and Dudinskaya repeatedly violated the rules of conduct of Soviet citizens abroad, engaged in unofficial contacts with foreigners and White émigrés, humiliating the dignity of Soviet man, (and) kowtowed to them to solicit gifts."[592]

It was alleged that under their control "an atmosphere of servility, opportunism and unprincipledness developed in the ballet collective, there was a tendency to level the leading artists, which caused them a feeling of discontent and resentment".[593]

Sergeyev was removed as Kirov director, but not cast out from the ballet establishment; blame did not mean disgrace. Indeed, in December 1970 he mounted his version of *Hamlet* to a score by Chervinsky which featured Baryshnikov ("...very young, suffering from shattered ideals"[594]) and subsequently Dolgushin (very romantic...lost in deep reflection"[595]) in

---

591   As quoted by Ogryzko, 'Isolation in art is a dead end', *Artists and Power*
592   ibid.
593   ibid.
594   Roslavleva, 'Two Hamlets in Russia', *Dancing Times*, July 1972
595   ibid.

the title role with Sizova and later Evteyeva as Ophelia. Sergeyev assumed the directorship of the Vaganova Academy in 1973 – he had, in fact, led it between 1938 and 1940 – a post he held until 1982, and he choreographed again at the Kirov in 1974, making *The Seasons* to Glazunov's score.

1970 – the defections of Filipov and Vostrikov

Natalia Makarova was not the only ballet defection of 1970. Prior to her decision in September to request asylum, Alexander Filipov, a twenty-two-year-old soloist with Moscow's Young Ballet, did the same during a company tour to Guadalajara, Mexico. Given his lack of profile and Makarova's London defection, it was scarcely reported. However, Filipov's reasons for leaving the Soviet Union were telling:

> "In Russia, only Russian ballet is best, and only certain kind of ballet. Like story of *Giselle*. Big pantomime, cemetery, everybody cry and big tragedy. Is fine, but for this time, I think it is a little bit funny. I want to learn Western style dance because is different, is more abstract, more careful, less emotional. Here, I am free to learn this and nobody say to me what I must do."[596]

He joined American Ballet Theatre almost immediately and developed an active career in the United States, rising to the rank of principal before joining San Francisco Ballet in 1978 and dancing opposite Makarova, his fellow defector of 1970, on Broadway in 1983 in the musical *On Your Toes*. He continues to live and now teach in the USA.

Another young company soloist, Gennady Vostrikov, spurred on by rumours that, given Filipov's behaviour, the ensemble was to be disbanded upon their return to Russia, requested asylum a few days later on 9th September. He joined the Mexico Ballet Company as a principal dancer before moving to the United States and Pittsburgh Ballet Theatre where he remained for his dancing career. He subsequently moved into teaching and has held numerous school and university posts.

The consequences of the two defections for the Young Ballet company were immediate: according to a State Security Committee investigation report, company co-founder Irina Tikhomirnova, "withdrew from the leadership of the collective (and) was conciliatory about the facts of violation of discipline and immoral misconduct on the part of individual artists who, during their stay abroad, entered into unofficial contacts with foreigners and abused alcohol".[597] Additionally, attention turned to co-founder Igor Moiseyev whom some accused of fostering an environment which encouraged defection;

---

596 As quoted by Zachary in *New York Magazine*, June 1971
597 As quoted by Ogryzko, 'Isolation in art is a dead end'.

Mikhail Suslov,[598] unofficially the 'Chief Ideologue of the Communist Party' noted: "Moiseyev even puts forward the idea of supranationality."[599]

Further investigations took place and on 15th September the report 'On serious shortcomings in the organization of touring trips of art groups to capitalist countries' was submitted to the Secretariat of the Central Committee. Deputy Minister Popov spoke for the Ministry of Culture at this meeting:

> "We considered at a closed meeting of the board the case of non-return of the artists. They gave it a very harsh assessment. We believe that the ministry made serious mistakes. We will change plans for sending artists abroad. First of all, you need to drastically reduce the travel of the ensembles. We mean to deal with each collective separately: with its composition, with the organization of educational work."[600]

The effect was felt not only by the world of ballet, but across the cultural spectrum. A tightening of restrictions, the elimination of multiple tours by companies or individuals and the curtailment of time spent away from the USSR were imposed on such world figures as cellist Mstislav Rostropovich[601] and violinist David Oistrakh.[602]

1971 – 'Choreographic Miniatures' in performance

'Choreographic Miniatures' presented its first all-Yakobson evening at the Maly Theatre in June 1971. The choreographer had had to deal with attempts at official interference and reprimands for using music by foreign composers, but at the core of his work was a quest for artistic freedom to create work for dancers whose main characteristic was individuality. A major coup for

---

598 Born in Shakhovskoye in 1902, Suslov left his job as a teacher to become a full-time official, rising through the ranks of the Communist Party under Stalin. By 1952, he had become a member of the ruling Presidium. A hard-line ideologue who opposed Khrushchev's 'thaw', he returned to greater influence at the accession of Brezhnev, whose second-in-command he was considered to be. He died in Moscow in 1982.

599 As quoted by Ogryzko, 'Isolation in art is a dead end'.

600 ibid.

601 Considered one of the twentieth century's greatest cellists, Rostropovich was born in Baku, Azerbaijan in 1927. He graduated from the Moscow Conservatoire in 1948 and became a professor there in 1956. Prokofiev and Shostakovich wrote works for him. He first appeared outside the USSR in 1963 and rapidly built an extensive international career. In 1974 he left the Soviet Union with his wife, Bolshoi leading soprano Galina Vishnevskaya, and settled in the USA. He returned to Russia after the fall of communism while living principally in Paris. He died in Moscow in 2007.

602 Born in Odessa, Ukraine in 1908, Oistrakh was one of the twentieth century's pre-eminent violinists. A child prodigy, he moved to Moscow in 1927 and established himself as one of the finest instrumentalists of the USSR. He travelled abroad from the end of the war, much in demand across the world. He died in Amsterdam in 1964.

his fledgling ensemble had been the arrival of Kirov ballerina Alla Osipenko and her husband John Markovsky as company members, both having spectacularly resigned from the Kirov in the autumn of the previous year. The evening comprised three 'collections' of miniature ballets, choreographed for the occasion with furious intensity and designed to take the audience on a journey through dance history. It started with the seven-part *Classicism-Romanticism*, made in the two historical ballet styles and which included *Taglioni's Flight*, made for Osipenko, as the great Romantic ballerina, Markovsky as her partner and four dancers dressed completely in black who thereby made her seem to float in the air. Next came five of the eight *Rodin Sculptures*, based on works by the famous French sculptor Auguste Rodin and on which Yakobson had initially worked between 1958 and 1962. The first three were made for the Kirov in 1958 and included Osipenko in *The Kiss*; the choreographer progressively added another five, which explored emotions in addition to the sensuality of the originals. *Five Russian Miniatures* followed, depicting both genre scenes and fairy tales and the evening concluded with *The Genre Triptych*, of which only one section, *Vagabond Circus*, made it through some eleventh-hour censorship on the evening of performance. The company was received with popular enthusiasm but official *froideur* which led initially to a ban on any performance outside Leningrad subsequently relaxed to exclusion from Moscow and foreign touring.

1971 – *Creation of the World*

In another attempt to inject some new work into the repertoire, the Kirov company invited Bolshoi choreographers Kasatkina and Vasilyov to Leningrad. Their choice for a new work was *Creation of the World*, a two-act ballet about the Creation, Adam and Eve, their fall from Grace and the birth of humankind. The libretto was of their own making and they chose to use a score by Andrey Petrov which had been commissioned by the Bolshoi, rather than Darius Milhaud's composition for the 1923 Ballets Suédois which had had choreography by Jean Börlin. Rehearsals had started at the Bolshoi but the project was cancelled by the management and so the Kirov decided to take it up, making Kasatkina and Vasilyov the first Moscow choreographers to create for the main Leningrad company. Following Soviet ideology, *Creation of the World* presented the religious story as something of a comic parody, inspired by the great 1945 cartoon cycle 'La Création du Monde' by French caricaturist Jean Effel. At the March première, Soloviev appeared as God, revealing comic talent in portraying the Almighty as a simple Russian peasant who created the world out of boredom and who executed dizzying virtuoso movements to alleviate the tedium. Mikhail Baryshnikov was a charming Adam who visibly grew up as the ballet progressed and added ever more spectacular leaps and turns as he did so; Kolpakova danced Eve, bringing great depth to the role. Another cast was also prepared for the first night but was not chosen: regular dance partners Vadim Gulyayev and Natalia Bolshakova[603] proved to be fine interpreters in subsequent performances. Valery Panov appeared as the Devil. The ballet was praised in *Pravda* by Igor Moiseyev for its modernity; he observed that it "once more demonstrated that new content is the only power capable of awakening creative thought and enriching the idiom of choreography".[604] *Creation of the World* proved popular with audiences and received 119 performances at the Kirov and was later staged in Tallinn, Tashkent, Sverdlovsk, Budapest and Berlin and entered the repertoire of Moscow Classical Ballet when the two choreographers assumed its directorship in 1977.

1971 – Vasiliev's *Icarus*

By the early 1970s Vladimir Vasiliev, the poster-boy not only for the Bolshoi but for Soviet ballet as a whole, began to expand his artistic horizons into choreography – in May 1971 he created his first dance work, *Icarus*, for the Bolshoi Ballet appearing at the Kremlin Palace of Congresses. Set to music by Sergey Slonimsky,[605] it featured Vladimirov in the title role and Nina Sorokina as the Girl but was not a success. Running to three acts, it was packed rather too much with technical virtuosity and was considered dramatically incoherent. Vasiliev was not helped by company director Grigorovich, who pointedly left the inexperienced dance-maker to his own devices. It was, nevertheless, an indication of the dancer's desire for his own artistic voice, a feeling which intensified as the decade progressed as he became increasingly disillusioned with Grigorovich's artistic sterility and deadening influence on the Bolshoi.

Alexey Chichinadze and the Stanislavsky

In 1971, Stanislavsky Ballet director Vladimir Burmeister died and was replaced by ex-company soloist turned choreographer Alexey Chichinadze.

---

603   Born in Leningrad in 1943, Bolshakova graduated into the Kirov in 1963 and rose to the rank of ballerina, performing roles across the repertoire with distinction and displaying both a lyrical quality and dramatic intelligence; over her career, she showed herself to have real affinity with contemporary work. She established a firm partnership with Vadim Gulyayev with whom she performed frequently. In 1987 she graduated from the ballet master department of the Leningrad Conservatoire, taught at the Vaganova Academy until 1990 and then at the Kirov from 1992 to 1994 when she and Gulyayev, left to teach and then open a dance school in Osaka, Japan.

604   As quoted by Roslavleva, '*Creation of the World* in Leningrad', *Dancing Times*, December 1971

605   Born in Leningrad in 1932, Slonimsky studied music firstly in Moscow and then composition at the Leningrad Conservatoire from where he graduated in 1955. He composed more than 100 works, including 34 symphonies, five operas and several song cycles in a variety of musical styles. He died in St Petersburg in 2020.

Chichinadze, who was born in 1917 in Tbilisi, Georgia, had been studying at a technical university when his father, a hydro-engineer and professor was arrested at part of Stalin's Terror against the intelligentsia. Losing his university place as a consequence, he initially worked to earn some money as an extra in performances by Viktorina Kriger's Moscow Art Ballet. Taken by the idea of dancing, he enrolled in evening classes at the Bolshoi Ballet School and graduated in 1941 and then the choreographic department of GITIS in 1953. Engaged briefly as a dancer with the Bolshoi from 1942 to 1944, he then joined the Stanislavsky where he remained for forty years, rising to the rank of principal – he was the first Siegfried in Burmeister's 1953 *Swan Lake*. After retirement from the stage in 1966, he headed the dance company at the Teatr Weikl in Warsaw until 1970 before returning to the Stanislavsky to lead the ensemble until 1984, working extensively with company prima ballerina Margarita Drozdova.[606] His choreographic style was heavily influenced by Burmeister's dramatic emphasis. He subsequently worked a great deal in his native Georgia, mainly at the Kutaisi Opera and Ballet Theatre. He died in Moscow in 1994.

1972-1974 – the Panovs

An awkward episode for the Soviet regime concerned the Jewish Kirov soloist Valery Panov and his dancer wife Galina (née Ragozina) who in 1972 applied for an exit visa to live in Israel. Their application was refused and the authorities proceeded to exact revenge on the couple. A campaign against him began within the Kirov Ballet, mostly of an anti-Semitic nature and virulent in the assertion that he sought to undermine them all. A company dancer asserted: "Panov wants to betray the greatest art in the world for the West's dirty degradation...if he wants to trade the best ballet in the world to rummage in moneymaking garbage, he is an animal, and we must treat him as such."[607] Panov was expelled from the Kirov Ballet, arrested and temporarily imprisoned. Their cause was taken up in the West, with several high-profile artists including the actor Laurence Olivier appealing on their behalf until, in June 1974, they were finally granted permission to leave. Their two-year fight seriously damaged the image the Soviet regime wished to portray internationally.

---

606 Born in Moscow in 1948, Drozdova graduated from the Bolshoi School into the Stanislavsky company in 1967. She rose to be their prima ballerina, encompassing a very wide range of styles from the classical to the experimental; she was considered a highly-polished virtuoso dancer. She retired from dancing in 1987 and has, since that time, coached and taught with the company.

607 Caute, *The Dancer Defects: The Struggle for Cultural Supremacy during the Cold War*, p.499.

1972 – *Anna Karenina*

Plisetskaya's initial favourable impression of Yuri Grigorovich rapidly soured after his assumption of the directorship of the Bolshoi and especially after his jettisoning of the classic Gorsky-Messerer production of *Swan Lake* in 1969 in favour of his own. The ballerina, now trusted by the authorities to travel abroad and, more importantly, to return, began to set her sights more on her international profile which was both glamorous and uncompromising and in her complete control. However, the Bolshoi remained her home company to whose standing she had contributed not inconsiderably, and she was not about to leave. Since 1967 she had nurtured the idea of a ballet version of Leo Tolstoy's 1877 novel *Anna Karenina* and she initially approached the Bolshoi choreographic duo Kasatkina and Vasilyov to create a libretto which, when completed, she subsequently judged too short. She then turned to experienced theatre director Boris Lvov-Anokhin who sketched out a full-evening, three-act structure. Plisetskaya fully understood the developments which were happening in ballet at the time and sought something of a middle ground between the old *drambalet* style with its detailed exposition of narrative, the increasing taste for technical virtuosity and even the avant-garde which mixed classical technique and "gymnastics, acrobatics and figure skating".[608] With a composite and re-orchestrated score by her husband Rodion Shchedrin of Tchaikovsky works composed at around the time of the novel's creation and help in creating the choreography from fellow dancers Natalia Ryzhenko and Viktor Smirnov-Golovanov,[609] Plisetskaya finally brought what was a loose, sprawling narrative to the Bolshoi stage in June 1972. *Anna Karenina* provided a splendid vehicle for the ballerina's unmatched histrionic talents, making the audience feel "as stunned as Anna was by forebodings of her downfall and death".[610] The première also featured Nikolai Fadeyechev as Karenin, Māris Liepa as Vronsky and Yuri Vladimirov as the Bearded Mujik. The second cast was led by Marina Kondratieva and a young company member, Alexander Godunov[611] as Vronsky who later

---

608   Plisetskaya quoted by Morrison in *Bolshoi Confidential*, p.384.

609   Son of ballet librettist Viktor Smirnov, Smirnov-Golvanov was born in Moscow in 1934 and graduated into the Bolshoi Ballet in 1953 where he danced as a soloist for some twenty years. A graduate of GITIS, he became a prolific choreographer at the Bolshoi and on television. Between 1970 and 1989 he was chief ballet master with the Odessa State Opera and Ballet Theatre before devoting himself to Moscow City Ballet. He died in Moscow in 2013.

610   Smakov, *The Great Russian Dancers*, p.142

611   Born on the north Pacific island of Sakhalin in 1949, Godunov initially started dancing in Riga, Latvia, a classmate of Mikhail Baryshnikov, before progressing to the Bolshoi School from where he graduated in 1967. After three years with Igor Moiseyev's Young Dancers Company, he joined the Bolshoi Ballet as a soloist, debuting as the poet in *Chopiniana*. Tall and handsome, he assumed many of the *danseur noble* roles and became

became a notable principal dancer with the company.

The ballet received a mixed reception but the reality of the stagnation of the Bolshoi and its repertoire was beginning to hit home; after an initial creative period, Grigorovich, once safely ensconced as director, had fallen into dullness and lack of genuine originality. The highly-respected Bolshoi ex-ballerina Viktorina Kriger was encouraged to write a critique in *Pravda* which included the offhand dismissal of the predictable repertoire: "...today is *Swan Lake*, tomorrow is *Giselle*",[612] while an anonymous denunciation accused him of being autocratic and rude, uninterested in new choreography (he had not made an original ballet since his arrival in 1964) and even a promoter of homosexuality within the Bolshoi. Minister of Culture Furtseva took no action.

1972 – Stuttgart Ballet in Russia

Under their director-choreographer John Cranko, the Stuttgart Ballet had scored a huge success in 1969 with their first tour to the United States, and *Gosconcert* subsequently set about negotiating a company tour to the Soviet Union. Given that the company was relatively unknown, it did not appear either at the Kirov or Bolshoi theatres but rather at the Maly and the Stanislavsky with a visit to Riga's Opera House in between. Expectations among the Russian audiences had been low prior to the company's arrival in the summer of 1972 but word quickly spread about the 'Stuttgart Miracle' which ensured full houses by the time the company opened. Great controversy was provoked by Cranko's insistence on bringing his production of *Onegin* based on Pushkin's 1833 verse drama *Eugene Onegin*. He had departed from the original in several ways which were deemed unacceptable by many in the audience – there was audible laughter that Tatiana's name-day was set in the summer and some left during performances. Nevertheless, the tour was deemed a success overall. Plans for Russian dancers to guest in Stuttgart and for further visits to Russia were stopped by Cranko's emphatic support of the Panovs' cause. The company next visited the Soviet Union in 1985.

Baryshnikov and defection

Anxious not to lose an artist rapidly becoming a star dancer, the Kirov accorded Mikhail Baryshnikov a gala at the end of 1973, allowing him to select his own music and programme. He chose to work with two young Soviet choreographers from the republics: Estonian Mai Murdmaa and Georgian Georgy Aleksidze. The evening was not deemed much of a success, although it was a clear demonstration of the young dancer's developing artistic

---

Plisetskaya's regular stage partner. He defected during the company's 1979 New York season and joined American Ballet Theatre and also developed a film career. He died in West Hollywood, California in 1995.

612 Morrison, *Bolshoi Confidential*, p.384.

tastes and style. Both choreographers opted for existing scores, Aleksidze choosing Mozart's *Les Petits Riens* for *Mozartiana*, a lively, abstract work in which Baryshnikov demonstrated zestful charm opposite Kolpakova, while Murdmaa chose two former Ballets Russes scores, the first *Daphnis and Chloe*, composed by Maurice Ravel for Fokine, the second Stravinsky's *The Prodigal Son* for Balanchine. *Daphnis* was deemed an empty essay in movement which somewhat perversely kept the usually airborne dancer firmly on the ground while *The Prodigal Son* was an uncertain reaction to the score, eschewing clear narrative and failing to invest the title role with either weight or meaning. During rehearsals for the second ballet, Baryshnikov quarrelled with principal dancer Valentina Gannibalova[613] who was scheduled to dance The Siren, and appealed to Alla Osipenko, who by that time had left the Kirov, to return to dance with him. She was finally persuaded and then permitted to return to the theatre, where she brought her experience of Yakobson's experimental choreography to bear. An independently-minded artist, she had previously spoken with Baryshnikov during the filming of a television ballet *The Tale of Serf Nikish*, warning him that he was likely to suffer the same artistic stagnation as Yuri Soloviev whose career had become an endless repetition of the same roles. Baryshnikov was indeed feeling stifled by the repressive Kirov structure and the Soviet state which, in part, came from continuing suspicion of the Leningrad ballet company by the Moscow-based regime. Additionally, the atmosphere at the Kirov had soured considerably, with a clear divide between dancers who were Communist party members and those who were not. Even though he was the company's brightest hope, Baryshnikov, who never became a party member, suffered multiple slights from his fellow dancers; at one *Prodigal Son* rehearsal, he was kicked as he lay on the floor of the studio. When asked by an incredulous Osipenko how that was even possible, he replied "You're just not used to it."[614]

Whilst Bolshoi stars like Plisetskaya and Vasiliev travelled frequently to the West and dutifully returned, the Kirov seemed to have an unfortunate habit of losing its star dancers when they allowed them to travel. Nevertheless, the twenty-six-year-old Baryshnikov was permitted, with Irina Kolpakova, to join a small-scale, foreign currency-earning tour to Canada in early summer of 1974 led by the Bolshoi's Raisa Struchkova and husband Alexander Lapauri. The cross-country tour included engagements first in Ottawa and Montreal, followed by a week in Toronto before finishing in Vancouver. It

---

613 Born in Tashkent, Uzbekistan in 1948, Gannibalova graduated into the Kirov alongside her classmate Baryshnikov in 1967, where she danced until 1989. A strong and expressive dancer, she was particularly successful as Kitri in *Don Quixote* and Zarema in *The Fountain of Bakhchisarai*. She also danced with Boris Eifman's ensemble. Since 1990, she has been the director of the St Petersburg Ballet Theatre.

614 Lobenthal, *Alla Osipenko: Beauty and Resistance in Soviet Ballet*, p.182.

was in Toronto in June 1964 that Baryshnikov took an impromptu decision to defect, hiding in a friend's house and claiming asylum, thereby sealing an unenviable hat trick of losses for his home company. Initially, the Soviet regime let it be known that Baryshnikov was on a state-approved prolonged tour of the West and that he was scheduled to return at a later date but, in time-honoured fashion, his name was then rapidly erased from records and publications. In 1981 the dancer observed in an interview that if he had not defected:

> "I think I would be broken mentally by now, but I am sure I would have adapted, like so many people there do. Life goes on and you go with it, you try to express yourself as best you can. You know, for years with the Kirov I was a very happy man. I loved the company, I had a very romantic view of it. But after a while, when I had traveled (sic) outside the country, I was able to look at it with more dispassion, and I realized I just couldn't be a part of it anymore."[615]

1974 – *Yaroslavna*

Choreographer Oleg Vinogradov assumed the directorship of the Maly Theatre in 1973, and in June of the following year, set out his artistic credo with a new ballet *Yaroslavna*. Its source was the ancient Russian epic *The Tale of Igor's Campaign* (the same Borodin used for his opera *Prince Igor*), a tale of feudal rivalries and foreign invasions. The ballet focussed on the theme of love for the motherland, a sentiment which could be said to have forged Russia as an entity, and also, tellingly, the suffering of those left behind as war is waged. Enlisting the skills of respected Moscow Taganka Theatre director Yuri Lyubimov,[616] Vinogradov used a variety of movement styles which he grafted onto classical technique – turned-in legs and soft shoes for the Russian characters brought to mind Mikhail Fokine's approach many decades before. Austerely designed by Vinogradov himself and intensely sober in atmosphere, *Yaroslavna* successfully evoked the tragedy of the events it depicted and communicated the pain and desperation of the characters. On the first night in June, Tatiana Fesenko[617] danced the title role and Nikita

615 As quoted by Ward in '20 Years after Nureyev's Leap for Freedom.' *New York Times*, June 1981

616 Born in Yaroslavl in 1917, Lyubimov studied at Moscow's Institute for Energy before joining the Second Art Theatre in 1934. After service in the Red Army, he joined the Vakhtangov Theatre in 1953 and started teaching in 1963. Influenced by the theories of Bertolt Brecht, he formed the Taganka Theatre in 1964. In 1977, he was the first to stage Mikhail Bulgakov's novel *The Master and Margarita*. In 1980, all of his productions were banned and in 1984, he was stripped of Soviet citizenship. He worked abroad before returning to the Taganka in 1989. He died in Moscow in 2014.

617 Born in Rostov-on-Don in 1948, Fesenko studied first at the Minsk Ballet School before moving to the Vaganova School from where she graduated into the Maly company

Dolgushin was Igor. The powerful score was by Boris Tishchenko.

1974 – *Chipolino*

In August 1974 a new children's ballet *Chipolino* premièred at the Kiev Opera House with choreography by Genrikh Mayorov[618] and music by Karen Khachaturian.[619] The story of the little onion Cipollino who fights against unjust treatment of his fellow vegetable townsfolk by the fruit royalty Prince Lemon and Lord Tomato in the garden kingdom came from the 1951 *Il romanzo di Cipollino* by Italian writer Gianni Rodari. It became well-known throughout the USSR as a story of the struggle of the underclass against the powerful, good versus evil, and the importance of friendship in the face of difficulties. Mayorov's ballet became a huge success and was mounted at the Bolshoi in 1977 with Mikhail Tsivin as Chipolino, Nina Sorokina as Radisochka, Marina Kondratieva as Magnolia and Sergey Radchenko[620] as Prince Lemon. Several more theatres around the Soviet Union took it into their repertoires, including at the Mikhailovsky (former Maly) Theatre in St Petersburg, where it was staged in 2007. Mayorov was very much of the new generation of choreographers who both wished and were permitted to mix classical dancing with other styles, in his case a quasi-vaudeville or music hall approach to create an enjoyable fusion.

1975 – *Ivan the Terrible*

In 1975, Grigorovich finally broke through his creative block with *Ivan the Terrible,* choreographed to a composite score of Prokofiev – Mikhail Chulaki drew on the music composed for Sergey Eisenstein's 1944 film to which he added elements of *Russian Overture,* the cantata *Alexander Nevsky*

---

in 1967. She danced there until 1990 as its prima ballerina, creating major roles in several productions including the title role in Nikita Dolgushin's *Giselle*. In 1994 she emigrated to Argentina where she founded Academy of Russian Classical Ballet.

618 Born in 1936 in the city of Ulan-Ude, Mayorov graduated from the Kiev Choreographic School in 1957 firstly into the Lvov company and then, from 1960 onwards, the Kiev ensemble where he danced until 1967. After studying choreography in Leningrad, he returned as a house choreographer, rising to become chief choreographer in 1977. He assumed the directorship of the Stanislavsky ensemble in 1983, became deputy head of the Department of Choreography at the Moscow State Academy of Choreography in 1988 and then was Artistic Director of the Moscow Art Theatre between 2004 and 2010.

619 Born in Moscow in 1920, Khachaturian studied composition at the Moscow Conservatoire and became a successful composer in various musical forms, from chamber music to symphonies. He was the nephew of Aram Khachaturian. He died in Moscow in 2011.

620 Born in Zhdanov (now Mariupol), Ukraine in 1944, Radchenko graduated into the Bolshoi in 1964 where he danced until 1989, becoming known as a character dancer of distinction. In 1982, he graduated from GITIS. He continues to lead the Moscow Festival Ballet which he founded in 1989.

and the Third Symphony. Yuri Vladimirov memorably created the title role alongside Natalia Bessmertnova as his consort Anastasia and Boris Akimov as Prince Kurbsky. It provoked mixed reactions, not least from those who saw the treatment of the sixteenth century tsar as an apology for the abuse of tyrannical power; Grigorovich's attitude was seen by some an acceptance of the oppressive Soviet regime which relied on censorship and the suppression of free thought and creativity. In dance terms, the choreographer had not moved on from his earlier works, and even some of his own dancers were not impressed; Vladimir Vasiliev, whose dislike of Grigorovich was intensifying, called *Ivan the Terrible* "campy and kitschy".[621]

The ballet fared poorly during the Bolshoi's New York season that year when it was shown in a season which included Grigorovich's second production of *The Sleeping Beauty*. *Ivan the Terrible* was said to be "cast in the same deadly mould as *Spartacus*" and in *The Sleeping Beauty* "the style eludes most of the dancers, from the principals down through the soloists to the corps de ballet".[622]

1975 – the emigration of Kaleria Fedicheva

1975 saw the departure from the Soviet Union of Kaleria Fedicheva, one of the Kirov Ballet's stalwarts. She had danced with the company for almost twenty years before marrying Martin Freedman, an American dance teacher, and emigrating to the United States. She had until then dominated the performing schedules because, it was said, of her intimacy with Pyotr Rachinsky,[623] Director of the Kirov Theatre, and she often secured first nights ahead of other company ballerinas. In 1970 Alla Osipenko left the Kirov and ultimately joined Yakobson's Choreographic Miniatures ensemble partly because of Fedicheva's seemingly unassailable position; she was referred to as the 'second Kschessinskaya', in an allusion to the company's pre-revolution *prima ballerina assoluta* who, as mistress to several Imperial Grand Dukes, wielded enormous power. Such was her influence, Fedicheva was able in 1964 to secure an unheard breach of protocol: the transfer of a dancer from the Maly to the Kirov. That dancer was Valery Panov with whom she danced successfully in many ballets until his fall from grace which, some said, was in part also her doing. When Rachinsky was found guilty of fraud and imprisoned, Fedicheva married Freedman and left the Soviet Union to live on Long Island, New York.

---

621   Vasiliev quoted in: *The Great Russian Dancers* p.330

622   Vaughan, 'Yuri the Terrible, George the Great', *Dancing Times*, October 1975

623   Born in St Petersburg in 1912, Rachinsky became involved in arts administration from 1937 onwards. He held numerous posts in Leningrad cultural institutions including being the Director of the Leningrad Television Studio. He was made Director of the Kirov Theatre in 1962, a post he held until 1973. He died in St Petersburg in 1994.

1976 – *The Infanta*

In what was to be his last notable appearance in a new work, in 1976 Yuri Soloviev created the Page in Leonid Lebedev's[624] *The Infanta* at the Maly Theatre alongside Irina Kolpakova, both dancers appearing as guest artists from the Kirov. To music by one of the company dancers, Lebedev constructed a twelve-minute piece concerning the unrequited love of a page for a Spanish princess and his ensuing suicide. Both dancers excelled in this highly challenging work, so much so that Lebedev refused to allow it to be danced by anyone else after the initial performances. It was never revived.

1976 – *Angara*

Grigorovich created another original work in April 1976, *Angara*, a two-act melodrama made for the Bolshoi's bicentenary celebrations. Based on Alexey Arbuzov's[625] 1960 play *The Irkutsk Story* and with a score by Andrey Eshpai,[626] it depicted young Siberian construction workers and the travails of a Soviet woman whose husband drowns in the eponymous river. The opening night featured Bessmertnova, Vasiliev and Mikhail Lavrovsky in the main roles of Valya, Sergey and Viktor. Vasiliev, notwithstanding the fact he was a member of the Bolshoi Art Committee, was outspoken in his criticism of the ballet, bringing his hostility towards the company director out into the open. At the time, he, his wife Ekaterina Maximova and Maya Plisetskaya served as de facto leaders of the Bolshoi's increasingly vocal anti-Grigorovich faction.

Maya Plisetskaya

Whilst on tour to Paris with the Bolshoi in 1977, Plisetskaya openly expressed her dissatisfaction with the status quo; "Are there choreographers in Russia who reach beyond the outdated rules? I don't know of any."[627] She was in a

---

624 Born in Kizel near Perm in 1943, Lebedev trained at the Perm Choreographic School and then the Kyrgyz Musical and Choreographic School in Frunze (Bishkek) from where he graduated in 1960. From 1960 to 1971 he danced at the Frunzenski Theatre. After graduating from the Leningrad Conservatoire in 1976, he was invited to the Maly Theatre, where he worked as a choreographer until 1991. He also worked extensively on television and in film. He died in Moscow in 2010.

625 Born in Moscow in 1908, Arbusov and his family moved to Petrograd in 1914. At the age of fourteen he was orphaned and found work at the Mariinsky Theatre. In 1928 he joined the Guild of Experimental Drama and then an agitprop group for which he started to write plays. Thereafter, he established himself as a successful playwright, creating dramas of transformation and redemption in the Soviet context. Several of his works were made into films. He died in Moscow in 1986.

626 Born in 1925 in Kozmodemyansk, Mari El Republic, Eshpai graduated from the Moscow Conservatoire in piano and composition and went on to create numerous instrumental concertos and songs in addition to nine symphonies. He died in Moscow in 2015.

627 Plisetskaya quoted by Morrison, *Bolshoi Confidential*, p.395.

better position to judge than most, given that that she was frequently allowed to travel abroad. In 1973, she had created Roland Petit's *La Rose Malade* pas de deux with the Ballet National de Marseille alongside company dancer Rudy Bryans. Inspired by William Blake's 1789 poem *The Sick Rose*, it was set to the *adagietto* of Gustav Mahler's Fifth Symphony and had costumes by Yves Saint Laurent; in 1977 Plisetskaya performed it at the Bolshoi with Alexander Godunov. In 1974 she had seen French choreographer Maurice Béjart's[628] choreography performed at the Dubrovnik Festival, and decided that she had to dance his work. They met in Brussels in 1975, an encounter which led to a long collaboration across the Iron Curtain with the ballerina travelling to western Europe to work on *Boléro*, which, along with Fokine's *The Dying Swan*, was to become her choreographic calling card. She created Béjart's *Isadora* in Monte Carlo in 1976 and *Leda* in 1979. In 1978, the Bolshoi presented a programme to mark the ballerina's thirty-five years with the company, and, as was customary, the celebrant chose her own programme. In addition to *Swan Lake* Act II, she indicated that she wished to dance two Béjart works, *Isadora* and *Boléro* but encountered stiff opposition from the theatre's General Director Georgy Ivanov[629] whose objections, as reported by Plisetskaya, indicated the stubborn stasis under Brezhnev's leadership:

"That loose pornographic ballet by the modernist Béjart cannot be shown to the public from the Bolshoi stage. A half-naked woman on a table with ogling men around her. It's a strip-tease! *Boléro* is for the Folies-Bergères or the Moulin Rouge, not the Bolshoi. As long as I am director, I will not allow our temple of art to be violated."[630]

By means of appeals to highly-placed officials, she managed to secure permission to perform *Boléro*. On the third night, Plisetskaya appeared as Isadora to great success and not a little official consternation.

---

628 Born in Marseille in 1927 as Maurice Berger, he studied dance in Paris and London before appearing as a dancer until 1952. His first acknowledged success as a choreographer was in 1959 with *Sacre du Printemps* for the Brussels Opera which led to the establishment of the Ballet du XXe Siècle at the Théâtre de la Monnaie in 1960 which remained in the Belgian capital until 1987 when he moved it to Lausanne. A controversial choreographer, he embraced new music and social trends and created popular expressionistic modern dance. He founded the Mudra Centre in 1970 as a training school. He died in Lausanne in 2007.

629 Born in Moscow in 1919, Ivanov was an actor in the Vakhtangov Theatre Ensemble from 1938 to 1949, after which he became a party official; he was the first deputy head of Moscow City of Culture from 1955 to 1957. He was director of the Theatre Office of the Ministry of Culture from 1970 to 1976 and was General Director of the Bolshoi between 1976 and 1979. From 1979 to 1987 he was Deputy Minister of Culture of the USSR. He died in Moscow in 1994.

630 Plisetskaya, *I, Maya Plisetskaya*, p.340.

Dancers of the third Golden Age

Kirov

Born in Stavropol in 1952, Galina Mezentseva graduated into the Kirov in 1970 and rapidly established herself as one of the ensemble's most distinctive artists. Unusual for the time, she possessed long, slender limbs and is now considered as one of the first dancers with a 'modern' elongated look. She was an intense performer who excelled in dramatic roles but also exuded a serenity which made her an exceptional interpreter of the role of Giselle. She left the Kirov in 1990 and appeared as a guest artist with Scottish Ballet until 1994 after which she toured to several countries as guest principal with the St Petersburg State Academic Leonid Yakobson Ballet Theatre. She now teaches and coaches.

Born in Leningrad in 1952, Tatiana Terekhova graduated into the Kirov in 1970 and quickly established herself as a brilliant representative of the Leningrad school. Displaying an impeccable virtuoso technique, she performed the classical repertoire with great distinction, especially Gamzatti in *La Bayadère*, Odette-Odile in *Swan Lake* and the Sylph in *La Sylphide*. She was notable in the growing Balanchine repertoire, appearing in *Theme and Variations*, *Symphony in C*, *A Midsummer Night's Dream* and *Tarantella*. She became a leading dancer during Oleg Vinogradov's directorship of the Kirov. She danced until 1998 after which she spent four years as a teacher and coach at Boston Ballet before returning to St Petersburg in 2002 to teach at the Vaganova Academy (until 2004) and then at the Mariinsky Ballet.

Olga Chenchikova was born in Moscow in 1956 and graduated from the Perm State Choreographic School in 1974, joining Perm Ballet with which she danced Juliet and also Beatrice in *The Servant of Two Masters* which earned her an invitation to join the Kirov Ballet in 1977. She quickly established herself as a fine principal dancer, noted for a large jump and tight spins, and she appeared in all the major roles of the standard repertoire as well as dancing in newly acquired works by Béjart and Balanchine. She began to teach in 1991 and, after an injury in the mid-1990s, retired from the stage to became a coach with the company.

Born in Alma-Ata, Kazakhstan in 1961, Altynai Asylmuratova graduated from the Vaganova Academy into the Kirov in 1978. She became a principal dancer in 1982 and was famed for her profound musicality and intelligence. A dancer of beautiful classical proportions, she excelled in the nineteenth century roles while also making her mark in twentieth century works by a variety of choreographers. After 1988, she guested with many companies outside Russia, including The Royal Ballet, American Ballet Theatre and Roland Petit's Marseille Ballet. She was appointed Director of the Vaganova Academy in 1999, a post she held until 2013. Since 2015, she has been director of the ballet company of Astana Opera in Kazakhstan.

Born in Petropavlovsk-Kamchatsky, Kamchatka in 1963, Elena Pankova graduated into the Kirov Ballet in 1981, establishing herself as a fine classical dancer, with a wide repertoire encompassing most of the major roles. She was in the first cast of the Kirov's production of Balanchine's *Scotch Symphony*. She was dismissed from the Kirov in 1990 and subsequently danced with the UK's English National Ballet between 1990 and 1992 and then became a principal dancer of the Bavarian State Ballet in Munich where she danced from 1993 to 2000. She was also a guest artist with London City Ballet. She returned to the Mariinsky as a guest artist in 1999 in the title role of *Giselle*. In 2004, she graduated from the choreographic department of the Vaganova Academy and has staged ballet worldwide since then.

Born in Leningrad in 1955, Konstantin Zaklinsky graduated into the Kirov in 1974, becoming a principal dancer in 1980. Tall and elegantly proportioned, he danced all the *danseur noble* roles in the repertoire, being a notable Siegfried in *Swan Lake*, Désiré in *The Sleeping Beauty* and Solor in *La Bayadère*. In London in 1988, Natalia Makarova asked Zaklinsky to partner her in the *Swan Lake* Act II pas de deux for her first appearance with the Kirov since her defection. He created roles in several Vinogradov ballets and guested frequently abroad. He retired from dancing in the late 1990s and now teaches in Kazakhstan.

Born in Tashkent, Uzbekistan in 1963, Farukh Ruzimatov graduated into the Kirov in 1981, performing his first major role, Basilio in *Don Quixote* in 1984 and becoming a principal in 1986. A controversial dancer who offended Kirov traditionalists because of his un-classical arched body line and over-extended limbs, he was nevertheless a dynamic and flamboyant performer who triumphed in such roles as Ali in *Le Corsaire*. He often danced with Altynai Asylmuratova. He was a guest principal with American Ballet Theatre for the 1990-91 season before returning to the Kirov. He was artistic director of the Mikhailovsky (former Maly) Ballet between 2007 and 2009 and since 2018 he has been director of the ballet company of the Navoi Theatre, Tashkent.

Bolshoi

Born in Leningrad in 1952, Ludmilla Semenyaka graduated into the Kirov in 1970 where she danced for two seasons before moving to the Bolshoi as a principal dancer. Coached by Ulanova, she added dramatic intensity and lyricism to her brilliant technique, which allowed her to excel in both nineteenth and twentieth century repertoire. She was a notable Aurora in *The Sleeping Beauty* and Raymonda as well as an intense Phrygia in *Spartacus*. From 1990 onwards, she began to guest with Western companies, joining English National Ballet for one season and appearing with the Paris Opéra

Ballet, the Royal Swedish Ballet and at the Teatro Colón, Buenos Aires. Between 2000 and 2004, she appeared as a stage actress in Moscow. She has been a teacher and coach at the Bolshoi since 2002.

Alla Mikhalchenko was born in Moscow in 1957 and graduated into the Bolshoi in 1976, where she performed until 1999. A tall, slender and highly musical dancer, she danced all the major roles in the classical and twentieth century repertoires, becoming a celebrated Giselle, less fluent in the Romantic style than some, but intense and moving nevertheless. After her retirement from dancing, she taught at the Department of Choreography of GITIS and was Head of the Department of Choreography (classical dance) at the Moscow State University of Culture and Arts from 2003 to 2004. In 2000 she was also instrumental in the establishment of the Bolshoi Ballet School in Joinville, Brazil.

Born in Tbilisi, Georgia in 1963, Nina Ananiashvili was a champion ice-skater as a child before moving to her home city's ballet school and then on to the Bolshoi School in 1977, debuting in 1980 as Swanilda in a school production of *Coppélia*. In 1981, she graduated into the company and rapidly assumed all the major roles in the repertoire. Known both for her dramatic ability and strong, unforced technique, she also showed a real desire for new experiences, guesting with New York City Ballet in 1988 and several other major companies thereafter. In 1993 she became a regular guest principal with American Ballet Theatre, and then in 1999 with Houston Ballet. She created her own ensemble, 'Nina Ananiashvili and the Stars of the Bolshoi', a prelude to becoming director of the National Ballet Ensemble of Georgia in 2004.

Vyacheslav Gordeyev was born in Moscow in 1948 and he graduated into the Bolshoi in 1968 where he danced all the major roles of the repertoire until 1989. He won the Gold Medal at the 1973 Moscow International Ballet Competition and, possessed of an immaculate technique, he was considered one of the company's most gracious principal male dancers, ideally suited to *danseur noble* roles. Since 1989 he has headed the Russian State Ballet Theatre of Moscow, taking time away to become artistic director of the Bolshoi Ballet between 1995 and 1997, and of the ballet company at the Ekaterinburg Opera and Ballet Theatre from 2003 to 2006. He is Head of the Department of Choreography at GITIS.

Son of ex-Bolshoi principal Nikolai, Alexey Fadeyechev was born in Moscow in 1960 and graduated into the Bolshoi in 1978, having already made his debut as Franz in *Coppélia*. Under his father's tutelage, he excelled in all the major roles of the repertoire as a valued principal dancer noted for his classical refinement and vivid stage presence. He appeared with many companies outside Russia, most notably with The Royal Ballet in London during the 1990-1991 season. He was Director of the Bolshoi Ballet from

1998 to 2000, reviving Gorsky's version of *Don Quixote* to great acclaim in 1999. He was artistic director of the Rostov Musical Theatre ballet company from 2004 to 2013. He continues to stage ballets.

Born in Kazan in 1960, Irek Mukhamedov graduated from the Bolshoi Ballet School in 1978 and joined the Moscow Classical Ballet, not having been invited to join the Bolshoi company. In 1981, however, on winning the Grand Prix at the Moscow International Ballet Competition, Grigorovich (who had been president of the jury) offered him a principal's contract. His first role with the company was Spartacus. He rapidly became the director's favoured male dancer and starred in many of his works, not least Ivan, Romeo and Boris (in *The Golden Age*). A powerful, athletic and heroic dancer, he became the star of several tours abroad. It was these tours which gave him sight of the possibilities life in the West would offer; having previously danced in London (where he debuted as Ivan) he decided to leave Russia in 1990 and claim asylum in the United Kingdom. He joined The Royal Ballet where he remained until 1998. In 1992 he formed 'Irek Mukhamedov and Company' and is now a respected coach and teacher.

Son of Bolshoi star dancer Māris, Andris Liepa was born in Moscow in 1962 and graduated into the Bolshoi in 1981. A handsome and lyrical dancer, he was well suited to the *danseur noble* roles of the repertoire; he was made a principal dancer in 1983. After dancing with American Ballet Theatre for the 1989 season, he transferred to the Kirov which had offered him a principal's contract with permission to guest elsewhere; in Leningrad he created works in Vinogradov ballets as well as dancing the full standard repertoire. He guested extensively abroad and moved into ballet production, with a focus on the restoration and reconstruction of Ballets Russes works. In 1997, he founded the Maris Liepa Charitable Foundation.

Moscow Classical Ballet

The company's leading male soloist from 1974 to 1990, Stanislav Isayev was born in 1956 in Gorky (now Nizhny Novgorod). He graduated from the Perm State Choreographic School in 1974, having appeared with the ballet company since 1970. On graduation he joined the Young Ballet, which became Moscow Classical Ballet in 1977 where he remained despite frequent offers to join the Bolshoi. An elegant virtuoso dancer with a pure classical line and an airy jump, he was also a powerful stage presence. In 1980 he was awarded the Gold Medal at the Varna Ballet Competition and received the Prix Nijinski in 1984. He excelled in the repertoire under directors Kasatkina and Vasilyov, being a notable Adam in *Creation of the World*. A favoured partner of Ekaterina Maximova, he partnered her with the company as well as around the world. He moved to Atlanta Ballet in 1990 where he danced for four years before progressing into teaching. Between 2014 and 2016, he taught at the Kirov Ballet Academy in Washington DC and since 2016 he has been teaching at the City Dance School in the capital.

1977 – the Death of Yuri Soloviev

Almost symbolic of the nadir of the Kirov Ballet's decline, Yuri Soloviev, the dancer whom Nureyev admired most, was discovered dead on 15th January at his country dacha, three miles from Leningrad. There was a gunshot wound to his body and the official verdict was that of suicide. Soloviev was thirty-seven years old and beginning to contemplate the end of a dancing career which increasingly seemed to him to have been an empty one. He had been very much a model Soviet artist, doing all that he asked to do, but it has been put forward that he was increasingly disillusioned with the hollowness of his achievements and that he was even considering defection during an upcoming Italian tour. Whatever his own thoughts and the circumstances of his death, the reality was that the Kirov was suddenly "bereft of its last prince".[631]

---

631 Smakov, *The Great Russian Dancers*, p.283

8

A Window on the West[632]

1977-1991

Oleg Vinogradov at the Kirov

Oleg Vinogradov took the helm of the Kirov Ballet in 1977. Born in Leningrad in 1937, he graduated from the Leningrad Choreographic School in 1958, joining the Novosibirsk Ballet with which he appeared in character roles until 1965. He began to make his name early on as a choreographer, initially under the tutelage of Pyotr Gusev. Vinogradov had been one of the young dance-makers who had met and spoken with Balanchine in 1962, a meeting which had led the older man to express 'some hope' for the future of ballet in the USSR. In 1967 Vinogradov was invited to create the Soviet-themed *Asel* for the Bolshoi, which was deemed a success. From 1973, he directed Leningrad's Maly company where for the four years he was in post he staged many original works as well as versions of the classics including *Coppélia* and *La Fille mal gardée*, after which he moved to the Kirov where he remained for almost twenty years.

In 1977, however, he was tasked with reinvigorating a company very much at a low artistic ebb, despite impressively-trained dancers drawn almost exclusively from the Vaganova Academy. On his arrival he dismissed half the ensemble of over two hundred dancers and over the next fourteen years reduced the roster of principals from twenty-one to just ten. Without personal political affiliation, he also sought to break the equation of communist party membership with security of tenure. In the late 1970s, close state control over the choice of ballets for performance slowly began to be relaxed and Vinogradov, increasingly freed from the strictures of repertory committee approval, explored styles and content in a way unthinkable to any director since the first few years immediately after the Russian revolution.

From the outset, he encouraged young choreographers to create work on the company. In 1977 Dmitry Bryantsev[633] put together an evening

---

632 The term ascribed by Tsar Peter I (the Great) to his newly-founded city of St Petersburg.

633 Born in 1947 in Leningrad, Bryantsev graduated from the Vaganova Academy in 1966 and joined Moscow's Young Ballet (later Classical Ballet) where he danced until 1977. He achieved choreographic fame with some televised ballets and worked with several ensembles before directing the Stanislavsky. An early success was with *An Optimistic Tragedy* in 1985 which demonstrated fluid movement and a sense of fantasy. He disappeared mysteriously, presumed murdered, in Prague in 2004.

of short works entitled 'Choreographic Novel' using music ranging from Tchaikovsky to Elton John; in 1987 a small-scale Kirov tour featured works by Boris Eifman, Bryantsev (who by then was Chief Choreographer of the Stanislavsky Ballet), and an excerpt from Béjart's *Our Faust* set to Bach's Mass in B minor.

1977 – Moscow Classical Ballet

In 1977 husband and wife Bolshoi dancers Natalia Kasatkina and Vladimir Vasilyov became joint artistic directors of the Moscow Classical Ballet (formerly the Young Ballet founded six years earlier by Igor Moiseyev and Irina Tikhomirnova) and began to present their own creations. These were characterised by their use of a wide range of music, from their striking version of Stravinsky's *Le Sacre du Printemps*, originally created in 1965 for the Bolshoi, to *Terpsichore's Tricks* set to Johann Strauss and *The Magic Suit* by composer Nikolai Karetnikov. They were open to co-operation with foreign choreographers and specifically took the first Soviet steps in the preservation and recreation of lost or near-lost dances; in 1980, Pierre Lacotte[634] worked with the ensemble to recreate Filippo Taglioni's[635] 1832 Paris ballet *Nathalie, ou la Laitière suisse* featuring guest ballerina Ekaterina Maximova in the title role and Stanislav Isayev as Oswald.

Boris Eifman

Born in in 1946 in Rubtovsk, Altai Krai on the Kazakhstan border, Eifman trained first at the Kishinev Ballet School and then at the choreographic faculty of the Leningrad Conservatoire from where he graduated in 1972. He had joined the Vaganova Academy the previous year as a ballet master and spent the following seven composing dances for the students before receiving state support to establish his own Leningrad Theatre of Modern Ballet (later known as New Ballet (1977-8), Leningrad Ballet Ensemble (1978-80) and from 1990 Leningrad (later St Petersburg) Eifman Ballet). He quickly established himself as one of the most dynamic dance-makers of his generation, drawing on a dizzying range of inspirations, sources and

---

634 Born in Chatou, France in 1932, Lacotte trained at the school of the Paris Opéra before joining the company in 1950 where he danced for ten years before beginning his career as a choreographer. In the early 1970s, he moved towards the 'reconstructions' of lost historic works, starting with Taglioni's original 1832 *La Sylphide* at the Opéra and worked worldwide on such recreations. He was director of several French dance companies throughout the 1980s and 90s.

635 Born in Milan in 1777 to a dancing family, Taglioni moved to Paris in 1799 where he studied under Coulon. In 1802, he became principal dancer and ballet master in Stockholm and subsequently travelled throughout Europe staging ballets. He created prolifically for Paris between 1830 and 1836 (including *La Sylphide* in 1832) before moving to St Petersburg with his daughter Marie between 1837 and 1842. He died in Como, Italy in 1871.

influences. His style was and remains an interweaving of "classical ballet, modern dance, ecstatic impulses and many other things".[636] His Soviet period works ranged from *Bivocality* in 1977, set to the music of Pink Floyd, to *Thérèse Raquin* in 1990 to J S Bach. As Soviet society began to relax under the policy of *perestroika*, he too started to explore more daring themes almost always in a narrative structure. He continues to create and to expand: in 2013, the purpose-built Boris Eifman Dance Academy in St Petersburg admitted its first pupils.

1978 – *Tsar Boris*

Throughout the 1970s, the Maly company continued to explore both movement and psychological drama in a way unthinkable at the Kirov or Bolshoi Theatres. Upon Oleg Vinogradov's move to the Kirov in 1977, the former MALEGOT dancer turned choreographer Nikolai Boyarchikov become the new ballet master in chief, returning from Perm where he had been director. In the spring of 1978, he premièred *Tsar Boris*, his two-act version of the story of the ill-fated sixteenth-century Russian monarch Boris Godunov using music by Sergey Prokofiev composed in 1937 for a theatre production as well as numbers for Sergey Eisenstein's[637] film *Ivan the Terrible*. It was a rethink of a one-act narrative ballet made three years previously in Perm. Closely following Pushkin's episodic treatment, he distilled the action to comprise five dancers and brought out the character of the Holy Fool to act as a dramatic counterpoint to the Tsar. Nikita Dolgushin danced Boris to great acclaim, investing the role with impressive detail, while Gennady Sudakov,[638] who had transferred from Perm to the Maly with Boyarchikov, reprised his now expanded role of the Holy Fool.

1978 – *Notre-Dame de Paris*

At the Kirov, the newly-arrived Vinogradov was decidedly more open to the work of foreign choreographers than any of his predecessors had been or indeed were allowed to be. In 1977 he obtained official permission to invite French choreographer Roland Petit to stage his 1965 *Notre-Dame de Paris* in

---

636 Eifman quoted in www.eifmanballet.ru

637 Born in Riga, Governate of Livonia (now Latvia) in 1898, Eisenstein was a major pioneer in film. He joined the Red Army at the revolution after which he worked as a theatre designer for Vsevolod Meyerhold. His first film *Strike* was made in 1925 which he followed the same year with the full-length *Battleship Potemkin*. He spent many years abroad in Europe, the USA and Moscow, leading to his denunciation by Stalin as a deserter. He returned to the USSR in 1933 and began to work again, producing *Alexander Nevsky* in 1938. He died in Moscow in 1948.

638 Born in Saratov in 1952, Sudakov graduated into the Perm company in 1971 where he danced until his move to Leningrad in 1977 to dance with the Maly company. A dancer of great expressive qualities, he excelled in a number of *demi-caractère* roles, which included many created for him by Nikolai Boyarchikov.

Leningrad. The ballet, set to music by Maurice Jarre[639] and based on the 1831 Victor Hugo novel (the narrative basis of the old Petipa ballet *Esmeralda*), had premièred at the Paris Opéra with Petit himself in the role of Quasimodo. It was Vinogradov's first victory in the choice of repertoire, despite mutterings in some official quarters about formalism, modernism and even pornography, and was the first staging at the Kirov by a Western choreographer. A great success with the Leningrad audience who were excited by the sight of a new artistic vision and approach, it was also a breath of fresh air for the dancers of the company who relished the challenges of a novel movement style and the demands of a choreographer whose experiences came from outside their world. Konstantin Zaklinsky danced Phoebus on first night opposite Galina Mezentseva's Esmeralda.

1979 – Grigorovich's *Romeo and Juliet*

In 1979 controversy hit the Bolshoi with Yuri Grigorovich's new *Romeo and Juliet*. Since its first performance in Moscow in 1946, Lavrovsky's version had been a staple of the repertoire, but, as he had done with *Swan Lake*, Grigorovich felt happy to jettison a company standard in favour of his own re-imagining. This *Romeo* was a far less literal take on the Shakespeare narrative, more filmic in quality, and provoked uproar among the company's traditionalists including Vasiliev, Maximova and Mikhail Lavrovsky who successfully petitioned the Minister of Culture to have the previous version reinstated so that both could run in the repertoire. Described after a New York performance by critic Arlene Croce as "an overlong, unsortably profuse three-act score blanketed in dance steps that no one can deny are dance steps",[640] it was a poor affair, even if identified in some quarters as a logical progression in the choreographer's output away from narrative towards 'formalism'. As such, it showed how far officially-sanctioned Soviet ballet had changed since the promulgation of *drambalet* and the condemnation of abstraction; it was only seventeen years earlier that many of Balanchine's works seen on the NYCB tour to Russia had been dismissed outright. Grigorovich had taken Soviet ballet was away from mime and detailed narrative but not fully towards true abstraction; his choreographic world remained something of an unsatisfying halfway house in which "he thinks emotions are contained in the steps". Croce asked the question: "Does everybody in Russian dance circles have this automatic trust in dancers as characters, steps as feelings? Are they going around in long hair and miniskirts spouting some Soviet version of

---

639   Born in Lyon, France in 1924, Jarre studied at the Paris Conservatoire. He became famous for his film music; his first major success was in 1962 with the score for *Lawrence of Arabia* and throughout the 1960s, 70s and 80s, he composed the music for numerous successful films. He died in Malibu, California in 2009.

640   Croce, *Going to the Dance*, p.217

'The medium is the message'?"[641] At the June première Bessmertnova danced Juliet (Nadezhda Pavlova in later performances), Romeo was Gordeyev (later Alexander Bogatyrev[642]) and Mercutio was Mikhail Tsivin.

1979 – Vasiliev and Plisetskaya in Paris

Dismissive of Balanchine as "a cold genius, revelling in the beauty of ice",[643] Vasiliev was drawn more to the work and styles of dance-makers Alvin Ailey, Paul Taylor and Maurice Béjart, which he had experienced as a result of his freedom to travel abroad and work in the West as a deputy of the USSR Supreme Council. In 1979, joining forces with Plisetskaya, he presented another face of the Bolshoi to a startled Parisian audience, brought up to expect *Swan Lake*, the 'classics' and Grigorovich: three Béjart works (*Isadora*, *Leda* and a pas de deux from his *Romeo and Juliet*) and three by Vasiliev himself – a second version of *Icarus* (his first was created in 1968), *Les Promenades* and a plotless ballet to Mozart's Symphony No.40.

1979 – Bolshoi defections

General dissatisfaction with life in Soviet Russia, the limitations placed on performing artists and the particular circumstances surrounding Grigorovich's regime at the Bolshoi came to something of a head in 1979. The Moscow company had not suffered the defections of dancers to the West as had the Kirov, but the 1979 USA tour saw three requests of asylum to the American authorities. In New York in August, principal dancer Alexander Godunov defected, leaving his wife, company soloist Ludmilla Vlasova,[644] to return to Russia (they had just danced their final performance of *Romeo and Juliet* at the Metropolitan Opera House). The company continued on to Los Angeles where a further two dancers, husband and wife Leonid Kozlov[645]

---

641   ibid.

642   Born in Tallinn in 1949, Bogatyrev trained locally before going to Moscow for the two last years, graduating into the Bolshoi in 1969 and rapidly rose to the rank of principal, dancing a wide repertoire. Tall and strong as partner, he was an elegant if undramatic dancer. He taught at GITIS' Department of Choreography from 1986. He retired from the Bolshoi in 1989 and died in Moscow in 1998.

643   Smakov, *The Great Russian Dancers*, p.330

644   Born in Moscow in 1942, Vlasova graduated into the Bolshoi in 1961 and rose to the rank of soloist, often partnered by her second husband Alexander Godunov. After his defection she returned to Moscow where she danced until her retirement from the stage in 1982, after which she became a successful ice dance choreographer.

645   Born in Moscow in 1947, Kozlov graduated into the Bolshoi in 1965 and rose to the rank of principal dancer, performing a wide range of roles in the repertoire. Initially, he pursued a freelance career in the West before joining New York City Ballet in 1983 where he remained as a principal dancer for eleven years. He has staged numerous ballets for companies around the world and in 1991 founded Kozlov Dance International.

and Valentina Kozlova[646] also requested asylum after the company's final performance of *Romeo and Juliet* at the Shrine Auditorium. In an interview shortly after they cited their reasons:

> "We also want to see the world more. We want to try modern dance, to express ourselves artistically in different ways. We want to explore new directions."[647]

They were also unhappy with internal Bolshoi politics which pitted the older, anti-Grigorovich guard against younger dancers who toed the line. Ironically, the latter were the very dancers who were permitted to travel on the 1979 tour. They also cited Grigorovich's attempts to split them up as a dancing couple:

> "We were firm in our refusal. That was one of our dissatisfactions: Grigorovich does not really respect dancers, not even dancers who save performances for him. He is a difficult man."[648]

After these defections, the Bolshoi company was not permitted to tour to the United States again until 1986.

1980 – Messerer defections

During the company's tour to Japan, the defection of one of the Bolshoi's star ballerinas of the 1930s and 40s and subsequently a prized teacher, Sulamith Messerer, along with her son, company soloist Mikhail,[649] was another blow to the Soviet ballet world. Sulamith, in Tokyo as a regular guest-teacher, was taken ill and needed hospital treatment. On asking the Soviet authorities for a few days recuperation and having been refused any delay to her return to Russia, she called her son at his hotel; he rapidly packed some personal effects and, slipping past his KGB minder, caught a late train from Nagoya to

---

646   Born in Moscow in 1957, Kozlova joined the Bolshoi School in 1966 and the company in 1973, becoming a soloist in 1975. She pursued a freelance career after defecting to the USA and in 1983 joined New York City Ballet as a principal, where she remained until 1995. In 2003 she founded Valentina Kozlova's Dance Conservatoire of New York (which moved to Connecticut in 2018) and her own eponymously-named international ballet competition in 2011.

647   Bernheimer, 'Defection: A Pursuit of Art', *Washington Post*, September 1979

648   ibid.

649   Born in Moscow in 1948, Messerer graduated into the Bolshoi Ballet in 1968 where he danced until his departure from Russia in 1980. He was also a guest dancer with the Kirov Ballet, Perm Opera and Ballet Theatre, and the National Theatre Ballet in Prague. He has become one of the world's most distinguished ballet teachers and has taught at all the major companies. In 2009 he became ballet master in chief of the Mikhailovsky Ballet where he stayed for ten years, creating a performing repertoire characterised by revivals of some of the most important Soviet ballets and productions. Since 2019 he has been the theatre's principal guest ballet master.

Tokyo to join her:

> "She got very annoyed," remembered Mikhail, "It reminded her yet again of USSR attitudes, a system that had put her sister in a cattle-truck and tried to put Maya (Plisetskaya, her niece and Mikhail's cousin) into an orphanage."[650]

The decision not to return in Russia was not an easy one for someone of Sulamith's profile and standing, but "...we talked the rest of the night, and when dawn came, and we had no more time for pros and cons, we said, it's time for action. At six in the morning, we went to the American Embassy,"[651] Mikhail recalled. Mother and son, fearful of the use of some form of poison on them (the Bulgarian dissident Georgy Markov had been murdered in London with a poisoned umbrella-tip the year before) insisted on a long table between themselves and the KGB agents who were sent to interview them, and the Japanese authorities, nervous at the reaction of the Soviet Union, insisted that they pay for their own flights to the United States.

1980 – *The Seagull*

Plisetskaya, as firm in her opposition to Grigorovich as ever, succeeded in getting permission to stage a new work herself at the Bolshoi, a dance adaptation of Anton Chekhov's 1896 drama *The Seagull*. Her struggle to bring her project to fruition was long indeed, as Mikhail Chulaki, the Bolshoi's General Director and Georgy Ivanov, his successor between 1976 and 1978, supported Grigorovich's *de facto* ban on her from the theatre. Lobbying by her husband Rodion Shchedrin, by then Chairman of the Union of Soviet Composers, and her own appeals to the minister of Culture Pyotr Demichev,[652] finally succeeded in overcoming the theatre's interdict and *The Seagull* was premièred in May 1980. Plisetskaya worked in effective secrecy from the Bolshoi management and contended with the fear among the dancers that involvement in her project would put an end to their careers. In its intimacy and use of modest stage forces – there were thirteen cast members – *The Seagull* was a conscious attempt to present an alternative vision to what Plisetskaya considered Grigorovich's empty bombast. The audience reaction was mixed, with some perplexed by the restricted, chamber quality of the action. The two-act work had a score by Shchedrin; Plisetskaya danced the dual part of the seagull and Nina Zarechnaya, while Treplyov was

---

650   As quoted by Brown, 'The Messerer Dynasty', www.theartsdesk.com.

651   ibid.

652   Born in Pesochnya, now Kirov, in 1919, Demichev became a civil servant and party administrator. He was First Secretary of the Moscow City Party Committee between 1960 and 1962 and was made Minister of Culture in succession to Ekaterina Furtseva in 1974, a post he held until 1986 after which he was First Deputy Chairman of the Presidium of the Supreme Soviet for two years. He died in Zhavoronky, near Moscow in 2010.

performed by Alexander Bogatyrev and Trigorin by Mikhail Gabovich. The ballet remained in the repertoire for several seasons.

1980 – *Revizor*

At the Kirov, director Vinogradov demonstrated that he was not averse either to using narrative from Russian literature as the basis for new works; in this he showed that an important feature of Soviet ballet which had begun in the 1930s still continued fifty years later. His choice fell on Nikolai Gogol's satirical 1836 play *Revizor* (or *The Government Inspector*, as it is known in the West), the tale of small-town corruption and petty rivalries, whose great challenge lay in the translation into dance of the author's biting wit. The quirky score was by Alexander Tchaikovsky[653] in his first ballet commission and the choreographer consciously adopted a magpie approach in his choice of movements, juxtaposing the classical and the grotesque. The cast was led by Vadim Gulyayev as Khlestakov, the foppish civil servant mistaken for the eponymous incognito official, Ninel Kurgapkina as the mayor's wife Anna Andreyevna and Natalia Bolshakova as her daughter Maria Antonovna.

1981 – Bolshoi criticisms: Gayevsky's *Divertissement*

In 1981, the ballet critic and writer Vadim Gayevsky[654] published *Divertissement – The Fate of Classical Ballet*, making the wider Russian public aware of the deep unhappiness within the Bolshoi company and laying the responsibility for the discontent squarely at the feet of the director, Yuri Grigorovich. At the end of his analysis of the 150-year development of Russian ballet, Gayevsky observed that the Bolshoi was now 'the home of false traditionalism'[655] and while the company dancers were longing for new ideas and directions in the choreography they had to perform, their director was moving in exactly the opposite direction. He concluded that the choreography for Grigorovich's *Ivan the Terrible* was bland and often undanceable. The book was subsequently banned by the authorities and its author forbidden to publish for a period of five years; official suppression of this work represented one of the last gasps of the 'old' Soviet approach to the arts.

---

653   Born in Moscow in 1946, Tchaikovsky graduated from the Moscow Conservatoire in 1972 and became a prolific composer in a variety of genres, producing some nine operas and several symphonies, concerti and vocal works. His first ballet score was for *Revizor*. He was Artistic Advisor at the Mariinsky Theatre between 1993 and 2002, Rector of the St Petersburg Conservatoire between 2004 and 2008 and has been Artistic Director of the Moscow Philharmonic Orchestra since 2003.

654   Born in Moscow in 1928, Gayevsky graduated from GITIS in 1951 and has occupied numerous university posts including being Head of the Department of Theatre Studies of the Russian State University since 1993. He has published since 1954, principally research and articles on choreographers of the 19th and 20th centuries.

655   As quoted by Willis, 'Bolshoi Ballet: Why there's discontent', *Christian Science Monitor*, February 1982

Divertissement's censorship notwithstanding, it seems that the regime's attitude towards Grigorovich was cooling rapidly. In 1982, dance writer Margaret Willis recorded:

'In a private interview last June one of the top authorities on Soviet ballet talked frankly about the shape of the Bolshoi and the problems just then emerging into the open. "The Grigorovich era has passed," she said. "He did wonders with his first ballet (*The Stone Flower*) and broke away from the solid, stale choreography of that time (1957). But we are now ready to develop a newer style and must once again look to the future."[656]

1981 – *La Sylphide*

In Leningrad, Kirov director Vinogradov maintained his policy of expanding the company's repertoire, not only in terms of newly-created dance works, but also in exploring ballet's heritage, an important part of which was the output of Danish choreographer August Bournonville[657] who had created an entire repertoire at Copenhagen's Royal Theatre in the mid nineteenth century. In the 1950s and then through the fame of Danish dancer Erik Bruhn, the West had become aware of this very specific style of dancing which preserved much of the early nineteenth century French school. Leningrad had its own link to Bournonville through the Swedish-born dance teacher Christian Johansson who worked at the Imperial Theatre School in St Petersburg from 1869 to 1903 and had brought many elements of his own studies under Bournonville himself to what he passed on to his pupils. In 1975, during his directorship of the Maly company, Vinogradov had invited the Swedish former ballerina Elsa-Marianne von Rosen[658] to set Bournonville's greatest work, *La Sylphide*, which opened in late November to great acclaim, featuring Tatiana Fesenko as the Sylph and Nikita Dolgushin as James. In 1980, Vinogradov invited von Rosen to the Kirov; in January 1981 the first night of *La Sylphide* featured Kolpakova and Sergey Berezhnoi[659] while Mezentseva and Evgeny

---

656   ibid.

657   Born in Copenhagen, Denmark in 1805, son of the French dancer Antoine, Bournonville studied firstly in Copenhagen and then in Paris under Vestris. He joined the Paris Opéra in 1826 and returned to Denmark in 1829 as a principal dancer and chief choreographer. With two brief spells abroad, he worked at the Royal Theatre until 1877, forging a repertoire and dance style which would make Copenhagen one of the world's great ballet centres. He died in the city in 1879.

658   Born in Stockholm in 1924, von Rosen trained at Valborg Franchi and at the Royal Theatre, Copenhagen. She debuted in 1941 with her own dance night in Stockholm's concert hall and then toured in Africa and to Spain. In 1950, she created the title role in Birgit Cullberg's *Miss Julie* and was a principal dancer at the Royal Theatre, Stockholm from 1951 to 1959, and afterwards led the Scandinavian Ballet which she had co-founded. Between 1970 and 1976 she was ballet director at Stora Teatern, Gothenburg and of Malmö Ballet from 1980 to 1987. She died in Copenhagen in 2014.

659   Born in Odessa in 1949, Berezhnoi graduated from the Kiev School in 1967 and

Neff[660] appeared in later performances. It was followed by a staging of the choreographer's *Napoli* which, unlike *La Sylphide*, did not remain long in the repertoire.

1982 – *The Golden Age*

The death in 1975 of Dmitry Shostakovich, the Soviet Union's most distinguished composer, prompted Bolshoi director Yuri Grigorovich to use his first ballet score, *The Golden Age*, which had unsuccessfully come to the GATOB stage in 1930. In November 1982 he premièred his new version at the Bolshoi, setting the action in a post-revolutionary Black Sea resort and its decadent night-club named 'The Golden Age'. A young fisherman Boris falls in love with the cabaret dancer Rita, girlfriend of the gangster Jashka. Fifty years on from its composition, Shostakovich's jazz-influenced score accompanied by Grigorovich's movement proved a huge hit. Irek Mukhamedov was the first Boris, alongside Natalia Bessmertnova's Rita and Gediminas Taranda[661] as Jashka. The choreographic language was stylised, almost caricatural, provoking one American critic to observe on seeing the ballet during the 1987 Bolshoi tour: "the corps struts, gesticulates, preens, twirls and contorts with an irresistible combination of Rockette precision and pristine Muscovite fervour."[662] Grigorovich's *The Golden Age* was the choreographer's last original work.

Six days after the ballet's Moscow première, General Secretary Leonid Brezhnev died; his tenure had been far from a golden age for the Soviet Union, but rather a period of stagnation which saw the apparatus of state grind to a near halt.

1983 – *The Legend of the Donenbai Bird*

The Maly company premièred a controversial new work in the spring of 1983: *The Legend of the Donenbai Bird*, Leonid Lebedev's parable of the suppression of the individual. Based on a literary work *And the Day lasts*

---

then the Vaganova Academy in 1970 from where he entered the Kirov company where he danced until 1990. He was Irina Kolpakova's regular stage partner across the repertoire. From 1990 until his death in St Petersburg in 2011 he taught at the Kirov Ballet.

660   Born in 1954 in the village of Mendol, Krasnoyarsk, Neff graduated from the Tallinn Choreographic School into the Estonian Ballet. In 1979 he moved to Perm and in 1980 joined the Kirov Ballet. A fine classical dancer, he was able to portray heroic characters through his strong stage presence. He danced all the leading roles of the repertoire.

661   Born in Kaliningrad in 1961, Taranda joined first the Voronzh Ballet School in 1974 and then the Bolshoi School in 1976, graduating into the company where he became a demi-caractère soloist, creating roles in several Grigorovich ballets, including the part of Abderakhman in *Raymonda*. He left the Bolshoi in 1993 and set up the Imperial Russian Ballet company the year after. He is now an entrepreneur and actor.

662   Bernheimer, 'Shostakovich Ballet; Bolshoi opens with 'The Golden Age', *Los Angeles Times*, August 1987

longer than a Century by the Kyrgyz author Chinghiz Aitmatov, it used a cast of five to depict a mother, her son, the Master and his two faceless assistants and told of the son's capture and transformation into a 'mankurt', a man whose identity has been erased. It was widely interpreted as an allusion to the wiping of the past to create the Soviet ideal and the ballet came to be seen as one of the decade's most important artistic creations in Leningrad. Lebedev's movement palate was resolutely unballetic which complemented Yuri Simakin's[663] experimental score. Vladimir Adzhamov[664] was the first 'son-mankurt'.

1984 – Grigorovich's *Raymonda*

The Golden Age may have been Grigorovich's last new ballet, but in 1984 he continued the remoulding of the classical repertoire in his own image with a production of *Raymonda*. Some identified a creeping conservatism in the choreographer in what was to prove an unfussy production of the Petipa classic, free from the re-imaginings of his 1969 *Swan Lake*. There was, however, a downplay of the character-dancing which is so central to the ballet, even if much of the old master's dances emerged unscathed in Grigorovich's new version. Raymonda was danced on the first night by Bessmertnova (later by Semenyaka), Jean de Brienne by Bogatyrev (then Mukhamedov) and Abderakhman was danced by Taranda (later Alexander Vetrov).[665]

1985 – *The Lady and the Lap Dog*

In 1985, Plisetskaya returned to Anton Chekhov, using his 1899 short story for her last ballet, *The Lady and the Lap Dog*, which faced opposition from Grigorovich but was allowed to be staged at the Bolshoi as part of the celebrations of the prima ballerina's sixtieth birthday. It premièred in Moscow in November with Plisetskaya as Anna Sergeyevna von Diderits

---

663 Born in Krasnodar in 1947, Simakin graduated in composition from the Leningrad Conservatoire in 1974. He became a noted composer in a variety of styles; ballet, drama, oratorios and song cycles. He was also a prolific composer for film. He died in 2015.

664 Born in Tbilisi in 1955 into an ethnic Yezidi family, Adzhamov trained firstly in his home city before moving to the Vaganova Academy from where he graduated into the Maly company in 1974. He was a dancer with the company for thirty years, rising to the rank of principal and noted for his versatility across both classical and contemporary repertoire. Since 2000 he has been the President and Artistic Director of the creative association 'Flying in Time'.

665 Born in Moscow in 1961, Vetrov graduated into the Bolshoi in 1979 where he danced as a soloist until 1997. In 1985 he took part in the Moscow International Ballet Competition and won First Prize. In 1997 he moved to the United States, where he danced with the International Ballet, Indianapolis. From 1999 onwards, he has been with Ballet Arlington (now Metropolitan Classical Ballet) of which he has, since 2002, been the artistic director. In 2011 he became a teacher and coach at the Bolshoi.

1968 - *Spartacus*, Act III, Bolshoi. Boris Akimov as Crassus. Courtesy of *Dancing Times*

1967 - Oleg Vinogradov in rehearsal for *Asel* with Nina Timofeyeva, Bolshoi. Courtesy of *Dancing Times*.

Galina Ulanova coaching *Swan Lake* with Maris Liepa, Bolshoi.

1969 - Mikhail Baryshnikov in *Vestris* at the first Moscow International Ballet Competition. Courtesy of *Dancing Times*

1969 - Jury members of I International Ballet Dancers Contest, Moscow RIA Novosti archive, image #842769 Alexander Makarov CC-BY-SA 3.0

1970 - *Hamlet*, Act II, Kirov. Mikhail Baryshnikov. Courtesy of *Dancing Times*

1970 - *Hamlet*, Kirov. Elena Evteyeva as Ophelia. Courtesy of *Dancing Times*

1970 - *Hamlet*, Act I, Kirov. Mikhail Baryshnikov in the title role. Courtesy of *Dancing Times*

1972 - Yuri Grigorovich, Pyotr Gusev, Galina Ulanova and Fyodor Lopukhov. Courtesy of *Dancing Times*

The Stone Flower, Kirov. John Markovsky and Alla Osipenko in rehearsal. Late 1960s. Courtesy of *Dancing Times*

1974 - *The Prodigal Son*, Kirov. Mikhail Baryshnikov in the title role.

1972 - *Anna Karenina*, Bolshoi. Maya Plisetskaya in the title role.

1974 - *Yaroslavna*, MALEGOT. Tatiana Fesenko in the title role. Courtesy of *Dancing Times*

1977 - Third Moscow International Ballet Competition "During contest days." RIA Novosti archive, image #843299 Alexander Makarov

1975 - Yuri Grigorovich during a rehearsal. Courtesy of *Dancing Times*

Natalia Kasatkina and Vladimir Vasilyov in rehearsal.

1975 - *Ivan the Terrible*, Bolshoi. Curtain call. Courtesy of *Dancing Times*

1976 - *Angara*, Bolshoi. Natalia Bessmertnova as Valya and Vladimir Vasiliev as Sergey.

Vladimir Vasiliev and Alexey Ermolayev in rehearsal, Bolshoi.

Yuri Grigorovich in rehearsal with Vladimir Vasiliev.

Stanislav Isayev in the studio.

1979 - Irina Kolpakova in the studio, Kirov. Courtesy of *Dancing Times*

1980 - *Nathalie ou la Laitière suisse*, Moscow Classical Ballet. Ekaterina Maximova as Nathalie and Stanislav Isayev as Oswald.

1978 - *Notre-Dame de Paris*, Kirov.

1979 - *Icarus*. Ekaterina Maximova and Vladimir Vasiliev. Courtesy of *Dancing Times*

1980 - *The Seagull*, Bolshoi. Maya Plisetskaya as Nina Zarechnaya and Alexander Bogatyrev as Treplyov. Courtesy of *Dancing Times*

1982 - *The Golden Age*, Bolshoi. Irek Mukhamedov as Boris and Natalia Bessmertnova as Rita. Courtesy of *Dancing Times*

above: 1984 - Stanislav Isayev - Moscow Classical Ballet. Courtesy of *Dancing Times*
below: 1982 - *The Golden Age*, Bolshoi. Yuri Vetrov, Tatiana Gorlikova and Vassily Vorokhobko. Courtesy of *Dancing Times*

above: *Ivan the Terrible*, Bolshoi. Irek Mukhamedov in the title role. Courtesy of *Dancing Times*
below: 1989 - *Petrushka*, Kirov. Andris Liepa in the title role.

Don Quixote, Kirov. Farukh Ruzimatov as Basilio and Elena Pankova as Kitri.

and Boris Efimov[666] as Dmitry Gurov, an unhappily married Moscow banker with whom she embarks upon an adulterous affair. The one-act ballet to Shchedrin's score opened on the day of Plisetskaya's sixtieth birthday and, after the interval, was followed by *Carmen Suite*. It was generally well received despite some disapproving observations about the unseemly discrepancy in age between the sixty-year-old Plisetskaya and the thirty-three-year-old Efimov.

1985 – *The Knight in the Tiger's Skin*

At the Kirov, amidst the invitations he was issuing to other dance makers to work with the company, Vinogradov did not ignore his own choreographic voice which increasingly expressed itself in a mix of styles combining classical dance with acrobatics, gymnastics, pantomime and grotesque movements, in a way echoing the experiments in Soviet choreography of the early 1920s. In 1985, in an effort to reinvigorate the repertoire, he created a new three-act ballet *The Knight in the Tiger's Skin*. Based on the medieval Georgian epic verse *The Knight in the Snow Leopard's Skin* by national poet Shota Rustaveli, it told of the friendship of two heroes, Avtandil and Tariel, and their quest to find the object of their love, Princess Nestan-Darejan. The jagged score was by Georgian composer Alexey Machavariani, who had composed it in 1974 for a Bolshoi production that had never materialised, and the libretto was by Yuri Grigorovich. Galina Mezentseva created the role of the Princess Nestan-Darejan, Olga Likhovskaya[667] was Queen Tinatin and Eldar Aliyev[668] and Evgeny Neff danced Tariel and Avtandil. The ballet received a favourable reception as a metaphorical work in which form and content were equally served by a choreographer who had clearly absorbed the influences of Western dance-makers, yet had also created a work which was both true to its literary inspiration and still identifiably Russian.

1986 – *Battleship 'Potemkin'*

Starting with his early *Yaroslavna* in 1974 for the Maly Theatre, Vinogradov

---

666 Born in Moscow in 1951, Efimov graduated into the Bolshoi company in 1970 where he danced until 1990, making a name as a character dancer. He worked extensively with Plisetskaya but managed to maintain his career under Grigorovich. He retired from the stage in 1990.

667 Born in Orenburg in 1958, Likhovskaya graduated from the Vaganova Academy into the Kirov in 1976 and performed a wide variety of major roles including Odette-Odile in *Swan Lake*, Giselle and the Girl in *Leningrad Symphony*.

668 Born in Baku, Aliyev graduated from the Baku Ballet School. He was principal dancer of the Kirov (the Mariinsky) between 1979 and 1992 where he danced leading roles in many ballets. In 1992 he became leading soloist with Ballet International based in Indianapolis, USA and subsequently its director, a post he held until 2005. Since then, he has taught and choreographed with many companies worldwide. In 2016 he was appointed chief ballet master of the Mariinsky's Primorsky Stage in Vladivostok.

often explored the theme of the Russian 'soul'. In 1986, he premièred *Battleship 'Potemkin'* at the Kirov with a score by Alexander Tchaikovsky. The ballet depicted the collective will of thirty-two sailors confined below decks on the ship famous for its 1905 mutiny, considered by Soviet historians as a precursor of the 1917 revolution. In *Potemkin*, the sailors finally rise up in revolt against their officers and the ruling class, tearing off their uniforms and streaming into the audience. It was an attempt by Vinogradov to say in a new way something about oppression by a regime of its own people and was deemed to have borrowed heavily from other works in so doing – Death, who stalks the bowels of the ship, was considered to be closely modelled on the figure in Kurt Jooss's[669] 1932 anti-war dance work *The Green Table*. It was, however, a powerful use of the male corps de ballet and it was deemed to have revealed "glimmerings of sensitivity and intelligence that are the antithesis of the I-know-better-than-Petipa attitude of Yuri Grigorovich".[670]

Gorbachev and *perestroika*

In 1985, Mikhail Gorbachev's accession as General Secretary of the Communist Party, the Soviet Union's most important political office, signalled a major societal shift. He instituted domestic reforms in the spirit of *glasnost* (openness) which allowed for greater freedom of speech and for the press; *perestroika* (restructuring) sought to decentralise the economic running of the country. The effects for the ballet companies of the Soviet Union were multiple: with greater freedom to travel and the increasingly desperate need for foreign currency, the Kirov and the Bolshoi embarked on ever more tours abroad without the need to sift the dancers who could and could not be trusted to return. Additionally, artists began to be permitted and trusted to accept guest contracts to dance abroad, which led to appearances by several notable Russian dancers with the major Western companies.

1986 – the Bolshoi in London and New York

The Bolshoi's currency-earning tours to London and New York in 1986 were its first since the 1979 US defections. However, the repertoire shown had not progressed and seemed increasingly preserved in Soviet aspic: *Swan Lake*, *Giselle*, *Romeo and Juliet*, plus programmes of excerpts which invariably included scenes from Grigorovich's *Spartacus* and *The Golden Age*.

---

669 Born in Wasseralfingen, Germany in 1901, Jooss studied dance in Stuttgart with Rudolf von Laban and in 1924 founded the experimental company Neue Tanzbühne. In 1930 he was appointed ballet master of the Essen Municipal Theatre and his company became the Folkwang Tanzbühne, Jooss creating several works in a synthesis of classical and modern dance. Jooss returned to Essen in 1949 and founded a dance school which outlived his company. His final company was the Tanzstudio which he founded in 1962; he retired as director in 1968. He died in Heilbronn in 1979.

670 Tobias, 'Worlds Apart', *The New York Magazine*, August 1989

Reactions were mixed, from "the greatest assemblage of dance talent anywhere on the face of the earth, dance's new elite",[671] to the view that it was a company "with an identity crisis, an agenda to defend at home, and a mystique to promote abroad".[672] It was generally deemed to be an ensemble which had changed in character, its members no longer the acrobatic supermen and women of before but more recognisably neo-classical dancers. The vexed question of tradition preserved or discarded was raised, with Grigorovich stating "For us, culture is, above all, memory." Certainly, both cities witnessed the triumph of Ludmilla Semenyaka as Raymonda, Phrygia in *Spartacus* and, in New York, as Giselle in Grigorovich's new production which itself was poorly received because of a lightweight dramatic focus.

Semenyaka was one of a new generation who were the products of Soviet training and the coaching of the dancers who had first come to the West thirty years previously. Nina Ananiashvili, Alla Mikhalchenko, Nina Semizorova,[673] Alexey Fadeyechev, Andris Liepa, Irek Mukhamedov and Yuri Possokhov[674] all made considerable impressions on British and American audiences. The company returned in 1989 and again in 1990.

The Kirov had never made the same mark as the Bolshoi in terms of foreign touring, the latter very much considered the 'official' Soviet ballet company, so their 1986 visit to the USA was the first in some twenty-two years. The company performed *Swan Lake, The Knight in the Tiger's Skin* and mixed bills which included *Chopiniana*, "The Kingdom of the Shades" from *La Bayadère*, the Grand Pas from *Paquita* and *Battleship 'Potemkin'*. It was a mark of how much the regime had relaxed under Mikhail Gorbachev that the defector ballerina Natalia Makarova danced again with her home company in the United States and the UK before appearing at the Kirov Theatre itself in 1989. The company returned in 1987 and 1989; before the 1987 visit, Vinogradov gave an interview to the *Chicago Tribune* which outlined his vision for the company:

---

671   Barnes in *The Post* quoted by Siemens, *Dancing Times*, October 1987

672   Croce in *The New Yorker* quoted by Siemens, *Dancing Times*, October 1987

673   Born in 1956 in Krivoy Rog, Dnepropetrovsk region, Ukraine, Semizorova graduated in 1975 into the Kiev Ballet from its school before joining the Bolshoi three years later where she remained until 2000. A stylish and accomplished technician, she rose to the rank of principal and danced the major roles of the repertoire, also creating ballets most notably by Andrei Petrov. She won First Prize and the Gold Medal at the 1977 Moscow International Ballet Competition. She graduated from GITIS in 1989 where she is now a professor. In 2000 she became a repetiteur at Moscow's Kremlin Ballet.

674   Born in Lugansk, Ukraine in 1964, Possokhov graduated into the Bolshoi Ballet in 1982, where he rose to the rank of principal. He joined the Royal Danish Ballet in 1992 and then San Francisco Ballet two years later. He began choreographing in 1990 and has created numerous ballets; when he retired from dancing in 2006, he became choreographer in residence at SFB. In July 2015, he created a full-length ballet *A Hero of Our Time* for the Bolshoi.

"Our theater (sic) is a sort of Hermitage, we store the traditions of ballet. But that doesn't mean we are a museum alone and do not reflect the progress of modern ballet. We are the best performers in the classical tradition in the world. But the company is capable of performing the most modern of works by any choreographer working with any trends. This, too, will be in our program."[675]

He also hinted that he was in negotiation with American choreographers Jerome Robbins and Robert Joffrey to work in Leningrad (neither of whom did, in fact), and commented on his brief for the management of the company: "I was invited to the Kirov to drag the theater out of the doldrums, out of a crisis of direction, a crisis of will." His mandate had been to reinvigorate and reshape the Kirov ensemble, sixty percent of whom were of retirement age, "because ballet is youth and beauty".[676]

The speed of change

For both companies, the income raised by touring abroad was vital – central funding shrank as economic reforms took hold in Russia, while individual dancers in all ranks welcomed the per diem allowances and the supplementary payments to their salaries they received on tour. The result back in Russia, however, was mounting dissatisfaction, as audiences found themselves deprived either of entire companies or their stars who were fulfilling lucrative guest contracts. In 1988 Bolshoi principals Nina Ananiashvili and Andris Liepa became the first Soviet dancers for several decades to receive permission to guest with an American company. They spent three weeks with New York City Ballet with which they appeared in Balanchine's *Symphony in C*, *Apollo* and *Raymonda Variations*, before returning to Moscow, artistically enriched by the experience of learning a new ballet style. Liepa went on to spend a full season with American Ballet Theatre.

The speed of change surprised everyone; with new-found freedom, ballet artists felt able to make decisions for themselves. In 1989 Kirov ballerina Altynai Asylmuratova observed to *The Washington Post*:

"So much has changed for the better, though. We can at last say what we think and maintain our self-respect. We can actually say what is on our minds without worrying about reactions, about repercussions. At last, too, we can demonstrate our value to the theatre, and what it means to us, through our work alone. It doesn't depend any longer on my being a party member or not. It's just based on my talent and my performances."[677]

The imperative to earn money abroad cannot be underestimated as a

---

675 Shanker, 'Kirov Regenerated', *Chicago Tribune*, May 1987
676 ibid.
677 Kriegsman, Dancing Diplomacy', *The Washington Post*, March 1989

factor in the artistic decisions of both companies and individual dancers. For the former, the earning potential of a new production on tour came to carry great weight, but for the latter, it literally changed the way they moved: "Dancers begin to turn into sportsmen. They strive to achieve more pirouettes, try to lift their legs that bit more or jump higher to be competitive, to get more financial dividends for the number of technical elements, but not for the spiritual satisfaction of the image they create," observed choreographer and ex-dancer Nikita Dolgushin in an interview in 1995, "but it is not just the highest jump or the biggest number of pirouettes that makes art great" he continued, "Galina Ulanova's jumps were low, she did not lift her legs high, and executed only a few pirouettes – but she is legendary, she is great."[678]

Soviet ballet repertoire in 1987

In an article in *Soviet Ballet*, the periodical then edited by ex-Bolshoi ballerina Raisa Struchkova, the repertoire of the fifty-odd ballet companies in the USSR was analysed. Little had changed since John Percival's analysis in 1962. There were some two hundred ballets performed with over one hundred and fifty given only in one or two locations – local works for local audiences. The general repertoire comprised, therefore, under fifty ballets. Of the 'classical' repertoire, *Swan Lake* was by far the most popular, with 450 performances to a quarter of a million people in just one year, followed by *Giselle*, *Don Quixote*, *The Nutcracker*, *Chopiniana*, *Vain Precautions*, *La Sylphide*, *Coppélia*, *The Sleeping Beauty*, *Esmeralda* and *La Bayadère*. Soviet ballets were also still widely performed: *Spartacus*, *The Fountain of Bakhchisarai*, *Romeo and Juliet*, *Cinderella*, *The Stone Flower* and *The Legend of Love*, while children's ballets such as *Chipolino*, *Snow White and the Seven Dwarfs*, *The Ugly Duckling* and *Veeni-Pukh (Winnie the Pooh)* received many performances, often in specially designated children's venues, such as Moscow's Natalia Sats Musical Theatre.[679] *Soviet Ballet* also examined the health of contemporary ballet and discussed the targets needed to maintain it: a need for greater local freedom, for decent pay for dancers, for the removal of 'dead wood' in ballet companies and for theatre outside Moscow and Leningrad to get recognition.

---

678   Borisova, 'The Ugly Side of Ballet', St Petersburg Press.
679   The Moscow Children's Theatre was opened in a former cinema in 1921. The concept was born out of touring ensembles which had started after the revolution and was taken up by Natalia Sats, the 15-year-old daughter of Moscow Art Theatre composer Ilya Sats. From 1921 until her arrest in 1937 she was director and artistic director of the Moscow Theater for Children; she commissioned *Peter and the Wolf* from Prokofiev in 1936 and, after the arrest of her husband, she spent five years in a gulag and was only permitted to return to Moscow in 1958. She taught at GITIS from 1981 and died in Moscow in 1993. The children's theatre was named after her in 1965. Ballet, opera and plays continue to be performed in a 1100 seat theatre built in 1979.

1987 – Béjart in Leningrad

Vinogradov was convinced that the Kirov should not exist in a Soviet bubble and needed exposure to outside influences. He fought to secure an invitation to Maurice Béjart and his Brussels-based ensemble Le Ballet du XXe Siècle, although Culture Minister Demichev insisted that he travel to the Belgian capital to vet works for any traces of sexuality. Vinogradov's wife went in his stead and Vinogradov delivered the requisite assurances to get permission, fully aware that Béjart's works were well-known for their eroticism. The visit went ahead, with the company appearing at the Kirov Theatre to great acclaim as part of Leningrad's summer White Nights Festival; they performed *Bakhti*, a ballet set to national Indian music, Opus No. 5, and the adagio from the ballet *Our Faust*. During the company's time in Leningrad, Vinogradov and Béjart came up with the idea of putting together a filmed co-production between their respective companies. The project took place over ten days of filming on stages erected in the city's Summer Gardens and at several palaces located nearby, with dancers of the Kirov and Le Ballet du XXe Siècle learning new choreography from each other's repertoires, as well as performing their own. The result was the film *White Night of Dance* in Leningrad which caused a sensation and was a major achievement of the policy of cultural glasnost. The programme comprised fifteen numbers, nine of which were by Béjart, two by Vinogradov, one by Vladimir Vasiliev, who had previously worked with the Frenchman and created a tribute to Fred Astaire, and the rest a selection from the Kirov's standard repertoire. The recording ended with a mixed cast performing Béjart's *Le Soldat Amoureux*.

1987 – *Quiet Don*

Nikolai Boyarchikov was another long-serving ballet director; he assumed the lead of the Maly Ballet in 1977, a post he held until 2007. He was a prolific choreographer, producing numerous works for the company. In 1987, he premièred the two-act ballet *Quiet Don*, based on Mikhail Sholokhov's[680] epic four-volume novel, known in English as *And Quiet Flows the Don*, written between 1925 and 1940. A romance set against the backdrop of civil and world wars, the story was chosen by Boyarchikov to mark the seventieth anniversary of the 1917 revolution. The score was the product of over twenty years work by its composer Leonid Klinichev[681] who had undertaken expeditions to the Don region to collect folk tunes and

---

680 Born in 1905 in Vyoshenskaya, Donetsky district, Sholokhov began writing at the age of seventeen. His first publication was a collection of autobiographical stories from the Don region. He spent fifteen years writing *And Quiet Flows the Don* which earned him the Nobel Prize for Literature in 1965. He died in his native village in 1984.

681 Born in Old Crimea in 1938, Klinichev studied composition at the Tashkent and Moscow Conservatoires before settling in Rostov-on-Don. His compositions range from operas and symphonies to chamber and choral works.

music, and incorporated authentic wedding song melodies and dances.

1987 – Bolshoi criticisms

In late 1987 a letter with sixty company signatures stating that 'ballet is in full crisis' was sent to Grigorovich who refused to respond. This led to an article in the weekly magazine *Ogonyok* (Spark) in which several major names in Russian ballet vented their unhappiness with his directorship. Observations were made about the stagnation in choreography and the company's archaic style and even that the size of the Bolshoi ensemble at 270 made it too big to be effectively managed. Perhaps the most surprising element was a critique by the then legendary teacher Asaf Messerer who commented that out of forty ballets nominally in the repertoire, only eighteen were performed and there was not a single work by such giants of the 20th century as Goleizovsky, Balanchine, Petit and Béjart.

1988 – Kirov criticisms

Oleg Vinogradov and the Kirov were not immune from criticism either. Discontent never reached the levels seen at the Bolshoi, however a letter signed by the distinguished former Kirov soloist Olga Zabotkina[682] in the weekly magazine *Literaturnaya Gazeta* lifted the lid on tensions and unhappiness in the Leningrad company. The refocussing of the company during the 1960s and 70s to satisfy the demands of Western impresarios is something she bitterly regretted, taking the company back, in her opinion, to its pre-revolutionary Mariinsky days when ballerina Matilda Kschessinskaya had complete control. She also lamented that the success of foreign tours was measured by the absence of defections, thereby encouraging the casting of lesser artists who would be guaranteed to return. Her attack was then directed towards Vinogradov whom she accused of creating an acquiescent 'collective' around him, dancers and collaborators desperate to be chosen to tour and to maintain their jobs. "General meetings" wrote Zabotkina, "became monologues, voting – unanimous, letters to high levels never answered. Complaining was only for those who had resigned or been removed."[683] Her criticisms then extended to the repertoire where she bemoaned the disappearance of some ballets, the revamping of classical works and the dearth of decent Soviet choreography; there was at the Kirov a "stagnation characteristic of Russia's choreographic culture of recent years". She continued that "it has become clear in the last fifteen years not

---

682 Born in Leningrad in 1936, Zabotkina graduated into the Kirov in 1953 where she danced until 1977 as a celebrated character artist. She was also a film actress, making her debut in 1956 as the female lead in director Vladimir Vengerov's *Two Captains*. Several films followed – her last major role was in a film version of the operetta of Shostakovich's musical comedy *Moscow-Cheryomushki*. She died in Moscow in 2001.

683 Devereux, *Dancing Times*, March 1988

one single ballet has been created on the stage of this famous theatre that is genuinely worthy of it, that the atmosphere of romanticism and poetry for which the Leningrad ballet was always famous has decayed away".[684]

In addition to providing an insight into what some Soviet dancers thought of the ballets they were called upon to perform, Zabotkina's letter is significant for the fact that it was published at all, an indication of the relaxation of censorship which was taking place under Gorbachev.

Bolshoi spasms

The nucleus of anti-Grigorovich sentiment, Plisetskaya, Maximova, and Vasiliev, left the Bolshoi Ballet during the 1987-8 season, ostensibly because they were past the notional retirement age for dancers at the ages of sixty-two, forty-nine and forty-eight respectively, but in truth because of their opposition. It was a considerable blow to the company which was magnified by the director's decision not to ask them to teach or coach the younger artists, thereby breaking the blood-line of performance and depriving them of the experience and knowledge of three of the Soviet Union's greatest dancers. They were stars enough to be able to pursue plans and projects elsewhere, but the calculated insult and their ensuing absence rebounded on the company itself. Plisetskaya continued in her vocal opposition to Grigorovich, observing in a 1992 interview:

> "At the moment, it's impossible to work at the Bolshoi Theatre because *Sovetskaia vlast* –Soviet power – is still in existence there. And there are no dancers, because there's no repertoire. Just one dictator, like Stalin."[685]

The polarisation of opinions at the Bolshoi continued apace, with what was often a generational divide between anti-Grigorovich older dancers and the younger artists who saw him as their ticket to professional advancement. Tensions ran so high that in March 1988 at a performance of *The Stone Flower*, several Bolshoi dancers refused to appear on stage until they had received assurances from none other than the General Secretary Gorbachev that the director would not be removed from his post. Irek Mukhamedov was deputised to speak on their behalf and received sufficient assurances from the Minister of Culture for the performance to begin.

1988 – *Cyrano de Bergerac*

The demands from several quarters for greater variety in the repertoire continued and led to an invitation to French choreographer Roland Petit to stage *Cyrano de Bergerac* at the Bolshoi, the Kirov under Vinogradov having successfully mounted his *Notre-Dame de Paris* some ten years previously. In

---

684   ibid.
685   Jennings, 'Nights at the Ballet', *The New Yorker*, March 1995

1959, Petit had himself created the title role at the première in the French capital by the Ballets de Paris and in casting the role in Moscow, he asked for Irek Mukhamedov, by then the company's star male dancer. The Russian dancer's eagerness to perform the part was seen by Grigorovich as something of a personal betrayal and signalled the beginnings of a cooling of relations between the two men.

1988 – Moscow City Ballet

In the spirit of burgeoning entrepreneurship in Russian society, choreographer and ex-Bolshoi soloist Viktor Smirnov-Golovanov founded a new privately-owned ballet company, originally called New Ballet of Moscow and renamed Moscow City Ballet in 1990, with the avowed aim to promote the original ideas of the great nineteenth and twentieth century Russian choreographers. Initially a small ensemble, it grew to about seventy dancers and used a concert hall in the Olympic Village situated on the outskirts of Moscow as its base. Moscow City Ballet began touring abroad from its inception, taking productions of the classics and original works by its director to numerous countries worldwide, including South Korea, Israel, Cyprus and Egypt. By 1991 the company was able to attract three notable guest ballerinas on its tour: Elena Pankova and Galina Mezentseva from the Kirov and the Bolshoi's Ludmilla Semenyaka.

1988 – the 'other' Bolshoi tour

Matters at the Bolshoi had deteriorated to such an extent in the second half of the decade that in March 1988 Plisetskaya led a splinter group of sixty-five dancers on a US tour starting in Boston, Massachusetts with an appearance at the 'Making Music Together' Soviet-American arts festival. The ballerina performed in her own work, *The Lady and the Lap Dog* and *Anna Karenina*, Petit's *La Rose Malade* pas de deux and Fokine's *The Dying Swan* while the other Bolshoi dancers, who included Andris Liepa and Nina Ananiashvili, danced *divertissements* from their standard repertoire including *Chopiniana* (*Les Sylphides*). The tour included *Sketches*, a new work by dancer Andrey Petrov[686] to music by Alfred Schnittke[687] which featured vignettes of several

---

686 Born in Moscow in 1947, Petrov graduated into the Bolshoi in 1965, where he danced for twenty years, mostly in character roles. In 1977 he graduated from GITIS and began his choreographic career, creating dances for opera productions at the Bolshoi before receiving commissions from elsewhere. In 1990 he founded the Kremlin Ballet based at the State Kremlin Palace auditorium which served as the Bolshoi's second stage. From the outset, the company mixed nineteenth-century works with new creations by Petrov, Vasiliev and others. Petrov remains the ensemble's Artistic Director.

687 Born in Engels, Saratov in 1934, Schnittke first studied music in Vienna before his family moved to Moscow in 1948. Heavily influenced by Shostakovich at first, he then developed an experimental 'polystylistic' approach which he developed in nine symphonies, several concerti and film scores. Often at odds with the Soviet regime, he

characters from Nikolai Gogol's novels and stories. The ballet, alongside those by Plisetskaya, served to show another side to the company, one which was unafraid of narrative and detail and stood as the antithesis of Grigorovich's approach.

Former Bolshoi stars Vladimir Vasiliev and Ekaterina Maximova accepted an invitation from the Kirov to appear with the company during a season in Paris in the spring of 1988 – they danced two performances of *Giselle* in what can only be seen as a gesture of defiance towards Yuri Grigorovich.

1989 – further Bolshoi troubles and Vasiliev's Jubilee

In January of 1989, members of the Bolshoi Ballet Collective met to discuss requesting a change of artistic leadership from the theatre's General Director Vladimir Kokonin. It was a heated meeting between those for and against Yuri Grigorovich's directorship; in the midst of fraught discussions, Vladimir Vasiliev requested a jubilee performance at the Bolshoi to mark his fiftieth birthday. Even Grigorovich could not block such an event, however, the animosity between the two was so intense that no Bolshoi dancers were made available to participate in a tribute to one of the company's greatest artists. Pointedly, Vasiliev turned his back on his Bolshoi repertoire and scheduled an evening of his own choreography in which he appeared alongside dancers from the Moscow Classical Ballet, a company with which he had by then begun to work. He danced in *Anyuta*, *Nostalgia* and *Fragments of One Biography*.

1989 – Moscow Festival Ballet

Hot on the heels of the founding of the Moscow City Ballet, the Russian capital saw another new company the following year: Moscow Festival Ballet. Under the directorship of ex-Bolshoi dancer Sergey Radchenko, it was formed as a reaction to the stagnation at the larger company, and based itself more on the Kirov approach of presenting the old Russian and Soviet repertoire which included works by Goleizovsky and Yakobson. A sister company, the Russian National Ballet Theatre was also established under Radchenko's wife, Elena, allowing both to tour to venues which would not otherwise be able to accommodate larger forces. Together they formed, and still form, the Russian National Ballet S. Radchenko. The company toured extensively abroad from the outset – in 1991 they performed a twenty-two-day UK tour, appearing in a different venue every day.

1989 – The Kirov dance Balanchine

In February 1989, the curtain of the Kirov Theatre rose on the first officially sanctioned Soviet Russian performance of choreography by George Balanchine. It was a significant moment; Balanchine, a graduate of the
emigrated to Germany in 1990 and died in Hamburg in 1998.

Petrograd Choreographic School and sometime dancer of GATOB, had left Russia in 1924 and had only returned in 1962 to lead the visit by New York City Ballet. Russian audiences were finally able to see Russian dancers in choreography by one of their most famous prodigal sons. Since his departure Balanchine had created notable works for Diaghilev's Ballets Russes before settling in the United States and establishing a new dance 'school', the American school, which was made real by the establishment of The School of American Ballet in 1934 and New York City Ballet, originally founded in 1946 as The Ballet Society. His works had never been performed by a Russian company principally because their abstraction had long been deemed the antithesis of narrative Soviet ballet. Balanchine died in 1983 since when a few unofficial pirated versions of his ballets had been staged in Russia: during the mid-1980s the Maly Theatre staged *Serenade*, *Symphony in C*, *Theme and Variations* and *The Four Temperaments* from video footage, while the Georgian State Ballet mounted *Serenade* in 1984, again from a video-recorded performance.

Kirov company director Oleg Vinogradov had long admired Balanchine and his work and indicated as early as 1982 that he wished for his ballets to be danced in Leningrad. In the autumn of 1988, he came to an agreement with The Balanchine Trust, the organisation which administers and curates the choreographic legacy, for two appointed stagers (Suzanne Farrell from NYCB and Francia Russell from Pacific Northwest Ballet) to set *Scotch Symphony* and *Theme and Variations* on the Kirov Ballet. In a television interview before the works' opening night in February 1989, Vinogradov observed tartly: "The Bolshoi should have had Balanchine years ago. But they waited for me to take the responsibility."[688] The challenging experience of dancing Balanchine for the first time emphasised how far the choreographer, who always acknowledged his own Russian training, had taken the art form. The Russian dancers knew very little of him: "I have seen very little of Balanchine's work. He was here once in person, you know, but that was about a hundred years ago,"[689] observed ballerina Altynai Asylmuratova, while her husband and fellow principal Konstantin Zaklinsky noted about *Theme and Variations*: "Even now, when I dance the *polonaise*, my brain knows what I should do, but my legs can't follow."[690] Opinions among the dancers about Balanchine were extremely mixed; Larisa Lezhnina,[691] who danced in

---

688   Reynolds, 'Setting Balanchine in Leningrad,' *Ballet Review* 71, no. 2, 1989
689   ibid., p.42
690   ibid., p.54
691   Born in Leningrad in 1969, Lezhnina graduated into the Kirov in 1987, becoming a First Soloist in 1990; she was noted for her interpretation of the role of Aurora in *The Sleeping Beauty*. In 1994 she left Russia and joined Dutch National Ballet as a principal dancer. She retired from the stage in 2014.

the first Leningrad cast, observed to *The New York Times*:

> "To me, Balanchine is a genius...but we cannot dance him as they do in the West. We interpret him in our own way; we have no choice. We have different souls, a different manner of performing than in the West. We look at him through our eyes."[692]

Principal dancer Farukh Ruzimatov saw things very differently, stating that Balanchine was not his "ideal of choreography" and that he found the works to be "without soul...I can't take a lack of soul. And in my personal opinion, his work is cold in some places, and paradey (sic) and showy in others. But I do think, all the same, that it's necessary to perform his works. It is difficult work, and difficult work enriches you."[693]

On the February first night a cast of young dancers performed *Scotch Symphony* (Lezhnina, Pankova and Yuri Zhukov[694]) while company principals Altynai Asylmuratova and Konstantin Zaklinsky were the central couple leading the company in *Theme and Variations*. The performances were, despite the sometimes-challenging learning process, a huge success in Leningrad, and established the beginnings of a growing Balanchine repertoire at the Kirov/Mariinsky. In the printed programme, director Oleg Vinogradov wrote:

> "We are happy that our dream is coming true. Finally, the first official première of Balanchine in the Soviet Union will take place, in the theatre where he grew up, where his aesthetics were nurtured. I see the origins of Balanchine's creativity in Petipa's works, in particular in (*La Bayadère's* Kingdom of the) 'Shadows', and in many other ballets. Of course, he was able to comprehend everything he saw, all the classics as a genius contemporary artist. And this is wonderful, because, in his words, 'tradition is much stronger than its denial. It fosters new things with incredible poignancy'."

1989 – Vinogradov's *Petrushka*

Soviet Russia had largely missed out on Mikhail Fokine's *Petrushka*, a masterly treatment of Stravinsky's score commissioned and first performed during Diaghilev's 1911 Ballets Russes Paris season. It had been staged in Petrograd in 1920 by Leonid Leontiev in what proved a short-lived revival and in 1961 at the Maly and subsequently for the Bolshoi by Konstantin

---

692   As quoted by Fein, 'The Kirov enters the World of Glasnost', *The New York Times*, July 1989

693   ibid.

694   Born in 1964, Zhukov trained at the Vaganova Academy and joined the Kirov Ballet, rising to the rank of soloist before becoming a principal of San Francisco Ballet and then Birmingham Royal Ballet. In 2008 he founded Zhukov Dance Theater, a contemporary dance ensemble based in San Francisco.

Boyarsky. Returning to his favoured theme of the oppression of the individual by outside forces, Vinogradov premièred his own new version in March 1989 not in Leningrad, but in Glasgow. He had been approached by the Chief Executive of Scottish Ballet during the Kirov's tour to Ireland in the summer of 1988 and had agreed to create a new version for the company to sit in a double bill alongside Scottish Opera's production of Stravinsky's *Oedipus Rex*. In the choreographer's mind, "It is a ballet about the fate of the little man. Any state, however big, consists of small people like us. This ballet will be about you and me."[695] The ballet subsequently received its Leningrad première in 1990 with Andris Liepa impressing in the title role.

1989 – The Kirov in the USA

In 1989, Vinogradov led the Kirov's first tour to New York for twenty-five years. After a month in Canada, it performed for three weeks at New York's Metropolitan Opera House before a fortnight at the Kennedy Center, Washington and further appearances in San Francisco and Orange County in Costa Mesa, California. The repertoire showed some of the fruits of the director's policy of refreshment: *The Sleeping Beauty*, Vinogradov and Gusev's production of *Le Corsaire* as well as *Potemkin* which shared a programme with the 'Kingdom of the Shades' scene from *La Bayadère* and mixed bills including Balanchine's *Scotch Symphony* and *Theme and Variations* as well as works by Roland Petit and Maurice Béjart. In interviews given before the company's departure on tour, Vinogradov described the previous two decades as a closed-off time in Soviet ballet:

> "We were deprived by absurd politics that declared that Western creativity doesn't need to exist here. This cultural cold war was a nightmare. And who did it hurt? The West? It hurt our people. It froze our development. It's ridiculous to live with such blinders on. What good did it do?"[696]

He also commented about the new generation of choreographers in Russia:

> "I consider the psychology of the new artists to be much freer. They were once scared off by elements of sex and acrobatics that were not supposed to be in ballet. But anything can be in ballet if it is justified by being good and beautiful. We now have abstract and concrete ballets, which are fundamentally realistic and pertaining to life."[697]

Vinogradov's comments were a sign of the significant loosening of state

---

695 *The Herald*, January 11th 1989

696 As quoted by Fein, 'The Kirov enters the World of Glasnost', *The New York Times*, July 1989

697 ibid.

control on both artistic policy and greater freedom to express personal opinion.

1989 – Defectors return

The rehabilitation of artists who had defected from the Soviet Union was part of the re-calibration of Russian culture in the light of Gorbachev's changes: the pianist Vladimir Horowitz[698] played in his native country in 1986, the first time since his departure in 1925. In February 1989, Natalia Makarova returned to Leningrad for the first time in some nineteen years; she appeared at the Kirov with French dancer Alexandre Sombart in two pas de deux from John Cranko's *Onegin*. In November of the same year, Rudolf Nureyev, who not been in the city for twenty-eight years, stepped out onto the same stage at the age of fifty-one as James in *La Sylphide* opposite Zhanna Ayupova[699] as the Sylph. A half-hour ovation followed the performance which had been rehearsed by his old partner Ninel Kurgapkina and watched by, among others, Alla Osipenko who spoke vehemently about what the company could learn from Nureyev and his experiences in the West, lamenting the fact that it had taken so long for him to be allowed to return. Mikhail Baryshnikov has never returned to Russia per se, only performing in his native Riga, by then capital of an independent Latvia, in 1997. Images of Nureyev, Makarova and Baryshnikov returned to the walls of their alma mater, the Vaganova Academy: Altynai Asylmuratova observed "there's a whole wall filled completely with their pictures. Now, people talk only about them. Before, it was as if they were all stuck in the Bermuda Triangle. Now, it's as if all of a sudden, they've been rediscovered."[700] The Kozlovs also made a return visit to Russia in 1991, appearing in a dance festival in Moscow.

1990 – La Classique

In 1990, a further ballet company was founded in Moscow. La Classique was established by Alexander Prokofiev,[701] formerly a highly-respected

---

698   Born in Kiev, Ukraine in 1903, Horowitz was recognised as one of the greatest pianists of all time. Already an acclaimed soloist, he left Russia in 1925, moving to the USA three years later. He appeared around the world and recorded extensively. He died in New York in 1989.

699   Born in Petrozavodsk in 1966, Ayupova graduated into the Kirov in 1984, becoming a principal dancer in 1987. Possessed of a fine technique and a winning stage presence, she rapidly became an audience favourite in a wide range of roles, from the nineteenth century classics to parts in Balanchine works and creations such as the bride in Alexey Ratmansky's *Le baiser de la fée*. From 2000 to 2013, she coached dancers at the Mikhailovsky Ballet and in 2013 became Artistic Director of the Vaganova Academy and First Vice-Rector.

700   Kriegsman, 'Dancing Diplomacy', *The Washington Post*, March 1989.

701   Born in Omsk in 1942, Prokofiev graduated from the Bolshoi School in 1961 and joined the Novosibirsk Ballet where he danced until 1966. He joined the Bolshoi School as

teacher of the graduating class at the Moscow Choreographic Institute (the Bolshoi School) who counted Andris Liepa, Irek Mukhamedov and Alexey Fadeyechev among his pupils. In 1989 Prokofiev and thirteen other teachers had resigned in protest at declining standards and intolerable internal politics. The formation of the new company was in response to the under-use of dancers at the Bolshoi and began with some seventeen members which soon grew to over forty. Prokofiev wished for a return to pure Russian ballet schooling as opposed to the corruptions of Grigorovich's style; in 1991 he staged *La Bayadère* for the company and secured Nadezhda Pavlova as a guest principal. In 1992, scenic artist Erik Melikov took over the directorship of the company which continues to present versions of the classics in Russia and on extensive foreign tours.

1990 – Kremlin Ballet

In 1990, yet another classical dance ensemble was established in Moscow. The Ballet Theatre of the Kremlin Palace of Congresses was headed by ex-Bolshoi choreographer Andrey Petrov who found ready support from Maximova and Vasiliev; the first production was a revival of the latter's *Macbeth* which had originally premièred at the Bolshoi in 1980 with Vasiliev himself in the title role and Timofeyeva as Lady Macbeth. The Kremlin production featured guest artists Andris Liepa and Svetlana Choi[702] and the score was by Kirill Molchanov.[703] In 1992 the company was renamed Ballet of the State Kremlin Palace or more simply Kremlin Ballet and continued with a programme of revivals of classical works and new creations. Since 2005 it has functioned in partnership with the Maris Liepa Charitable Foundation – Russian Seasons XXI Century with the intention of reviving the Ballets Russes repertoire.

Russian Winds of Change

During the late 1980s, the Soviet regime's control over the conglomeration of states comprising the USSR started to falter and several republics began to agitate for independence. In 1988, the three Baltic states declared the supremacy of their own laws and in the spring of 1989 the first, albeit

---

a teacher in 1969 and graduated from GITIS in 1971. He taught internationally from the early 1970s. He stepped down from La Classique in 1992, emigrated to Germany in 1993 and taught at Munich's Ballet School thereafter. He died in Munich in 2007.

702 Born in Chimbay, Karakalpak in 1959, Choi trained at the Tashkent Ballet School until 1976 and then the Bolshoi School from where she graduated in 1978. She joined the Stanislavsky Ballet in the same year and rose to the rank of principal, dancing a wide variety of roles. From 1990 onwards she danced regularly with the Kremlin Ballet.

703 Born in Moscow in 1922, Molchanov graduated from the Moscow Conservatoire in 1949. Primarily a composer for the voice – he created numerous songs and seven operas – he was Director of the Bolshoi Theatre between 1973 and 1975. His third wife was ballerina Nina Timofeyeva. He died during a performance of *Macbeth* at the Bolshoi in 1982.

limited, exercise in democracy took place with elections to the new Congress of People's Deputies. Gorbachev abandoned the oppressive and expensive 'Brezhnev Doctrine' which mandated Russian intervention in the six Warsaw Pact states (East Germany, Poland, Czechoslovakia, Hungary, Romania and Bulgaria), paving the way for elections and the subsequent loss of a majority for local communist parties. In 1990, the Central Committee of the party voted to give up its monopoly on political power and all fifteen republics of the USSR went on to hold their first competitive elections. The Communist Party lost the elections in six republics: Lithuania, Latvia, Estonia, Moldova, Armenia and Georgia.

By the middle of 1990, brisk winds of change were to be felt in all areas of Soviet society; ballet was not exempt. During the summer, the Kirov toured first to London and then New York. In an interview, Vinogradov observed: "Our artists at last are no longer isolated from the outside world. They have total freedom, they work in theaters (sic) they choose, they make their own contracts and they dance whatever works they like." Farukh Ruzimatov had recently left the company to join American Ballet Theatre. Vinogradov continued: "Our dancers do what was totally impossible even one year ago and these changes have affected considerably the psychology of the company, the atmosphere in the theater. We must now enter a period of re-evaluation. This is only natural, and I'm happy that this new generation will enjoy this."[704]

However, there were many voices being raised against Vinogradov and his artistic policy which, despite his acquisition of outside choreographies and the promotion of a new generation of Russian dance-makers, had not convinced everyone. During a conference for dance writers arranged in Moscow by the magazine *Soviet Ballet*, a prominent Leningrad critic expressed his opinion that tours by the Kirov, the Maly and Boris Eifman's company served to empty his city of dance and that, at the Kirov in particular, Vinogradov's eye on the touring value of productions compromised artistic standards. "Classical ballet is being turned into brilliant, attractive popular productions to sell abroad" said Arkady Sokolov-Kaminsky, referring to Vinogradov's 1987 alterations to *Le Corsaire*, adding that they were "fascinating for most, but for me this is the death of classical ballet".[705]

As the Soviet system creaked and groaned into the 1990s and through the major reforms under Mikhail Gorbachev, it became clear that the state coffers were empty for ballet. This was the first time since the privations and ideological questionings of the early years after the 1917 revolution that it was seriously threatened financially – even during the Second World War

---

704   Silverman, 'Politics Pervade the Kirov's New 'Petrouchka', *The New York Times*, July 1990

705   Kaminsky quoted by Willis, *Dancing Times*, February 1990

money was found as classical dancing was designated as essential for the morale of troops and populace alike. The imperative to make money sent the Bolshoi and Kirov ensembles out on lucrative foreign tours during which the quality of the dancers' training and their mesmerising 'old-school' quality in performance outweighed dull repertoire and poor theatrical standards in terms of set and costume design. There was, as Western critics and audiences noted, something extraordinary about Russian dancers which overcame their views on choreography and visual presentation. Presented by Western producers, the dancers performed, no longer in promotion of the Soviet ideal or to play their part in the creation of a Soviet utopia, but rather to earn hard currency to keep themselves and their companies afloat. Discontent among the artists was high, so much so that during the 1990 USA tour by the Bolshoi, the dancers went on a one-day hunger strike in protest. Grigorovich observed gloomily to dance critic and writer Anna Kisselgoff "everything is going downhill...what is happening in the theater reflects what is happening in the entire country".[706]

Dissatisfaction reigned about the financial terms of foreign tours with impresarios and organisations accused of profiting from the visits rather more than the companies themselves. In 1990, a story broke in the UK's *The Times* reporting that "the Soviet cultural establishment (was) up in arms over reports that the Bolshoi has been 'sold' to foreigners".[707] The row concerned the London-based Entertainment Corporation which presented the Bolshoi and stood accused of taking the same level of profits, 42.5%, as the company itself, with 15% going to the Soviet cultural management organisation *Gosconcert*. The row was in the context of wider disquiet over the running of the company and poor reviews that season in London and Paris.

Westward Ho!

The wish to dance more roles and more frequently was often at the heart of a steady stream of dancers from both the Bolshoi and the Kirov either leaving Russia for good or at least securing lengthy contracts to dance abroad. At the beginning of 1990, Andris Liepa joked in the magazine *Ogonyok* that "in eighteen months time there will be no dancers left at the Bolshoi".[708] Liepa himself had left Moscow to join American Ballet Theatre before returning to dance with the Kirov and observed: "In seven years at the Bolshoi I danced *Swan Lake* only three times and Romeo three times. In just one season in America, I performed *Swan Lake* twenty-five times and Romeo six times."[709]

---

706 Morrison, *Bolshoi Confidential*, p.405
707 Quoted in *Dance and Dancers*, May 1990
708 Quoted in *Dance and Dancers*, April 1990
709 ibid.

Kirov soloist Yuri Zhukov arranged a full season with San Francisco Ballet, while two Bolshoi principal dancers, wife and husband Alla Khaniashvili[710] and Vitaly Artiushkin[711] spent a year with the Ballet of Los Angeles. Alexander Monakhov joined the Lucerne Ballet in Switzerland, swapping his only Bolshoi featured role, Paris in *Romeo and Juliet*, for Romeo himself in Valery Panov's staging. Stanislav Tchassov,[712] who had left the Bolshoi in 1989 and was subsequently granted leave to remain in the United Kingdom with his family, was dancing with the small-scale London City Ballet by the following year.

The biggest departure to hit Soviet ballet since the defection of Mikhail Baryshnikov in 1974 was the emigration of Irek Mukhamedov in 1990, who, having spoken with The Royal Ballet management about guest appearances in London the following season, announced to them that he would rather not return to Russia. Permission to remain in the UK having been sought and duly obtained, he sent a telex to the Bolshoi resigning from the company; on June 12th he arrived for morning class with his new company; The Royal Ballet had offered him a five-year contract on the spot. He subsequently refused a guest contract to appear in his scheduled Bolshoi performances during their United States tour that summer.

A Bolshoi principal who chose not to emigrate was Alexey Fadeyechev who nonetheless appeared alongside Nina Ananiashvili with The Royal Ballet at Covent Garden during the 1990-1991 season as the Salamander Prince in Kenneth MacMillan's *The Prince of the Pagodas* and Romeo as well as the Sugar Plum Fairy's Cavalier in *The Nutcracker*.

With months of the Soviet Union to go, at the invitation of Stalingrad-born company director Galina Samsova,[713] Kirov principal dancer Galina

---

710   Born in 1958, Alla Khaniashvili graduated from the Bolshoi School as a principal into the Stanislavsky company in 1976. In 1980 she was invited to join the Bolshoi Ballet where she danced all the major roles of the repertoire. In 1989 she left Russia for the United States with her husband and continued to dance as a guest artist until her retirement from the stage in 2004. She now teaches in the United States.

711   Artiushkin danced with the Stanislavsky Ballet in the 1970s before moving to the Bolshoi in 1980.

712   Born in Moscow in 1963, Tchassov graduated into the Bolshoi in 1981 where he danced until his departure from Russia in 1989. He danced with London City Ballet and Birmingham Royal Ballet before taking a lead dance role in Kenneth MacMillan's production of *Carousel* at the National Theatre in 1992/3. He founded European Ballet in 1994 for which he choreographed a number of works.

713   Born in Stalingrad in 1937, Samsova graduated into the Kiev Ballet from its school in 1956, rising to the rank of soloist. In 1960, after her marriage to a Canadian, she moved to Canada and danced with the National Ballet of Canada for a season. She danced with London Festival Ballet from 1964 to 1973 and distinguished herself in lyrical roles. She co-founded the New London Ballet in 1972 with which she appeared until 1977. She joined Sadler's Wells Royal Ballet in 1979 and danced with the company until 1990 after

Mezentseva decided to swap the gold and blue auditorium of her home theatre for touring with Scottish Ballet on a one-year contract. It was an indication of the West's attractiveness to dancers in the dying days of the regime not only because of an expanded repertoire but also for financial stability.

---

which she became Artistic Director of Scottish Ballet from 1991 to 1997. She staged a number of acclaimed productions of the classics.

Postscript

Soviet Russia collapsed on 25th December 1991 but the ballet, as it had done in 1917, lived on. As dawn broke on a country liberated from over eighty years of state communism, there was, however, no comparable ideological belief in the future, no new world to forge. The social and political merits and demerits of the Soviet period are material for the study and comment of others, but for ballet, it was an extraordinary time. From having been the property of the Emperor and a source of entertainment of the elite, ballet had, often painfully, sometimes brutally, expanded and transformed itself to become the darling art of the Russian people and state and a totem for their cultural achievements around the world. Russia's golden age of ballet is a remarkable story and an extraordinary journey for the artists, known and unremembered, who peopled it along the way.

In the turmoil of post-Soviet Russia, artists did leave, much as their predecessors had done in 1917, the West as hungry for dancers as they had been some seventy-four years previously. However, the majority stayed on and continued to perform. The social upheavals were huge, as Russian society lurched into a form of unregulated capitalism, leaving behind much of the population, born and brought up in a world in which the state provided everything.

After the fall of communism, Moscow's Bolshoi Ballet continued with Yuri Grigorovich at the helm, who offered a limp and poorly received new production of *Don Quixote* in 1994. The loss of the confidence of the theatre's General Director Vladimir Kokonin and threats of industrial action prompted him to resign in March 1995, but not before a strike by pro-Grigorovich dancers caused the cancellation of a performance of *Romeo and Juliet*. Grigorovich's arch-critic Vladimir Vasiliev then arrived as artistic director for the Bolshoi Theatre as a whole, appointing Vyacheslav Gordeyev as director of the ballet company, a post he held for two years before being replaced for a year by Alexander Bogatyrev as acting artistic director. Alexey Fadeyechev, in post from 1998 to 2000, commissioned several new productions including asking Pierre Lacotte to stage a popular reconstruction of Petipa's *La Fille du Pharaon* (*The Pharaoh's Daughter*). Vasiliev lasted five years, learning of his own dismissal in 2000 from a radio broadcast. Boris Akimov then took over the ballet company and himself remained for four years, acquiring works by Ashton and Neumeier; he subsequently relinquished his directorship to choreographer Alexey Ratmansky who, from 2004 to 2009, widened the repertoire further with his own new ballets including new versions of *The Bright Stream* and *The Bolt*. In 2002 a second New Stage auditorium was opened with a capacity of some 900 seats. 2009 saw the return of Yuri Grigorovich as company choreographer and the appointment of Yuri Burlaka[714] as director, who focussed on the restoration of classical ballets (*Paquita*, *Coppélia* and *Esmeralda*). In 2011 former principal dancer Sergey Filin[715] replaced him as director. The Bolshoi closed its doors in 2005 for a major structural rebuild which took six years and some twenty-five million roubles. With a seating capacity of 2,153, the theatre reopened with a gala in October 2011; the first ballet was a new production of *The Sleeping Beauty* by Yuri Grigorovich which saw the dancing of American principal David Hallberg who had joined the company. Sergey Filin was seriously injured in an acid attack in 2013 and partially blinded; he remained director until 2016 when he stood down in favour of Makhar Vaziev[716] who remains in post.

In 1991, the change of Leningrad's name back to St Petersburg prompted the rebranding of the Kirov Ballet and Theatre and a return to their pre-revolutionary name of Mariinsky, even if the former was used for some time after on foreign tours. Oleg Vinogradov remained in post as the company's director until 1997 when he was accused of advancing the career of a young ballerina with whom he was having an affair and of bribery in receiving the sum of $10,000 from a Canadian impresario. He was arrested and released without charge after three days. After a suspected heart attack,

---

714 Born in Moscow in 1968, Burlaka graduated from the Bolshoi Ballet School into the Russian Ballet Company with whom he danced many major roles. Drawn to historic choreography, he arranged numerous evenings of revivals of excerpts, and graduated from the Moscow State Academy of Ballet to be a teacher-choreographer in 1999. He was company répétiteur from 2006 and director the year after. He continues to reconstruct historic ballets around the world and is currently director of the Samara Opera and Ballet Theatre.

715 Born in Moscow in 1970, Filin graduated into the Bolshoi Ballet in 1988 and achieved the rank of principal two years later. He was noted for his noble and intense stage presence and he excelled as the Classical Dancer in Alexey Ratmansky's *The Bright Stream*. After an injury in 2004 stopped his dancing career, he devoted himself to teaching and direction, becoming the director of the Stanislavsky Ballet between 2008 and 2011 when he assumed the directorship of the Bolshoi company. An acid attack in 2013 and his incapacitation led to his contract at the Bolshoi not being renewed in 2016.

716 Born in 1961 in Alagir, North Ossetia, Vaziev graduated into the Kirov Ballet in 1981 and was made a principal dancer in 1989, appearing in major roles across the repertoire. From 1995 to 2008 he directed the company, expanding the repertoire to include more by Balanchine and acquiring works by notable Western choreographers. He also explored the company's old repertoire and oversaw reconstructions of 'original' Petipa ballets *The Sleeping Beauty*, the 1900 *La Bayadère* and *Le Réveil de Flore*. He was Director of the Ballet of La Scala, Milan from 2008-2016 after which he became Director of the Bolshoi Ballet, where he remains.

Vinogradov left his post. In 1998 he became director of the Universal Ballet in Seoul, as well as the Kirov Ballet Academy in Washington DC, and he staged productions such as *La Fille mal gardée* for the Stanislavsky Ballet. He left Seoul Ballet in 2008 to join the Mikhailovsky Ballet as an associate choreographer.

Conductor Valery Gergiev had become the Music Director of the Kirov Theatre in 1988 and in 1996 was appointed Artistic and General Director meaning that he led the orchestra, the opera and the ballet companies. He remains in post. Subsequent ballet directors have answered to Gergiev. Vinogradov was replaced with ex-company dancer Makhar Vaziev who remained until 2008 when Yuri Fateyev[717] became Acting Director of the company in which post he currently remains. In 2013 the Mariinsky Theatre Second Stage was opened close to the original theatre with a seating capacity of 1,830 to add to the Mariinsky's 1,625 seats.

Leningrad's Maly Theatre (along with its opera and ballet companies) was renamed in 1989 in honour of the composer Modest Mussorgsky and in 1991, at the collapse of communism, became The St Petersburg Mussorgsky State Academic Opera and Ballet Theatre. In 2007, it returned to its original nomenclature of the Mikhailovsky Theatre. Following the retirement that year of Nikolai Boyarchikov after thirty years as director, ex-Kirov dancer Farukh Ruzimatov replaced him as head of the ballet company; he remained for two years. Mikhail Messerer, who had defected to the West with his mother Sulamith in 1980, was then made ballet master in chief, a post he held for nine years, during which time the artistic and technical standards of the ensemble soared, attracting notable dancers from both the Mariinsky and Bolshoi companies. Messerer also instituted a policy of the revival of important Soviet ballets and productions, including Chabukiani's *Laurencia*, Vainonen's *The Flames of Paris*, Zakharov's *Cinderella* and the Gorsky/Asaf Messerer *Swan Lake*. Spanish contemporary choreographer Nacho Duato[718] held the post of Artistic Director from 2011 to 2014 and returned to the post in 2019. The Mikhailovsky Theatre currently seats 1,151.

The Stanislavsky Ballet was headed by choreographer Dmitry Bryantsev

---

717 Born in Leningrad in 1964, Fateyev graduated into the Kirov Ballet in 1982 where he performed as a lively character dancer, notably as the Jester in *Swan Lake*. He became a company répétiteur in 2003 and has been a guest teacher with major companies worldwide. Since his appointment as Acting Director, he has sought further to expand the repertoire of the Mariinsky company.

718 Born in Valencia, Spain in 1957, Duato trained at the Rambert School in London, Maurice Béjart's Mudra School in Brussels and Alvin Ailey American Dance Theater in New York City. In 1981, he joined Nederlands Dans Theater under choreographer Jiří Kylián where he remained for ten years. His first work was *Jardí tancat* in 1983, since when he has choreographed many works. He was the artistic director of Spain's Companía Nacional de Danza from 1990 to 2011; after his first spell at the Mikhailovsky, he was director of the Berlin Staatsballett from 2014 to 2019.

from 1985 to 2004 when he mysteriously disappeared in Prague, presumed murdered. Ex-Bolshoi principal Mikhail Lavrovsky was then director between 2005 and 2008, followed by Sergey Filin who remained in post until 2011 when he took charge of the Bolshoi Ballet. From 2011 to 2016 the Stanislavsky company was led by ex-Kirov/Mariinsky principal dancer Igor Zelensky[719] who was also director of the Novosibirsk Ballet, a role he had taken up in 2006. He brought in several ballets by choreographers whose work he had encountered as a guest artist abroad. In 2017, when Zelensky left Russia to take over the direction of Munich's Bavarian State Ballet, Laurent Hilaire,[720] ex-*danseur étoile*, ballet master and associate artistic director of the Paris Opéra Ballet, was appointed to replace him. Two major fires in 1989 and 2005 seriously damaged the fabric of the building, but the Stanislavsky and Nemirovich-Danchenko Moscow Music Theatre reopened after extensive restorations; it currently seats 1,100 people.

The Moscow and Leningrad ballet schools continued to train fine dancers after the fall of communism, providing the companies with a steady supply of artists and, indeed, future principal dancers, although from the 1990s onwards, there were increasing numbers of company members from other conservatoires, such as Svetlana Zakharova who graduated from the Kiev Choreographic School in 1995 and Ivan Vasiliev who left the Belarusian Ballet School in 2006, both becoming Bolshoi principals. Certainly, the majority of dancers continued to live and work in Russia while the freedom to accept guest engagements abroad satisfied all but the most globe-trotting of star dancers. Notable Moscow State Academy of Choreography (Bolshoi Ballet School) graduates have included Nikolai Tsiskaridze (graduation in 1992), Svetlana Lunkina (1997) and Natalia Osipova (2004), while Ulyana Lopatkina (1991), Diana Vishneva (1995), Vladimir Shklyarov (2003) and Olga Smirnova (2011) have emerged from the Vaganova Academy.

The Bolshoi School was led by Igor Uksusnikov[721] from 1988 until 1993 when he was succeeded by Genrikh Mayorov. In 2001 Boris Akimov acted as

---

719 Born in Labinsk, Krasnodar Krai in 1969, Zelensky trained first in Tbilisi and then in Leningrad, graduating into the Kirov in 1988, rising to the rank of Principal in 1991. He danced all the major roles of the repertoire with the company until 2013. He was a principal with New York City Ballet between 1992 and 1997 and a guest artist around the world.

720 Born in 1962 in France, Hilaire graduated into the Paris Opéra Ballet from its school in 1979, rising to become a *danseur étoile* in 1985 and dancing for a further twenty-two years as one of its most accomplished and admired stars.

721 Born in Moscow in 1931, Uksusnikov graduated into the Bolshoi Ballet in 1948. He danced there until 1952 when he transferred to the Kirov where he remained until 1968, known as a classical dancer with a fine jump and an heroic stage presence. He taught at the Leningrad Choreographic School from 1953 to 1967. He returned to Moscow in 1968 to work with the Young Ballet. In 1988 he was appointed director of the Bolshoi School. He died in Moscow in 2009.

interim Rector before Maria Leonova[722] assumed the directorship in 2002, a post she still holds. At the Vaganova Academy, Konstantin Sergeyev died in 1992 and was replaced by Igor Belsky who was director until his own death in 1999. Altynai Asylmuratova was appointed to replace him in 2000 and was in post until 2014 when ex-Bolshoi star dancer Nikolai Tsiskaridze[723] took over.

---

722 Born in Moscow in 1949, Leonova graduated from the Bolshoi School in 1968 and joined the company the year after, remaining as a dancer until 1989, rising to the rank of soloist. She started to teach at the Bolshoi School upon her retirement and rose to become Rector in 2002, a post she continues to occupy.

723 Born in Tbilisi in 1973, Tsiskaridze started at the Tbilisi Ballet School in 1984 before moving to the Bolshoi School in 1987. On his graduation in 1992, he joined the company, rising to the rank of principal in three years. A long-limbed dancer of considerable elegance, he excelled across the full repertoire and became a hugely popular company artist. In 2011, he was not successful in his application to lead the company and subsequently left. He became Rector of the Vaganova Academy in November 2014.

Conclusion

The fall of the communist state led to an acceleration of the internationalisation of ballet in the major Russian companies with the acquisition of Western works progressing apace. An important feature of this phenomenon was the reclaiming of the repertoire of those Russians who had left at, or soon after, the 1917 revolutions. First and foremost were the ballets of George Balanchine which established a dance tradition from which Soviet Russian ballet had been excluded; they were acquired with undisguised eagerness, despite the difficulties inherent in mastering what was a foreign style. The Mariinsky in particular also sought to lay claim to the heritage of Diaghilev's Ballets Russes whose most important works were also brought into the repertoire, albeit in decidedly unconvincing versions. Thirdly, the 1990s and 2000s saw a trend in the recreation of 'original' versions of the great Petipa classics from notations – in an attempt to emphasise the heritage of Russian ballet, the two main companies chose to jettison the accretions and re-imaginings of the Soviet era, as if to expunge its perceived choreographic sins. In so doing, the companies largely divested themselves of the major works of the communist era repertoire, the *drambaleti* which had for so long been staples of the repertoire. In Moscow, that process was far slower, given the returned presence of Yuri Grigorovich, whose ballets remain a prominent part in the company's performing schedule. It was at the Mikhailovsky Ballet in St Petersburg and at its sister company in Novosibirsk that some of the jewels of the Soviet era were revived with care.

The belief that Soviet dancers were 'good' but that the ballets they danced were not has been widely held since the first Russian forays into the West in the 1950s, but this view must be seen in the wider context of the Cold War, which also had its cultural front of conflict. Soviet ballet functioned very much as it had in the late imperial era – it remained a Russian art form for Russian consumption. Under the Soviet regime, ballet came to represent an underlying political ideal in a way impossible to imagine in the West, and the peoples of Russia identified with it as an art form in a way inconceivable to the audience members of the Paris Opéra, the New York State Theatre or The Royal Opera House, Covent Garden. Where Soviet ballet could not be criticised was in the way it spread to cover the entire country, with schools and companies established across the USSR. That phenomenon, with the degree of control it required to come about, is something which could never realistically be witnessed anywhere other than in a totalitarian state; it remains, nevertheless, Soviet ballet's greatest and most long-lasting achievement.

Russian ballet's current relationship with its Soviet past remains complicated. There is a tendency to portray the history of classical dancing as seamless, somehow forgetting the upheavals of the twentieth century. In St Petersburg in particular, the Mariinsky Ballet emphasises its links with its Imperial past, part of the narrative of which is that it is the curator of an unbroken tradition; the Bolshoi in Moscow is far less focussed on its pre-revolutionary past, given that it was during the Soviet era that it was lifted out of the Mariinsky's shadow and elevated to the position of the Soviet Union's senior ballet company. The ballet ensembles of the states of the Russian Federation and those which seceded from the old USSR forge their own artistic paths, although many owe their original existence to the Soviet policy of spreading 'Russian' culture across the nation.

Ballet in Soviet Russia was, for much of the duration of the USSR, a highly valued cultural prize and a propaganda tool used both internally and on the international stage. The achievements in classical dance of this extraordinary political and social entity were impressive indeed; the mistake would lie in forgetting those achievements when considering the sometimes-negative social, political and economic consequences of the Russian Soviet experiment. They are the achievements of a truly golden age in dance.

Appendices

A   **Checklist of Soviet Ballet 1959-60 – Soviet theatres with a ballet company**
John Percival in *The Ballet Annual* 1962, No. 16

1. Bolshoi Theatre, Moscow
2. Stanislavsky and Nemirovich-Danchenko Theatre, Moscow
3. Kirov Theatre, Leningrad
4. Maly Theatre, Leningrad
5. Pushkin Theatre, Gorky
6. Kuibyshev State Opera and Ballet Theatre
7. Novosibirsk Opera and Ballet Theatre
8. Perm State Opera and Ballet Theatre
9. Chernishevsky Theatre, Saratov
10. Lunacharsky Theatre, Sverdlovsk
11. Glinka Theatre, Chelyabinsk
12. Bashkir Opera and Ballet Theatre, Ufa
13. Buryat Opera and Ballet Theatre, Ulan-Ude
14. Moussa Jalil Tatar Theatre, Kazan
15. Shevchenko Theatre, Kiev
16. Ivan Franko Theatre, Lvov
17. Stalino Opera and Ballet Theatre
18. Lysenko Theatre, Kharkov
19. Byelorussian Opera and Ballet Theatre, Minsk
20. Alisher Navoi Uzbek Theatre, Tashkent
21. Abay Kazakh Theatre, Alma-Ata
22. Paliashvili Georgian Theatre, Tbilisi
23. Akhundov Azerbaijan Theatre, Baku
24. Lithuanian Opera and Ballet Theatre, Vilnius
25. Kaunas Musical Theatre

26. Pushkin Moldavian Theatre, Kishinev
27. Latvian Opera and Ballet Theatre, Riga
28. Kirghiz Opera and Ballet Theatre, Frunze
29. Aini Tadjik Theatre, Stalinabad
30. Spendiarov Armenian Theatre, Yerevan
31. Makhtum Kuli Theatre, Ashkhabad
32. Estonian State Theatre, Tallinn

B   Names of the Mariinsky Theatre

(1860) – 1917	Imperial Mariinsky Theatre
1917 – 1920	State (ex-) Mariinsky Theatre
1920 – 1924	State Academic Theatre of Opera and Ballet (GATOB)
1924 – 1935	Leningrad State Academic Theatre of Opera and Ballet (LATOB or GATOB)
1935 – (1992)	Kirov State Academic Theatre of Opera and Ballet
(1992 –)	State Academic Mariinsky Theatre

C   Directors of the ex-Mariinsky/GATOB/Kirov Ballet

1917	I N Ivanov
1918-1920	Boris Romanov
1920	Leonid Leontiev
1922-1925	Leonid Leontiev
1925-1931	Fyodor Lopukhov
1931-1937	Agrippina Vaganova
1938-1944	Leonid Lavrovsky (1942-3 in Yerevan)
1941-1944	Vladimir Ponomarev (in Molotov)
1944-1945	Fyodor Lopukhov
1945-1950	Pyotr Gusev
1951-1955	Konstantin Sergeyev
1955-1956	Fyodor Lopukhov
1956-1959	Boris Fenster
1960-1970	Konstantin Sergeyev (some sources indicate he took over from an ailing Fenster in 1959)
1970–1973	Vladilen Semyonov (acting director)
1973-1977	Igor Belsky
1977-(1997)	Oleg Vinogradov

D Names of the Petrograd / Leningrad Choreographic School / Vaganova Academy

(1738)-1917	Imperial Theatre School (Imperial Petersburg Theatrical Institute)
1917-1928	State Petrograd Theatre College (Petrograd Choreographic School)
1928-1937	Leningrad Choreographic Training College (Leningrad Choreographic Institute) LKhU or LGKhU
1937-1957	Leningrad Choreographic School (LHU)
1957-1991	Vaganova Ballet Academy
1991-	Vaganova Academy of Russian Ballet

E Directors of the Petrograd / Leningrad Choreographic School / Vaganova Academy

1917-1918	A N Maslov?
1918-1920	Leonid Leontiev
1919-1926	Andrey Oblakov
1927-1929	Viktor Semyonov
1930-1938	Boris Shavrov
1938-1940	Konstantin Sergeyev
1941-1943	Lydia Tager (acting director in Leningrad)
1940-1952	Nikolai Ivanovsky
1952-1954	Tatiana Vecheslova
1954-1961	Nikolai Ivanovsky
1962-1973	Feya Balabina
1973-(1992)	Konstantin Sergeyev

F Directors / Chief Ballet Masters of the Bolshoi Ballet

1917-1919	Vasily Tikhomirov (head of the ballet company)
1919-1926	An Artistic Council was in place
1926-1930	Vasily Tikhomirov
1930-1935	?
1935-1936	Fyodor Lopukhov
1936-1939	Rostislav Zakharov
1942-1944	Mikhail Gabovich (Moscow)
1941-1943	Asaf Messerer (Kuibyshev)
1944-1955	Leonid Lavrovsky
1955-1957	Pyotr Gusev
1957-1959	Alexander Tomsky?
1957(9)-1964	Leonid Lavrovsky
1964-(1995)	Yuri Grigorovich (Chief Ballet Master 1964-1988, Artistic Director 1988-1995)

G   Names of the Bolshoi Ballet School

(1806)-1920	Moscow Imperial School
1920 - 1931	State Ballet School of the State Academic Bolshoi Theatre
1931 - 1932	State Moscow Ballet College at the Bolshoi Theatre
1932 - 1937	State Moscow Choreographic College at the Bolshoi Theatre
1937 - 1948	Bolshoi Ballet School
1948 - 1961	Choreographic School of the State Academic Bolshoi Theatre
1961 - 1987	The Moscow Academic School (MAHU)
1987 - 1995	The Moscow State Choreographic Institute
1995 -	Moscow State Academy of Choreography (MGAKh)

H   Directors of the Bolshoi Ballet School

1917 - 1920	Alexander Gorsky (AD)
1920 - 1924	Alexander Gorsky and Vasily Tikhomirov (AD)
1924 - 1931	Vasily Tikhomirov (AD)
1931 - 1936	Viktor Semyonov (AD)
1936 - 1937	Elizaveta Gerdt (AD)
1937 - 1941	Pyotr Gusev (AD)
1941 - 1945	Nikolai Tarasov (AD and D)
1945 - 1947	Rostislav Zakharov (AD and D)
1948 - 1953	Leonid Lavrovsky (AD)
1948 - 1952	Rafailov, Iosif (D)
1953 - 1960	Elena Bocharnikova (D)
1953 - 1954	Nikolai Tarasov (AD)
1954 - 1958	Mikhail Gabovich (AD)
1959 - 1964	Yuri Kondratov (AD)
1960 – (2001)	Golovkina, Sofia (1960-1987, Director of the Moscow Academic Choreographic School; 1987-1995, Rector-Director of the Moscow Academic Choreographic School and the Moscow State Choreographic Institute; 1995-2001, Rector of the Moscow State Academy of Choreography.)
1964 - 1967	Leonid Lavrovsky (AD)
1968 - 1972	Alexey Ermolayev (AD)
1973 - 1987	Maxim Martirosyan (AD)
1988 - (1993)	Igor Uksusnikov (AD)

AD – Artistic Director, D – Director

I   Directors of the Ballet Company of the Maly Theatre

1932-1935	Fyodor Lopukhov

1935-1938	Leonid Lavrovsky
1938-1939	Vladimir Ponomarev
1941-1943	Vladimir Varkovitsky
1943-1944	Fyodor Lopukhov
1945-1953	Boris Fenster
1954-1960	Galina Isayeva
1960-1962	Pyotr Gusev
1962-1973	Igor Belsky
1973-1977	Oleg Vinogradov
1977-(2007)	Nikolai Boyarchikov

Bibliography

Abyzova, L. (2000) *Игорь Бельский. Симфония жизн»и.* (Igor Belsky: Symphony of Life) St Petersburg: Vaganova Academy

Abyzova L. (2015) *Военные хроники ленинградского балета* (Military chronicles of the Leningrad ballet) St Petersburg: Vaganova Academy

Acocella, Joan (1998) 'The Reluctant Prodigal.' In: *The Guardian*, February 28th 1998

Baer, Nancy (1986). *Bronislava Nijinska; a dancer's legacy*. San Francisco: The Fine Arts Museums of San Francisco

Bakrushin, Y. (1947) 'Dance in Soviet Schools.' In: *The Art Education of Soviet Schoolchildren*. Moscow: Issue 1

Barghoorn, Frederick (1960). *Soviet Cultural Offensive. The Role of Cultural Diplomacy in Soviet Foreign Policy*. Princeton: Princeton University Press

Barker, Diana (1960) 'The Russian Heritage.' In: *Dancing Times*, Vol. 60, April 1970, pp. 358-359, 361

Baryshnikov, Mikhail (1976) 'Giselle.' In: *Reading Dance*, ed. R. Gottlieb. New York: Pantheon Books, 2008

Barnes, Clive (1961). 'Cinderella.' In: *Dance and Dancers*, January 1961 pp.18-19, 34

Barnes, Clive (1961) 'Prelude to the Kirov.' In: *Dance and Dancers*, June 1961

Barnes, Clive (1974) 'What Has the Bolshoi Done for Us Lately?' *The New York Times*, July 21st, 1974, page 104

Barnes, Clive, Kerensky, Oleg (1988) 'Another Bolshoi Ballet'. In: *Dance and Dancers*, June 1988

Beaumont, Cyril (1938). *Complete Book of Ballets*. London: Putnam

Beaumont, Cyril (1942). *Supplement to the Complete Book of Ballets*. London: C. W. Beaumont

Bellew, Hélène (1956). *Ballet in Moscow Today*. London; Thames and Hudson

Bernheimer, Martin (1979) 'Defection: A Pursuit of Art.' In: *The Washington Post*, September 22nd, 1979

Bernheimer, Martin (1987) 'Shostakovich Ballet; Bolshoi opens with 'The Golden Age'. In: *Los Angeles Times*, 13th August 1987

Bocharnikova, Yelena and Gabovich, Mikhail (195?) *Ballet School of the Bolshoi Theatre*. Moscow: Foreign Languages Publishing House

Bogdanov-Berezovsky, Valerian (1962) 'The History of "Petrushka".' In: the Sunday supplement of the newspaper *Izvestia* for January 14-20, 1962

Bonitenko, A.D. 'Ленинградский балет в годы Великой Отечественной войны' (Leningrad Ballet during the Great Patriotic War) https://spbarchives.ru/-/-leningradskii-balet-v-gody-velikoi-otecestvennoi-voiny-

Boriosova, Yevgenia (1995) 'The Ugly Side of Ballet.' St Petersburg Press. http://www.friends-partners.org/oldfriends/spbweb/lifestyl/127/uglyside.html

Borome, Joseph (1965). 'The Bolshoi Theatre and Opera.' In: *The Russian Review*, Vol.24, No.1 pp.52-64

Bourgeois, J. (1961) 'La Fleur de Pierre, un ballet contestable danse à la perfection', *Arts*, 31st May 1961

Bowl, John (1977). 'Constructivism and Russian Stage Design.' In: *Performing Arts Journal*, Vol.1, No.3 pp.62-84

Bradley, Lionel (1947) 'News from Abroad – Russia' In: *Ballet*, Vol.3, No.4, pp.42-43

Bremser, Martha ed. (1993) *International Dictionary of Ballet*. Farmington Hills: St. James Press

Brooks, Jeffrey (2019). *The Firebird and the Fox: Russian Culture under the Tsars and Bolsheviks*. Cambridge: Cambridge University Press

Brown, Ismene (2007). 'Dynasty: The Messerer Dynasty.' In: *Dance Now* Vol.16, No.4. pp.25-35

Brown, Ismene (2009). 'The Messerer Dynasty' In: *The Arts Desk*, September 9th 2009. https://theartsdesk.com/dance/messerer-dynasty

Buckle, Richard (1988) *George Balanchine – Ballet Master*. London: Hamish Hamilton

Buckle, Richard (1993) *Diaghilev*. London: Weidenfeld

Buxton, Jennifer (2013) 'Perestroika Pirouettes and Glasnost Glissés: The Kirov and the Bolshoi Ballet, 1977-1991.' University of North Carolina at Chapel Hill

Cashin, Kathryn (2005) 'Alexander Pushkin's Influence on the Development of Russian Ballet.' The Florida State University College of Arts and Sciences. https://diginole.lib.fsu.edu/islandora/object/fsu:182279/datastream/PDF/view

Caute, David (2005) *The Dancer Defects: The Struggle for Cultural Supremacy during the Cold War*. Oxford: Oxford University Press

Chao, Eveline (2017) 'The ballet that caused an international row.' https://www.bbc.com/culture/article/20170628-the-ballet-that-caused-an-international-row

Clarke, Mary (1956). 'The Bolshoi Ballet: 'The Four Ballets.' *Dancing Times*, Vol. 48, No. 554, pp.69-72

Clarke, Mary (1958). 'The Stanislavsky Ballet in Paris.' In: *The Ballet Annual* Vol.12. London: A. and C. Black

Clarke, Mary (1961). 'The Leningrad State Kirov Ballet: The Season Reviewed' *Dancing Times*, Vol.51, No.611, pp.662-665, 678

Clarke, Mary and Crisp, Clement (1973) *Ballet: An Illustrated History*. New York: Universe Books

Cohen, Selma Jeanne (1978) 'Yuri Slonimsky (1902-1978)' In: *Dance Chronicle*, Vol. 2, No. 2, pp. 148-156

Coton, A.V. (1960). 'Russian Journey.' In: *Dance and Dancers*, August 1960, pp.8-11

Coton, A.V. (1960). 'Return to Moscow.' In: *Dance and Dancers*, September 1960, pp.22-25

Craine, Debra and Mackrell, Judith (2000) *The Oxford Dictionary of Dance*. Oxford: Oxford University Press

Crisp, Clement (1970) 'Kirov Dancers in London.' In: *Dancing Times*, Vol. 60, September 1970, pp.634-635

Croce, Arlene (1982) *Going to the Dance*. New York: Alfred A. Knopf

Croce, Arlene (2000) *Writing in the Dark, Dancing in The New Yorker*. New York: Farrar, Straus and Giroux

Croft, Clare (2009). 'Ballet Nations: The New York City Ballet's 1962 US State Department-Sponsored Tour of the Soviet Union.' In: *Theatre Journal*, Vol. 61, No. 3, Theatre and State / Theatre and Law, pp. 421-442

Croft, Clare (2015). *Dancers as Diplomats – American Choreography in Cultural Exchange*. New York: OUP

Crofton, Kathleen (1961). 'The Leningrad State Kirov Ballet: The Leningrad Style' *Dancing Times*, Vol.51, No.611, pp.666-667

Cross, Jonathan (2016). 'Telling Tales: The Myths of Stravinsky.' https://calperformances.tumblr.com/post/151341966062/telling-tales-the-myths-of-stravinsky

Culp, Lydia (2018) 'Resisting Arrest: Soviet Ballet as Protest from 1955-1980.' https://cducomb.colgate.domains/globaltheater/europe/resisting-arrest-soviet-ballet-as-protest-from-1955-1980/

Danilova, Alexandra (1986). *Choura – The memoirs of Alexandra Danilova*. New York: Fromm International Publishing Corporation

Demidov, Alexander (1977). *The Russian Ballet – Past and Present*. London: A&C Black Ltd

Denby, Edwin (1959) "The Bolshoi at the Met." In: *The Hudson Review*, vol. 12, no. 4, 1959, pp. 582–586

Devereux, Tony (1987) 'Russia Then and Now.' In: *Dancing Times*, October 1987

Devereux, Tony (1988)' Legend of a Lost Choreographer – Feodor Lopukhov Part 1.' In: *Dancing Times*, January 1988, pp. 339-340

Devereux, Tony (1988) 'Legend of a Lost Choreographer – Feodor Lopukhov Part 2.' In: *Dancing Times*, February 1988, pp. 432-434

Devereux, Tony (1998) 'Ballet in Russia since 1917.' In: *Dancing Times*, February 1998, pp. 453- 457

Dikovskaya, Lily and Hill, Gerard (2008) *In Isadora's Steps: The Story of Isadora Duncan's school in Moscow, told by her favorite pupil*. London: Book Guild Ltd.

Dimitrievitch, Nina (1983) Review of: 'Vadim Gayevsky, Divertissement'. Moscow: Iskousstvo, 1981. In: *Dance Research*, Volume 1, Issue 2

Dolfus, Ariane (2017) *Béjart. Le démiurge (La Traversée des Mondes)*. Kindle Edition: Arthaud

Dolgopolov, Mikhail (1953) 'Olga Moiseyeva' *Dancing Times*, No. 515, August 1953, pp.665-666

Dunning, Jennifer (1988)' Kirov to Dance in New York After 25 Years.' In: *The New York Times*, September 1, 1988, Section C, Page 19

Ershova, Tatiana (2013). 'Балеты долго я терпел' (I endured ballets for a long time). https://lenta.ru/articles/2013/07/19/onegin/

Ezrahi, Christina (2007) 'The Thaw in Soviet Culture and the Return of Symphonic Dance' (paper presented at the International Symposium of Russian Ballet, The Harriman Institute, New York, NY, October 12-13, 2007), 1, http://www.harrimaninstitute.org/MEDIA/01228.pdf

Ezrahi, Christina. (2012). *Swans of the Kremlin: ballet and power in Soviet Russia*. Binsted: Dance Books Ltd

Ezrahi, Christina (2015) 'Experiments in Character Dance: From Leningrad's "Estrada" to the Kirov Ballet. In: Russian Movement Culture of the 1920s and 1930s.' Barnard College Dance Department and the Harriman Institute, Columbia University pp.59-62

Fay, Laurel ed. (2004) *Shostakovich and His World*. Princeton: Princeton University Press

Fein, Esther (1989) 'Makarova, Home Again, Dances at the Kirov.' In: *The New York Times*, February 3, 1989, Section A, Page 1

Fein, Esther (1989) The Kirov Enters the World of Glasnost.' In: *The New York Times*, July 2, 1989, Section 2, Page 1

Filanovskaya, Tatiana (2017) 'The State Petrograd Theater School in the mirror of the October Revolution of 1917.' *Bulletin of the Vaganova Academy*, 2017, Vol.3, pp.147-155. https://vaganov.elpub.ru/jour/article/view/432/424

Finch, Tamara (1989) 'Sulamith Messerer'. In: *Dancing Times*, November 1989

Fisher, Hugh, ed. (1953) Violetta Elvin – Dancers of Today. London: A & C Black

Fitzpatrick, Sheila (2002) *The Commissariat of Enlightenment. Soviet Organization of Education and the Arts under Lunacharsky, October 1917-1921*. Cambridge: Cambridge University Press

Fokine, Mikhail (1961). *Fokine: Memoirs of a Ballet Master*. London: Constable and Company Ltd

Fradkin, Herman (1956) *Raisa Struchkova*. Moscow: Foreign Languages Publishing House

Frangopulo, Marietta (1948) 'The Kirov Theatre of Opera and Ballet /

Leningrad Theatres during the Great Patriotic War.' Moscow-Leningrad: Isskustvo, 1948,

Galaïda, Anna (2019) 'Comment la passion du ballet a donné naissance à l'union unique de Béjart et des étoiles russes.' https://fr.rbth.com/art/82715-maurice-bejart-ballet-russe

Garafola, Lynn (2011) 'An Amazon of the Avant-Garde: Bronislava Nijinska in Revolutionary Russia'. In: *Dance Research*, February 2011, pp.109-166. Edinburgh University Press

Garafola, Lynn (2015) 'Soviet Bodies, Emigré Bodies: Bronislava Nijinska's Career in the 1920s and 1930s.' Barnard College Dance Department and the Harriman Institute, Columbia University pp.93-98

García-Márquez, Vicente (1995) *Massine: A Biography*. New York: Alfred A Knopf, Inc

Gasimov, Zaur (2017) *Historical Dictionary of Azerbaijan*. Rowman & Littlefield Publishers

Godzina, Natalia (1986)' Fanny Elssler's Russian Seasons.' *Sovietsky Balet*, Issue No.1, 1986

Gonçalves, Stéphanie (2012) 'Les tournées dansées pendant la guerre froide: danser pour la paix?' ILCEA [http://journals.openedition.org/ilcea/1402]

Gonçalves, Stéphanie (2015) 'Une guerre des étoiles – Les tournées de ballet dans la diplomatie culturelle de la Guerre froide (1945-1968)' bictel.ulb.ac.be:ULBetd-03192015-174303; ulbcat.ulb.ac.be:1094975

Gonçalves, Stéphanie (2016). 'Les Danseurs Soviétiques à Paris et à Londres pendant La Guerre Froide: Entre Travail, Tourisme Et Propagande Politique, 1954-1968.' « Les Cahiers Sirice » pp.69-82

Gonçalves, Stéphanie (2019). 'Dien Bien Phu, Soviet Ballet, and the Cold War: The First Paris Tour, May 1954.' *Dance Chronicle*, Volume 42, 2019 – Issue 1, pp. 53-77

Gonçalves, Stéphanie (2019)' Ballet, propaganda, and politics in the Cold War: the Bolshoi Ballet in London and the Sadler's Wells Ballet in Moscow, October–November 1956.' *Cold War History*, 19:2, pp.171-186, DOI: 10.1080/14682745.2018.1468436

Goodwin, Noel (1956) 'And, onstage, a Mammuth Murder', *The Daily Express*, 4th October 1956

Goodwin, Noel (1977) 'Dance beside the Danube.' In: *Dance and Dancers*, August 1977 pp.22-24

Gregory, John (1970) 'Natalia Dudinskaya.' In: *Dancing Times*, Vol. 61, October 1970, pp.20-21

Gregory, John and Ukladnikov, Alexander (1980) *Leningrad's Ballet - Mariinsky to Kirov*. London: Robson Books Ltd

Greskovic, Robert (1975) 'The Grigorovich Factor and the Bolshoi.' In: *Ballet Review*, Vol.5, No.2

Greskovic, Robert (2005) *Ballet 101: A Complete Guide to Learning and Loving the Ballet*. Wisconsin: Hal Leonard Corporation

Grey, Beryl (2017). *For the Love of Dance*. London: Oberon Books

Grigorovich, Yuri ed. (1981) Энциклопедия балета (*Ballet Encyclopaedia*) Moscow: Soviet Encyclopedia

Gunther Kodat, C. (2014) *Don't Act, Just Dance: The Metapolitics of Cold War Culture*. New Brunswick: Rutgers University Press

Hakobian, Levon (2016) *Music of the Soviet Era: 1917–1991*. Abingdon: Routledge

Hamm, K (2009) "The Friendship of Peoples": Soviet Ballet, Nationalities Policy, and The Artistic Media, 1953-1968.' https://core.ac.uk/download/pdf/4823617.pdf

Haskell, Arnold L. (1961). 'The Leningrad State Kirov Ballet: A Sorry Affair' *Dancing Times*, Vol.51, No.611, p. 676

Holter, Howard (1970) 'The Legacy of Lunacharsky and Artistic Freedom in the USSR.' *Slavic Review*, Vol. 29, No. 2 (Jun., 1970), pp. 262-282

Homans, Jennifer (2010) *Apollo's Angels – A History of Ballet*. New York: Random House

Hunt, Marilyn (1993) 'George Balanchine and the Russian Avant-Garde.' In: Näslund, E. (1993). Ed. *Teater Revolution – Det Ryska Avantgardet på Scen 1913-1930*, 1st ed. Stockholm: Centraltryckeriet I Borás, pp. 184-187

Illarionov, Boris (2008) три века петербургского балета (Three Centuries of the St. Petersburg Ballet). St Petersburg: Petropol

Ilyicheva, Marina (1988) 'The First One Hundred Years of Life of the St. Petersburg School.' *Sovietsky Balet*, Issue No.3, 1988

Jennings, Luke (1995) 'Nights at the Ballet: The Czar's Last Dance' In: *The New Yorker* 71, March 27th 1995)

Jordan, Olga (1947) 'Ballet and the Blockade.' In: *The Soviet Ballet*, pp.169-176 New York: Philosophical Library

Jordan, Olga (1948) From diaries / Leningrad Theatres during the Great Patriotic War. Moscow-Leningrad. Iskusstvo. 1948, pp. 505–506

Jowitt, Deborah (1988) *Time and the Dancing Image*. Berkeley and Los Angeles: University of California Press

Kant, Marion (2015) 'The Russians in Berlin, 1920-1945.' In: Russian Movement Culture of the 1920s and 1930s'. Barnard College Dance Department and the Harriman Institute, Columbia University pp.73-79

Karsavina, Tamara (1950) *Theatre Street*. London: Readers Union

Kasow, Joel (1978) 'American Ballet Theatre – A Chronology, 1959-1964.' In: *Dance Chronicle*, vol. 2, no. 4, pp. 279–326

Kavanagh, Julie (2007) *Rudolf Nureyev*. London: Penguin Books

Kavanagh, Julie (2001). 'The Alexander Technique.' In: *Talk*, October 2001

Kelly, Catriona (2014) *St Petersburg: Shadows of the Past*. Yale: Yale University

Press
Kendall, Elizabeth (1992) 'The Kirov.' In: *The New Yorker*, June 8th 1992
Kendall, Elizabeth (1999) 'A Doorway to Revolution: The Revolution in dance that was underway in 1900 mirrored the upheavals to come in this century.' *Dance Magazine*, January 1999, p.80
Kendall, Elizabeth (2013). *Balanchine and the Lost Muse*. Oxford: Oxford University Press
Khan, Albert (1962) *Days with Ulanova*, London: Collins, 1962
Khazieva, Diana (2017) 'Ballet "Joseph the Beautiful" by K. Goleizovsky' Bulletin of the Vaganova Academy, 2017, Vol.4, pp.60-66 https://vaganov.elpub.ru/jour/article/view/446/438
Khimicheva, Angelica (2019) 'Ballet School and Choreographic College' https://adresaspb.ru/category/theme/uchrezhdenie/baletnoe-uchilishche-i-khoreograficheskiy-tekhnikum
Kholfina, Serafima (1990) *Remembering the Masters of the Moscow Ballet*. http://www.bol-theatre.su
Kim, Angela (2018) 'Making of Nationalistic Dance: Agrippina Vaganova and Choi Seung-Hee.' https://core.ac.uk/download/pdf/215548101.pdf
Kirstein, Lincoln (1934). *Fokine*. London: British-Continental Press
Kirstein, Lincoln (1978) *Thirty Years – The New York City Ballet*. New York: Albert Knopf
Kisselgoff, Anna (1975) 'Aleksandr Lapauri Obituary' In: *The New York Times*, Aug 7th, 1975
Kisselgoff, Anna (1990) 'Ballet Theater welcomes back a pair of longtime Bolshoi stars.' In: *The The New York Times*, May 16th, 1990
Klirova, Ksenia (2017) 'The Ballet *Petrushka* on the Leningrad stage' *Bulletin of the Vaganova Academy*, 2017, Vol.4, pp.40-46. https://vaganov.elpub.ru/jour/article/view/444/436
Koegler, Horst (1982) *Dictionary of Ballet*. London: Oxford University Press
Koegler, Horst (1990) Review of: 'Soviet Choreographers in the 1920s.' In: *Dance and Dancers*, December 1990
Koegler, Horst (1996)' Socialist Realism in East Germany.' In: *Dance Now*, Vol.5, No.1
Krasovskaya, Vera (1961). 'The Leningrad State Kirov Ballet: Our Beauty in Leningrad' *Dancing Times*, Vol.51, No.611, pp.668-670
Krasovskaya, Vera. (1976) 'The Middle of the Century.' In: Советский балетный театр: 1917-1967 (*Soviet Ballet Theater: 1917-1967*). Isskustvo Moscow
Krasovskaya, Vera (2005) 'Vaganova: A Dance Journey from Petersburg to Leningrad'. Gainsville: University Press of Florida
Kriegsman, Alan (1989)' Dancing Diplomacy.' In: *The Washington Post*, March 8th 1989

Krylovskaya, Isabella (2018) 'Dancers of the Leningrad ballet in the Far East in the 1920s-1930s' *Bulletin of the Vaganova Academy*, 2018, Vol.5, 54-77. https://vaganov.elpub.ru/jour/issue/view/31/showToc

Kun, Zsuzsa (1966) 'The Bolshoi's Rite of Spring.' In: *Dancing Times*, Vol. 61, February 1966, pp. 232-233

Lavrenyuk, B (1987). *The Soviet Ballet*. Moscow: Novosti Press Agency

Lawson, Joan (1943).' A Short History of Soviet Ballet: 1917-1943.' In: *Dance Index*. Vol II, Nos 6, 7 June-July 1943 pp. 77-93. https://eakinspress.com/danceindex/issueDetail.cfm?issue=danceindexunse_13

Lawson, Joan (1939) 'The Heart of the Hills' In: *Dancing Times*, No. 346, July 1939, pp. 389-392

Lawson, Joan (1968) 'New Developments in Russia.' In: *Dancing Times*, Vol. 68, July 1968, pp.524-527

LeBere, Kathryn (2019) 'Red Swans: The Transformation of Ballet after the Russian Cultural Revolution (1924-1937).' BA Thesis – University of Victoria

Ledeneva, Alena, et al., editors. "The Unlocking Power of Non-Conformity: Cultural Resistance vs Political Opposition." Global Encyclopaedia of Informality, Volume 1: Towards Understanding of Social and Cultural Complexity, UCL Press, London, 2018, pp. 336–384. JSTOR, www.jstor.org/stable/j.ctt20krxh9.14. Accessed 2 Dec. 2020

Legat, Nikolai (1932). *The Story of the Russian School*. London: British-Continental Press

Leonova, Maria (2008). 'Роль московской балетной школы в творческой жизни Большого театра: 1945-1970' (The role of the Moscow Ballet School in the creative life of the Bolshoi Theatre (1945-1970)

Lincoln, Bruce (2001) *Sunlight at Midnight: St. Petersburg and the Rise of Modern Russia*. Basic Books

Linkova, Lyudmila (1985) 'Arthur Saint-Leon.' *Sovietsky Ballet*, Issue No.1, 1985

Lobenthal, Joel and Whitaker, Lisa (2021) *Red Star White Nights: The Life and Death of Yuri Soloviev*. New York: Ballet Review Books

Lobenthal, Joel with Whitaker, L. (2010) 'Tatiana Legat on Yuri Soloviev.' In: *Ballet Review*, Fall 2010 pp.55-67

Lobenthal, Joel (2016). *Alla Osipenko. Beauty and Resistance in Ballet*. Oxford: OUP

Lopukhov, Fyodor (2002). 'Writings on Ballet and Music (Studies in Dance History).' Wisconsin: The University of Wisconsin Press

Macaulay, Alastair (1986) 'Bolshoi Balletomania.' In: *Dancing Times*, October 1986

Mackenzie, John (1995) *Orientalism – History, Theory and the Arts*. Manchester; Manchester University Press

Makarova, Olga (2017) 'Shostakovich's "Golden Age". Chronicle of the education of young choreographers of the Soviet ballet.' *Bulletin of the Vaganova Academy*, 2017, Vol.2, pp.161-164. https://vaganov.elpub.ru/jour/article/view/406

Makaryk, Irene and Tkacz, Virlana (2010). *Modernism in Kyiv: Jubilant Experimentation.* Toronto: University of Toronto Press

Manchester, P W and Morley, Iris (1949) *The Rose and the Star.* London; Victor Gollancz Ltd

Marcy, Rachel (2014) 'Dancers and Diplomats: New York City Ballet in Moscow, October 1962.' In: *The Appendix*, Futures of the Past, Vol. 2, No. 3

Massine, Leonid (1968). *My Life in Ballet.* London: MacMillan

McDaniel, Cadra (2015) *American-Soviet Cultural Diplomacy: the Bolshoi Ballet's American Première.* Lanham: Lexington Books

McMahon, D.' 'Corridor to the Muses' Myth and Realism in Leningrad's Ballet.' *Ballet Review*, 12:1 Spring 1984-Winter 1985

Meinertz, Alexander (2007). *Vera Volkova – a biography.* Alton: Dance Books Ltd

Meisner, Nadine (1988). 'Questions of Style'. *Dance and Dancers*, January 1988 pp.19-20

Meisner, Nadine (2019). *Marius Petipa.* Oxford: Oxford University Press

Melovatskaya, Anna (2012) 'The Ballet "Geologists" staged by N. Kasatkina And V. Vasilyov' https://cyberleninka.ru/article/n/balet-geologi-v-postanovke-n-kasatkinoy-i-v-vasilyova

Melovatskaya, Anna (2016) 'The Rite of Spring' (1965) staged by choreographers N. D. Kasatkina and V. Yu. Vasilyov: the originality of the authors' solution'. https://cyberleninka.ru/article/n/spektakl-vesna-svyaschennaya-1965-v-postanovke-horeografov-n-d-kasatkinoy-i-v-yu-vasilyova-svoeobrazie-avtorskogo-resheniya

Messerer, Asaf (1979) Танец. Мысль. Время (Dance. Think. Time)

Messerer, Asaf (2007) *Classes in Classical Ballet.* Limelight

Messerer, Azary (1989) 'Maya Plisetskaya: Childhood, Youth and First Triumphs, 1925-59' In: *Dance Chronicle*, Vol.12, No.1 (1989), pp. 1-47

Messerer, Azary (2005) 'Asaf and Sulamith Messerer's 1933 European Tour' In: *Dance Chronicle*, Vol. 28, No. 2, pp. 201-217

Mikhailov, L. and Volkov, N (1946) 'Ballet in the USSR' In: *USSR Information Bulletin*, Volume 6., pp. 15-17

Mikhailova, E.A. (2019) 'Performance of Stravinsky's music in the Soviet Union before the arrival of the Maestro.' http://expositions.nlr.ru/ex_manus/stravinsky/before.php

Mikhailova, E.A. (2019) 'I.F.Stravinsky's arrival in the USSR.' http://expositions.nlr.ru/ex_manus/stravinsky/arrival.php

Misler, Nicoletta (1993) 'Designing Gestures in the Laboratory of Dance.'

In: Baer, N, ed. Russian *Avant-Garde Stage Design*, 1st ed. New York and London: Thames and Hudson; San Francisco: The Fine Arts Museums of San Francisco, In: Näslund, E. (1993). Ed. *Teater Revolution – Det Ryska Avantgardet på Scen* 1913-1930, 1st ed. Stockholm: Centraltryckeriet I Borás, pp. 165-173

Misler, Nicoletta (2015) 'Feeling, Sentiment, and the Soviet Body: From Isadora Duncan to the Russian Avant-Garde.' In: 'Russian Movement Culture of the 1920s and 1930s'. Barnard College Dance Department and the Harriman Institute, Columbia University, pp.15-32

Moore, Lillian (1961). 'The Kirov Ballet in New York'. In: *Dancing Times*, Vol. 52, November 1961, pp. 84-85, 77

Morley, Iris (1945). *Soviet Ballet*. London; Collins

Morley, Iris (1947) '*Romeo and Juliet* in Moscow' In: *Ballet*, Vol.4, No.2, pp.19-24

Morrison, Simon (2004). 'Shostakovich as Industrial Saboteur: Observations on The Bolt.' In: *Shostakovich and His World*, Fay, L. Princeton: Princeton University Press

Morrison, Simon (2009). *The People's Artist. Prokofiev's Soviet Years*. Oxford: Oxford University Press

Morrison, Simon (2015) 'The Bolshoi and the Revolution.' In: Garafola. Lynn, ed. Russian Movement Culture of the 1920s and 1930s. New York: Harriman Institute, Columbia University, pp.15-32

Morrison, Simon (2016). *Bolshoi Confidential*. London; 4th Estate

Morrison, Simon (2017). 'Dance of Steel.' In: *The Paris Review*, February 13, 2017. https://www.theparisreview.org/blog/2017/02/13/dance-of-steel/

Moynahan, B (2013). *Leningrad: Siege and Symphony*. London: Quercus Editions Ltd

Nagy, Peter, Rouyer, Phillippe, Rubin, Don (2001) *World Encyclopedia of Contemporary Theatre: Volume 1: Europe*. London: Routledge

Näslund, Erik (1993) *Teatr i Revolution. Det ryska avantgardet på scen 1913-1930*. Stockholm: Dansmusei Skrifter

Nicholas, Larraine. 'Fellow Travellers: Dance and British Cold War Politics in the Early 1950s.' In: Dance Research: *The Journal of the Society for Dance Research*, Vol. 19, No. 2 (Winter 2001) pp. 83-105

Norton, Leslie (2004). *Leonide Massine and the 20th Century Ballet*. London: McFarland & Company

Ogryzko, V (2020) 'Isolation in art is a dead end.' *Artists and Power*, No. 2020/19, 05/21/2020. https://litrossia.ru

Percival, John (1962) 'A Check List of Soviet Ballet, 1959-60.' In: *The Ballet Annual* 1962 pp. 122-133

Percival, John (1983). *Theatre in my blood – A biography of John Cranko*. New

York: Franklin Watts
Percival, John (1990) 'Prodigal Son.' In: *Dance and Dancers*, January 1990 p.5
Percival, John (1990) 'No Strings.' In: *Dance and Dancers*, April,1990 p.8
Percival, John (1990) 'Seeing red.' In: *Dance and Dancers*, May 1990 p.5
Percival, John (1990) 'Mukhamedov joins the Royal Ballet.' In: *Dance and Dancers*, July 1990 p.5
Percival, John (1990) 'Travelling Men.' In: *Dance and Dancers*, August 1990, pp.11-12
Percival, John (1991) 'No messing about.' In: *Dance and Dancers*, April 1991 p.5
Percival, John (2005) 'A Symphonic Variation.' In: *Dance Now*, Vol.14, No.1, Spring 2005 pp. 45-51
Peters, K (1954) 'Russian Dancers in Berlin.' In: *Dancing Times*, July 1954, p.607
Petrov, Ivan (2017) 'Dancing here – In the centenary year of the October Revolution – six stories about how the revolution took place in Soviet opera and ballet' https://vtbrussia.ru/culture/gabt/zdes-tantsuyut/#3
Plisetskaya, Maya (2001) *I, Maya Plisetskaya*. Yale: Yale University Press
Poarskaâ, Milica, Volodina, Tat'âna (1990) *L'Art des Ballets Russes à Paris: Projets de Décors et de Costumes (1908-1929)* Paris: Gallimard
Pollaud-Dulian, Emmanuel. 'Chas Laborde à Moscou (1935) Un témoignage oublié.' *Revue des Études Slaves*, vol. 83, no. 1, 2012, pp. 251–267
Poudru, Florence (2007). *Serge Lifar. La danse pour la patrie*. Paris: Hermann Danse
Poudru, Florence (2010). 'Les tournées du Ballet de l'Opéra de Paris au temps de Lifar (1930-1958).' In: Le repertoire de l'Opéra de Paris (1671-2009) ed. Michel Noiray and Solveig Serre. Paris
Pouncy, Carolyn (2005) 'Stumbling toward Socialist Realism: Ballet in Leningrad 1927-1937.' In: *Russian History*, Vol.32, No.2 pp.171-193; Brill
Press, Stephen (2006) *Prokofiev's Ballets for Diaghilev*. London: Routledge
Prevots, Naima (1998) *Dance for Export: Cultural Diplomacy and the Cold War*. Middletown, Connecticut: Wesleyan University Press
Priest, Douglas (2016) *The Bolshoi meets Bolshevism: Moving Bodies and Body Politics, 1917-1934*. Michigan State University
Pudelek, Janina (1990)' 'Swan Lake' in Warsaw 1900'. In: *Dance Chronicle*, Vol 13, No.3 (1990-1991) pp.359-367
Pudelek, Janina (1992). 'Fokine in Warsaw 1908-1914.' In: *Dance Chronicle* Vol.15, No.1 (1992) pp.59-71
Rappaport, Helen (2016) *Caught in the Revolution: Petrograd, 1917*. London: Hutchinson

Ratanova, Maria (2010) 'The Choreographic Avant-Garde in Kyiv, 1916-1921.' In: Modernism in Kyiv: Jubilant Experimentation, Toronto: University of Toronto Press, pp. 311-321

Rene (Roslavleva), Natalia (1960). 'Lavrovsky's 'Paganini' may start a new trend in Soviet Ballet.' In: *Dance and Dancers*, October 1960, pp.7-9

Rene (Roslavleva), Natalia (1961). 'New Choreographer in Leningrad.' In: *Dance and Dancers*, March 1961, pp.14-15, 34

Reynolds, Nancy (1989) 'The Kirov Claims Its Balanchine Legacy.' In: *The New York Times*, March 15 1989

Reynolds, Nancy (1989) 'Setting Balanchine in Leningrad.' *Ballet Review* 71, no. 2 (1989): 38-60

Reynolds, Nancy and McCormick, Malcolm (2003). *No Fixed Points: Dance in the Twentieth Century*. New Haven and London: Yale University Press

Richmond, Yale (2003) *Cultural Exchange and the Cold War: Raising the Iron Curtain*. Penn State University Press, 2003

Roca, Octavio (2010) *Cuban Ballet*. Layton, Utah, Gibbs-Smith

Rosenberg, Victor (2015) *Soviet-American Relations, 1953-1960: Diplomacy and Cultural Exchange During the Eisenhower Presidency*. Jefferson: McFarland

Roslavleva, Natalia (1960). 'Nadia Nerina in Russia.' *Dancing Times*, Vol.51, October 1960, pp.234

Roslavleva, Natalia (1960). 'Soviet Reactions to the American Ballet Theatre.' In: *Dancing Times*, Vol.51, October 1960, pp.296-298

Roslavleva, Natalia (1961). 'The Leningrad State Kirov Ballet.' In: *Dancing Times*, Vol.51, June 1961, pp.534-537, 543

Roslavleva, Natalia (1962). 'A New Petrushka – Rebirth of the ballet in Russia.' In: *Dancing Times*, Vol.52, June 1962, pp.553-557

Roslavleva, Natalia (1962). 'A Rewarding Experience: The Royal Ballet in Moscow.' In: *Dancing Times*, Vol.51, September 1961, pp.734-737

Roslavleva, Natalia (1962). 'The Royal Ballet in the USSR.' In: *The Ballet Annual* 1962 pp. 38-46, 145-146

Roslavleva, Natalia (1964). 'The Legacy of Fokine.' In: *Dancing Times*, Vol. 54, October 1964, pp.16-17

Roslavleva, Natalia (1966). *Era of the Russian Ballet*. London: Victor Gollancz

Roslavleva, Natalia (1969). 'The Bolshoi's Spartacus.' In: *Dancing Times*, Vol. 59, June 1969, pp.462-465, 481

Roslavleva, Natalia (1970). 'The Grigorovich Swan Lake.' In: *Dancing Times*, Vol.60, April 1960, pp.352-353, 360

Roslavleva, Natalia (1971) "Creation of the World' in Leningrad.' In: *Dancing Times*, Vol. 62, December 1971, pp. 134-135

Roslavleva, Natalia (1972) 'Two Hamlets in Russia.' In: *Dancing Times*, Vol. 62, July 1972, pp. 528-530

Roslavleva, Natalia (1972) 'Plisetskaya as Anna Karenina.' In: *Dancing Times*, Vol. 63, November 1972, pp. 76-78

Roslavleva, Natalia (1975) "Ivan" through Russian Eyes.' In: *Dancing Times*, Vol. 65, July 1975, p. 534

Ross, Alex (2007) *The Rest is Noise*. London: Fourth Estate

Ross, Janice (2015) *Like a Bomb Going Off*. New Haven and London; Yale University Press

Ross, Janice (2015) 'Aestheticizing Sport: Leonid Yakobson's Muscular Choreography and "The Golden Age".' In: 'Russian Movement Culture of the 1920s and 1930s'. Barnard College Dance Department and the Harriman Institute, Columbia University, pp.47-55

Ross, Janice (2017) 'Outcast as Patriot: Leonid Yakobson's *Spartacus* and the Bolshoi's 1962 American Tour.' In: 'Dancing the Cold War – An International Symposium'. Barnard College Dance Department and the Harriman Institute, Columbia University pp.47-44

Rozanova, Olga (2016) 'Drambalet – a view from the XXI century'. *Bulletin of the Vaganova Academy*. 2016, Vol.1, pp.79-87. https://vaganov.elpub.ru/jour/article/view/490/482

Šabasevičius, Helmutas 1945–1967: 'The First Post-War Decades.' Online: http://www.mmcentras.lt/cultural-history/cultural-history/dance/19451967-the-first-post-war-decades/19451967-the-first-post-war-decades/77208

Sadie, Stanley and Tyrrell, John (Editors) (2001) *The New Grove Dictionary of Music and Musicians*. USA: Oxford University Press

Sakhnovskaya, N (2004) 'From siege-time diaries / Remembering Again.' In: Anthology. Saint Petersburg. Vaganova Academy of Russian Ballet, p.34. https://www.mariinsky.ru/en/about/ww2/

Sapanzha, O.S. (2020). 'The first tour of the Soviet ballet of the Bolshoi Theater of the USSR in Japan (1957): Memories by Olga Lepeshinskaya.' *Bulletin of Vaganova Ballet Academy*. 2020, Vol. 2, pp.62-73. https://vaganov.elpub.ru/jour/article/view/1359?locale=en_US#

Sargsyan N.G. (2017). 'On the staging of the legend of "Ara the Beautiful and Shamiram" by choreographer Ashot Asaturyan.' In: *Fundamental Armenology*, No.1 (5) 2017. http://www.fundamentalarmenology.am/datas/pdfs/455.pdf

Schaikevitch, André (1954) *Olga Spessivtzeva – Magicienne Envoutée*. Paris: Librairie Les Lettres

Scheijen, Sjeng (2009). *Diaghilev : A Life*. London : Profile Books

Schepeleva, Elizaveta (2019) 'Akim Volynsky on the verge of establishing The School of Russian Ballet.' http://www.russianballet.ru/dissertacii/kafedra_06_19_1.pdf

Scheuer, L.F. (1933) 'Messerer in Paris.' *Dancing Times*, May 1933, p.103

Scheuer, L.F. (1936) 'Semonova in 'Giselle'.' *Dancing Times*, February 1936, p.637

Scholl, Tim. 'Dancing Ballet in Baku.' https://pdfs.semanticscholar.org/4b16/66827973fd471fb17c56efff06166171b60d.pdf

Scholl, Tim (1994) *From Petipa to Balanchine: Classical Revival and the Modernisation of Ballet*. London: Routledge

Scholl, Tim (2015) 'The Bolshoi and the Revolution'. In: Russian Movement Culture of the 1920s and 1930s'.' Barnard College Dance Department and the Harriman Institute, Columbia University pp.56-58

Scholl, Tim (2015) 'From Moscow and Back: Creating and Assessing the "National" Ballets of Caucasia in the 1930s.' In: Russian Movement Culture of the 1920s and 1930s'. Barnard College Dance Department and the Harriman Institute, Columbia University pp.56-58

Scholl, Tim (2017) 'Traces: What Cultural Exchange Left Behind.' In: 'Dancing the Cold War – An International Symposium'. Barnard College Dance Department and the Harriman Institute, Columbia University pp.45-46

Schwall, Elizabeth (2016) *Dancing with the Revolution: Cuban Dance, State, and Nation, 1930-1990*. Columbia University

Schwall, Elizabeth (2017). 'Azari Plisetsky and the Spectacle of Cuban-Soviet Ballet Exchanges, 1963-1973.' In : 'Dancing the Cold War – An International Symposium'. Barnard College Dance Department and the Harriman Institute, Columbia University, pp.72-77

Searcy, Anne (2016). 'Soviet and American Cold War Ballet Exchange, 1959–1962.' http://nrs.harvard.edu/urn-3:HUL.InstRepos:

Searcy, Anne (2016) "The Recomposition of Aram Khachaturian's Spartacus at the Bolshoi Theater, 1958–1968." *The Journal of Musicology*, vol. 33, no. 3, 2016, pp. 362–400.

Searcy, Anna (2020). *Ballet in the Cold War: A Soviet-American Exchange*. New York : OUP

Scherr, Apollinaire (2015) 'The Soviets' Cold War Choreographer.' *The Atlantic*: June 2015

Senelick, Laurence and Ostrovsky, Sergey (2014) *The Soviet Theater: A Documentary History*. Yale : Yale University Press

Serdyuk, Natalia (2016) 'Ballet of the Mikhailovsky Theatre: from the organisation of the troupe to the first performance'. *Bulletin of the St. Petersburg State Institute of Culture*. https://cyberleninka.ru/article/n/balet-mihaylovskogo-teatra-ot-organizatsii-truppy-k-pervomu-spektaklyu

Serdyuk, Natalia (2018) 'The first ballet dancers of the Maly Opera House (1918-1935)'. *Bulletin of the Vaganova Academy*, 2018, Vol.4, pp.37-48. https://vaganov.elpub.ru/jour/issue/view/30/showToc

Serdyuk, Natalia (2018) 'Ballet of the Leningrad State Academic Maly Opera House in evacuation (1941-1944)' *Bulletin of the Vaganova Academy*, 2018, Vol.1, pp.4-19. https://vaganov.elpub.ru/jour/article/view/743/723

Shanker, Thom (1987) 'Kirov Regenerated.' In: *Chicago Tribune*, May 24th 1987

Shay, Anthony (2019). ' The Igor Moiseyev Dance Company: Dancing Diplomats.' Intellect

Siegel, Marcia (1978) 'Panov: The Making of a Myth.' In: *The Hudson Review*, Vol. 31, No. 4, pp. 644-648

Siemens, R (1987) 'Bolshoi Here and There.' In: *Dancing Times*, October 1987

Silverman, Jill (1990) 'Politics Pervade the Kirov's New 'Petrouchka'.' In: *The New York Times*, July 15th 1990

Sivashinsky, Terry, Panov, Valery (2013). *Scene from the Wings*. Xlibris Corporation

Slonimsky, Yuri and others (1947). *The Soviet Ballet*. New York: Philosophical Library

Slonimsky, Yuri (1950) *Soviet Ballet*. Leningrad: Isskusstvo

Slonimsky, Yuri (1956) *The Bolshoi Theatre Ballet*. Moscow: Foreign Languages Publishing House

Slonimsky, Yuri (1957) 'In Pursuit of the New.' In: *The Ballet Annual*, Vol. 12. London: A. and C. Black

Slonimsky, Yuri (1958) A Letter on Soviet Ballet. In: *The Ballet Annual*, Vol. 13. London A. and C. Black

Slonimsky, Yuri (1972-3) 'Balanchine: The Early Years'. In: *Ballet Review*, Volume 5, Number 3

Smakov, Gennadi (1984) *The Great Russian Dancers*. New York: Alfred A Knopf

Smorodinskaya, Tatiana, Goscilo, Helena, Evans-Romaine, Karen (2006) *Encyclopedia of Contemporary Russian Culture*. London: Routledge

Snodgrass, Mary (2015) *The Encyclopedia of World Ballet*. Lanham: Rowman and Littlefield

Sokolov-Kaminsky, Arkady (2018) 'The Choreographer Overcomes the Scenarist: Ballet *Shore of Hope*'. Bulletin of the Vaganova Academy, 2018, Vol.6, pp.32-40

Sollertinsky, Ivan (2015)' 'Bolt' and the problem of Soviet ballet, 1931.' https://www.grad-london.com/blog/bolt-and-the-problem-of-soviet-ballet-i-sollertinsky-1931/

Souritz, Elizabeth (1985). 'Fyodor Lopukhov: A Soviet Choreographer in the 1920s.' In: *Dance Research Journal*, Vol. 17/18, Vol. 17, no. 2 – Vol. 18, no. 1 (Autumn, 1985 – Spring, 1986), pp. 3-20

Souritz, Elizabeth (1988) 'Soviet Choreographers in the 1920s: Kasian Yaroslavich Goleizovsky.' *Dance Research Journal*, vol. 20, no. 2, 1988, pp. 9–22

Souritz, Elizabeth (1990). *Soviet Choreographers in the 1920s*. Duke University Press
Souritz, Elizabeth (1991). 'Constructivism and Dance' In: Baer, N, ed. *Russian Avant-Garde Stage Design*, 1st ed. New York and London: Thames and Hudson; San Francisco: The Fine Arts Museums of San Francisco
Souritz, Elizabeth (1994) 'Moscow's Island of Dance, 1934-1941.' In: *Dance Chronicle*, vol. 17, no. 1, 1994, pp. 1–92
Souritz, Elizabeth (1995) 'Isadora Duncan's Influence on Dance in Russia.' In: *Dance Chronicle*, vol. 18, no. 2, 1995, pp. 281–291
Souritz, Elizabeth (1998) 'The Achievement of Vera Krasovskaya.' *Dance Chronicle*, vol. 21, no. 1, 1998, pp. 139–148
Spalva, Rita (2013). 'Innovation in Choreography of Leonid Yakobson.' *Journal of Literature and Art Studies*, October 2013, Vol. 3, No. 10, pp. 657-662
Starikova, Ludmilla (1988) 'From the Biography of the First Russian Ballet Company.' *Sovietsky Balet*, issue No.5, 1988
Stites, Richard ed. (1995) 'Culture and Entertainment in Wartime Russia', Bloomington: Indiana University Press
Svetlov, V (1934). in: *Archives Internationales de la Danse*, No.1 1934. Paris
Swift, Mary Grace (1968). *The Art of the Dance in the USSR*. University of Notre Dame Press
Swift, Mary Grace (1968) 'How Russian Ballet Survived.' In: *Dancing Times*, Vol.59, November 1968, pp.74-78
Taper, Bernard (1984). *Balanchine – A biography*. New York: Times Books
Taylor, Jeffrey (1994) *Irek Mukhamedov: The Authorized Biography*. London: Fourth Estate
Thévenon, Patrick (1961) 'Le ballet de Leningrad est le plus bourgeois du monde', *Paris Presse L'intransigeant*, 18th May 1961.
Thorpe, Richard (1992) 'The Academic Theaters and the Fate of Soviet Artistic Pluralism, 1919-1928'. *Slavic Review*, Vol. 51, No. 3 (Autumn, 1992), pp. 389-410
Tobias, Tobi (1982) 'Ballet à la Russe.' In: *The New Yorker*, 28th June 1982 pp.44-45
Tobias, Tobi (1989) 'Worlds Apart.' In: *The New York Magazine*, August 7th 1989
Twysden, Aileen (1945) *Alexandra Danilova*. London: C W Beaumont
Tyerman, Edward (2015) 'The Red Poppy and 1927: Translating Contemporary China into Soviet Ballet.' In: 'Russian Movement Culture of the 1920s and 1930s'. Barnard College Dance Department and the Harriman Institute, Columbia University p.46
Ulanova, Galina (1959) *Galina Ulanova: The Making of a Ballerina*. Moscow: Foreign Languages Publishing House
Vaganova, Agrippina (1965) *Basic Principles of Classical Ballet: Russian Ballet*

Technique. London: Adam and Charles Black

Van Praagh, Peggy and Brinson, Peter (1963) *The Choreographic Art.* London: Adam and Charles Black

Vaughan, David (1975). 'Yuri the Terrible, George the Great'. *Dancing Times,* Vol.65, No. 778, pp. 532-533

Vecheslova, Tatiana (1964) *I am a Ballerina.* Moscow-Leningrad, Isskustvo, 1964, pp.145-6

Vlasova, Ekaterina (2013) 'Stalinist leadership of the Bolshoi Theater' http://opentextnn.ru/music/epoch%20/XX/?id=4768

Volkov, Nikolai (1946) 'Raymonda revived in Moscow' *Dancing Times,* No. 424, January 1946, pp.171-172

Volkov, Nikolai (1948) 'Soviet Choreography.' In: *USSR Information Bulletin,* Vol. 8., p.265

Volkov, Nikolai (1951) 'The Bolshoi's Famed Ballet.' In: *USSR Information Bulletin,* Vol. 11, No.1

Volkov, Solomon (1997). *St. Petersburg: A Cultural History.* New York: Free Press

Volkov, Solomon (2018) 'Saving the Bolshoi Theater: Lenin and Stalin.' https://regnum.ru/news/2394387.html

Volynsky, Akim (2008) *Ballet's Magic Kingdom.* New Haven and London: Yale University Press

Ward, Alex (1981) '20 Years after Nureyev's Leap to Freedom.' *The New York Times,* June 28, 1981, Section 2, Page 1

Williams, Peter (1961). 'Prelude to the Kirov.' In: *Dance and Dancers,* June 1961 pp.6-8

Willis, Margaret (1982)' Bolshoi Ballet; Why there's discontent.' *Christian Science Monitor,* February 10, 1982

Willis, Margaret (1988) 'Two Bolshoi veterans shine in Paris. Age and a company rift limit visibility at home.' *Christian Science Monitor,* March 2, 1988

Willis, Margaret (1990) 'Moscow Magazine Conference.' In: *Dancing Times,* February 1990

Willis, Margaret (1991) 'Russian Roulette.' In: *Dance and Dancers,* September 1991, pp.8-9

Willis, Margaret (2008) 'Assoluta: Marina Semyonova at 100.' In: Vol.17 No.4 *Dance Now*

Willis, Margaret (2008) 'Spartak.' In: Vol 17, No.1 *Dance Now*

Windreich, Leland (1986) 'The Kirov of Expo.' In: *Dancing Times,* July 1986

Wood, Daniel (1981) 'A friend's close-up of Baryshnikov.' In: *Christian Science Monitor,* June 17 1981.

Yaschenkov, Pavel (2018) 'Ballet aristocrat Kasatkina: "They demanded we remove thirty-degree sex"' https://www.mk.ru/culture/2018/12/21/

baletnaya-aristokratka-kasatkina-ot-nas-trebovali-ubrat-tridcatigradusnyy-seks.html

Zachary, R (1971) 'The ABT's Other Russian.' In: *New York Magazine*, 28th June 1971, p.48

Zamostyanov A. (2011) 'Mirandolina for war veterans.' In: National Security Journal, October 2011. https://web.archive.org/web/20120119075505/http://psj.ru/saver_national/detail.php%3FID%3D68943&usg=ALkJrhikFohQ8YxukkDssd1R23Al98tF8A

Unattributed

(2002) 'Nikolai Ivanovich Tarasov.' Online: http://www.russianballet.ru/line/2002/line0210.htm

(2015) 'How the "Wizard of Dance" took New York by Storm.' 6th March 2015 Online: https://www.georgianjournal.ge/culture/29867-how-the-wizard-of-dance-took-new-york-by-storm.html

(2015) '100-летие хореографа Константина Боярского' (100th anniversary of choreographer Konstantin Boyarsky). Online: https://mikhailovsky.ru/press/news/centenary_of_konstantin_boyarskys_birth/

(2015) 'The triumph of the muses during the war.' https://www.bolshoi.ru/about/press/articles/exhibition/3295/

(2017) 'MALEGOT: Thoughts on the Revolution.' https://mikhailovsky.ru/en/press/news/malegot_thoughts_on_the_revolution/

(2018) 'Soviet ballet: dancing the heritage of humanism.' https://thecommunists.org/2018/06/27/news/culture/soviet-ballet-dancing-the-heritage-of-humanism/

'Opera and Ballet Theater during the Great Patriotic War (Samara).' http://www.opera-samara.net/novosti/art3089.html

'Activities of the Bolshoi Theater during the Great Patriotic War.' http://moscowars.mozello.ru/1941-1945/ku/bolshoj-teatr-v-vov/

'Kirov theater in evacuation.' http://expositions.nlr.ru/proriv_blokada/dudinskaya4.php

Online Sources

Soviet Ballet Encyclopaedia 1981: https://ballet-enc.ru/
Russian Ballet Encyclopaedia 1997: http://www.pro-ballet.ru
https://www.belcanto.ru/genre_balet.html
https://www.kino-teatr.ru
https://russiainphoto.ru
http://gallery-mt.narod.ru/pages/balet_v.html&usg=ALkJrhib6pEikymr82yiPyrkpnkk3Tcy8Q

British Pathé newsreel footage: https://www.britishpathe.com/workspaces/df699ffd537d4e0c74710ad015dfd64d/1w3iYAQX

Index

Abirov, Dauren 186
Abrahams, Peter 151
Abramova, Anastasia 75, 77, 89
ABT, *see* American Ballet Theatre
Abyzova, Larisa 132
Adam, Adolphe 94
Adashevski, Valentin 192
Adyrkhaeva, Svetlana 208
Adzhamov, Vladimir 244
Aftonbladet 81
Aitmatov, Chinghiz 204, 243-244
Ak, *see* GATOB
Akhmatova, Anna 122
Akimov, Boris 208, 210, 226, 264, 267
Aleksidze, Georgy 193, 197, 222-223
Alexander Nevsky (Prokofiev) 225
Aliyev, Eldar 245
All-Union Committee for Affairs of the Arts in the Council of People's Commissars 96, 100
All-Union Choreographic Conference 146
Alma-Ata 187, 229
Almaszade, Qamar 192-193
Alonso, Alberto 205
Alonso, Alicia 148, 177, 200, 205, 211
American Ballet Theatre 94, 163, 166, 171-172, 176, 214, 216, 229-232, 248, 260-261
Amicis, Edmondo de 196
Ananiashvili, Nina 231, 247-248, 253, 262
And Quiet Flows the Don (Shokolov) 250
And the Day lasts longer than a Century (Aitmatov) 243-244
Andersen, Hans Christian 61
Andreyanova, Elena 8
Andreyev, Alexey 132
Anisimova, Nina 100, 106, 111, 183
Anna Karenina (Tolstoy) 221
Anna, Tsarina 4
Arbuzov, Alexey 227
Arends, Andrey 88, 213
Art Theatre Ballet 72-73 *see also* Moscow Art Ballet, Stanislavsky Ballet
Artiushkin, Vitaly 262
Asafiev, Boris 30, 61, 89, 91, 96, 99-101, 120
Asaturyan, Ashot 192
Ashton, Frederick 13, 149, 169, 180-181, 208, 264
Astaire, Fred 250
Astana Ballet 230
Asylmuratova, Altynai 229-230, 248, 255-256, 258, 268
Atlanta Ballet 232
Atovmyan, Levon 133
Aybolit and Barmaley (Chukovsky) 124
Ayupova, Zhanna 258

B Minor Mass (Bach) 235
Bach, Johann Sebastian 235-236
Badalbeyli, Afrasiyab 193
Baku 132, 191-192
Balabina, Feya 69, 72, 93, 97, 111, 120
Balanchine Trust, The 255
Balanchine, George 13, 16, 33, 36-37, 102, 136, 169-170, 171, 177, 182-186, 190, 223, 229-230, 234, 237-238, 248, 251, 254-257, 269
see also Balanchivadze, Georgy
Balanchivadze, Andrey 102, 129, 169, 193
Balanchivadze, Georgy 34, 36-38, 41, 47, 50, 55 *see also* Balanchine, George
Balasanian, Sergey 170
Balashova, Alexandra 28, 80
Ballet 123
Ballet Annual 186
Ballet du XXe Siècle, Le 250
'Ballet Fraud' 97, 99, 103, 131
Ballet Masters' Course 106
Ballet Museum (Leningrad) 185
Ballet National de Marseille 228
Ballet of Los Angeles 262

Ballet schools
Baku School of Choreography 192
Ballet Studio (Perm) 194
'Baltflot' 46-47
see also School of Russian Ballet
Belarusian Ballet School 267
see also Belorussian Ballet School
Belorussian Ballet School 190
see also Belarusian Ballet School
Bolshoi Ballet School 6, 18, 38, 48-49, 66, 69-70, 72, 104, 110, 130, 157-161, 183, 206, 220, 231-232, 267
Bolshoi Ballet School (Brazil) 231
Boris Eifman Dance Academy 236

INDEX 295

City Dance School (Washington) 233
École de Mouvement, L' 49-51
GITIS 49, 73, 121, 130, 159, 220, 231
  see also Lunacharsky State Institute for Theatre Arts GITIS
Imperial Theatre School 4-5, 9-10, 14, 16, 18, 28, 31, 33, 44-47, 49, 102, 242
  see also Petrograd Choreographic School, Leningrad Choreographic School, Vaganova Academy
Kaunas Ballet School 188
Kiev Choreographic School 191, 267
Kirov Ballet Academy (Washington) 233, 266
Kishinev Ballet School 235
Leningrad Choreographic School 41, 65-69, 90, 106, 110-111, 113-114, 129, 143-144, 162-165, 194, 212, 234
  see also Imperial Theatre School, Petrograd Choreographic School, Vaganova Academy
Lermontov School 130
Lunacharsky State Institute for Theatre Arts GITIS 49, 121
  also see GITIS
Molotov Ballet School 112
  see also Perm State Choreographic School
Moscow Choreographic Institute 259
  see Bolshoi Ballet School
Moscow Imperial Theatre College 6, 48
  see also Bolshoi Ballet School
Perm State Choreographic School 194, 229, 232 see also Molotov Ballet School
Petrograd Choreographic School 18, 36, 41, 45-46, 66, 212, 255
  see also Imperial Theatre School, Leningrad Choreographic School, Vaganova Academy
Petrograd State Choreographic Technical School (or Technicum) 47
  see Petrograd Choreographic School
Riga Ballet School 187
School of American Ballet, The 40, 255
School of Russian Ballet 46-47, 67 see also 'Baltflot'
State Choreographic School (Tbilisi) 193
State Practical Institute of Choreography 49
  see GITIS
Vaganova Academy 6, 67, 129, 157, 162-163, 206, 212, 216, 229-230, 234-235, 258, 267-268
Vaganova Ballet Academy see Vaganova Academy
  see also Imperial Theatre School, Petrograd Choreographic School, Leningrad Choreographic School
Ballet Society 255 see also New York City Ballet
Ballet Theatre of the Kremlin Palace of Congresses 259 see Kremlin Ballet

Ballets and other dance presentations
Acis and Galatea (Fokine) 41
Agon (Balanchine) 184
Ali-Batyr (Yakobson) 128 see also *Shuraleh*
Amulet of Freedom (Changa) 187-188
Andalusiana (Romanov) 15
Angara (Grigorovich) 227
Anna Karenina (Plisetskaya/Ryzhenko/Smirnov-Golovanov) 221, 253
Antony and Cleopatra (Chernishev) 163, 209
Anyuta (Vasiliev) 254
Apollo (Balanchine) 177, 248
Asel (Vinogradov) 204, 234
Asiyat (Vinogradov) 207 see also *Goryanka*
Bakhti (Béjart) 250
Ballet Class (Messerer) 70, 183 see also *Class Concert*
Battleship 'Potemkin' (Vinogradov) 245-247
Bayadère, La 71, 112, 249
Bayadère, La (Gorsky) 15, 18, 20-21
Bayadère, La (Petipa) 9, 13, 48, 59, 67, 125, 160, 162, 229, 230, 259
Bayadère, La, 'Kingdom of the Shades' (Petipa) 178-179, 181, 183, 247, 256-257
Bayadère, La, Golden Idol solo (Zubkovsky) 125
Bedbug, The (Yakobson) 164, 198, 202
Bela (Fenster) 110
Billy the Kid (Loring) 171
Bivocality (Eifman) 236
Black Gold (Berdovsky/Efremov) 191
Bluebeard (Fokine) 172
Bluebeard (Petipa) 21
Boléro (Béjart) 228
Bolt, The (Lopukhov) 83-84, 98
Bolt, The (Ratmansky) 265
Bright Stream, The (Lopukhov) 97-100
Bright Stream, The (Ratmansky) 265

Bronze Horseman, The (Zakharov) 125, 131, 134-135
Carmagnole, La (Virsky) 73
Carmen Suite (Alonso) 204-205, 245
Carnaval, Le (Fokine) 14, 21, 49, 174
Chipolino (Mayorov) 225, 249
Chopiniana (Fokine) 11, 14, 26, 36, 43, 66, 70, 72, 159, 161, 183, 214, 247, 249, 253
Christmas Eve (Lopukhov/Burmeister) 102
Christmas Eve (Varkovitsky) 101-102
Cinderella 249
Cinderella (Sergeyev) 120-121, 135, 162-163, 170
Cinderella (Zakharov) 73, 119, 131, 158-159, 161, 213, 266
Class Concert 70, 183 see also Ballet Class
Classicism-Romanticism (Yakobson) 218
Cléopâtre (Fokine) 174 see Nuit d'Égypte, Une
Coast of Happiness. See Shore of Happiness
Coast of Hope (Belsky) 163, 165-166
Combat, Le (Dollar) 172
Comedians, The (Chekrygin) 103
Coppélia 81, 188, 194, 208, 213, 231, 249
Coppélia (Gorsky) 21, 73
Coppélia (Lopukhov) 86, 114-115
Coppélia (Petipa) 41, 234
Coppélia (Petipa/Cecchetti) 265
Coppélia (Saint-Léon) 9, 13
Corsaire, Le 70, 72, 112
Corsaire, Le (Burmeister) 130
Corsaire, Le (Gorsky) 21, 38
Corsaire, Le (Mazilier) 13
Corsaire, Le (Petipa) 27, 66, 160, 230, 257, 260
Corsaire, Le pas de deux 68, 163-164, 182, 206
Creation of the World (Kasatkina/Vasilyov) 163, 207, 218-219
Crimson Sails (Radunsky/Pospekhin/Popko) 104, 116
Cyrano de Bergerac (Petit) 177, 252
Dance of Machines (Foregger) 27
Dance Symphony or The Magnificence of the Universe (Lopukhov) 33, 55
Dance with a Hoop (Messerer S.) 81
Dante Sonata (Ashton) 153
Daughter of the Port, The 62 see Red Poppy, The
Diana and Actéon pas de deux (Petipa) 96, 164-165 see also Esmeralda, Pas de Diane
Distant Planet (Sergeyev) 170
Divertissement 155
Doctor Aibolit (Moiseyev M.) 124
Don Quixote 71, 112, 114, 249
Don Quixote (Gorsky) 15, 21, 28, 35, 69, 73, 158, 160-161, 232
Don Quixote (Gorsky/Anisimova) 162, 206, 230
Don Quixote (Grigorovich) 264
Don Quixote (Petipa) 9, 41, 43, 48, 68
Don Quixote pas de deux 80-81, 135, 171
Donizetti Variations (Balanchine) 184
Dream of Pierrot, The (Romanov) 15
Dying Swan, The (Fokine) 14, 135, 228, 253
Eleventh Symphony (Belsky) 152
Episodes (Balanchine)184
Eros (Fokine) 14 ,21 ,40
Esmeralda 72, 112, 249
Esmeralda (Perrot) 8, 13, 96
Esmeralda (Petipa) 21, 43, 59-60, 66, 96, 165, 237, 265
Eternal Idol (Yakobson) 156
Eternal Spring (Yakobson) 156
Études (Lander) 155
Eunice (Fokine) 11
Ever Fresh Flowers (Gorsky) 30
Fadetta (Lavrovsky) 92-93 ,114-115
Fairy Doll, The (Legat) 71
Fall River Legend (de Mille) 171
False Bridegroom, The (Fenster) 119
Fancy Free (Robbins) 172
Fantasia pas de deux (Yakobson) 179
Faun (Goleizovsky) 32, 56-57
Fear (Nijinska) 50
Fille du Pharaon, La (Lacotte) 264
Fille du Pharaon, La (Petipa) 13
Fille mal gardée, La 48, 73 see also Vain Precautions
Fille mal gardée, La (Dauberval) 13
Fille mal gardée, La (Ashton) 149, 180-181, 208
Fille mal gardée, La (Ivanov/Petipa) 187
Fille mal gardée, La (Vinogradov) 266
Firebird, The (Fokine)14, 25, 160, 174, 180 ,183 ,200
Firebird, The (Lopukhov) 33, 41
Five Russian Miniatures (Yakobson) 218
Flames of Paris, The (Vainonen) 66, 88-89, 91, 100-101, 136, 143, 162, 266
Flames of Paris, The pas de deux (Vainonen) 179, 182
Fleetingness (Lukin) 27

Footballer, The (Moiseyev/Lashchilin) 74-75, 95
Fountain of Bakhchisarai, The 186, 249
Fountain of Bakhchisarai, The (Goleizovsky) 190
Fountain of Bakhchisarai, The (Zakharov) 66, 77, 91-92, 98, 120, 135, 141, 155, 158
Four Temperaments, The (Balanchine) 255
Fragments of One Biography (Vasiliev) 254
Francesca da Rimini (Chichinadze) 161
Francesca da Rimini (Fokine) 40
Gavroche (Varkovitsky) 151
Gayaneh 123
Gayaneh (Anisimova) 105-106, 111, 135, 164, 183
  see also *Happiness*
Gayaneh (Asaturyan) 192
Genre Triptych, The (Yakobson) 218
Giselle 70, 72, 94, 139, 186, 188, 194, 216, 222, 246, 249
Giselle (Coralli/Perrot) 7, 9, 13
Giselle (Dolgushin) 164
Giselle (Gorsky) 15, 30
Giselle (Petipa) 21, 43, 49, 118, 141, 148-149, 155, 159-161, 164, 166, 179, 181-182, 207, 214, 230, 254
Golden Age, The (Grigorovich) 232, 243, 246
Golden Age, The (Vainonen/Yakobson/Chesnakov) 73-74, 84
Goryanka (Vinogradov) 206-207 see also *Asiyat*
Gossiping Women (Yakobson) 179
Graduation Ball (Lichine) 172
Graziella (Gerdt) 55
Green Table, The (Jooss) 246
Gudule's Daughter (Gorsky) 59 see also *Esmeralda*
Halte de Cavalerie, La (Petipa) 21
Hamlet (Sergeyev) 215
Happiness (Arbatov) 105 see also *Gayaneh*
Heart of the Hills, The (Chabukiani) 102-103, 193 see also *Mzechabuki*
Heroic Poem (Geologists) (Kasatkina/Vasilyov) 161, 199
Icarus (Belsky) 176
Icarus (Vasiliev) 219, 238
Ice Maiden, The (Lopukhov) 61-62
In the Chains of the Harem 73
Infanta, The (Lebedev) 227
Interplay (Robbins) 184
Isadora (Béjart) 228, 238
Islamey (Fokine) 14

Ivan the Terrible (Grigorovich) 161, 225-226, 241
Jeune Homme et la Mort, Le (Petit) 153
Joan of Arc (Burmeister) 131
Joseph the Beautiful (Goleizovsky) 57-58
Jota Aragonesa (Fokine) 14
Kalevipoeg (Tohvelman) 189
Kambar and Nazym 186
Katerina (Lavrovsky) 93-94
Kiss, The (Yakobson) 156, 218
Knight in the Tiger's Skin, The (Vinogradov) 245, 247
Krakoviak from *Ivan Susanin* 135
Kratt (Olbrei) 189
Lady and the Fool, The (Cranko) 180
Lady and the Lap Dog, The (Plisetskaya) 244, 253
Lady from the Sea (Cullberg) 172
Laima (Tangieva-Birzniek) 187
Land of Miracles (Yakobson) 205
Laurencia (Chabukiani) 67, 103-104, 118, 135, 161, 266
Leda (Béjart) 228, 238
Legend of Love, The 249
Legend of Love, The (Grigorovich) 146, 159, 161, 163, 174-175, 199, 210
Legend of the Donenbai Bird, The (Lebedev) 243
Leili and Majnun (Goleizovsky) 160-161, 170
Leningrad Symphony (Belsky) 152, 175-176, 182, 214 see also *Seventh Symphony*
Life (Lavrovsky) 169
Lilac Garden (Tudor) 172
Lithuanian Rhapsody (Petrov) 188
Little Humpbacked Horse, The 71, 113
Little Humpbacked Horse, The (Gorsky) 21, 143
Little Humpbacked Horse, The (Radunsky) 161, 168
Little Humpbacked Horse, The (Saint-Léon) 8, 13
Little Stork, The (Radunsky/Pospekhin/Popko) 104
Lola (Burmeister) 118
Lost Illusions (Zakharov) 96-97
Love is Quick! (Gorsky) 21
Macbeth (Vasiliev) 259
Magic Flute, The (Ivanov) 13, 72
Magic Lotus Lantern, The (Li/Wan) 194
Magic Mirror, The (Gorsky) 21
Magic Suit, The (Kasatkina/Vasilyov) 235
Maiden's Tower, The (Almaszade/Vronsky/) 192

Maltakva (Chabukiani) 193
Medea (Murdmaa) 190
Medtneriana (Goleizovsky) 36
Merry Wives of Windsor, The (Burmeister) 117-118
Midsummer Night's Dream, A (Balanchine) 229
Millions d'Arlequin, Les (Petipa) 21, 85
Mirages, Les (Lifar) 153
Mirandolina (Vainonen) 126-127, 155
Mistress into Maid (Fenster) 120
Mistress into Maid (Zakharov) 120
Moszkowsky Waltz pas de deux (Vainonen) 135, 158
Mother (Yakobson) 124
Mozartiana (Aleksidze) 223
Mzechabuki (Chabukiani) 193 *see also Heart of the Hills*
Napoli (Bournonville) 243
Nathalie, ou la Laitière suisse (Lacotte) 235
Native Fields (Andreyev/Stukolkina) 132
Night (Balanchivadze) 36
Night City (Lavrovsky) 169
Night Shadow (Balanchine) 153
Nightingale, The (Ermolayev/Lopukhov) 190
Nostalgia (Vasiliev) 254
Notre-Dame de Paris (Petit) 236, 252
Nuit d'Égypte, Une (Fokine) 14, 174
Nutcracker, The 249, 114, 189
Nutcracker, The (Gorsky) 29, 77
Nutcracker, The (Grigorovich) 203
Nutcracker, The (Ivanov) 13, 21, 35, 47, 66, 262
Nutcracker, The (Lopukhov) 36, 41, 57
Nutcracker, The (Vainonen) 94, 159, 161, 163, 203
Nutcracker, The, Rose Waltz (Vainonen) 179
On the Seashore (Messerer) 188
Ondine (Ashton) 180
Onegin (Cranko) 222, 258
Opus No. 5 (Béjart) 250
Orpheus (Boyarsky) 174, 183
Othello (Chabukiani) 147
Our Faust (Béjart) 235, 250
Paganini (Lavrovsky) 159, 169, 183, 202
Pages of Life. See *Life*
Palais de Cristal, Le (Balanchine) 185 *see also Symphony in C*
Pan Koniowski (Litvinienko) 191
Paquita, Grand Pas (Petipa) 143, 247, 265
Partisan Days (Vainonen) 100

Pas d'acier, Le (Massine) 57, 80 *see also Ursignol*
Pas de Diane (Petipa) 96 *see also Diana and Actéon* pas de deux, *Esmeralda*
Path of Thunder, The (Sergeyev) 151
Patineurs, Les (Ashton) 181
Pavillon d'Armide, Le (Fokine) 14
Petits Riens, Les (Aleksidze) 223
Petrushka (Fokine) 14, 25, 49, 143, 173-174, 183
Petrushka (Vinogradov) 256-257
Pictures at an Exhibition (Lopukhov) 171
Pierrot et Pierrette (Messerer A.) 81
Pilules magiques, Les (Petipa) 5
Polovtsian Dances (Fokine) 14
Prince of the Pagodas, The (MacMillan) 262
Prisoner of the Caucasus, The (Lavrovsky) 101, 114-115
Prisoner of the Caucasus, The (Zakharov) 70, 103
Prodigal Son, The (Murdmaa) 190, 223
Promenades, Les (Vasiliev) 238
Pulcinella (Lopukhov) 60
Quiet Don (Boyarchikov) 250
Rake's Progress, The (de Valois) 154, 180
Raymonda 188
Raymonda (Gorsky) 21, 38
Raymonda (Petipa) 13, 35, 72
Raymonda (Petipa/Gorsky/Lavrovsky) 120, 135
Raymonda (Petipa/Grigorovich) 244
Raymonda Variations (Balanchine) 248
Red Flower, The 64 *see also Red Poppy, The*
Red Poppy, The 72
Red Poppy, The (Lavrovsky) 63
Red Poppy, The (Lopukhov/Ponomarev/Leontiev) 63
Red Poppy, The (Tikhomirov/Lashchilin) 62-64, 70, 81, 151, 190-191
Red Poppy, The (Zakharov) 63
Red Sails. See *Crimson Sails*
Red Whirlwind, The (Lopukhov) 55
Revizor (Vinogradov) 241
Revolutionary Étude (Duncan) 124
Rivals, The 73
Rodeo (de Mille) 172
Rodin Sculptures (Yakobson) 218
Rodin 'Triptych' (Yakobson) 156
Roi Candule, Le (Petipa) 96
Romance of the Rose (Chekrygin) 42
Romeo and Juliet 249, 262
Romeo and Juliet (Chernishev) 206, 209, 214

Romeo and Juliet (Grigorovich) 237-239, 246, 264
Romeo and Juliet (Lavrovsky) 66, 69, 94, 107-108, 110, 134, 140-141, 155, 166, 213
Romeo and Juliet (Vinogradov) 195
Romeo and Juliet pas de deux (Béjart) 238
Rose Malade, La pas de deux (Petit) 228, 253
Ruby Stars (Lavrovsky) 129
Sacre du Printemps, Le (Kasatkina/Vasilyov) 161, 202-203, 235
Salambo (Moiseyev) 76, 88
Salomé (Goleizovsky) 32, 36, 56
Sarcasms (Lukin) 27
Scarlet Sails. See *Crimson Sails*
Schéhérazade 73
Schéhérazade (Burmeister) 118
Schéhérazade (Fokine) 11, 25
Scotch Symphony (Balanchine) 230, 255-257
Scriabiniana (Goleizovsky) 36, 170, 185
Seagull, The (Plisetskaya) 240-241
Seasons, The (Sergeyev) 216
Serenade (Balanchine) 184, 255
Serf Ballerina, The (Lopukhov) 93
Servant of Two Masters, The (Fenster) 119, 229
Seven Beauties (Gusev) 132-133
Seventh Symphony (Belsky) 175-176 see also *Leningrad Symphony*
Shore of Happiness (Burmeister) 123, 139
Shuraleh (Adashevski) 192
Shuraleh (Yakobson) 128, 135, 165 see also *Ali-Batyr*
Sketches (Petrov) 253
Sleeping Beauty, The 54, 249
Sleeping Beauty, The (Petipa) 9, 13, 20-22, 32, 34, 38, 40-41, 43, 59, 65, 67-68, 70, 98, 114, 123, 130, 151, 160, 162-163, 165, 177-179, 181, 226, 230, 257, 265,
Smerch (Goleizovsky) 55-56 see also *Whirlwind, The*
Snow Maiden, The (Yakobson) 156
Snow Maiden,The, solo (Yakobson) 179
Snow Maiden, The (Burmeister) 130
Snow White and the Seven Dwarfs 249
Soccer Player, The (Messerer A.) 81
Soldat Amoureux, Le (Béjart) 250
Source, La (Saint-Léon) 18
Spartacus 162, 249
Spartacus (Elizariev) 190
Spartacus (Grigorovich) 160-161, 208-210, 226, 230, 246-247
Spartacus (Moiseyev) 152-153, 182
Spartacus (Yakobson) 67, 136-137, 149, 182
Spring Waters pas de deux (Messerer) 70, 135, 158
Stenka Razin (Gorsky) 28
Stone Flower, The 249
Stone Flower, The (Grigorovich) 144-146, 159-161, 163, 166-167, 174, 179, 210, 242, 252
Straussiana (Burmeister) 117
Stronger than Death (Yakobson) 124
Stronger than Love (Varkovitsky) 152
Suite en blanc (Lifar) 155
Svetlana (Radunsky/Pospekhin/Popko) 104, 116
Swan Lake 135, 183, 186, 188-189, 191, 213, 249, 261
Swan Lake (Burmeister) 130, 139, 220
Swan Lake (Gorsky) 15, 21, 29, 63, 65-66, 70
Swan Lake (Gorsky/Messerer) 116, 123, 141, 148-150, 155, 158, 160, 210, 221-222, 266
Swan Lake (Grassi)11
Swan Lake (Grigorovich) 210, 237-238, 244
Swan Lake (Petipa/Ivanov) 9, 13, 21, 67-68, 72, 89, 94, 111, 141, 159, 163, 179, 181, 188, 229-230, 247
Swan Lake (Serebrovskaya) 192
Swan Lake Act II 228, 230
Swan Lake Act III pas de deux 171-172
Swan Lake Act IV (Messerer) 70
Sylphide, La 249
Sylphide, La (Bournonville) 59, 229, 242-243, 258
Sylphide, La (Taglioni) 7, 13
Sylphides, Les (Fokine) 11, 171, 253 see also *Chopiniana*
Sylvia 93
Symphony in C (Balanchine) 185, 229, 248, 255
Taglioni's Flight (Yakobson) 218
Tale of Serf Nikish, The 223
Tale of the Priest and his Workman Balda, The (Varkovitsky) 106, 114-115
Tale of the Stone Flower, The (Lavrovsky) 133-134, 144
Talisman, Le (Petipa) 21, 48, 67
Tarantella (Balanchine) 229
Taras Bulba (Fenster) 109
Taras Bulba (Lopukhov) 108-109, 179,

182
Taras Bulba (Zakharov) 109
Tatiana, or Daughter of the People (Burmeister) 123
Teolinda (Goleizovsky) 58
Terpsichore's Tricks (Kasatkina/Vasilyov) 235
Theme and Variations (Balanchine) 171-172, 229, 255-257
Thérèse Raquin (Eifman) 236
Three Fat Men (Moiseyev) 95
Toady (Yakobson) 156
Transience or Visions fugitives 56
Triumph of the Republic, The 89 see *Flames of Paris, The*
Tsar Boris (Boyarchikov) 236
Twelve, The (Yakobson) 202
Ugly Duckling, The 249
Ursignol 78 see *Pas d'acier, Le*
Vagabond Circus (Yakobson) 218
Vain Precautions 249
Vain Precautions (Gorsky) 15, 21, 69, 72-73, 77
Vain Precautions (Petipa/Ivanov) 48
Vain Precautions (Vinogradov) 234 see also *La Fille mal gardée*
Valse-Fantaisie (Grigorovich) 144
Vanina Vanini (Kasatkina/Vasilyov) 197-198
Variations on a Theme by Mozart (Aleksidze) 193
Veeni-Pukh 249
Vestris (Yakobson) 206, 211
Walpurgis Night (Lavrovsky) 127, 183
We Stalingraders (Varkovitsky) 123
Western Symphony (Balanchine) 184
What happened to The Ballerina, the Chinese and the Jumpers (Romanov) 15
Whirlwind, The (Goleizovsky) 55-56, 71 see also *Smerch*
Yaroslavna (Vinogradov) 224, 245
Young Lady and the Hooligan, The (Boyarsky) 196-197
Youth (Fenster) 127

Ballets de Paris 253
Ballets Russes 9, 11, 14, 19, 23, 25, 40, 43, 49-50, 57, 60, 78-79, 138, 154, 173-174, 183, 200, 223, 232, 255-256, 259, 269
Balzac, Honoré de 96-97
Bank, Lyubov 58-59, 77, 80, 92, 120
Barber, Samuel 190
Barnes, Clive 178

Bartók, Bela 169
Baryshnikov, Mikhail 51, 94, 158, 161-162, 206, 211-212, 215, 218, 222-224, 258, 262
Basil, Colonel de 169
Bat, The (cabaret) 31
Bavarian State Ballet 230, 267
Beaumont, Cyril 80
Beccari, Filippo 6
Beethoven, Ludwig van 33-34
Begak, Dmitry 152, 182
Béjart, Maurice 228-229, 235, 238, 250-251, 257
Belkin Tales (Pushkin) 120
Belsky, Igor 128, 146, 151-152, 165, 175-176, 182, 214, 268
Benesh, Joan and Rudolf 173
Benois, Alexandre 35
Berezhnoi, Sergey 242
Berg, Olga 60
Berlin 25, 37, 42, 78, 80-81, 137, 219
Berlin, East 69, 134
Berlioz, Hector 209
Bessmertnova, Natalia 158-161, 170, 175, 208, 210, 226-227, 238, 243-244
Bitov, Boris 151
Blake, William 228
Blok, Alexander 202
Blok, Lyubov 90
Bobishov, Mikhail 126
Bocharov, Alexander 35
Bogatyrev, Alexander 238, 241, 244, 264
Bogdanov-Berezovsky, Valerian 174
Bogolyubskaya, Marianna 101
Boléro (Ravel) 170, 228
Bolshakova, Natalya 219, 241
Bolshaya Sovietskaya Entsiklopediya 153
Bolshoi Art Committee 227
Bolshoi Ballet 15, 20, 22-23, 28-33, 38, 40-41, 56, 58, 62-63, 65-66, 69-70, 72-74, 76-77, 80, 88, 94, 98-100, 103-104, 106, 108-110, 115-118, 120-123, 127-131, 133-134, 137-146, 148-153, 155, 158-161, 166-175, 179-183, 185, 188, 190, 194, 197, 199-200, 202-205, 210, 213, 218-223, 225-228, 230-232, 234-235, 237-249, 251-256, 259, 261-262, 264, 266-268
Bolshoi Ballet Collective 254
Bolshoi Theatre Museum 73
Bolt, The (Shostakovich) 197
Borodin, Alexander 14, 224

INDEX

Boston 253
Boston Ballet 229
Bourgeois, J 177
Bourget, Le (airport) 178
Bournonville, Auguste 59, 242 242
Bovt, Violetta 130
Boyarchikov, Nikolai 143, 197, 236, 250, 266
Boyarsky, Konstantin 143-144, 173-174, 196, 200, 256-257
Bradley, Lionel 123
Brams, Jacques 82
Bregvadze, Boris 128, 147
Brezhnev, Leonid 201, 228, 243, 260
Bright Stream, The (Shostakovich) 197
Brno 107
Bruhn, Erik 172, 176, 201, 242
Bruni, Tatiana 121
Brussels 228, 250
Bryans, Rudy 228
Bryantsev, Dmitry 234-235, 266
Buckle, Richard 179
Budapest 48, 160, 219
Bulgakov, Alexey 29, 58, 60, 62
Burlaka, Yuri 265
Burmeister, Vladimir 102, 117-118, 123, 130-131, 139, 189, 219-220

Cairo Ballet School 155
Catherine II (the Great), Tsarina 4, 6
Caute, David 150
Cavos, Alberto 5
Cecchetti, Enrico 11
Central Theatre Committee 23
Chabukiani, Vakhtang 51, 68, 82-83, 89, 96, 100, 102-104, 109, 119, 125, 139, 147-148, 158, 161, 193, 211, 266
Chamber Ballet 211 *see also* Choreographic Miniatures
Chamber Ballet (Goleizovsky) 56
Changa, Eugeni 187
Chauviré, Yvette 211
Chekhov, Anton 240, 244
Chekrygin, Alexander 42, 103
Chelyabinsk 111
Chenchikova, Olga 229
Cherevichki 101 *see also Vakula the Smith*
Chernishev, Igor 156, 163, 202, 206, 209, 214
Chervinsky, Nikolai1 32, 215
Chicago 82, 162
Chicago Tribune 247
Chichinadze, Alexey 106, 121, 130, 161, 219-220
Chikvaidze, Elena 101
Chingiz, Aitmatov 204
Chkalov 110, 114-115
Choi, Svetlana 259
Chopin, Fryderyk 11, 26, 193
Choreographers' Course (GITIS) 121
Choreographers' Course (Leningrad Choreographic School) 143
Choreographers' Course (Leningrad Conservatoire) 197
Choreographic Miniatures 123, 155, 163, 199, 209-211, 217, 226
'Choreographic Symphonism' 136, 145
Chukovsky, Korney 124
Chulaki, Mikhail 106, 119, 153, 196, 200, 225, 240
Clarke, Mary 179
Classical Ballet Concert Ensemble of the USSR 203 *see also* Young Ballet, Moscow Classical Ballet, State Academic Theatre Classical Ballet of N. Kasatkina and V. Vasilyov
Classique, La 258
Columbus, Ohio 131
Comédie Française 134
Commissariat for Enlightenment 45, 49, 75 *see also* Narkompros, Peoples' Commissariat for Enlightenment
Copenhagen 81, 242
Corps des Cadets 4
Council of People's Commissars 19, 45, 96, 100 *see also Sovnarkom*
Cranko, John 13, 180, 222, 258
Création du Monde, La (Milhaud) 218
Crisp, Clement 179, 206, 214
Croce, Arlene 237
Cuban Ballet 204
Cullberg, Birgit 172

Daily Express 141
Dalcroze, Eugene 27, 50
Dancing Times 135, 141
Danilova, Alexandra 16, 34, 38, 43, 55
Daphnis and Chloe (Ravel) 223
Dauberval, Jean 7, 13, 180
Daydé, Liane 148
Debussy, Claude 32, 155-156
dekada/dekadi 95, 105, 187-188, 190
Delibes, Léo 93
Demichev, Pyotr 240, 250
Derzhavin, Konstantin 105
Deshevov, Vladimir 110
Detskoe Selo 46 *see also* Tsarskoe Selo

Diaghilev, Sergey 9, 11, 14, 25, 32 , 42-43, 49, 51, 60, 78-79, 140-141, 154, 181, 183, 255-256, 269
Didelot, Charles-Louis 7, 101
Diên Biên Phu 134
Dimitrov, Emil 200
Divertissement - The Fate of Classical Ballet (Gayevsky) 241-242
Dmitriev, Vladimir 57, 89
Doctor Aybolit (Chukovsky) 124
Dolgushin, Nikita 164, 195, 201, 215, 224-225, 236, 242, 249
Dollar, William 172
Dr Doolittle (Lofting) 124
drambalet 64, 87, 91-92, 107, 122, 131-133, 135-136, 145-146, 169, 175, 196, 210, 221, 237
Dresden 177
Drigo, Riccardo 85
Drozdova, Margarita 220
Duato, Nacho 266
Dubinin, Sergey 93, 101
Dubrovnik Festival 228
Dubrovska, Felia 37
Dudinskaya, Natalia 51, 66-67, 69, 89, 104, 106, 109, 111, 114, 120, 125-126, 128, 130, 132, 134-135, 151, 158, 162, 182, 206, 215
Dudko, Mikhail 35, 41, 63, 92, 96, 109
Duncan School 124
Duncan, Isadora 11, 26-27, 36, 50, 124, 136, 143

Eden, Anthony 138
Effel, Jean 218
Efimov, Boris 245
Efimov, Vasily 58
Egorova, Lyubov 37, 43
Eifman, Boris 106, 160, 163, 235-236, 260
Eisenstein, Sergey 225, 236
Ekaterinburg 110 *see* Sverdlovsk
Ekskuzovich, Ivan 23-24, 44-45
Eleventh Symphony (Shostakovich) 152
Elizariev, Valentin 190
Elssler, Fanny 8
English National Ballet 230
Entertainment Corporation, The 261
Epikur 18
'Era of Stagnation, The' 201
Erdman, Boris 57-58, 121
Ermolayev, Alexey 63, 65, 67-68, 76, 89, 94-95, 98, 108, 118, 120, 126, 134, 161, 190, 192

Eshpai, Andrey 227
Estonian Theatre Ballet Company 189
Eugene Onegin (Pushkin) 142, 222
Evdokimova, Eva 201
Evteyeva, Elena 207, 216

Fadeyechev, Alexey 231, 247, 259, 262, 264
Fadeyechev, Nikolai 118, 141, 145, 149, 152, 160, 200, 204-205, 210, 221, 231
Faier, Yuri 59, 99, 213
Farmanyants, Georgy 126
Farrell, Suzanne 255
Fateyev, Yuri 266
Faust (Gounod) 127
Fedicheva, Kaleria 170, 226
Fedorova, Alexandra 187
Fedorova, Sofia 38
Fedotov, Viktor 213
Femilidi, Vladimir 73
Fenster, Boris 109-110 ,115, 119-120, 125, 127, 136, 189
Fesenko, Tatiana 224, 242
Field, John 91
Fifth Symphony (Mahler) 228
Filin, Sergey 265, 267
Filipov, Alexander 216
Financial Times 206, 214
First Symphony (Khachaturian) 105
Firtich, Georgy 198
Flaubert, Gustave 88
Fokina, Vera 25, 81
Fokine, Mikhail 11, 14-15, 21, 25-28, 33-34, 36, 40, 49, 62, 81, 136-137, 143, 169, 171-174, 180-181, 200, 223-224, 228, 253, 256
Fonteyn, Margot 164, 181
Foregger, Nikolai 27, 57
Formalism 87-88, 135, 153, 184, 206, 237
Forty-First, The (Lavrenyev) 152
Fourth Symphony (Beethoven) 33
Frangopulo, Marietta 111, 114
Free Ballet Studio 27 *see also* Moscow Free Ballet
Freedman, Martin 226
Freud, Sigmund 154
Fuenteovejuna (Vega) 103
Fundamentals of Classical Dance, The (Vaganova/Blok) 90
Furtseva, Ekaterina 142, 178, 199, 210, 222

INDEX

Gabovich, Mikhail 58, 70, 92, 101, 108-109, 115, 119-120, 172, 180, 185, 241
Galkin, Vladimir 22
Gambler, The (Prokofiev) 79
Ganjavi, Nizami 133
Gannibalova, Valentina 223
GATOB (ballet company) 14, 24, 33, 36-37, 40-42, 47-48, 54-55, 63-66, 68, 72, 82, 84, 86, 89, 91, 94, 212, 255 *see also* Mariinsky Ballet, Kirov Ballet
Gayevsky, Vadim 241
Gazette of the Bolshoi Theatre 197
Gazmatov, Rasul 207
Geltser, Ekaterina 28, 31, 38-39, 59-60, 62-63
Gerbek, Robert 108, 112, 128,
Gerdt, Elizaveta 35, 41-43, 60, 157
Gerdt, Pavel 42, 47, 55, 157
Gergiev, Valery 266
Giuri, Adelina 181
Glasgow 257
glasnost 246
Glazunov, Alexander 13, 28, 88, 120, 216
Glière, Reinhold 59, 62, 103, 125
Glinka, Mikhail 144
Godunov, Alexander 221, 228, 238
Godunov, Boris 236
Gogol, Nikolai 101, 108, 241, 254
Golden Age, The (Shostakovich) 197
Goldoni, Carlo 119, 126
Goleizovsky, Kasyan 31-32, 36-37, 50, 55-58, 63, 71, 76-77, 79, 88, 119, 160-161, 170, 185, 190, 203, 251, 254
Golovashenko, Yuri 185
Golovin, Alexander 61, 200
Golovkina, Sofia 168, 206
Golyubov, Vladimir 89
Goncharova, Natalia 180, 200
Goodwin, Noel 141
Gorbachev, Mikhail 147, 246-247, 252, 258, 260
Gordeyev, Vyacheslav 231, 238, 264
Gorky 232 *see also* Nizhny Novgorod, Vasilsursk
Gorky, Maxim 86
Gorky Park 103
Gorsky, Alexander 15, 18, 21-22, 28-31, 33, 35-36, 39, 59, 69, 71, 76-77, 88, 94, 120, 168, 210, 221, 232, 266
Gosconcert 171, 222, 261
Gould, Morton 184

Gounod, Charles 127
Government Inspector, The (Gogol) 241 *see Revizor*
Grand Ballet du Marquis de Cuevas, Le 51
Grassi, Rafael 11
Grey, Beryl 147-148
Gribov, Alexander 113, 145, 175
Gridin, Anatoly 145
Grieg, Edvard 61
Grigorovich, Yuri 67-68, 118, 137, 144-146, 159-162, 166-167, 174-175, 199-200, 203-204, 208, 210-212, 219, 221-222, 225-227, 232, 237-247, 251-254, 259, 261, 264-265, 269
Grin, Alexander 116
Grisi, Carlotta 8
Grivickas, Vytautas 188
Guadalajara (Mexico) 216
Gulyayev, Vadim 209, 219, 241
Gurilyov, Alexander 91
Gusev, Pyotr 34, 36, 41, 55, 61, 76, 86, 92, 97-98, 122, 130, 132-133, 173, 195, 197, 204, 211, 234
Gvozdev, Alexey 71

Hallberg, David 265
Harlequinade see Les Millions d'Arlequin
Haskell, Arnold 179-180, 200
Havana (Cuba) 205
Heidenreich, Ekaterina 194
Henze, Hans-Werner 180
Hermitage Museum 137, 248
Hikmet, Nazym 175
Hilaire, Laurent 267
Horowitz, Vladimir 258
Houston Ballet 231
How the Steel was Tempered (Ostrovsky) 127
Hugo, Victor 8, 59, 151, 237

Ilyushchenko, Elena 29
Imperial Directorate 4
Imperial Theatres of Moscow 7
'Irek Mukhamedov and Company' 232
Iordan, Olga. See Jordan, Olga
Irkutsk 191
Irkutsk Story, The (Arbuzov) 227
Isayev, Stanislas 232, 235
Isayeva, Galina 85, 115, 128, 151
Ivan the Terrible (Eisenstein) 236
Ivanov, Georgy 228, 240
Ivanov, Lev 10, 13, 21, 34, 72, 94, 130, 136, 183, 210

Ivanova, Lydia 37, 43, 55
Ivanovsky, Alexander 73-74
Ivanovsky, Nikolai 157
Izvestia 98, 129, 146, 185

Jacobson, Leonid. See Yakobson, Leonid
Jarre, Maurice 237
Joffrey, Robert 248
Johansson, Christian 38, 242
John, Elton 235
Joinville (Brazil) 231
Jooss, Kurt 246
Jordan, Olga 65, 74, 89-90, 92, 94, 112-114
Juzeliūnas, Julius 188

Kahn, Albert 142
Kalinin, Mikhail 63
Kama (river) 112
Kambar batyr 186
Kandaurova, Margarita 77
Kaplan, Semyon 144
Kapp, Eugen 189
Karamanov, Alemdar 152
Karavaichuk, Oleg 198
Karayev, Kara 132, 151
Karelskaya, Rimma 168
Karetnikov, Nikolai 197, 199, 235
Karsavina, Tamara 10, 23, 37, 40, 122
Kasatkina, Natalia 106, 161, 163, 197, 199, 202-203, 207, 218, 221, 232, 235
Kastendieck, Miles 167
Kaunas (Lithuania) 188
Kazan 128, 232
Kazhlayev, Murad 207
Kemenov, Vladimir 136
Kevorkov, Sergey 191-192
Khachaturian, Aram 105, 122, 137, 152, 185, 192, 208
Khachaturian, Karen 225
Khaniashvili, Alla 262
Kharkov (Ukraine) 58, 66, 191
Khodasevich, Valentina 74, 137
Kholfin, Nikolai 125
Khrushchev, Nikita 135, 138, 149, 166-167, 178, 201
Kiev 49-50, 69-70, 148, 171, 190-191, 204, 213
Kiev Ballet 191
Kikaleishvili, Zurab 147
Kirillova, Galina 93, 101, 106
Kirov Artistic Council 136
Kirov Ballet 4, 41-42, 48, 63, 66-67, 69, 93-94, 96, 99-101, 104-105, 107, 109-111, 113-114, 117-118, 120, 122, 124-125, 128-132, 135-139, 143-144, 147-148, 150-152, 155, 158-159, 161-165, 170, 174-182, 192, 194-195, 198, 202-203, 206-210, 212, 214-216, 218, 220, 222-224, 226-227, 229-230, 232-238, 241-242, 245-248, 250-257, 260-262, 265-267
see also GATOB, Mariinsky Ballet
Kirov, Sergey 96
Kirova, Vera 201
Kisselgoff, Anna 261
Klebanov, Dmitry 104
Klein, Alexander 118, 130
Klimov, Alexander 175
Klimova, Larisa 196
Klinichev, Leonid 250
Knight in the Snow Leopard's Skin, The (Rustaveli) 245
Kochetovsky, Alexander 50
Kokonin, Vladimir 254, 264
Kolpakova, Irina 42, 121, 145, 147, 156, 162-163, 170, 175-176, 178, 182, 218, 223, 227, 242
Komarov, Boris 60
Komisārs, Voldemārs 187
Komleva, Gabriela 145, 170, 207
Komsomol 74, 84-85, 177
Kondratieva, Marina 145, 158-159, 169, 221, 225
Kondratov, Yuri 104, 106, 126, 129, 134, 148, 151
Koren, Sergey 108-109, 112, 140
Kornblit, Evgeny 151
Koshlev, Vladimir 199
Kosterovo 161
Kostroma 111
Kosygin, Alexey 201
Kozlov, Leonid 238-239, 258
Kozlova, Valentina 239, 258
Krasnoyarsk 191
Krasnoye Znamya 72
Krasovskaya, Vera 154, 167
Kravchenko, Boris 156
Krein, Alexander 103
Kremlin Ballet 121, 259
Kriger, Viktorina 72-73, 80, 138, 220, 222
Kroshner, Mikhail 190
Kschessinskaya, Matilda 10, 18, 37, 60, 72, 96, 226, 251
Kschessinsky, Joseph 60, 72

Kudryavtseva, Valentina 29, 77
Kuibyshev 70, 110, 115-116, 123 *see also* Samara
Kuibyshev Ballet 67
Kurgapkina, Ninel 162, 177, 182, 241, 258
Kurilko, Mikhail 62
Kurilov, Ivan 102, 117
Kuznetsov, Anatoly 93, 141
Kuznetsov, Svyatoslav 139, 147

Laborde, Chas 94
Lacotte, Pierre 235, 264
Lady Macbeth of Mtsensk District (Shostakovich) 97
Landé, Jean-Baptiste 4
Lapauri, Alexander 134, 139-140, 158, 223
Lashchilin, Lev 62, 74, 109
Lavrenyev, Boris 152
Lavrovsky, Leonid 34, 63, 66, 69, 92-94, 101, 107-108, 118, 120, 127, 129,133-134, 143-144, 152, 155, 159-161, 167, 169-170, 182-184, 200, 202, 237
Lavrovsky, Mikhail 160-161, 208, 227, 237, 267
Lazarev, Eduard 209
Le Picq, Charles 7
Lebedev, Leonid 227, 243-244
Legat, Nikolai 38, 40, 46-47, 212
Legat, Sergey 71
Legat, Tatiana 113, 166
Lenin, Vladimir 19, 21, 23, 30, 53-54, 59, 109, 137
Lenin Prize 160, 204
Leningrad 35, 41-42, 48-49, 51, 55, 57, 60, 63-69, 72, 76-77, 79, 89-93, 95-96, 98, 103, 107-108, -115, -120, -126, 128-129, 134, 138, 143-145, 148-150, 157, 159, 162-165, 171, 174-176, 178-183,185-186, 188-189, 191, 193-196, 200, 204, 211-212, 218, 223, 229-230, 232-234, 237, 242, 244, 248-252, 255-258, 260, 265-266
 see also St Petersburg, Petrograd
Leningrad Ballet Ensemble 235 *see also* New Ballet, Leningrad Theatre of Modern Ballet, Leningrad Eifman Ballet, St Petersburg Eifman Ballet
Leningrad Conservatoire 197, 213-214, 235
Leningrad Eifman Ballet 235 *see also* New Ballet, Leningrad Theatre of Modern Ballet, Leningrad Ballet Ensemble, St Petersburg Eifman Ballet
Leningrad Ice Ballet 144
Leningrad Symphony (Shostakovich) 152
Leningrad Theatre Institute 143
Leningrad Theatre of Modern Ballet 235
 see also New Ballet, Leningrad Ballet Ensemble, Leningrad Eifman Ballet, St Petersburg Eifman Ballet
Leonova, Maria 268
Leontiev, Leonid 14, 33-34, 46, 60, 63, 94, 96, 173, 256
Lepeshinskaya, Olga 69, 76, 93, 95, 101, 104, 109, 116-117, 119, 126-127, 149, 151, 158
Levashov, Vladimir 128, 145, 200
Levitan, Joseph 81
Lezhnina, Larisa 255-256
Li, Tshen Len 194
Lichine, David 172
Liepa, Andris 232, 247-248, 253, 257, 259, 261
Liepa, Māris 131, 159-161, 169, 175, 188, 200, 208, 221, 232
Liepiņš, Anatols 188
Lifar, Serge 38, 50-51, 83, 140, 153-155, 178, 200
Likhovskaya, Olga 245
Literaturnaya Gazeta 86, 251
Litvinenko, Vasily 191
Litvinienko, Yuri 133
Lofting, Hugh 124
London 40, 43, 59, 80, 134, 138-143, 149, 153, 159, 162, 166-167, 174, 177-178, 180-181, 188, 206, 214, 216, 230-232, 240, 246, 260-262
London City Ballet 230, 262
London Festival Ballet 130, 143
Lopatkina, Ulyana 267
Lopokova, Lydia 32, 43
Lopukhina, Valentina 93
Lopukhov, Andrey108
Lopukhov, Fyodor 14, 19-20, 32-36, 39, 41, 47, 50, 54-57, 60-61, 63-64, 67-68, 71, 83-87, 90, 93-94, 97-99, 102, 106, 108, 115, 118-119, 135-137, 143-144, 146, 159, 165-166, 168, 171, 173-174, 188, 190, 197, 200, 209-210
Loring, Eugene 171
Los Angeles 51, 82, 130, 238
Love of Three Oranges, The 79
Lucerne Ballet 262

Lukin, Lev 27
Lukom, Elena 14, 33, 41-43, 63, 110
Lunacharsky, Anatoly 16, 19, 22-24, 26, 30, 39, 44-45, 49, 53, 58-59, 62, 72, 75, 78-80, 84, 150
Lunkina, Svetlana 267
Lvov, Mikhail 18
Lvov-Anokhin, Boris 205, 221
Lyubimov, Yuri 224

Machavariani, Alexey 147, 245
MacMillan, Kenneth 262
Maddox, Michael 6
maestrina degli operai, La (De Amicis) 196
Mahler, Gustav 228
Maisel, Boris 170
Makarov, Askold 109, 128, 137, 166, 182, 199, 212
Makarova, Natalia 51, 157, 162-165, 198, 205-207, 209, 214-216, 230, 247, 258
Making Music Together Soviet-American arts festival 253
Malachite Box, The 134
MALEGOT Ballet 41, 48, 84-85, 110, 114-115, 136, 143, 151, 164, 168, 173, 176, 183, 196-197, 234, 236, 243, 250, 260 including references to Maly Ballet, *see also* Mikhailovsky Ballet
Malevich, Kazimir 26, 56
Malinovskaya, Elena 22-23, 50, 75, 81
Maly Ballet *see* MALEGOT Ballet
Maly Opera Ballet *see* MALEGOT Ballet
Mammoth Workshop of Monumental Theatre 54
Maria Alexandrovna, Tsarina 5
Mariinsky Ballet 4, 10-11, 14-15, 18, 21, 24-25, 28, 31, 33, 38-49, 65-66, 91, 94, 121, 149, 157, 188, 197, 229-230, 251, 256, 265-267, 269-270 *see also* GATOB, Kirov Ballet
Maris Liepa Charitable Foundation 232, 259
Markov, Georgy 240
Markovsky, John 209, 218
Marseille Ballet *see* Ballet National de Marseille
Martin, John 83, 184-185
Massine, Léonide 33, 60, 79-80, 140
Maximova, Ekaterina 157-159, 167, 173, 200-201, 203, 208, 227, 232, 235, 237, 252, 254, 259
Mayakovsky, Vladimir 26, 78, 196, 198

Meyerbeer, Giacomo 181
Mayorov, Genrikh 225, 268
Mazilier, Joseph 13
Mazun, Maria 173
Medtner, Nikolai 32
Melikov, Arif 175
Melikov, Erik 259
Mérimée, Prosper 205
Messerer, Asaf 39, 62, 69-70, 75, 77, 80-83, 88, 95, 115, 117, 139, 141, 148, 158, 181, 183, 188, 203 210, 221, 251
Messerer, Boris 205
Messerer, Mikhail 239-240, 266
Messerer, Sulamith 20, 80-83, 98, 101, 158, 239-240, 266
Mexico Ballet 216
Meyerhold, Vsevolod 31, 49, 79, 199
Mezentseva, Galina 229, 237, 242, 245, 253, 262-263
Mikhailov, Mikhail 63, 109, 157
Mikhailovsky Ballet 164, 230, 266, 269 *see also* MALEGOT Ballet
Mikhalchenko, Alla 231, 247
Milhaud, Darius 218
Mille, Agnes de 171-172
Ministry of Culture Decree, The 149
Minkus, Léon (or Ludwig) 5, 15
Minsk Ballet 190
Mir iskusstva 25
Miraculous Mandarin, The (Bartók) 169
Misérables, Les (Hugo) 151
Mobile Ballet Collective 72
Moiseyev, Igor 58, 74, 76, 88, 90, 95, 97, 131, 137, 152-153, 182, 203, 208, 216-217, 219, 235
Moiseyev, Mikhail 124, 188
Moiseyeva, Olga 124, 134, 175, 178, 182
Molchanov, Kirill 259
Molotov 48, 105, 110-112, 114, 130, 194 *see also* Perm
Monakhov, Alexander 262
Monde, Le 134
Monte Carlo 228
Montreal 223
Mordkin, Mikhail 38, 69, 73, 187, 190
Morley, Iris 65, 107, 116-117
Morozov, Igor 125
Moscow 4, 6, 15-16, 21-23, 26, 28, 31, 33, 38-40, 42, 48-49, 51, 53, 55, 63-66, 68-71, 73, 76-79, 86, 89-91, 94-96, 98, 101, 103, 106-107, 110, 116-118, 120, 123-126, 128-130, 133-134, 138, 140-141, 146-150,

153, 155, 158-163, 166-168, 171, 177-178, 180-184, 186, 188, 190-195, 197, 199-200, 203-205, 208, 210-211, 213-214, 218, 220, 223, 229, 231-232, 237-238, 243-244, 248-249, 253, 258-261, 264, 267, 269-270
Moscow Art Ballet 72, 102, 117, 130, 220 *see also* Art Theatre Ballet, Stanislavsky Ballet
Moscow Art College 40
Moscow Chamber Ballet 56 *see also* Moscow Chamber Studio
Moscow Chamber Studio 32, 36, 77
Moscow City Ballet 253
Moscow Classical Ballet 106, 203, 219, 232, 235, 254 *see also* Young Ballet, Classical Ballet Concert Ensemble of the USSR, State Academic Theatre Classical Ballet of N. Kasatkina and V. Vasilyov
Moscow Conservatoire 213
Moscow Festival Ballet 254 *see also* Russian National Ballet S. Radchenko
Moscow Foundling Home 6
Moscow Free Ballet 27 *see also* Free Ballet Studio
Moscow International Ballet Competition 194, 206, 211, 231-232
Moscow State University of Culture and Arts 231
Mozart, Wolfgang 223, 238
'Muddle instead of Music' 97, 99
Mukhamedov, Irek 51, 212, 232, 243-244, 247, 252-253, 259, 262
Mukhanova, Valentina 209
Mungalova, Olga 36, 61, 74, 94
Munich 158, 230, 267
Murdmaa, Mai 189, 222-223
Musatov, Nikolai 56
Mussorgsky, Modest 171, 266
My Little Poplar in a Red Scarf (Aitmatov) 204

Nagoya 239
Narkompros 19, 70 *see also* Commissariat for Enlightenment, People's Commissariat for Enlightenment
Narkompros School of Drama 45
National Ballet Ensemble of Georgia 231
National Conservatoire (Argentina) 42
Nebolsin, Vasily 88
Neff, Evgeny 242-243, 245
Nemirovich-Danchenko, Vladimir 29

Nerina, Nadia 148-149, 181
Neumeier, John 264
New Ballet 235 *see also* Leningrad Theatre of Modern Ballet, Leningrad Ballet Ensemble, Leningrad Eifman Ballet, St Petersburg Eifman Ballet
New Ballet of Moscow 253 *see also* Moscow City Ballet
New York 40, 82, 141, 166-167, 181-182, 184, 186, 214, 226, 237-238, 246-247, 257, 260
New York City Ballet 13, 171, 182-186, 231, 237, 248, 255
New York Daily Mirror 83
New York Post, The 83
New York Times, The 83, 172, 256
Newsweek 167
Nicholas II, Tsar 4, 17, 20
Nijinska, Bronislava 38, 49-51
Nijinsky, Vaslav 32, 40, 42, 49, 67, 161
Nikitina, Tamara 168
'Nina Ananiashvili and the Stars of the Bolshoi' 231
Nisnevich, Anatoly 156
Nizhny Novgorod 110, 232 *see also* Gorky, Vasilsursk
Nizhnyaya Kurya 112
Notre-Dame de Paris (Hugo) 8, 59
Noverre, Jean-Georges 7
Novoalexandrovka 213 *see also* Serebryansk
Novosibirsk 41, 124, 164, 194-195
Novosibirsk Ballet 41, 204, 234, 267
Nureyev, Rudolf 51, 67, 158, 163-165, 175-181, 206, 212, 233, 258
NYCB *see* New York City Ballet

Oblakov, Andrey 45-46
Odessa 58
Odessa Ballet 191
Oedipus Rex (Stravinsky) 257
Office of the Imperial Theatres 6
Ogonyok 251, 261
Oistrakh, David 217
Okasha, Tharwat 155
Olbrei, Rahel 189
Olesha, Yuri 95
Olivier, Laurence 220
On Your Toes 216
One Day in the Life of Ivan Denisovich (Solzhenitsyn) 202
Oransky, Viktor 75, 95, 117
Orenburg 110 *see also* Chkalov
Orlov, Alexander 86, 106

Osaka 149
Osipenko, Alla 139, 145, 147, 156, 162-163, 166, 178-179, 182, 209, 214, 218, 223, 226, 258
Osipova, Natalia 267
Ostrovsky, Nikolai 127
Ostrovsky, Vasily 209
Ostrozsky, Konstantin 21
Otkazov, F. 198 see Karavaichuk, Oleg
Ottawa 223

Pacific Northwest Ballet 255
Pakhomov, Vasily 142
Pankova, Elena 230, 253, 256
Panov, Valery 144, 173, 196, 205-207, 212, 219-220, 222, 226, 262
Panova, Galina 220
Paradis, Léopold 6
Paris 8-9, 19, 42, 49, 51, 60, 78-83, 134-135, 139, 141, 153, 155, 177-179, 181, 227, 235, 238, 254, 256, 261
Paris Opéra Ballet 148, 153-154, 164-165, 185, 230-231, 267
Paris-Presse L'intransigeant 177
Paths of the Ballet-Master (Lopukhov) 34
Pavlova, Anna 10-11, 55, 73, 80
Pavlova, Nadezhda 194, 212, 238, 259
Pavlovsk 4
People's Commissariat for Enlightenment 18-19 see also Commissariat for Enlightenment, *Narkompros*
Percival, John 249
perestroika 236, 246
Pergamon Altar 137
Pergolesi, Giovanni 60
Perm 110, 112, 114, 193-194, 236 see also Molotov
Perrot, Jules 8, 13, 59-60, 96, 210
Peter I (the Great), Tsar 4
Peters, Kurt 135
Petipa, Lucien 9
Petipa, Marius 5, 9, 13, 15, 21, 27-28, 34, 39, 59, 62, 67, 85, 87, 94, 96, 120, 125, 136, 143, 171, 183, 185, 210, 237, 244, 246, 256, 264, 269
Petit, Roland 176, 228-229, 236-237, 251-253, 257
Petite Fadette, La (Sand) 92
Petrograd 14, 18-19, 21-24, 33, 36-36, 39-46, 49, 51, 53, 55, 57, 90, 143, 170, 256
    see also Leningrad, St Petersburg
Petrograd Young Academic Ballet 36 see *also* Young Ballet
Petropavlovsk-Kamchatsky 230
Petrov, Andrey 165, 218, 253, 259
Petrov, Leonid 173
Petrov, Pavel 61, 188
Petrova, Ninel 156
Pink Floyd 236
Pittsburgh Ballet Theatre 216
Platoshino 112
Pleshcheyev, Alexander 21
Plisetskaya, Maya 51, 104, 116, 118-119, 128-129, 134, 140, 145, 152, 157-158, 160, 166-168, 175, 182, 199-200, 204-205, 210-211, 221, 223, 227-228, 238, 240, 244-245, 252-254
Plisetsky, Azary 205
Podgoretskaya, Nina 76, 88
Poland (Ballet in) 10-12
Polazna 112
Polish Ballet 51
Ponomarev, Vladimir 48, 63, 68, 125, 212
Ponomareva, Nina 140
Popko, Nikolai 104, 116
Posledniye Novosti 81
Pospekhin, Lev 104, 116, 168
Possokhov, Yuri 247
Poulenc, Francis 202
Prague 267
Prague Spring 201
Pravda 23, 98-99, 129, 136, 219, 222
Preobrazhenskaya, Olga 38, 41, 45-46, 55
Preobrazhensky, Vladimir 93, 117, 119-120, 126, 134, 149
Prince Igor 14, 224
Prix Nijinski 178, 232
Prodigal Son, The (Prokofiev) 190, 223
Prokhorova, Violetta 122
Prokofiev, Alexander 258-259
Prokofiev, Sergey 27, 56, 78-80, 107-108, 119, 122, 131, 133, 144, 156, 183, 225, 236
Prophète, Le (Meyerbeer) 181
Proust, Marcel 154
Psota, Ivo 107
Pugni, Cesare 8, 59, 168
Pushkin, Alexander (ballet teacher) 157-158, 164, 206, 212
Pushkin, Alexander (poet) 91, 101, 106, 120, 125, 142, 222, 236
Pyotrovsky, Adrian 107

Quest, The 31
Quo Vadis (Sienkiewicz) 11

Rachinsky, Pyotr 226
Rachmaninov, Sergey 169
Radchenko, Elena 254
Radchenko, Sergey 225, 254
Radlov, Sergey 31, 91, 107
Radunsky, Alexander 63, 104, 116, 126, 168, 182
Rassadin, Konstantin 156, 199
Ratmansky, Alexey 264
Ravel, Maurice 156, 170, 223
Red Banner Ensemble 40
Reisen, Maria 29-30
Renault, Michel 148
Revizor (Gogol) 241
Rhapsody on a theme by Paganini (Rachmaninov) 169
Riga 80, 148, 160, 187, 206, 258
Rite of Spring, The 202 see *Sacre du Printemps, Le*
Robbins, Jerome 171-172, 184, 248
Rodari, Gianni 225
Rodchenko, Alexander 56
Romanov, Boris 14, 40, 42
Romanov, Grand Duke Andrey 18
romanzo di Cipollino, Il (Rodari) 225
Romanova, Maria 46, 66
Rosenberg, Valentina 85
Roslavleva, Natalia 172, 181
Rossi Street 4, 44-45, 114
Rossi, Carlo 6
Rostropovich, Mstislav 217
Royal Ballet, The 147, 149, 153, 169, 180-1, 200, 214, 229, 231-232, 262 see also Sadler's Wells Ballet
Royal Swedish Ballet 231
Rubinstein, Anton 36, 94
Rubtovsk 235
Rues et visages de Moscou (Laborde) 94
Russell, Francia 255
Russian Academy of Theatre Arts – GITIS 49 see also GITIS
Russian Musical Society 5
Russian National Ballet S. Radchenko 254
Russian National Ballet Theatre 254 see also Russian National Ballet S. Radchenko
Russian Overture (Prokofiev) 225
Russian Romantic Theatre 42
Russian State Ballet Theatre of Moscow 231

Rustaveli, Shota 245
Ruzimatov, Farukh 207, 230, 256, 260, 266
Ryabinkina, Elena 198, 204
Rybatsev, Vladimir 60, 94
Ryzhenko, Natalia 152, 182, 221

Sadler's Wells Ballet 13, 123, 153, see also Royal Ballet, The
Saint Laurent, Yves 228
Saint-Léon, Arthur 8, 13, 18, 65, 168
Sakhnovskaya, Natalia 112
Salammbô (Flaubert) 88
Salimbaeva, Olga 112
Samara 110 see also Kuibyshev
Samsova, Galina 262
San Francisco 82, 257
San Francisco Ballet 216, 262
Sand, Georges 92
Saratov 191
Sartre, Jean-Paul 154
Scarlet Sails (Grin) 116
Schnittke, Alfred 253
Schollar, Ludmilla 38
Schubert, Franz 58
Scottish Ballet 229, 257, 263
Scriabin, Alexander 124
Seagull, The (Chekhov) 240
Sekh, Yaroslav 169, 204
Semenyaka, Ludmilla 173, 230, 244, 247, 253
Semizorova, Nina 247
Semyonov, Viktor 40, 43, 68
Semyonov, Vladilen 121, 170, 178, 212
Semyonova, Marina 40, 51, 65-68, 76, 83, 89, 94, 100-101, 109, 120, 126, 139, 141, 148, 158, 181-182, 213-214
Seoul 266
Serebrovskaya, Lyubov 192
Serebryansk 213 see also Novoalexandrovka
Serenade for Strings (Tchaikovsky) 184
Sergeyev, Konstantin 51, 67-69, 72, 89-90, 92, 94, 97, 106-107, 109, 111, 114, 119-121, 126, 128-130, 132, 134-136, 144, 146, 149, 151, 162, 164, 170, 174, 177-178, 182, 187, 197-198, 206-207, 211, 213-216, 268
Sergeyev, Nikolai 35
Servitore di due padroni, Il (Goldoni) 119
Seventh Symphony (Shostakovich) 175
Seventh World Communist Youth Festival

176
Shakespeare, William 147, 237
Shavrov, Boris 33, 41, 43, 74, 90, 94, 96-97, 130, 212
Shchedrin, Rodion 168, 205, 221, 240, 245
Shcherbinina, Alla 168
Sheina, Svetlana 127
Shelest, Alla 67, 74, 109, 112, 120, 128, 130, 134, 137, 156, 168, 177, 182
Sheremetyevskaya, Natalya 115
Sheveleva, Ekaterina 141
Shiryaev, Alexander 45, 68
Shklyarov, Vladimir 267
Sholokhov, Mikhail 250
Shostakovich, Dmitry 74, 83-84, 97-99, 102, 122, 152, 175, 197, 199, 202, 243
Shuraleh (Yarullin) 192
Shvarts, Isaac 124, 156, 205
Sick Rose, The (Blake) 228
Sienkiewicz, Henryk 11
Simakin, Yuri 244
Sixty Years in Ballet (Lopukhov) 20
Sizova, Alla 162-163, 170, 176, 178, 182, 200, 216
Skulte, Ādolfs 187
Slonimsky, Sergey 219
Slonimsky, Yuri 68, 89, 106, 127, 146, 151, 166, 190
Smena 85
Smirnov, Viktor 83
Smirnova, Elena 41-42
Smirnova, Olga 267
Smirnov-Golovanov, Viktor 221, 253
Smoltsov, Ivan 60, 62
Smoltsov, Viktor 77, 80
Socialist Realism 56, 86-87, 89, 94, 126, 129-130, 135, 166, 185, 201
Sofia National Opera 160
Sokolov, Nikolai 106, 115
Sokolova, Evgenia 5, 44
Sokolov-Kaminsky, Arkady 176, 260
Sokolow, Anna 139
Sollertinsky, Ivan 71, 92
Solodovnikov, Alexander 154
Soloviev, Yuri 162-165, 170, 176, 178, 182, 212, 218, 223, 227, 233
Solovyov-Sedoy, Vasily 108
Solzhenitsyn, Alexander 202
Sombart, Alexandre 258
Sorokina, Maria 73, 102, 118
Sorokina, Nina 199, 203, 212, 219, 225
Soviet Art 175

Soviet Ballet 249, 260
Sovietskaya Muzika 154
Sovietskaya Zhenshchina 149
Sovietsky Balet 159 *see also Soviet Ballet*
Sovnarkom 19, 49 *see also* Council of People's Commissars
Spadavecchia, Antonio 123
Spessivtseva, Olga 35, 38, 42-44, 83, 96, 125
Splendeurs et misères des courtisanes (Balzac) 96
Squire's Daughter, The (Pushkin) 120
St Petersburg 4-11, 13, 17-18, 26, , 32, 36, 38, 40-42, 47-48, 51, 65-69, 72, 84, 129, 150, 162-164, 168, 184, 193, 225, 229, 236, 242, 265, 269, 270
see also Leningrad, Petrograd
St Petersburg Conservatoire 5
St Petersburg Eifman Ballet 235
see also New Ballet, Leningrad Theatre of Modern Ballet, Leningrad Ballet Ensemble, Leningrad Eifman Ballet
St Petersburg State Academic Leonid Yakobson Ballet Theatre 229
Stalin, Joseph 53-54, 56, 70, 75-78, 82, 86, 96, 98, 100, 105, 109, 119, 122, 129, 131-132, 135-136, 138-139, 149, 157, 167, 183, 187, 201, 220, 252
Stanislavsky and Nemirovich-Danchenko Music Theatre Ballet 73, 117, 130
see also Stanislavsky Ballet
Stanislavsky Ballet 106, 117, 121, 130, 139, 160-161, 171-172, 219-220, 235, 266-267
Stanislavsky method 92
Stanislavsky Opera 117
Stanislavsky, Konstantin 15, 26, 28, 31, 39, 68, 73, 135
Stankevich, Vera 133
State Academic Theatre Classical Ballet of N. Kasatkina and V. Vasilyov 203
see also Young Ballet, The Classical Ballet Concert Ensemble of the USSR, Moscow Classical Ballet
State Institute of Musical Drama 49
State Kremlin Palace Ballet 259 *see also* Kremlin Ballet
State Theatrical Workshops 49
Stavropol 229
Stendhal 197
Stock Market News 46
Strauss, Johann 81, 235

Stravinsky, Igor 33, 60, 79, 174, 183-184, 203, 223, 235, 256-257
Stray Dog (cabaret) 15
Struchkova, Raisa 104, 106, 116, 134, 139-140, 157-158, 161, 169, 223, 249
Studio of Vera Maya 26
Stukolkina, Nina 132
stulchik 180
Stuttgart Ballet 13, 222
Sudakov, Gennady 236
Suite bergamasque (Debussy) 156
Sunday Times, The 179
Suslov, Mikhail 217
Sverdlovsk 90, 110-111, 219
Sylphides, Les (Fokine) 11 *see also* Chopiniana
Symphony No.40 (Mozart) 238

Taglioni, Filippo 235
Taglioni, Marie 7, 66
Taktakishvili, Shalva 193
Tale of Igor's Campaign, The 224
Tallinn 189, 219
Tallchief, Maria 172
Tangieva-Birzniek, Elena 187-188
Tanz, Der 81
Taranda, Gediminas 243-244
Tatlin, Vladimir 56
Taylor, Paul 238
Tbilisi 41, 68, 102, 147-148, 158, 161, 171, 193, 204, 220, 231 *see also* Tiflis
Tbilisi Ballet 161
Tchaikovsky Piano Competition 211
Tchaikovsky, Alexander 241, 246
Tchaikovsky, Pyotr 13, 30, 70, 101, 130, 184, 192, 204, 221, 235
Tchassov, Stanislav 262
Teatr 47
Terekhova, Tatiana 229
Terry, Walter 137
The Art of the Choreographer (Zakharov) 135
Theatres and auditoria
Baku: Akhundov 192
Brno: State 107
Chkalov: Operetta 114
Copenhagen: Royal 242
Dnepropetrovsk: Opera and Ballet 191
Ekaterinburg: Opera and Ballet 231
Kharkov: Opera 191
Kiev: Russian Opera 190
　Kiev Young 190
　Opera 225

Kuibyshev: Palace of Culture 115-116
Kutaisi: Opera and Ballet 220
Leningrad: Comedy 112-113
　Cultural Cooperative Centre 171
　GATOB 61, 68, 74, 76, 87, 92, 96, 243
　see also Mariinsky, Kirov
　Hermitage 85
　House of Culture 206
　Kirov 96, 100, 102, 107-108, 112, 117, 121, 123, 125-126,128-129, 131-132, 148, 155, 165, 168, 171, 193-194, 199, 205, 207-209, 211, 213-214, 219, 222, 226, 236, 247, 250, 254, 258, 265-266
　see also GATOB, Mariinsky
　MALEGOT 84 *see* Maly
　Maly 41, 84, 86, 93, 97, 101, 106, 113-114, 119-121, 125, 127-129,132-133, 143-144, 173, 194, 197, 200, 209, 217, 222, 224-225, 227, 245, 255-256, 266
　see also MALEGOT, Mikhailovsky
　Maly Petrograd State Academic 84 *see* Maly
　Musical Comedy 143
　Palace of Congresses 183
　State Academic Maly Opera 84 *see* Maly
　State Academic Theatre of Comic Opera 84 *see* Maly
London: Alhambra 188
　Covent Garden, The Royal Opera House 138, 140-141, 149, 153, 169, 214, 262, 269
Minsk: Bolshoi 190
　National Drama 190
　Opera and Ballet 190
Molotov: Molotov Opera and Ballet 112
Moscow: Aquarium Garden 28
　Arbat 6 *see also* New Imperial
　Bolshoi 4, 6, 15, 16, 18, 19, 20, 22-23, 29, 30, 55, 57, 59, 63-64, 72, 75-77, 80, 89, 92-93, 94, 95, 105, 117, 119, 123, 126-127, 150, 153-154, 161, 168, 171, 184, 194-195, 197, 200, 208, 213, 221-222, 227-228, 236, 240, 252, 264-265
　Experimental 58 *see also* Filial
　Filial 93, 104, 116, 120, 126 *see also* Experimental
　Kremlin Palace of Congresses 173, 200, 204, 219

Lenin Palace of Sports 171
Mamontovsky Theatre of Miniatures 31
MKhAT-2 (Second Moscow Academic Arts Theatre) 83
Moscow Arts 15, 26, 29, 75
Natalya Sats Musical 249
New 30
New Imperial 6 *see also* Arbat
Bolshoi New Stage 265
Petrovsky 6
Stanislavsky and Nemirovich-Danchenko Musical *see* Stanislavsky and Nemirovich-Danchenko
Stanislavsky and Nemirovich-Danchenko 40, 117, 123, 125, 130, 171-172, 222,
Taganka 224
New York: Carnegie Hall 82
Metropolitan Opera 166, 181, 238, 257
New York State 269
Novosibirsk: Opera and Ballet 194
NOVAT 194 *see also* Novosibirsk Opera and Ballet
Odessa: Opera 191
Paris: Opéra 9, 43, 83, 130, 237, 269
Opéra Palais Garnier 177 *see also* Opéra
Palais des Sports 177
Petrograd: GATOB 23, 43, 48, 173 *see also* Mariinsky, Kirov
Mariinsky 28
Mikhailovsky 44
Petrograd Private Opera 49
Riga: Opera 82, 187, 213, 222
Rostov: Musical 232
Saratov: Opera 191
St Petersburg
Alexandrinsky 18, 22
Hermitage 4, 85
Bolshoi Kamenny 5
Equestrian Circus 5
Mariinsky 5, 10, 16, 18-24, 26, 28, 171, 265-266
Mariinsky Second Stage 266
Mikhailovsky 18, 44, 84, 164, 225, 266 *see* Maly
St Petersburg Mussorgsky State Academic Opera and Ballet 266 *see* Maly, Mikhailovsky
Tallinn: Opera 189
Tashkent: Navoi 230

Tbilisi: Paliashvili 158, 161, 193
Tiraspol: Moldovan music-drama 126
Warsaw: Weikl 4, 11, 220
Washington: Kennedy Center 257

Thévenon, Patrick 177
Third Symphony (Prokofiev) 226
Thirteenth Symphony (Shostakovich) 202
Tiflis 68, 193 *see also* Tbilisi
Tikhomirnova, Irina 116-117, 139, 203, 216, 235
Tikhomirov, Vasily 28, 31, 38-39, 49, 59-60, 62-63, 70
Tikhonov, Vladimir 198
Times, The 179, 261
Timofeyeva, Nina 158-159, 169, 204, 208, 259
Tishchenko, Boris 202, 225
Tohvelman, Helmi 189
Tokyo 149, 239
Tolsky, Anatoly 102
Tolstoy, Leo 221
Tomsky, Alexander 118
Topping, Seymour 172
Toronto 223-224
Trefilova, Vera 37, 43
Trotsky, Leon 53, 70
Tsarskoe Selo 4, 46 *see also* Detskoe Selo
Tsentroteatr 23 *see* Central Theatre Committee
Tsfasman, Alexander 81, 88
Tsignadze, Vera 147
Tsiskaridze, Nikolai 267-268
Tsïtovich, Vladimir 156
Tsivin, Mikhail 173, 225, 238
Tubin, Eduard 189
Tudor, Antony 171-172
Tulubiev, Viktor 115, 128

Ufa 111, 191
Ukhov, Vsevolod 156
Uksusnikov, Igor 267
Ulanov, Sergey 66
Ulanova, Galina 51, 63, 66, 69-70, 74, 76, 90, 92, 94, 96-97, 107-108, 114, 118-119, 131, 134, 138-142, 146, 158-159, 161, 167, 182, 197, 200, 211, 230, 249
Union of Soviet Composers 87, 174, 240
Union of Soviet Writers 87, 91
Universal Ballet 266
Urusov, Prince Pyotr 6
Urusova, Angelina 102

USSR Folk Dance Ensemble 131
USSR-Great Britain Friendship Society 173

Vaganova, Agrippina 46-48, 51, 64-66, 71, 84, 87, 89-90, 94, 96-99, 112, 129, 162-163, 212
Vainonen, Vasily 74, 89, 94, 100, 106, 118, 120, 126, 179, 194, 203, 266
Vakula the Smith (Tchaikovsky) 101 *see also Cherevichki*
Valois, Ninette de 154, 180-181
Valse, La (Ravel) 170
Vancouver 223
Vanslov, Viktor 132
Varkovitsky, Vladimir 102, 106, 123, 151-152
Varna 200
Varna Ballet Competition 200-201, 211, 232
Vasilenko, Sergey 58, 118, 126
Vasiliev, Ivan 267
Vasiliev, Vladimir 51, 121, 159-161, 167-170, 173, 200, 203, 208, 219, 223, 226-227, 237-238, 250, 252, 254, 259, 264
Vasilieva, Tatiana 80
Vasilieva, Vera 75, 92
Vasilieva, Zinaida 86, 97-98, 190
Vasilsursk 110 *see also* Gorky, Nizhny Novgorod
Vasilyov, Vladimir 106, 161, 163, 197, 199, 202-203, 207, 218, 221, 232, 235
Vazem, Ekaterina 44, 47
Vaziev, Makhar 265-266
Vecheslova, Tatiana 63, 66, 82-83, 96-97, 103-104, 106, 111, 120, 139, 214
Vega, Lope de 103
Velikanov, Vasily 186
Verikovsky, Mikhail 191
Vetrov, Alexander 244
Vienna 25, 51, 139, 176
Vikulov, Sergey 201
Vilna 69 *see also* Vilnius
Vilnius 69, 188 *see also* Vilna
Vilzak, Anatoly 38
Vinogradov, Nikolai 54
Vinogradov, Oleg 121, 164, 195, 203-204, 206-207, 224, 229-230, 232, 234, 236-237, 241-242, 245-247, 250-252, 255-257, 260, 265-266
Virsaladze, Simon 103, 145

Virsky, Pavel 73
Vishneva, Diana 267
Vladimirov, Pyotr 37, 40, 67-68
Vladimirov, Yuri 160-161, 199, 203, 212, 219, 221, 226
Vlasova, Ludmilla 238
Voix Humaine, La (Poulenc) 202
Volgograd 204
Volkonsky, Prince Sergey 81
Volkov, Nikolai 122, 137
Volkova, Vera 47
Volynsky, Akim 37, 46-47, 55, 67
Von Rosen, Elsa-Marianne 242
Vostrikov, Gennady 216
Voyshnis, Lyubov 109
Vronsky, Vakhtang 191-192

Wan, Si Sun 194
War and Peace (Prokofiev) 119
Warsaw 4, 10-11, 150, 220
Washington 233, 257, 266
Washington Post, The 248
Webster, David 138
White Night of Dance 250
White Nights Festival 250
Williams, Pyotr 108
Willis, Margaret 242

Yakobson, Leonid 67, 71, 74, 123-124, 128-129, 136-137, 149, 152, 155, 163, 165, 179, 182, 192, 197-199, 202, 205-206, 208-209, 210-211, 217-218, 223, 226, 254
Yakulov, Georgy 57
Yankovsky, Mikhail 84
Yarullin, Farhid 192
Yastrebova, Nonna 199
Yerevan 105
Yermolayev, Alexey. *See* Ermolayev, Alexey
Young Ballet (Balanchivadze) 36-37, 41, 50, 55
Young Ballet (Moiseyev/Tikhomirnova) 164, 203, 216, 232, 235
  see also Classical Ballet Concert Ensemble of the USSR, Moscow Classical Ballet, State Academic Theatre Classical Ballet of N. Kasatkina and V. Vasilyov
Yurovsky, Vladimir 116
Yusupova, Princess Zinaida 46

Zaakov, Rafael 171
Zabotkina, Olga 251-252
Zakharov, Rostislav 63, 73, 76-77, 91-

92, 96-97, 99, 101, 103, 107, 109,
  119-121, 125, 135, 146, 184, 266
Zakharova, Svetlana 267
Zaklinsky, Konstantin 207, 230, 237,
  255-256
Zelensky, Igor 267
Zhdanov, Andrey 119, 122,174
Zhdanov, Yuri 140, 169, 203
Zhizn iskusstva 64, 71, 73
Zhukov, Alexey 126
Zhukov, Leonid 30
Zhukov, Yuri 256, 262
Zimin, Veniamin 133, 197
Zubkovskaya, Inna 125, 128, 137,
  175,178
Zubkovsky, Nikolai 86, 93, 97, 106, 119,
  125,182
Zvonareva, Nonna 202

www.ingramcontent.com/pod-product-compliance
Lightning Source LLC
Chambersburg PA
CBHW060107230426

43661CB00033B/1430/J